A GUIDE TO
OLD TESTAMENT THEOLOGY
AND EXEGESIS

A GUIDE TO
OLD TESTAMENT THEOLOGY AND EXEGESIS

The Introductory Articles from the
*New International Dictionary of
Old Testament Theology and Exegesis*

**Willem A. VanGemeren
General Editor**

ZondervanPublishingHouse
Grand Rapids, Michigan

A Division of HarperCollins*Publishers*

A Guide to Old Testament Theology and Exegesis
These introductory articles are also published in the *New International Dictionary of Old Testament Theology and Exegesis* © 1997 by Willem A. VanGemeren

Preface to *A Guide to Old Testament Theology and Exegesis* © 1999 by Willem A. VanGemeren

Zondervan Publishing House
Grand Rapids, Michigan 49530

Library of Congress Cataloging-in-Publication Data
    A guide to Old Testament theology and exegesis / Willem VanGemeren, general editor.
            p.   cm.
    Includes bibliographical references.
    ISBN 0-310-23193-0 (pbk.)
    1. Bible. O.T.—Hermeneutics. 2. Bible.   O.T.—Theology   I. VanGemeren, Willem.
    BS476.G85   1999
    221.6'01—dc21   99-26266
                                                                                          CIP

Printed in the United States of America

99 00 01 02 03 04 /❖ DC / 10 9 8 7 6 5 4 3 2 1

A GUIDE TO OLD TESTAMENT THEOLOGY AND EXEGESIS

Contributors   *6*

Preface
    Willem A. VanGemeren   *7*

Abbreviations   **10**

Introduction: Hermeneutics, Text, and Biblical Theology   **11**
1.   Language, Literature, Hermeneutics and Biblical Theology:
    What's Theological About a Theological Dictionary?
    Kevin Vanhoozer   *12*

Part I. The Reliability of the Old Testament Text   **48**
2.   Textual Criticism of the Old Testament and Its Relation to
    Exegesis and Theology
    Bruce K. Waltke   *48*

Part II. History, Theology, and Hermeneutics   **65**
3.   Old Testament History: A Theological Perspective
    Eugene H. Merrill   *65*
4.   Old Testament History: A Hermeneutical Perspective
    V. Philips Long   *83*

Part III. Literature, Interpretation, and Theology   **100**
5.   Literary Approaches and Interpretation
    Tremper Longman III   *100*
6.   Narrative Criticism: The Theological Implications of Narrative Techniques
    Philip E. Satterthwaite   *122*

Part IV. Semantics, Interpretation, and Theology   **131**
7.   Linguistics, Meaning, Semantics, and Discourse Analysis
    Peter Cotterell   *131*
8.   Principles for Productive Word Study
    John H. Walton   *158*

Part V. Canon, Literature, Interpretation, and Biblical Theology   **169**
9.   The Flowering and Floundering of Old Testament Theology
    Elmer A. Martens   *169*
10. Integrating Old Testament Theology and Exegesis: Literary, Thematic,
    and Canonical Issues
    Richard Schultz   *182*

Appendix   *203*

CONTRIBUTORS

ALLEN, LESLIE C.
M.A., Ph.D., D.D.; Professor of Old Testament, Fuller Theological Seminary, Pasadena, California

COTTERELL, PETER
B.D., B. Sc., Ph.D., D.Univ.; Former principal, London Bible College, London, United Kingdom; Fellow of the Institute of Linguists, Fellow of the Royal Society of Arts

GORDON, ROBERT P.
M.A., Ph.D.; Regius Professor of Hebrew and Fellow of St. Catharine's College, University of Cambridge, Cambridge, United Kingdom

KRUGER, PAUL A.
D.Litt., B.Th.; Senior Lecturer, The University of Stellenbosch, Stellenbosch, South Africa

LONG, V. PHILIPS
B.A., B.S., M.Div., Ph.D.; Professor of Old Testament, Covenant Theological Seminary, St. Louis, Missouri

LONGMAN, TREMPER, III
B.A., M.Div., M.Phil, Ph.D.; Professor of Old Testament, Westminster Theological Seminary, Philadelphia, Pennsylvania

MARTENS, ELMER A.
B.A., B.Ed., B.D., Ph.D.; Professor Emeritus of Old Testament, Mennonite Brethren Biblical Seminary, Fresno, California

MERRILL, EUGENE H.
B.A., M.A., M.Phil., Ph.D.; Professor of Old Testament Studies, Dallas Theological Seminary, Dallas, Texas

NOLL, STEPHEN F.
B.A., M.A., Ph.D.; Associate Professor of Biblical Studies, Academic Dean, Trinity Episcopal School for Ministry, Ambridge, Pennsylvania

SATTERTHWAITE, PHILIP E.
B.A., M.A., Ph.D.; Affiliated Lecturer at the Faculty of Oriental Studies, University of Cambridge; Research Fellow at Tyndale House, Cambridge, United Kingdom

SCHULTZ, RICHARD
B.A., M.Div., M.A., Ph.D.; Associate Professor of Old Testament, Wheaton College, Wheaton, Illinois

SELMAN, MARTIN J.
B.A., M.A., Ph.D.; Deputy Principal, Spurgeon's College, London, United Kingdom

VANGEMEREN, WILLEM A.
B.A., B.D., M.A., Ph.D; Professor of Old Testament and Semitic Languages, Trinity Evangelical Divinity School, Deerfield, Illinois

VANHOOZER, KEVIN
B.A., M.Div., Ph.D.; Senior Lecturer in Theology, New College, Edinburgh University, Edinburgh, Scotland

WALTKE, BRUCE K.
Th.D., Ph.D.; Marshall Sheppard Professor of Biblical Studies, Regent College, Vancouver, British Columbia, Canada; Professor of Old Testament, Reformed Theological Seminary, Orlando, Florida,

WALTON, JOHN H.
A.B., M.A., Ph.D.; Professor of Bible, Moody Bible Institute, Chicago, Illinois

PREFACE

I am pleased that the editors at Zondervan Publishing House have decided to publish separately "The Guide," which forms the introductory essays to the *New International Dictionary of Old Testameant Theology and Exegesis* (*NIDOTTE*). These ten essays summarize methodological concerns. This is important, because interpreters of the OT differ in their approach to interpretation and because advances in hermeneutical orientation, textual criticism, biblical history, linguistics, and biblical theology have created a paradigm shift in interpretation. The approach is in line with the customary historical-grammatical method, but includes refinements in its nuanced concern for linguistics, literary analysis, and a historical-theological synthesis of the text. It advances the issue of method by a fourfold thrust.

1. *The interpretation of the **whole** Bible involves the text and the interpreter.* Vanhoozer ("Language, Literature, Hermeneutics and Biblical Theology: What's Theological About a Theological Dictionary?" sec. 3, p. 42) reminds us that interpretation involves both the text and the reader. On the one hand, the language of the Bible is God's means of communicating in order to discover what is real. It is the source of truth because it refers to God as the ultimate source of reality. However, as a means of communication it requires interpretation of the genres (story, law, genealogy, poetry, etc.) and of the literary forms (simile, metaphor). The student of the text must involve himself or herself with the acts of "hearing" the Word, of relating the Word to the world, and of experiencing a personal transformation.

2. *Interpretation is perspectival.* The reader-interpreter aims at the search for truth, but realizes that his apprehension of that truth requires a bringing together of several perspectives. The historical-grammatical approach supposes the reader's competence with matters of history and grammar. History is more than the study of acts and facts. It has a theological dimension and thus requires interpretation (see Eugene H. Merrill's essay, "Old Testament History: A Theological Perspective,"sec. B: The Structure of the OT as a Historical Record, p. 72) as well as a method of working with the exegetical evidence (see V. Philips Long's essay, "Old Testament History: A Hermeneutical Perspective," sec. C: Historical Interpretation of the OT: Four Steps in the Process, p. 93). History is also a story (narrative). God communicates truth through stories, narrative techniques, and literary genres. The biblical stories permit the reader to view God's activity in human affairs by the narrative approach and by application of the literary technique. While history calls for active engagement by reconstructing God's ways in human affairs, the literary approach calls forth an engagement of the

imaginative faculties. The biblical text assumes familiarity with such literary conventions or writings strategies and richly rewards all who familiarize themselves with the categories of Hebrew prose and poetry (see Tremper Longman III, "Literary Approaches and Interpretation," sec. G: Literary Conventions, p. 111, and Philip E. Satterthwaite, "Narrative Criticism: The Theological Implications of Narrative Techniques," p. 122).

3. *Interpretation provides a detailed and nuanced assessment of the exegetical possibilities of the text*. The exegetical data are many. As interpreters study the text, they need to concern themselves with the reliability of the text (see Bruce K. Waltke, "Textual Criticism of the Old Testament and Its Relation to Exegesis and Theology," p. 48), issues of grammar and syntax (see *IBHS*, and also commentaries based on the Hebrew text), the meaning of the words (semantics), and the context of communication. The science of linguistics makes a significant contribution as it links grammar and syntax (syntactics) with the meaning of words (semantics) and the context of communication (pragmatics). The article by Peter Cotterell ("Linguistics, Meaning, Semantics, and Discourse Analysis," p. 131) provides the reader with a carefully argued defense for a larger place for linguistics than is usually allocated (see sec. A: Linguistics and Biblical Interpretation, p. 131). Linguistics locates the meaning of words in the triad of Author-Text-Reader, and while penetrating the text for meaning, it reminds the reader of one's subjectivity in all of his or her questions, deliberation, searching, analysis, and synthesis (see sec. B: The Source of Meaning, p. 137).

Semantics or the discovery of meaning (see sec. C: Lexical Semantics, p. 144) sets the stage of interpretation at the broader levels of linguistics and of textual interpretation. While the common concern in traditional interpretation has been with grammar and syntax, linguistics sets forth rules of interpreting human communication that also incorporates semantics and pragmatics. To this end, the meaning of a word as a symbol of communication is to be determined in its relation to other words (lexical semantics; see further John H. Walton, "Principles for Productive Word Study," p. 158), in its place within the sentence or verse, and at the level of a literary unit or discourse (see Cotterell, sec. D: Discourse Analysis, p. 151). The goal of interpretation is to understand the more precise meaning of a word at the level of the discourse, i.e., a literary unit (in contrast to the level of word or sentence).

The discourse is held together at three levels: syntactics, semantics, and pragmatics. Grammar and syntax help in seeing "grammatical and syntactical cohesion" of a text, but the study of the meaning of words enhances the study by two additional dimensions: semantic coherence and intentionality. The lexical entries in a theological dictionary may enhance the reader's sense of the potential meanings of a Hebrew word, but the text (discourse unit) as well as the intention of the text should lead the reader to limit the possibilities and to engage with the text as a coherent whole. Pragmatics as the third dimension of linguistics helps the reader of the text to connect the author with his intended audience, by raising several questions: (a) How does the author communicate and move his audience? (b) What does he communicate and in what manner is this message unique? (c) When and where does the communication take place?

4. *The text has theological meaning and significance*. Changes have taken place in scholarly positions with regard to biblical theology. The somewhat axiomatic posi-

tion as reiterated by Krister Stendahl separates the text from the reader. He argued that there is a difference between what the ancient text *meant* (the job of biblical theology) and what the text *means* (the job of systematic theology). He argued further that the connection between what the text *meant* and what the text *means* is the job of hermeneutics and not that of exegesis or interpretation (see Elmer A. Martens, "The Flowering and Foundering of Old Testament Theology": A. Divergent Objectives, p. 170). The historical model (what is meant) has undergone a shift. The paradigm shift from occupation with historical issues has brought about a renewed awareness of other vantage points, such as the sociological, literary, and linguistic approaches (see sec. B. Shifting Orientations, p. 173).

Another impetus for a theological interpretation of the text has come from the canonical approach inaugurated by Brevard S. Childs (see Richard Schultz, "Integrating Old Testament Theology and Exegesis: Literary, Thematic, and Canonical Issues," p. 182). The interpretation of the text is not an issue merely of origins—attempting to go back to the original form, analyzing the process of redaction, and/or tracing of the sources. For Childs, theological reflection was an inherent part of the canonical shaping of each OT book as the community of God's people received that book and accepted it as authoritative for their faith and life. The book's authority extends beyond that generation to subsequent generations, as each generation interacts with the book's teaching, exhortation, and rebuke.

Each generation can and must interact with the Bible. On the one hand, it has received the legacy of past interpreters. On the other hand, it can make a contribution by interacting honestly with the cultural challenges. To this end, we affirm that while the traditional interpretations of the Bible are important and appropriate, the Bible itself opens up perspectives that may challenge past interpretations and invites the traveler to journey into exciting, but not always known, landscapes of literary and linguistic possibilities. This journey requires interpretation—a detailed and nuanced assessment of the exegetical possibilities of the text, and an openness to the text as well as to one's self. In between these two horizons (text and self), the text presents a message of God afresh to a new generation. The ancient text is the bearer of theological meaning and significance.

I trust that these essays will encourage many students of the Bible to explore the exegetical and theological perspectives of the biblical text. While these essays stand on their own, they make a larger contribution as introductory essays to *NIDOTTE*. The publisher has provided several samples of lexical, biblical, and topical articles from *NIDOTTE* in the Appendix. After perusing these articles, I encourage you to examine the five-volume set for yourself. The articles open up vistas to the biblical text.

I am most grateful to the authors, the editors, and the staff at Zondervan Publishing House for my involvement as general editor.

Willem A. VanGemeren

Professor of Old Testament and Semitic Languages

Trinity Evangelical Divinity School

ABBREVIATIONS

In general, standard abbreviations are used in the book. The following is a list of some of the more common abbreviations of books, journals, and series. For a complete listing, see *NIDOTTE*, xxi to xlviii in vols. 1-4.

ANET	*Ancient Near Eastern Texts Relating to the Old Testament*
AUSS	*Andrews University Seminary Studies*
BSac	*Bibliotheca Sacra*
CBQ	*Catholic Biblical Quarterly*
ExpTim	*Expository Times*
FOTT	*The Flowering of Old Testament Theology*
HALAT	*Hebräisches und aramäisches Lexicon zum Alten Testament*
HALOT	*The Hebrew and Aramaic Lexicon of the Old Testament*, 1994- (ET of *HALAT*)
HBT	*Horizons in Biblical Theology*
JAOS	*Journal of the American Oriental Society*
JBL	*Journal of Biblical Literature*
JETS	*Journal of the Evangelical Theological Society*
JSOT	*Journal for the Study of the Old Testament*
NIDNTT	*The New International Dictionary of New Testament Theology*
NIDOTTE	*The New International Dictionary of Old Testament Theology and Exegesis* (the present work)
OTL	Old Testament Library
OTT	G. von Rad, *Old Testament Theology*
RB	*Revue biblique*
SJOT	*Scandinavian Journal of the Old Testament*
TDOT	*Theological Dictionary of the Old Testament*
TOT	W. Eichrodt, *Theology of the Old Testament*
TRE	*Theologische Realenzyklopädie*
TWAT	*Theologisches Wörterbuch zum Alten Testament*
TynBul	*Tyndale Bulletin*
VT	*Vetus Testamentum*
WTJ	*Westminster Theological Journal*

INTRODUCTION: HERMENEUTICS, TEXT, AND BIBLICAL THEOLOGY

How does the ancient text (the Bible) make an impact on our modern theological mind-set? Is theology a separate discipline from biblical interpretation? Many interpreters are highly skeptical of the truth claims of the Bible as well as of its use in shaping the way in which we interact with "the modern world." Vanhoozer posits that since Jesus Christ is "the Word incarnate," words are God's means of sanctioning a truthful way of life, politics, and values. Deconstruction and postmodernity notwithstanding, the student of the ancient text must learn to let the text speak meaningfully to a new context.

The ancient text has inherent problems. The obstacles to understanding are many. Some are textual (see the article on textual criticism by Bruce Waltke). Others are cultural (historical, social situation, language, and literature). Yet all the issues are in the words of the text. But instead of aiming at the interpretation of individual words (for the dangers inherent in word studies, see also the essays by Cotterell and Walton), the interpreter must learn to look at the "discourse" as a basic level for interpretation and for practice. Modern linguistics—especially semantics (theory of meaning, a branch of linguistics)—is a corrective to the openness in interpretation of the text, because it seeks to answer relevant questions, such as: What is the nature of human language? How do we communicate and process the information we receive? What are the proper ways of listening to the Bible?

The Old Testament also requires familiarity with its varied literary genres (see the essays by Longman and Satterthwaite) and encourages the integration of language with literature and of literature with history (see the essays by Merrill and Long).

These are the issues with which Kevin Vanhoozer deals in the essay below. His engagement with the philosophy and history that shape one's interpretation, though somewhat complex, is fascinating. In this essay you will discover how difficult the art of interpretation is. Further, he will open up the vista of the integration of language and literature with theology.

Vanhoozer concludes that the interpreter can have confidence in hearing the truth claims of the Bible. After all, the text (*sola Scriptura*) is sufficient for salvation and for living to God's glory. This text is not only sufficient, it is the totality of God's revelation in "written form" (*tota Scriptura*). However, more than hearing these claims, the interpreter will come to know God. Here is the theological dimension of the interpretive process (see the essays by Martens and Schultz).

Simply learning to read and interpret words and even concepts in the Bible is never sufficient. Studying God's Word is intended to bring students of the Word closer to God and to hearing his claims on their lives. In the process of interpretation, readers undergo several shifts. They undergo changes in their perception of the text, of themselves, of God, and, consequently, of the world. In the light of this concern, you will discover that Vanhoozer's essay is provocative in calling forth a generation of disciples. (VanGemeren)

1. LANGUAGE, LITERATURE, HERMENEUTICS, AND BIBLICAL THEOLOGY: WHAT 'S THEOLOGICAL ABOUT A THEOLOGICAL DICTIONARY?

> "I am not yet so lost in lexicography, as to forget that words are the daughters of the earth, and that things are the sons of heaven. Language is only the instrument of science, and words are but the signs of ideas: I wish, however, that the instrument might be less apt to decay, and that signs might be permanent, like the things which they denote.
> —Samuel Johnson, "Preface" to *Dictionary of the English Language* (1775)

Why should anyone consult a dictionary of OT terms, or even NT terms for that matter, in order to do Christian theology? Can words—daughters of the earth, according to Samuel Johnson—speak of things (the "sons of heaven"), not to mention God and the Son of God?

The dictionary definition of "definition" lists "the statement of the meaning of a word or the nature of a thing," and "the degree of distinctness in outline of an object or image" as possible meanings.[1] Definitions mark out the boundary or limits of something. Yet this definition raises two fundamental problems for the project of a theological dictionary: (1) Are definitions about words or the world? That is, do dictionaries talk only about language, or do they give us insight into the nature of reality as well? (2) What actually defines or gives a word its determinate meaning? Do words have a natural sense, or a supernatural sense imposed by God? Is meaning a matter of individual decision ("When *I* use a word ... it means just what I choose it to mean"—Humpty-Dumpty[2]) or of social convention? And are definitions forever, or do they change? As Samuel Johnson knew all too well, words and meanings alike change over time:

> Words strain,
> Crack and sometimes break, under the burden,
> Under the tension, slip, slide, perish,
> Decay with imprecision, will not stay in place,
> Will not stay still.
> (T. S. Eliot, *Four Quartets*, "Burnt Norton")

The purpose of this article is to survey some of the leading ways in which language and literature have been thought to serve either as an access or as an impediment to talking about God. Is language the antechamber or prison-house of theology, its handmaid or its warden? Can any language—prophetic, Pauline, pietistic, or philosophical—ultimately achieve transcendence and so speak of something other than itself?

These fundamental questions about the language of theology lead to questions about the theology of language. For questions about meaning and interpretation are themselves implicitly theological, and sometimes explicitly so. Is language a human construct or a gift of God? Is language basically an instrument the human creature uses to cope with its environment, or is it a means for interacting with what is other than itself? To some extent, the way one answers this question bears on how one conceives the relation between language and reality.

I begin with a survey of some important theories about words and their meaning, from Plato to postmodernity, and of how they have proven influential in biblical and theological studies. I then make good on my twofold claim that theology is largely a matter of language and language largely a matter of theology. Next I trace the fate of meaning by considering ever more complex levels of language: words, sentences, and literary texts. I suggest that meaning and interpretation are most properly located on the level of the sentence and the text, for meaning is less a matter of words in the abstract than of words put to certain kinds of use. Hermeneutics, I shall contend, seeks the meaning of communicative action, and for this we need to look at language as discourse—as something said to someone about something. I then look, in the following section, at the ways in which the Bible says something about God through its many kinds of literature.

Finally, I examine how an integrated hermeneutics of the Bible's language and literature can be theologically fruitful. While language and literature in general raise implicitly theological questions, the language and literature of the Bible make explicit theological claims—claims about God as well as claims on the reader. A dictionary of OT terms and themes provides an important service in aiding contemporary interpreters in achieving biblical literacy and canonical competence. The Christian theologian is one who has learned his or her craft through an apprenticeship to biblical literature. In learning what to say of God when, the biblical interpreter gains theological competence—not only theoretical knowledge of God (*epistēmē*), but a practical wisdom (*phronesis*) that can be applied to new situations as well.[3] Dictionaries, far from being dull records of past communicative action, thus serve a more dynamic purpose, namely, of informing contemporary speech and thought about God. Biblical interpretation ultimately leads not only to biblical theology, but to systematic and practical theology too.

A. On the Very Idea of a Dictionary Definition: From Cratylus to Cupitt

1. *Word and thing. Premodernity and the imitation of the world.*

(a) *Plato's* Cratylus—*on philology and philosophy.* Many of Plato's philosophical dialogues take the form of a search for definitions: What is justice? What is knowledge? What is goodness? In one of his lesser known dialogues, the *Cratylus,* Plato treats the nature of meaning and language. The three participants in the dialogue—Hermogenes, Cratylus, and Socrates—each represent different positions, positions that anticipate, often in extraordinary fashion, theories about language that have been, and continue to be, influential in ancient, modern, and postmodern times. For instance, Socrates' speculations about etymologies bears a certain resemblance to how the Biblical Theology Movement of the 1940s and 1950s interpreted biblical words. Similarly, the figure of Cratylus, after whom the dialogue takes its name, is a precursor of sorts to certain postmodern themes.

The main issue at stake in the *Cratylus* is whether or not we can speak truly: Do words give us knowledge of the world? Just what is the relation between philology (the study of words) and philosophy (the study of reality)? Hermogenes (a disciple of the Sophists) argues that names are conventional; like the names of slaves, they may be given or changed at one's pleasure. As such, words are unreliable guides to the nature of things, for there is no necessary connection between a word and the thing it names.

13

As we shall see, this position foreshadows Saussure's linguistics, a theory that has come to dominate much twentieth-century thinking about words.

The figure of Cratylus is less straightforward. He holds that a name is either a true name, the perfect expression of a thing, or else it is a mere inarticulate sound, not a name at all. Cratylus neatly encapsulates both the modern emphasis on meaning as reference and the postmodern emphasis on the indeterminacy of meaning. Cratylus thus resembles the skeptic who has such high requirements as to what counts as knowledge that nothing can meet it.[4] According to Aristotle, Cratylus was a follower of Heraclitus, the philosopher who said that one cannot step into the same river twice and who believed that change is the fundamental reality. From Heraclitus's notion that "all is flux," Cratylus concludes that one ought not to say anything, but only point with one's finger, since no true statement can be made about what is always changing. Cratylus is more pessimistic than Samuel Johnson: Whereas Johnson bemoans the impermanence of signs, Cratylus ascribes the same transitoriness to things in themselves. On the one hand, then, Cratylus espouses, if only for the sake of argument, the belief that everything has a right name of its own, fixed (made determinate) by nature. On the other hand, because he apparently maintains that nature is constantly in flux, no true names can be given; neither the world nor language is determinate.

It is to counter such skepticism that Socrates enters the discussion.[5] He first points out that if names are only conventional and if there are different conventions for different people, then people name things differently. But do the things to which the names refer differ as well? In other words, is what is in the world a matter of convention too? Socrates is unable to conceive of this—he did not have the advantage of reading Derrida or Foucault—and argues that things cannot be relative to individuals. The things of which we speak therefore have their own proper essence, and the successful speaker is the one who speaks of things "naturally." In other words, when we name things, we are also defining their natures. Who is able to do this? He who knows "how to put the true natural name of each thing into sounds and syllables, and to make and give all names with a view to the ideal name."[6] The business of a name is to express a nature. One might here cite 1 Sam 25:25 (RSV) in support: "He is just like his name—his name is Nabal [Fool], and folly goes with him."

Most of the dialogue is devoted to Socrates' exploration of Cratylus's suggestion that a word names a thing. Dictionary definitions are not only about words but about the world. Indeed, in another dialogue Socrates asks: "Do you think anybody understands the word for anything, if he doesn't know the thing, what it is?"[7] Plato evidently finds it difficult to distinguish the definition of a word from the definition of a thing. But how is it that words are the "proper names" for things? Here Socrates launches into what at times appears to be a tongue-in-cheek attempt to answer this question by means of an appeal to etymologies. A name is considered appropriate if its root meaning, its etymology, says something about the nature of the thing named. For instance, the etymology of the Greek term for "understanding" (*synesis*) means "to go along with." Understanding is thus a matter of "following" an argument or a story. The etymology of the term, its constituent parts, defines the nature of the thing (e.g., understanding) itself. There is not much that separates Socrates' use of etymologies from many theological dictionaries, and much preaching besides.

14

Once names have been analyzed into their constituent parts, however, the task remains to analyze the parts, for otherwise one falls into an infinite regress. Socrates, consistently enough, maintains that the parts of words—the consonants and vowels—are themselves imitations of things. "R," for example, expresses rapidity and motion, for "the tongue was most agitated and least at rest in the pronunciation of this letter."[8] And "l" expresses liquidity, because its pronunciation requires the tongue to slip. Thus, in the Eng. word "roll," we are to think of liquid motion or of rapid slipping (the "o," of course, represents the circular nature of the rapid motion!). Socrates' serious philological point, and it is a brilliant one, is that language is *imitative* sound. Resemblance of sounds to things is the first principle of language.

Socrates confesses to no little doubt as to the correctness of his theory, but what are the alternatives? If one rejects the imitation theory, the only alternatives are to appeal to the "Deus ex machina" (i.e., the gods gave the first names) or to the "veil of antiquity" (i.e., we don't know who gave things their names). Plato is clearly unhappy with either alternative, for each requires him to acknowledge that he has no reason to believe that we can speak truly (e.g., according to a thing's nature). At the same time, Socrates is aware that names can be wrongly given; one might call a tomato a vegetable rather than a fruit. There is a distinction, then, between a name and the thing itself.

Here Socrates grants Hermogenes's point, that naming is, at least in part, a matter of convention. After all, "tomato" does not really sound like a tomato, nor is there anything in its etymology that requires it to be linked with a glossy red fruit that grows on a vine. It is because there is unlikeness, as well as likeness, to things that requires a combination of nature and convention in naming. This is particularly true of numbers. The names of numbers do not resemble them. Socrates concedes this point reluctantly; one gains the distinct impression that Plato would be happier if language worked exclusively by imitation of nature, as this would fit in better with his theory of the Forms, according to which things on earth imitate eternal Ideas. To his credit, however, we find Plato at the end of the *Cratylus* suggesting that it is dangerous to try to find philosophy in words (e.g., etymologies). One cannot argue from name to nature, from philology to philosophy, from morphology to metaphysics: "He who follows names in the search after things, and analyses their meaning, is in great danger of being deceived."[9] We can only trust names to reveal the nature of things if names are God-given, but Socrates finds little way of making sense of this suggestion. On this account, how could one account for the variety of languages and for the fact that the meanings of words change over time? Better by far to view meaning as a joint product of natural imitation and social convention.

(b) *Augustine's* On Christian Doctrine. Augustine, the most important biblical interpreter in the early church, held a view of language that owed much to Plato. In his *Confessions*, Augustine recalls how his parents taught him to speak. "When they named some object, and accordingly moved towards something, I saw this and I grasped that the thing was called by the sound they uttered. Thus, as I heard words repeatedly used in their proper places in various sentences, I gradually learnt to understand what objects they signified."[10] This is a classic exposition of the "meaning as reference" theory. On this view, the meaning of a word is the object for which it stands. "All doctrine concerns either things or signs, but things are learned by signs."[11] Some things, however, signify other things. This accords with Plato, for whom earthly things are but pale imitations of eternal Ideas. Things are nevertheless learned by signs, and this includes things spoken of in Scripture. However, the relation between sign and thing may be obscured because some signs are ambiguous.

Augustine contrasts literal signs, which designate the things to which they refer directly, with figurative signs, which occur "when the thing which we designate by a literal sign is used to signify something else."[12] The literal meaning is often the least interesting, the least edifying, and the least theologically significant meaning. Literalistic interpretation often leads to poor results:

> When that which is said figuratively is taken as though it were literal, it is understood carnally. . . . There is a miserable servitude of the spirit in this habit of taking signs for things, so that one is not able to raise the eye of the mind above things that are corporeal and created to drink in eternal light.[13]

In other words, interpretation is carnal when one fails to see that the thing signified by a sign is itself a sign of something higher. To read spiritually is to recognize that the things referred to by the literal sense themselves refer to something higher, namely, the things of God. Ambrose had freed Augustine from his difficulties with the OT by showing that many of its stories, while distinctly unedifying on the literal level, carried a higher, spiritual meaning.

In an allegory, one thing is said but another meant. The early Christians applied this method of interpretation to the OT; on this level, the Law and the Prophets refer to Christ. Augustine's rule for deciding when to take a passage literally and when figuratively was brilliant in its simplicity: "Whatever appears in the divine Word that does not literally pertain to virtuous behavior or to the truth of faith you must take to be figurative."[14] If a literal reading fosters neither the love of God nor the love of neighbor, then one must choose the spiritual interpretation that does. Multiple readings are not dangerous so long as none of them contradicts the rule of faith, hope, and love.

Augustine later came to interpret 2 Cor 3:6, "the letter kills, the spirit gives life," differently: The law kills the soul unless the Spirit regenerates and enables it to love God. However, Augustine gives to this principle of the priority of grace a hermeneutic application as well: Words will convey their true meaning only as God himself illumines the heart and mind. In contemporary times this has become the insight that one can only read the Bible aright if one reads as an active participant in the Christian community (i.e., in the life of the church, and only then in the life of God).

What should be noted is the essentially Platonist theory of meaning that underlies Augustine's theory: As words signify things, so things signify higher things. Augustine's penchant for spiritual meanings and the general medieval tendency towards allegorical interpretation still work within a largely Platonic view of the language-world relation, where signs imitate things, and earthly things imitate heavenly Forms. Plato and Augustine serve as excellent illustrations of my working hypothesis that theories of interpretation presuppose theories of how God, world, and language are all interrelated. Such an integration between words and worldviews is as true of modern and postmodern theories as it is of the premodern theories we have just surveyed. I thus turn now to consider the language-world relation in modern biblical studies.

16

2. *Word and thought. Modernity and the turn to the subject.* In modern thinking about language, explanations of how language speaks truly have recourse to the mind rather than the world. It was Immanuel Kant who revolutionized philosophy by insisting that the mind does not know the world directly but supplies the categories and concepts that shape experience and so make reality determinate. Kant's so-called "Copernican Revolution" reversed the traditional relation between ideas and objects in the world. The mind, Kant argued, plays an active role in the language-world relation, contributing the structure to human experience. Words express thoughts. This "turn to the subject" implied that language expresses an individual's experience of the world rather than the world itself. What words represent in the first instance is not the world itself, nor Plato's eternal ideas, but rather human ideas or subjectivity. Words are signs not of things but of thoughts.[15] The legacy of Kant's revolution was that subsequent thinkers became trapped by what appeared to be an insoluble dilemma: Either language is subjective, eclipsing the world, or objective, eclipsing the subject.

(a) *Frege and the Biblical Theology Movement.* In a famous article entitled "On Sense and Reference," Gottlob Frege distinguished "sense," *what* someone says, from "reference," that *about which* one says something.[16] The sense is the ideal object, the idea one has in mind; the referent is the real object in the world that the sense or idea represents. The logic of interpretation is clear: One has first to determine the sense of a word or sentence before then going on to determine whether it refers to something real (i.e., whether it is true or false). The same referent may have a number of senses or connotations, but a sentence should refer to only one object.

(i) "Sense" and "reference." Frege's distinction highlights the two directions in which modern philosophy of language has tended to go. What Frege called "sense" calls attention to the intentionality of the speaker or author and to what he or she had in mind. "Reference," by contrast, calls attention to the external objects in the world towards which one's mind may be directed. Accordingly, language was thought to express thoughts and events—the meaning of a word is the state of affairs that it represents. Samuel Johnson speaks for modernity when he says that words are the signs *of ideas* (e.g., mental representations). The language of the Bible is now used as (1) direct evidence for reconstructing the mentality of the authors and (2) as indirect evidence for reconstructing what actually happened in history. As Hans Frei has observed, however, meaning in both instances is still associated with reference: reference to what the writers had in mind or reference to what happened "behind" the text. Language is still a matter of naming and representation, only now what is "imitated" in words are internal thoughts and external (earthly) states of affairs. Language thus performs an essentially informative function.

(ii) Theology as etymology? It was the Biblical Theology Movement in particular that became preoccupied with the notion that dictionaries and word studies provided a privileged access to the distinctive mentality and concepts of the biblical authors. The Biblical Theology Movement gave theological privilege to "sense."[17] Some suggested that the very structure of Heb. syntax expresses a peculiarly Heb. mentality: The structure of the Heb. language was taken as evidence of Heb. patterns of thought, including thought about God. On the basis of differences in syntax and grammar, for instance, Greek thought was said to be static and abstract in contrast to the dynamic and concrete thought of the Jew. It was then suggested that the theology of the

17

Bible pictured a more dynamic sense of time, of history, and of divine activity than in Greek thought. In other words, it became fashionable to read theology off of etymologies and syntax.[18]

Biblical scholars were particularly tempted by etymological analyses because Semitic languages, including Heb., are built around usually three consonants that serve as the root of a family of related words (e.g., in Arab., the root SLM is common to *salam,* peace; *islam,* submission; and *muslim,* one who submits). Moreover, the consonantal script in which Heb. is written also calls attention to a word's root. An eighteenth-century philologist, A. Schultens, suggested that the Heb. word *hôšîa'* (save, help) is derived from an Arab. word meaning give room to. He then moved, mistakenly, from Barr's point of view, from word to concept by arguing that salvation consequently carries with it some connotation of spaciousness.[19]

Kittel's *Theological Dictionary of the New Testament,* perhaps the greatest scholarly product of the Biblical Theology Movement, had a profound impact on modern theology, at least until James Barr published his scathing critique, *The Semantics of Biblical Language,* in 1961. Barr showed that a word's etymology may or may not affect its meaning in a particular instance. Much more important is the immediate context in which a word is used. Only careful contextual study will prove whether words of the same consonantal family always carry a "root meaning." David Kelsey concurs: "In ordinary discourse, surely, a word does not have one structure of systematically interrelated senses that goes with the word in every context of use."[20] One cannot move smoothly from a study of the various words for "to save" to a discussion of "the biblical concept of salvation," for instance. Moreover, some words (e.g., tomato) have no significant etymology. Others have etymologies that explain how terms were once used but have nothing to do with the meaning of a term today (e.g., nice). In general, Barr cautioned against identifying the various uses of a word with its root meaning (the "word-concept fallacy"). Barr correctly observed that the new content in the Judeo-Christian Scriptures was expressed at the level of the sentence, rather than the sign (e.g., the individual words) or the syntactical structure (e.g., the language as a whole).

Barr's critique of the Biblical Theology Movement represents modernity's attack on the premodern penchant to move from language to reality too fast. Barr insists that language only refers to the world as mediated through the mind. There can be no linguistic shortcut to God that bypasses historical criticism and authorial intention. Barr writes: "Modern biblical theology in its fear and dislike of the 'proposition' as the basis of religious truth has often simply adopted in its place the smaller linguistic unit of the word, and has then been forced to overload the word with meaning in order to relate it to the 'inner world of thought.'"[21]

(b) *Old Vienna and Old Princeton: Wittgenstein and Warfield.* Kant's turn to the subject has produced mixed results in modern biblical scholarship. On the one hand, as we have seen, modern biblical critics have redirected their attention to the mentality of the human authors and to "what it meant." Meaning is still reference, though now the reference to the world is always indirect, that is, through the mind of the author. For other modern scholars, however, the turn to the subject constitutes a dangerous turn towards subjectivity. Modernity is a victim of its own position: To conceive of the language-world relation with the categories of objectivity and subjectivity

18

is to be doomed always to be veering between the one pole and the other. Does language represent the self's thought (subjectivity) or the world itself (objectivity)? James Barr is typical of much modern biblical criticism in his insistence that one only reaches the objective (what actually happened) through the subjective (what it meant). Not all biblical critics, or philosophers for that matter, however, have been as sanguine about making the mind and its thought-forms the source of the world's determinations.

(i) Interpretation and logical positivism. Ludwig Wittgenstein's early philosophy of language is an outstanding example of modernity's quest for objectivity. Wittgenstein, together with Bertrand Russell, a colleague at Cambridge, was concerned to render ordinary language less misleading. Like other modern thinkers, Wittgenstein was under the impression that the job of a word was to name a thing, and that the chief occupation of sentences must be to picture states of affairs. Why cannot all language be as clear as the language of logic and mathematics, he wondered. Why indeed? Upheld by this ideal of a formal language that would perfectly mirror the world, Wittgenstein argued that every proposition corresponds to a basic fact in the world. A fact is a state of affairs, and a state of affairs is a combination of objects.[22] The world is made up of the sum total of facts. Wittgenstein's basic insight is that language pictures facts. If the picture agrees with reality, then it is true.[23] As to thought, it is a logical picture of facts, and a proposition is an expression of a thought. The purpose of language is to formulate true propositions, that is, to paint a verbal picture of or to represent the world.[24] Meaning is a matter of reference, but for Wittgenstein reference must always be to a factual state of affairs: "A name means an object. The object is its meaning."[25] Wittgenstein's early philosophy of language has been called "logical atomism" to highlight the central place he accords to propositions that picture basic facts. An object is like an "atom." What is "logical" is the ordering of objects and names. A true proposition thus pictures a state of affairs, that is, a set of objects and their arrangement (e.g., "The book is on the table").

Wittgenstein wrote his *Tractatus* in Austria during World War I. Soon after, a group of philosophers in Vienna seized upon Wittgenstein's work and used it as a basis for a whole philosophy—Logical Positivism. According to this philosophy, the nature of language itself rendered metaphysics—the study of ultimate reality—logically impossible. As Wittgenstein had shown, language referred only to states of affairs in the world. Metaphysics attempts to go beyond experience. But if language cannot speak of that which exceeds experience, then metaphysics, strictly speaking, has literally nothing to say. Accordingly, the Vienna Circle formulated the "Verifiability Criterion of Meaning." Reference now becomes a criterion for meaning: Unless we can show how and to what we refer, what we say is meaningless. For a sentence to be meaningful, it must be possible, at least in principle, to verify it—to check it against experience. The world is limited to what we can sense (empiricism), and language is rendered clearer by means of logic—hence the name Logical Positivism. Meaning is swallowed up by empirical reference. We are still working with a picture theory of language, only now what language imitates can never be heavenly realities, as Plato thought, but only what can be verified and falsified by science.[26] As we shall see, Wittgenstein later came to be his own harshest critic, rejecting his attempt to clarify ordinary language and coming to see instead that ordinary language has its own kind of logic.

(ii) Interpretation and biblical positivism? At first blush, it may seem odd to pair Old Princeton—the thought of such theologians as Benjamin Warfield and Charles Hodge—with Old Vienna and logical positivism. However, both James Barr and David Kelsey have accused the Princetonians (and implicitly, several generations of conservative biblical scholars as well) of succumbing to a kind of "biblical atomism" or "biblical positivism."[27] Barr and Kelsey suggest that the Princetonians unwittingly held to a distinctly modern philosophy of language, namely, one that privileges meaning as reference, and this despite their high view of biblical authority and their antimodernist polemic.

According to Barr, a theory of meaning as reference is presupposed every time the biblical narratives are read as history. Barr says that evangelicals tend to assume that the meaning of the biblical narrative lies in historical events. It is hermeneutically unwarranted, however, to insist that all biblical sentences must convey information. Barr believes that it is inerrancy that forces evangelicals to assume that every biblical statement corresponds to some "fact" in the world. I suggest, against Barr, that it is not the doctrine of inerrancy so much as a modernist philosophy of language that equates meaning with reference that does so. It is a theory of meaning as reference, not of biblical truth, that ultimately leads the Princetonians to privilege the proof-texting method. A proof text is simply a "biblical atom"—a proposition that pictures a fact.

With regard to theology and the interpretation of Scripture, then, the Princetonians resembled the logical positivists, though their primary source of data was not empirical experience but biblical propositions. As Hodge stated: "The Bible is to the theologian what nature is to the man of science. It is his storehouse of facts."[28] Warfield, similarly, interpreted the Bible as a verbal means of access to the facts of Christianity: "What Christianity consists in is facts that are doctrines, and doctrines that are facts."[29] Both Hodge and Warfield believed that God had so constituted the mind so as to enable it to apprehend the facts as they are.[30]

Hodge considers theology a science because it examines biblical facts and arranges them in a logical order. To be precise, theology is an inductive science that aspires to the same kind of objectivity as that found in the natural sciences. The man of science, be he physicist or theologian, must assume the trustworthiness of his sense perceptions and the trustworthiness of his mental operations. Lastly, the inductive approach derives principles (theories) from the facts and does not impose them upon the facts. Hodge assumes, in short, that interpretation is not necessary; it is enough to observe and deduce. The Princetonians differed, of course, from the members of the Vienna Circle in their conception of reality; for Warfield and Hodge language can refer to the supernatural as well as the natural. But in their attitude towards language and meaning, Princeton and Vienna concur: The meaning of language is the facts to which they refer.

3. *Word and sign. Postmodernity and the indeterminacy of meaning.* With the advent of postmodernity we have perhaps to speak of the turn *away* from the subject and of the turn towards language. For according to a number of postmodern thinkers, what gives rise to definitions and determinate reality is not the world itself, nor the subject who assigns names, but rather language itself. It is language that shapes both the world and our thought about the world. Language is less a mirror than a screen that pictures reality, not in the sense of representing it but rather of inventing it.

(a) *Derrida's poststructuralism.* Deconstruction, a movement associated with Jacques Derrida, is perhaps the most significant of the postmodern approaches to language and theology. In order to make sense of Derrida and deconstruction, we have first to discuss the structuralist approach to language.

As we have seen, for both the Platonists and propositionalists, truth is a matter of correspondence to the real. Language is true when it faithfully represents the real—either the Idea (for Plato) or the empirical (for the positivist). The Swiss linguist Ferdinand de Saussure worked out a very different account of language. He saw a word as a sign that means what it means not because it represents an object, but because it differs from other signs. For example: "hot" means what it means because it differs from "lot," "cot," or "dot," as well as from "cold," "lukewarm," and "tepid." Unlike Plato, who saw sounds imitating things, Saussure suggested that what makes a sign determinate is its place in a system of signs. A word does not resemble anything else but another word. The few, mostly minor, exceptions prove the rule. Words acquire meaning not by representing things but by differing from other words. Meaning is thus a matter of absences rather than presences, of arbitrary conventions rather than natural imitations. And, most important, what a person can say (*parole*) is limited, perhaps even determined by, the possibilities of the language system (*langue*) in which one works. The way to study language, according to Saussure, is to examine the structure of the language system. The actual use of language in the world (*parole*) is eclipsed by the world of language alone (*langue*). Language here swallows up both mind and world.

Derrida's poststructuralism takes Saussure's insights into language one step further—a step that unfortunately leads one to the brink of an abyss, if not actually over it. While agreeing that language is made up of differences between signifiers, Derrida rejects Saussure's idea that these differences can be contained in a system. Not only is meaning a function of differences, it is also deferred, because the play of signifiers never comes to an end. Signs refer to signs refer to signs, *ad infinitum*. Signs never do come to rest, never do cast anchor onto the real world. On the contrary, language is an ever-changing social construct that forcefully imposes different determinations onto the world, which has no more definition than a blank slate.

There is a certain despair of language in much postmodern thought. According to the poststructuralist, one can only stabilize sense and fix reference by an illegitimate use of force that imposes a sense of closure on language, which language, by its very nature, inherently resists. Derrida criticizes all attempts to bring the play of language to a halt. He calls the attempt to find some stable reference point outside of language "logocentrism." Platonism and positivism, despite their vast differences, share an underlying logocentrism, insofar as each position tries to ground language in the world.[31] Deconstruction is an attempt to display the groundlessness of language. It is the undoing of the covenant between language and reality that has characterized Western philosophy's belief that we can speak the truth.

Derrida's philosophy is significantly informed by literary criticism. Literary critics view the language-world relation quite differently from historians and traditional philosophers. For Erich Auerbach, for instance, the meaning of a literary work is not that to which it refers.[32] Rather, a literary work creates its own world; a story is its own meaning. Form and content are inseparable. Without the story, one simply does not have the meaning of, say, Henry James' novel *Portrait of a Lady*. More significantly, one does not have the referent, the lady mentioned in the title, without the story. She simply does not exist apart from the whole story. In Derrida's terms, all we have are such "texts." All uses of language, not only the poetic, are similarly textual. For Derrida, both the world and the mind are ineradicably textual, that is, structured by language, which is to say by an arbitrary set of social conventions. Whereas modern thinkers like Descartes began philosophy in human consciousness ("I think, therefore I am"), Derrida claims that consciousness itself is structured by language. Though we may think that we use words to express thoughts, Derrida maintains that the way we think is determined by the language we use. Writing (by which he means the *system* of language) precedes speech (by which he means a person's conscious *use* of language).

If language is a product of social forces and political power that imposes ideologies (e.g., systems of hierarchically organized distinctions) onto ultimately unknowable things, then perhaps Cratylus was right: We may as well point at things rather than try to speak of them. Even worse, if language is no longer an adequate medium of communication, human intercourse may degenerate into the making of inarticulate gestures—either threatening or defensive—as persons seek to negotiate a common world without the benefit of common words. For the postmodern poststructuralist, language is less a neutral medium of thought than thought's hostile and polluted environment.

(b) *Don Cupitt's aesthetic antirealism.* Increasingly, biblical scholars and theologians are showing every sign of accepting postmodernity's view of the language-world relation.[33] The operative term now is neither imitation nor information, but indeterminacy. If words do not have a determinate meaning, however, the very idea of a definition is called into question.

Don Cupitt is one such theologian who rejects both fixed definitions and fixed essences in the name of creative indeterminacy. We simply have no access to a world of timeless essences, he says. Like other intellectual disciplines—such as physics, psychoanalysis, and literary criticism—theology too must begin to dismantle its object of study. Of course, from another angle, undoing may look like a process of continual redoing. And this is precisely what Cupitt thinks theology should be about: reinventing faith for our time, engaging in make-believe. Words, says Cupitt, do not hook up to things. Words refer to other words and in this way generate a meaningful world. In other words, what gives reality shape or determinate meaning are the distinctions we draw and articulate in words. In Welsh, for instance, the color spectrum is divided up differently than in English. The color *glas* (blue) includes elements that in English would be called green or gray. In learning its native language the child learns a set of differentiating concepts that identify not *given entities* but *socially constructed signifieds*.[34] Whereas for Plato words imitate things, one might say that for the postmodernist, things imitate words.

The postmodernist does not believe in a "super-language" that gives us the true story. Indeed, François Lyotard defines the postmodern condition in terms of an "incredulity towards metanarratives."[35] That is, the postmodern thinker no longer believes that we can attain a perspective outside of and above language from which we can then check to see if our language really does correspond to the way things are or not. Reality is merely "the sum of all that our language makes generally accessible and discussable."[36]

For Cupitt, the way forward for theology is to accept that its language is essentially aesthetic and creative. Instead of trying to speak truly, we should be more concerned with speaking creatively, in ways that make human experience meaningful. Theology's task is to develop symbols and metaphors that will enable us to dwell meaningfully in the world. Cupitt neatly reverses Hodge: Theories invent facts and impose forms upon them. We have no access to the world as it is apart from some language or other. To inhabit a language is to abandon all attempts to attain a God's-eye point of view. Again, it is not that words imitate the world, but that the world imitates words. Socrates' notion that sounds imitate things, which Cupitt dubs the "bow-wow theory" of language, got it backwards: "Words shape the way we see the world, we fancy that the world has shaped our words. In reality, language determines perception."[37]

B. God, Language, and Literary Theory: What's Theological About Language and Hermeneutics?

1. *The fundamental issue: realism and nonrealism.* Ought language represent reality? Can it? Questions about language and meaning are inextricably tied up with larger philosophical and theological issues. What dictionaries were thought to be and do has changed over time. In the ancient world, the dictionary gave insight not only into language but ultimately into things themselves, not only spoken and written words but the real world. For both Plato and Augustine, language is true when it imitates the world. In more modern times, words give us insight into what people are feeling and thinking, into an individual's mind.[38] Henceforth, philosophers would guard against mistaking the linguistic description for the thing itself. With postmodernity's turn towards language, the gap between language and world becomes an unbridgeable "ugly ditch": The dictionary tells us not how language represents the world or human thought, but rather how language shapes and determines human thinking, and thus what we take to be the world.[39] Language is less a window onto the world or a mirror of the soul than it is a system that shapes both the world and subjectivity. The disappearance of the third-person-masculine singular pronoun as a term for humanity in general is not only a lexical but a political event. Our brief survey confirms the thesis that the various methods of biblical interpretation are compelling for those who practice them because of the underlying worldview that they presuppose.[40] One's understanding of the relation between language and reality ultimately involves theological assumptions. This brings us back to my initial twofold claim, namely, that theology has to do with language and that language has to do with theology.

Let us return to the idea of a definition. To define something is to determine what something is: its nature, character, and outline. In its ocular sense, "definition" has to do with clarity, with the distinctness of an object or image. But a word can have a clear definition only if the thing in the world that it names has a determinate nature. The alternative would lead to Cratylus' position: If things do not have a fixed nature, definitions are no good; we could only point with our fingers at the flux. Two larger questions, therefore, haunt our discussion of language: (1) Are things in the world determinate? (2) If reality is determinate, what makes it so? What stamps a determinate nature onto things so that language can speak truly of them? Is it God, human subjectivity (e.g., reason), social convention, or perhaps artistic creation (e.g., language)?

23

Does the world (and God) have a fixed character, or do human speakers differentiate the world (and God) by inventing linguistic distinctions?

To repeat my thesis: Views of language presuppose views of God (or of God's absence). In the premodern world, the nature of reality was fixed and revealed by God. In early modern philosophy, reality was thought to have an eternal order that was knowable by reason. In later modern philosophy, Kant suggested that what reason knows is its own workings on experience, not the world itself. In our postmodern context, the tendency is to radicalize Kant's insight and to follow Nietzsche by saying that we can never get beyond our languages to an extralinguistic reality. The challenge today is to explain how language can be used to talk truly about reality.

Today little is taken as "given," since everything is thought to be constructed—"graven." The world—the sum total of "natural" kinds and "natural" orders, not to mention the explicitly cultural ones—is now thought to be a product of our language systems. Instead of language mirroring the way things are, the world is rather like a blank screen onto which language projects its system of distinctions. Nonrealism—the position that there is no such thing as a real world independent of language—takes an implicitly theological (or rather, countertheological) position. According to the nonrealist, not only is there no God's-eye point of view, but God is absent. That is, there is no reference point from which to make true distinctions and definitions. For the nonrealist, the world simply does not exist independent of our linguistic representations of it. This is the sense in which one must understand Derrida's maxim: "There is nothing outside the text." There is, in other words, no determinate reality that stands "over against" our language systems. Cupitt readily acknowledges the consequences of the notion that thought is radically dependent on, perhaps even determined by, language. He calls his position "semiotic materialism," to underline his thesis that language is a mind-shaping and world-creating social force.[41]

Cupitt's view of language is consistent with his nonrealist faith: "'Reality'?—feelings fixed by conventional noises, and systematized."[42] Being postmodern means facing up to the fact that language is free-floating, grounded neither in the world, nor in reason, nor in revelation. It means facing up to the arbitrariness of all our talk, including our God-talk. For the nonrealist, God has no being or definition apart from the language we use to speak of him. Nonrealists thus think of meaning the way Feuerbach thought of God: Both meaning and God are merely projections of language.[43] Cupitt, mindful of the creative nature of language, thus calls for Christians to reinvent faith for their time, to formulate new images and metaphors for talking about God, that is, about our highest human aspirations. The crisis and confusion in contemporary theories of language, literature, and interpretation is directly related to the crisis in contemporary theology. Why is theological nonrealism a threat? Because it means that there is no extralinguistic reality—God—that can serve as a criterion and check for what we say and do in the name of God. The word "God" is the ultimate designer label, the supreme sanction for moral values and political programs. It is precisely because the word "God" is so powerful that theology is necessary—to make sure that talk of God corresponds to the way God really is as revealed in the event of Jesus Christ as attested in the Scriptures.

2. *Language and theology: the analogy of being and the analogy of faith.* As John Macquarrie reminds us, "Theology is language," inasmuch as theology is "rea-

soned talk about God."[44] But how can language have to do with God? For much of its history, theology's primary concern has been with its own possibility, with how its words are related to an original Word of God. Two examples of how views of language and views of God are mutually supportive must suffice. Each tries to take account of the fundamental problems of presence and absence—of how human words can refer to God truly and of how the reality of God ultimately transcends human language.

(a) *Thomas Aquinas and the analogy of being.* Twelfth-century theologians were among the most sophisticated with regard to their understanding of the relation of language to theology. Their primary problem was how human words could signify God. As G. R. Evans observes: "Unless we can show that what we are saying has some meaning in connection with God, or that it refers to him in some way, we cannot be sure that we are saying anything about God at all. We may be talking about an imaginary being."[45] If language is humanly devised, a system of social conventions, as many of the medieval theologians believed, how can it refer to God?

When we say "God is good," does "good" mean the same as it means when applied to creatures (in which case God loses his transcendence and is reduced to an earthly object), or does it mean something entirely different (in which case we do not know what it means)? Thomas Aquinas evades this either-or and suggests that some words may be used *analogically* of God.[46] If a thing can be a sign for God, there must be some similarity between the thing and God. If there were not, then how could, say, fatherhood or kingship be meaningful terms to ascribe to God? Language about things may be applied analogously to God insofar as the created things share certain qualities (e.g., perfections such as goodness, justice, beauty, etc.) with their Creator, though only to a lesser degree.

Aquinas's view of language thus relies on a picture of how God is related to the world. God is present in the world as the source of Being.[47] Aquinas claims, reasonably enough, that we can only speak of God as we know him, but then he goes on to say that "we know him from creatures."[48] God is the ground of being, the source of all that is. God is the reference point for all that is. He is the transcendent Presence and perfection that creaturely things analogically (and thus imperfectly) represent. Aquinas states: "When we say God is good or wise we do not simply mean that he causes wisdom or goodness, but that he possesses these perfections transcendently."[49] The confidence that language may refer analogically to God is based on the analogy of being that posits a similarity between creaturely reality and the Creator. What creatures and Creator share is Being, though God is the highest Being, endowed with all the perfections of Being, and has Being in and of himself.[50] "Good" has the meaning it has only because there is an extralinguistic reference point (viz., the goodness of God) that fixes language (viz., the term "good"). The analogy of being thus accords with a natural theology that maintains that we can say true things about God on the basis of our experience of and reflection about nature.[51]

(b) *Karl Barth and the analogy of faith.* Karl Barth conceives of the presence of God very differently from Aquinas and thus provides another instructive example of how one's view of God and one's view of language each have a bearing on the other.

Barth rejects the *analogia entis* as a massive theological error. Natural theology implies that God is in fundamental continuity with the world and so denies the "wholly otherness" of God. Barth's dialectical theology, on the other hand, affirms an "infini-

25

tive qualitative difference" between God in heaven and eternity on the one hand and humanity on earth and in time on the other. But if God is wholly other than the world, how then can human language speak of God truly? Barth's short answer is: It cannot. Left to its own devices, human language can speak only of the world. Dialectical theology prevents any illegitimate or premature synthesis of God and humanity from the human side. However, there is nothing to stop human language from revealing God *from God's side*. Barth's dialectical theology therefore recognizes an *analogia fidei* (analogy of faith)—an analogy "from above," initiated by divine grace. Only in this way can God remain God (e.g., the wholly other) as well as the referent of human words.[52]

Barth's dialectical theology appears to lead to two incompatible views of human language. On the one hand, human talk about God, like justification by works, degenerates into a hopeless human activity—the meaningless play of signifiers. Barth accepts the Kantian point that concepts, or in this case language, always intrude on the relation between the human knower and the object of knowledge. If left to its own devices, Barth seems to imply, language is as the poststructuralists conceive it—an indeterminate play of signs. Only by God can God be known. Only in the act of revelation do the words of Scripture disclose the Word of God. For Barth, human words only refer to God when God in his revelation uses them to do so.[53] Only by reading in faith, through an *analogia fidei*, can we follow the biblical word from sense, from what it says, to referent, to what it is about.

The goal of biblical interpretation for Barth is to discern the Word in the words. "Without revelation there can only be semantic agnosticism—for all acts of signification make arbitrary connection between words and what is."[54] God's language, on the other hand, is wholly adequate to its object. Without divine activity, however, the process of interpreting the Scriptures is short-circuited. "That human language can become a bearer of divine revelation is a divine possibility, not a human possibility."[55] Exegetical labor alone cannot catch the sacred fish. Successful reference—the disclosure of the Word by the words—is ultimately God's own achievement in the interpreter. If there is revelation—successful reference to the Word—it is not a function of the Bible's language so much as an event of divine grace.

Barth's view of God thus gives rise to a particular view of language and interpretation: the *analogia fidei*. The theological motive behind Barth's refusal of the analogy of being is his concern to forestall any kind of linguistic natural theology. God would not be God if he could be the referent of human discourse or if he could simply be read off of the biblical texts. As wholly other, God is hidden in his revealedness; only in this way can God be Lord of the process of revelation. The unresolved question for Barth concerns the status of the economy of signification (viz., language): Is it a God-given gift, or a sinful postlapsarian product that has nothing to do with God? Is language human or divine in origin? Barth seems to be saying both: Language is socially constructed and divinely elected, both arbitrary and adequate in relation to the reality of God. Behind Barth's view of language lies his view of God as dialectially present: hidden to reason, revealed to faith. Both Barth and Aquinas seek a view of language that does justice to divine immanence (presence) and transcendence (absence) alike. For Aquinas, however, God's presence is the stable ground of Creation, whereas for Barth, God's presence is more dynamically conceived, a revealing presence only to an active faith.[56]

3. *Literary theory as a theology?* Is hermeneutics without theological presuppositions possible? Whereas Bultmann argued that exegetical work always involves presuppositions, I would go further and claim that our hermeneutical theories themselves are dependent on theologies (or atheologies). If I am right, then we should expect to find some sort of correlation between various theological positions (e.g., classical theism or natural theology, dialectical theology, pantheism, etc.) on the one hand, and various approaches to interpretation (e.g., feminism, historicism, deconstruction, etc.) on the other. I turn to post- structuralist literary theory as the chief exhibit in defense of this working hypothesis.

(a) *The death of the author.* Deconstruction, it has been said, is the death of God put into hermeneutics.[57] For Derrida, presence—the presence of meaning, an author, God—is always illusory, an effect or projection of writing. Without an Author, the world has no fixed meaning; without the author, the text has no fixed meaning. God's death in the nineteenth century precipitated the author's death in the twentieth century—a similarly theological event. "Both deaths attest to a departure of belief in authority, presence, intention, omniscience and creativity."[58] Derrida and other deconstructionists celebrate the death of the author as a counter-theological event which frees the reader for creative play.[59]

To declare the author dead is to abandon the search for a stable home for linguistic meaning. For Barthes and Foucault, the death of the author means that there is nothing outside the play of writing that guarantees determinate sense or that our words refer to the world. The turn to language involves a turn away from the subject: The author's consciousness is no longer thought to be able to control the sense and reference of his words. Consequently, the author has lost all "authority"—the ability to say of x that it is y, the power of say-so.

With the death of the author comes the birth of the reader. Readers benefit from the power vacuum that follows from the author's absence. It is the reader's will-to-power that bestows meaning on texts. Derrida agrees with Nietzsche: If God (stable meaning) does not exist, it would be necessary to invent him (it). This is precisely the role of the reader: to create meaning out of a sea of indeterminate signs. Atheism thus leads to nonrealism in literary theory and philosophy alike. In much literary theory, God, self, and world are all alike reduced to modes of textuality.[60] In Derrida's words: "There is nothing outside the text."[61]

(b) *Hermeneutics or grammatology?* Derrida, to his credit, acknowledges the tie between hermeneutics and theology. "The sign and divinity have the same place and time of birth. The age of the sign is essentially theological."[62] The sign is theological insofar as it is taken to represent presence, that is, insofar as it is a sign of an extra-linguistic reality that transcends it. Meaning, and hermeneutics in general, is theological insofar as it refers to the belief that there is something in what we say, that is, if it refers to the belief that our God-talk is not merely talk about talk but talk about God. Derrida, however, pits grammatology over against hermeneutics. Grammatology is the "science of writing," that is, the study of signs in their material and differential relation to one another rather than of the relation between signs and things or thoughts. It is the dream of hermeneutics that meaning (the transcendental signified) will some-

27

how be made present through the process of deciphering signs. Grammatology is to language as atheism is to religion; it reminds us that there is only writing, only absence, only signs referring to other signs—never voice, presence, or the fullness of being.

George Steiner, another literary critic, agrees that meaning is ultimately a theological affair yet claims, against Derrida, that the actual practice of speaking and writing necessarily presupposes a belief in meaning: "Any coherent account of the capacity of human speech to communicate meaning and feeling is, in the final analysis, underwritten by the assumption of God's presence."[63] Steiner admits that the sense of an other's "real presence" in language may be only a rhetorical flourish, as the deconstructionists say, rather than "a piece of theology," but any significant encounter with the text as other must make a wager of faith in transcendence.[64] Interpretation is "theological" for Steiner because he believes that there is something that transcends the play of signs in language. The alternative for Steiner is a "deconstructionist and postmodernity counter-theology of absence," where the reader discovers only herself.[65]

C. Biblical Exegesis, Theology, and Hermeneutics: What Are We Interpreting?

What precisely are we after as linguists or interpreters? "Meaning" is too glib an answer, for what is the meaning of meaning? Krister Stendahl drew what has become a celebrated distinction between "what it meant" and "what it means" in order to distinguish the respective tasks of biblical and systematic theology.[66] It is the role of the biblical theologian to describe "what it meant" for the original authors and readers. The systematic theologian's job is to find a suitable language and conceptuality to explain "what it means" in a manner faithful to the text and intelligible to contemporary culture. But what, we may ask Stendahl, is "it"? Is "it" a word, and meaning its definition, perhaps the thing it refers to? This, by and large, was the answer of premodern biblical scholars. Subsequent suggestions for what we are trying to describe include the things referred to historically, the things referred to allegorically, and the thoughts of the original authors. To ask what interpreters are after is thus to raise two questions: "What is meaning?" and "Of what precisely are we asking the question of meaning?"

1. *From semiotics to semantics.* What has emerged from our survey of views of language—from premodern imitation theories through the modern focus on language as information about empirical or subjective reality to the postmodern emphasis on indeterminacy—is that the object of study has been, for the most part, either isolated words or the language system as a whole. Interpretation has gravitated more towards *signs* and *systems* of signs than *sentences*, towards *langue* rather than *parole*. To put it yet another way: To this point we have been examining *semiotics* rather than *semantics*. We have seen the importance accorded to signs as imitations of things, of signs as expressions of thought, and of signs as constituent elements in what is ultimately an arbitrary language system. And whether the emphasis was on words as imitative, informative, or indeterminate, all the theorists assumed that the major task of language was to refer to the world. Where theorists differed was over whether they thought language was up to its task. To generalize, the question of reference (ideal, historical, indeterminate) has swallowed up the question of meaning. *What is conspicuous by its absence is any study of signs as used by human beings in particular contexts to accomplish specific tasks.*

(a) *Langue/parole; sign/sentence; semiotics/semantics.* "For me, the distinction between semantics and semiotics is the key to the whole problem of language."[67] I am inclined to agree with Ricoeur. While semiotics (the science of signs or *semeia*) focuses on linguistic rules and conventions, semantics examines linguistic performance and intentions. For semiotics, meaning is a matter of the relations between signs with the system of *langue.*

One may, of course, study words or texts as elements in a structure of language. Similarly, one may study language systems as a whole in relation to the social and political systems of which they are a part. The study of signs and codes (*langue*), however, effectively ignores the speaking subject and the act of communication. Semiotics studies language as constituting a self-contained world of its own. On this view, systems of language perform an ideological function insofar as they shape how people will differentiate and experience the extralinguistic world. Language, far from being a neutral instrument for naming the world, is instead an indispensable instrument of indoctrination. In learning a language a speaker also learns a system of differences and distinctions—an ideology.

(b) *Parole/sentences/semantics.* According to Ricoeur, speech—in particular, the sentence—introduces a level of complexity and uniqueness that cannot be described by semiotics. He sees semiotics and semantics "as the two sciences which correspond to the two kinds of units characteristic of language, the sign and the sentence."[68] The sentence is not merely a larger sign but a distinct entity, requiring new methods of description. A sentence, composed of at least a name and a vb., connects words in a synthesis that displays a new level of complexity and requires a new and higher level of description than the semiotic. Though one can analyze a sentence and break it down into its constituent parts, a sentence "is a whole irreducible to the sum of its parts."[69] Ricoeur defines semantics as "the science of the sentence."

2. *Language and literature: the covenant of discourse.* As the function of words in premodernity and modernity has been to (a) name things or (b) stand for or label thoughts, so the sentence has been thought to function as a pictorial representation of a state of affairs. A picture of language as composed of signs rather than sentences has held us captive. To focus on the semantics of sentences, however, is to create a new picture of language as "discourse"—as something someone says to someone about something. To conceive of language and literature as discourse is to view speech and text as the communicative acts of communicative agents.[70] John Fiske defines language as a means of communication, of "social interaction through messages."[71]

(a) *Language as discourse: an interaction theory.* Ludwig Wittgenstein was one of the first philosophers to free himself from the picture of language as a means of referring to objects in the world. Wittgenstein came to see that language can be used for many different purposes and that there are a variety of different "fits" between word and world. J. L. Austin similarly believed that the task of the philosopher was not to improve upon ordinary language by showing how it corresponded to the world so much as to understand how it performed many other tasks as well.[72] Austin discovered that the situation in which language was used was every bit as important as the words themselves.

Discourse has to do with the actual use of words, with words in action. For the sake of analysis, we may distinguish four levels of communicative action. (i) Locutionary. While language systems are merely virtual, discourse pertains to an actual use of words. The locutionary act refers to the act of saying something.[73] (ii) Illocutionary. Sentences, besides saying something (e.g., identifying and predicating), also *do* something (e.g., warn, assert, promise, etc.). The illocutionary act refers to what we do when we say something.[74] It is the illocutionary aspect of discourse that semiotics overlooks, to damaging effect. For it is the illocution that makes a set of words into a particular type of communicative action (e.g., an assertion, a question, a warning, a command, etc.). The words "It's hot," alone, are indeterminate; it is not clear what illocutionary act is being performed, be it assertion, or warning, or promise. The words alone cannot render the meaning determinate; the interpreter needs contextual clues before deciding what it means. (iii) Perlocutionary. This dimension of communicative action refers to what a speaker brings about by saying something. For instance, by asserting something, a speaker may also persuade. (iv) Interlocutionary. Discourse is always addressed *to* someone. Every illocutionary act is a kind of invitation to which the reader or listener is invited to respond (e.g., by assent, by action, by further discourse, etc.). Thanks to discourse, we are able to communicate meaning to one another. The interlocutionary aspect of discourse reminds us that language is ultimately a medium for interpersonal interaction.

It follows from the nature of discourse that language is both a means for relating to other persons and a means for relating to one's world. To speak is to incur certain privileges as well as responsibilities vis-à-vis one's hearers and the world. To view language as discourse is to see it as a medium for personal interaction. Speech or *parole*, unlike *langue*, cannot be dissociated from its speaker. Take, for example, a promise. Here the speaker explicitly implicates herself in what she says. As J. L. Austin puts it: "Our word is our bond."[75] There is, I believe, a similarly "covenantal" aspect in all discourse. As agents of communicative action, authors are tied to their texts and responsible for what they say. Words are instruments of communicative interaction. Some communicative interactions concern the way the world is or the way the speaker feels. Others pertain to the speaker's wishes or requests. Still others have to do with the actions and promises of God. In all cases, our word is our bond: an intersubjective bond between speakers and an objective bond between language and reality.

(i) Conventions and intentions. Meaning, as a function of the process of communicative interaction, involves both intentions and conventions. On the one hand, speakers cannot simply make their words mean what they want them to mean through a sovereign intention. In this sense, the poststructuralists are right to call attention to the fact that language precedes speech. Yet the mere existence of *langue* does not condemn its speakers to some kind of linguistic determinism, for the speaker is able to put the language system to different kinds of use. By invoking particular conventions, speakers intend to communicate something and to make sure that their intention will be recognized by others. The communicative agent intends to reach understanding through the use of linguistic conventions. Discourse is thus an intersubjective phenomenon that requires both subjective intentions and public ("objective") conventions. By invoking a particular linguistic or literary convention, an author enacts his or her intention and so renders it public, a legitimate object of understanding.[76]

(ii) Understanding or explanation? In the nineteenth century, Wilhelm Dilthey developed a distinctive method for the human as over against the natural sciences.[77]

The latter, he argued, seek explanations while the former seek understanding. Explanation works with universal laws and is well-suited to studying the natural world. Understanding, on the other hand, is the attempt to grasp the significance of human experience and action, that is, the life of an individual. Dilthey believed hermeneutics to be concerned with grasping the meaning, not the cause, of human action via its expression in history: Both the deeds and the discourse of the past call for understanding.

Dilthey himself believed that the aim of the human sciences was to recover the mind of the author, his or her psychic life. But this is to search for some meaning behind the discourse. A better goal for interpretation is to seek the meaning of, not the motive behind, the discourse. Understanding a discourse means grasping the meaning of the whole considered as a communicative act. To understand a discourse is to apprehend both its propositional content (e.g., the matter) as well as its illocutionary force (e.g., the energy). The illocutionary act is the touchstone, the aspect that breathes semantic life into what otherwise would be a lifeless chain of signifiers. It is the illocutionary level that distinguishes discourse from signs and language systems. Understanding is essentially the recognition of one's illocutionary act. To understand discourse is to grasp the nature and content of a communicative act, and this can only be done when the illocutionary intent is recognized. Understanding discourse is, I suggest, the proper aim of interpretation, for only on this level do we achieve understanding of the discourse as a whole as opposed to knowledge of its elementary parts.

What effect does the newer picture of language as discourse have on the role of a dictionary? If language is discourse, then dictionaries are best viewed as descriptions of discourse, that is, as records of linguistic usage. A good dictionary usually lists several entries for well-known words and is a good source of information for how words are, and have been, habitually used. Dictionaries cannot, of course, anticipate how words will be used in the future.

(iii) Divine speech acts. If, as I have claimed, theology informs views of language and hermeneutics, what theology informs the present discussion of language as communicative interaction (e.g., discourse)? This is a perfectly appropriate question. The short answer is "evangelical" theology, where evangelical stands for theology oriented to "good news"—news of divine action on behalf of the world. The gospel concerns the communication of what has happened in the event of Jesus Christ. Accordingly, the theology behind my view of language and interpretation is a theology of communicative interaction. God's Word is something that God *says*, something that God *does*, and something that God *is*. The God of the Christian Scriptures and Christian faith is the kind of God that can enter into relation with human beings through Incarnation and through verbal communicative action.[78] Moreover, the God portrayed in the Scriptures has given to humans the dignity of communicative agency and communicative responsibility. Consequently, meaning is first and foremost something persons *do*.

(b) *Literature as discourse: the meaning of texts.* The text is an extended and unified discourse, fixed by writing. As such, it is a complex whole, admitting of many kinds of investigation. Literary texts "are best viewed as actions performed on a variety of levels for our contemplation."[79] Texts are speech acts of a higher order. They have mass (e.g., subject matter) and energy (e.g., illocutionary force). Like sentences, texts call for semantics, not just semiotics. As an extended and unified discourse, a text calls for understanding, not merely analysis. One cannot say that one has understood a biblical text, for instance, when one has parsed every word or even after one has analyzed the overall structure. On the contrary, understanding is only achieved when one interprets a text as a communicative act and receives the message that the author has transmitted for our consideration.

What, for instance, is Paul *doing* in his letter to Ephesians? Several possible answers come to mind: putting words together, dictating a letter, addressing the Ephesians, sending greetings, reflecting on the significance of the event of Jesus Christ. A historical approach that examines the situation behind the text could do justice to some aspects of the communicative action but not others. A semiological approach could do justice to others. If used exclusively, however, a semiotic study of Ephesians would not merely explain but explain away, as all reductionistic theories always tend to do. Much to be preferred is a description that incorporates the semiotic but then go on to do justice to the semantic. For one cannot describe an action simply by describing its components parts. It is one thing to describe an action as moving one's finger or producing sounds, and another to describe the moving of one's fingers as performing a Beethoven piano sonata. One cannot correctly understand a person's bodily movements (or words) without reference to an agent's intentions. What we are ultimately trying to understand as biblical interpreters, I would contend, is the intention enacted in the text—the sense and significance of a communicative act.[80]

D. Interpreting Scripture: The Semantics of Biblical Literature

In the sixteenth century, renewed interest in the Bible's original languages contributed to the Reformation. At the end of the twentieth century, we are on the verge of a similar recovery, not of the languages but of the literature of the Bible. An appreciation of the biblical texts as forms of extended discourse makes two important contributions to biblical interpretation. It encourages us to treat biblical texts as certain kinds of literary wholes (viz., genres). It also requires us to treat the literary form more seriously, as the only access to the text's content. To claim that the proper object of interpretation is neither individual words nor atomic proof texts but rather discourse is to imply that biblical exegetes and theologians should attend to the whole text as a unified though extended piece of discourse.[81]

1. *Literary whole and context:* sola scriptura *as a hermeneutical principle.* To say that language and literature are forms of discourse does not solve all interpretive problems. What, for instance, of the problem of indeterminacy of meaning? It is one thing to say that meaning is communicative action, quite another to determine what kind of communicative act has been performed. As with *langue*, so with *parole*: The general principle is that *context* disambiguates. We know what sense to make of "he's hot" once we are clear about the context: Is he lying on a bed in a hospital, in the midst of a family argument, or playing a great game of tennis? The situation of a discourse provides important interpretive clues.

But if the meaning of texts depends on their contexts, have we not simply pushed the problem of semantic indeterminacy back one step, for who determines the relevant context, and how? Derrida and other deconstructionist critics argue for a pluralism of meanings precisely because texts have as many contexts as they have readers.[82] The search for determinate textual meaning thus appears to founder on the question of context. Which contexts makes texts determinate? How large a context must we establish in order to interpret a text correctly? In reply to these questions, I contend that the most important context for understanding biblical discourse is its literary (e.g., generic) and canonical context.

(a) *The issue:* sola scriptura *and hermeneutical sufficiency.* "The infallible rule of interpretation of Scripture is the Scripture itself."[83] The question is whether, and to what extent, the interpreter must have recourse to extrabiblical information in order to interpret Scripture correctly. What is at stake is not so much the material sufficiency of Scripture (e.g., does the Bible contain all things necessary for salvation?) but rather what one could call the *hermeneutical sufficiency* of Scripture.[84] According to the framers of the Westminster Confession of Faith, Scripture itself is the best context for interpreting Scripture. In modernity and postmodernity alike, however, interpreters have tended to provide Scripture with extrabiblical interpretive contexts.

(i) The reconstructed historical context. In his magisterial study of biblical hermeneutics in the eighteenth and nineteenth centuries, Hans Frei documents the loss of the literal sense of Scripture in modern historical criticism.[85] Under the influence of an antisupernaturalistic bias, many modern critics distinguished between the biblical accounts and "what actually happened." The effect of this critical distinction was to pry apart the story from its meaning, the sense of the text from its historical reference. Henceforth biblical interpretation meant reading the text in light of extrabiblical information, which was thought to be more reliable. This led, ironically, to a confusion between the biblical text itself and what lay behind it. Thus, the meaning of a biblical text was thought to be its historical reference (e.g., the events to which it refers), and the prime interpretive context, the critically reconstructed original situation.[86] Such was the "great reversal" that took place, according to Frei, in modernity: "Interpretation was a matter of fitting the biblical story into another world with another story rather than incorporating that world into the biblical story."[87] Frei particularly objects to historical criticism's relative neglect of the most important context for determining meaning, namely, the form of the text itself.

(ii) The context of the reader. A second mode of hermeneutical insufficiency is characteristic of postmodern approaches to the Bible. We can read Exodus in its original historical context (insofar as this can be established), or we can read it in the contemporary context of Latin America or South Africa, of feminist or womanist experience, of the poor (and the wealthy). According to the hermeneutical nonrealist, however, there is no communicative perspective in the text itself; this is projected onto the text by the reader. For all intents and purposes, therefore, it is the reader's aims and interests that control the process of textual interpretation. The immediacy and intensity of the contemporary context overpowers and overshadows the voice of the text.[88] Like historical criticism, then, reader-oriented criticism makes sense of the biblical text only by first placing the text in an extrabiblical context. Neither approach allows the text to make sense on its own terms.

(b) Sola scriptura; tota scriptura. The purpose of context is to disambiguate textual meaning. Is there a sense in which Scripture may serve not only as its own interpreter, but also as its own context?

(i) The literary context. The immediate literary context of a biblical text has the advantage of being both available and fixed. One does not have to search for the literary context *behind* the text, as it were. The text itself is its own best context for interpretation. Indeed, could it be that a text might only yield its meaning—its sense and its reference—on its own terms? The biblical text itself is probably the best evidence even for reconstructing the situation behind the text. The literary context is not only necessary but often sufficient for the purposes of interpretation if it enables one to answer the question, "What is the author doing here?" In other words, the contexts relevant for the purposes of interpretation are those that enable the interpreter to describe the nature of the communicative action under consideration (e.g., "he's prophesying"; "he's telling a story"; "he's composing a love song," etc.). Conversely, the most spectacular errors in interpretation are those that miss the prime communicative function. For instance, those who read *Gulliver's Travels* as a children's story miss the (primary) aspect of political satire. Similarly, those that read the book of Jonah as a story about a great fish miss the (primary?) aspect of prophetic satire.[89]

(ii) The narrative context. Hans Frei argues that the biblical narratives make sense on their own terms. That is, they provide all the information and clues that the interpreter needs in order to follow the story. For Frei, the meaning of the biblical story is the story itself, not some history behind the story. Furthermore, we cannot gain the message of the story apart from the story's form; the medium is the message. That is, the meaning of the story is held within the story world, the sum total of characters and events that figure in the story. There is no gap between the story and its meaning. Following the biblical narratives is more than a matter of appreciating the story on its own terms, however. It involves reading one's own world (or story) in light of the story world of the biblical text. Frei calls this interpretive approach "intratextual": "Intratextual theology redescribes reality within the scriptural framework rather than translating Scripture into extrascriptural categories. It is the text, so to speak, which absorbs the world, rather than the world the text."[90] Meir Sternberg argues similarly that the OT narratives are interpretive frameworks that draw the reader and the reader's world into the world of the text.[91]

(iii) The canonical context. "Scripture interprets Scripture." How large is a literary context? On the one hand, there are sixty-six books, or literary wholes, in the Bible. On the other hand, the scope of the biblical story reaches back to the beginning of time and stretches forward to its conclusion. In the Gospels, the story of Jesus is a kind of retelling of the story of Israel.[92] The rest of the NT examines the story of Jesus as the story of the church, and of the whole cosmos. Because of its peculiar subject matter, the acts of the one Creator-Covenant God, the biblical narratives take on the status of a unified metanarrative. That means that the individual biblical stories have to be interpreted in light of the set of stories taken together. The literary whole I now have in mind is, of course, the Christian canon.[93] Childs argues that the canon provides the appropriate context for biblical interpretation. Indeed, in his commentary on Exodus he devotes a section to analyzing the material in light of its NT context.[94]

2. *Literary whole and content: genre as object and form of understanding.* "Every piece of writing is a kind of something."[95] It may be that the best way to do justice to the principle that "Scripture interprets Scripture" is to focus not simply on the

34

literary context of Scripture but in particular on the distinctive way in which the Bible's message is mediated by its literary forms.[96]

(a) *The centrality of literary genre.* A genre is a literary kind ("genus"), a conventional and repeatable pattern of written discourse.[97] Genre thus refers to discourse of a higher order: to communicative *practices* rather than to communicative acts: "A practice is any form of socially established cooperative human activity that is complex and internally coherent ... and is done to some end."[98] To write in a certain genre, one might say, is to engage in a form of rule-governed social practice. If understanding is a matter of recognizing the nature of communicative action (e.g., what it *is*), and if the literary context is the best clue to the meaning of the text as a whole, then identifying a text's genre is of the utmost importance: "Our stance about the literary genre of the book determines our entire interpretation of the book."[99] Our decision as to a text's genre determines how we read it: Do we read it *as* history or fiction, *as* prophecy or apocalyptic, *as* seriously intended or ironic? In what follows I will present genres as communicative strategies for using words to interact with other people and to engage reality.

(i) Form and meaning: following conventional rules. First, genres use words to create larger verbal forms. E. D. Hirsch compares literary genres to games: "Coming to understand the meaning of an utterance is like learning the rules of a game."[100] This is also the metaphor that Wittgenstein chose when he revised his earlier position on language and interpretation. Each genre has its own rules for making sense. A reader will achieve understanding only if he grasps the kind of game the text is playing. It is not enough to know the meaning of individual words; one must have some sense of the illocutionary point of the whole discourse. If the reader is not playing the same game, if, say, history is read as if it were myth, then the result is misunderstanding. A generically correct reading is one that follows the formal rules or conventions that make a communicative act one kind of thing rather than another. Genre thus acts as a bridge between the author's interpretive framework and that of the reader. For communication to be successful, for meaning to be disambiguated, the generic context must be shared.

(ii) Form and function: following conversations. Second, genres create literary form in order to facilitate social interaction. Language, as we have seen, is an instrument for interpersonal interaction. Speech and writing are the chief means of interpersonal interaction known to humanity.[101] In his *Philosophical Investigations*, Wittgenstein denies that any one "language game" (e.g., referring) represents the essence of language. On the contrary, there are as many ways of using language as there are human activities, and many of these activities have developed their own rules for using language, not to mention their own distinct vocabulary. Wittgenstein compared words to tools: "Think of the tools in a tool-box: there is a hammer, pliers, a saw, a screw-driver, a rule, a glue-pot, nails and screws. The function of words are as diverse as the function of these objects."[102] If words are like tools, then genres may be thought of as the projects on which these tools are put to work. "Picturing reality" is only one such project among many others.

Genres facilitate interpersonal interaction by offering relatively stable types of communication. They are distinguished according to their prime communicative function (e.g., love song, prophecy, history, apocalyptic). They offer the reader an interpretive framework with which to process their particular content. Once one knows that one is listening to sports commentators rather than political commentators, it is easier to follow their respective discourse. Interpreting genre thus requires a certain sensitivity to the social situations in which particular forms of language (and literature) are employed.

(iii) Rationality and reference: following routes to the real. Lastly, literary genres are adapted not only to serve particular social functions but also to engage with and think certain aspects of reality more than others. Literary genres are not only communicative but *cognitive* strategies. Each genre constitutes a distinct mode of cognition, a unique form for thinking about (and experiencing) the world in ways that, without it, would not be possible. This insight exposes the shortcomings of the proof-texting method; biblical texts yield not only propositional information, but ways of seeing and processing information. Literary genres are verbal maps, each with its own "key" and "scale." The "key" tells you what a piece of discourse is about. Just as there are different kinds of maps—of roads, of geological characteristics, of historical incidents, of the stars—so different literary genres select and attend to various features of reality more than others.[103] Similarly, every literary genre has its own "scale" or manner of fitting words to the world. The aim of history, for instance, is to make our words fit or correspond to the world, viz., the past; the aim of utopias is to make the world fit or correspond to our words. The point is that words do not naturally refer to reality in uniform fashion. Rather, every genre has its own conventions and strategies for relating to the real.

(b) *The centrality of narrative.* Among the various genres in Scripture, none illustrates the significance of literary form better than narrative. Narrative is an indispensable cognitive instrument for learning about the world, the identity of Jesus Christ, and our own identity as Christians.

(i) With regard to the world, what we know, by and large, is not a set of discrete propositions or items of knowledge, but particulars that form part of a larger story. This is as true of science as of theology. Our theories are not abstract views from nowhere, but concrete views from where we are in our particular histories and traditions. Theories are stories that cultures believe in. According to N. T. Wright, knowledge occurs "when people *find things that fit* with the particular story or (more likely) stories to which they are accustomed to give allegiance."[104] *Stories, in other words, provide an indispensable interpretive framework through which we view the world, ourselves, and God.* When a story claims to make sense of all others stories and the whole of reality, it becomes a "metanarrative."

(ii) According to Frei, the Gospels are neither straightforward histories or myths but rather "realistic narratives" whose intent is to render the identity of Jesus by relating what he did and what happened to him. The meaning of a realistic narrative is "in large part a function of the interaction of character and circumstances."[105] Who Jesus is inseparable from his actions and his passion. In other words, without the narrative we would not be able to identify Jesus. The meaning is inextricably tied up with the story form itself: "not *illustrated* (as though it were an intellectually presubsisting or preconceived archetype or ideal essence) but *constituted* through the mutual, specific determination of agents, speech, social context, and circumstances that form the indispensable narrative web."[106] Only the Gospel narratives can render Jesus' specific uniqueness as a person, for personal identity, enacted over time, bears the shape of a narrative.

(iii) Narrative has to do with interpretation, lastly, insofar as the biblical story can clash with and subsequently transform those stories that readers may prefer to tell about themselves. Biblical interpretation is ultimately a dangerous enterprise, to the extent that readers risk having their own identities challenged by what they read. This critique of one's old understanding is the condition for a new understanding of God, the world, and oneself. For the Christian interpreter is the one who reads the story of Israel, and especially the story of Jesus, as his or her own story, that is, as constitutive of his or her own identity. The apostle Paul understood himself in the light of the story of Jesus: "I have been crucified with Christ" (Gal 2:20). The Bible calls, similarly, not only for understanding but for personal appropriation on the part of interpreters. In other words, Scripture calls for intratextual interpretation, where the interpreter's world is itself interpreted in terms of the biblical text, as part of the biblical story. What is ultimately at stake in biblical interpretation is not simply the meaning of the text, but the identity of the interpreter.

E. Sacra Littera, Sacra Pagina, and Sacra Doctrina: From Dictionary to Theology

The trajectory of interpretation, and of this essay, is from the letter through literature to doctrine (and life). But what precisely is the relation between philology, the study of words, and theology, the study of God? Just what is the connection between the sacred letter, the sacred page, and sacred doctrine?

1. *Literacy and the "sacred letter."* Throughout this essay I have assumed that biblical interpreters should strive for literacy rather than letterism. What is interesting theologically happens on the level not of the letter, nor of the word, but rather of the whole text. In other words, it is not the word or the concept alone, but the word/concept as used in the context of the literary whole that is the object of understanding. The general thrust of most contemporary linguistics has been to demythologize etymologies. The letter has lost its sacred aura.[107]

Does my argument render the notion of a theological dictionary contradictory? Not at all. On the contrary, I have argued that language is a God-given human capacity that enables complex communicative competence and interaction. The task of the biblical interpreter is not to define individual terms but rather to achieve biblical literacy, by which I mean not simply the ability to read and write, but above all the ability to *follow* a text. Literacy in this sense refers to a certain body of background information, a certain set of skills, and to an inclination on the part of the reader to recover, respect, and respond to a text's communicative intention. Biblical literacy thus refers to everything that the Christian reader needs to know and to do in order to follow the text from page to practice. One important ingredient in this task is to know how biblical words were habitually used in their particular historical, literary, canonical, and narrative contexts. Another, equally important aspect of the interpretive task, however, is to become familiar with the rules governing larger forms of biblical discourse, with the diverse generic practices that comprise the Old and New Testaments.

2. *Sense, meaning, and the "sacred page."* If theology cannot be squeezed out of sacred letters, what about the "sacred page"? In medieval theology, to be a theologian was to be a master of the sacred page. Thomas Aquinas, for instance, affirmed the content of the Bible as the place where sacred teaching was to be found. He could thus

speak of *sacra scriptura* and *sacra doctrina* interchangeably.[108] According to modern biblical scholars, however, theology may not simply be "read off" of the Bible, as though one could simply take over biblical words today and be saying the same thing: "Theology is no longer simply biblical interpretation."[109] What then is the role of the sacred page?

(a) *The page as collection of propositions.* The sacred page should not be confused with a reference book or a compendium of theology, that is, with a collection of theological propositions. Nor should sacred doctrine be confused with the attempt to substitute clearly formulated propositions for the metaphors, stories, and other literary forms in Scripture. This would be to confuse the Bible's meaning with its (ideal or historical) reference. The sacred page is not a blank space on which inerrant propositions are arbitrarily parked, nor is it merely grist for the propositional mill. The page, far from being a place on which to paste proof texts or deduce propositions, is rather the context in which a group of sentences make sense as a whole. It is important to bear in mind that the propositional function of language (e.g., to make statements) is only one of many uses to which language can be put.[110] One of the functions of genre is to provide a clue as to what illocutionary force a given proposition bears (e.g., is it part of a story, a parable, a warning, a question, etc.). Only when one first determines the sense of a sentence can one then go on to inquire after its truth. The sacred page may or may not be a page of information; that depends on the kind of book of which the page is a part. According to Bernard Ramm: "Much harm has been done to Scripture by those within and without the Church by assuming that all statements in the Bible are on the same logical level, on which level they are either true or false."[111]

(b) *The page as pedagogue.* "All Scripture is God-breathed and is useful for teaching ... and training in righteousness" (2 Tim 3:16). I do not wish to deny that the sacred page contains sacred teaching, that is, true information about God and God's actions in history. I do, however, wish to call attention to the significance of other uses of biblical language and literature. For to equate the sacred page with propositional information is to subscribe to a picture theory of meaning that ultimately reduces the many ways in which Scripture is profitable to one. Whereas the "meaning as reference" approach focuses on the teaching or propositional aspect of Scripture, I believe that "meaning as communicative action" better shows how the Bible can also be profitable for "training in righteousness."

(i) Technology and the sacred page: *savoir.* Words are instruments of communicative action. To focus on the nature of the instruments rather than what they are being used for, however, is to lose the forest for the trees. Interpretation is neither a matter of mere technical information about the text (e.g., textual criticism) nor even of the propositional information a text conveys. Interpretation is about following texts, and this involves practical know-how too. How do we learn to follow or understand communicative action? It is just here that the notion of genre as a communicative practice is significant. One masters a practice by learning its implicit rules, and one learns the rules by participating in the practice (e.g., by engaging in a certain kind of language or literature game).

(ii) Sanctification and the sacred page: *connaître.* "I would far rather feel remorse than know how to define it."[112] Biblical interpretation is a matter of participating in the canon's communicative practices to the point of grasping not only the conventions, but the point of the text. To take biblical narrative as an example: It is not enough simply to know about the conventions that narrative employs. Understanding biblical narrative means being able to *dwell* in what Ricoeur calls "the world of the text," and to read one's own life in terms of the biblical story. A text is not understood until its discourse is appropriated.[113] The understanding reader must expose himself or herself to the effects of the text. To use C. S. Lewis's well-known distinction: The reader must not only "see" but "taste" the meaning of the text.[114] Understanding is short-circuited when the interpreter achieves only seeing or apprehension (i.e., *savoir,* or "objective knowledge about") rather than tasting and appropriation (i.e., *connaître,* or "knowledge by personal acquaintance").

What is theologically normative in Scripture are not the words, nor even isolated proof texts, but the various rules for conceiving and speaking about God embedded in biblical genres. Each of the biblical genres engages with and leads us to divine reality, albeit in different ways. The task of biblical theology is to make clear how the various literary forms in the Bible are ways of seeing, and *tasting*, the reality of God. The Bible, as a collection of books, functions as a pedagogue that teaches us not only what to say about God, but *when* and *where* to say it, and under what conditions. Knowing how to use ordinary words so that they say something true about God is to be "wise in speech." Christian thinkers today achieve theological wisdom when they have been trained in the school of Scriptures and when they learn the grammar of faith—what is appropriate to say about God in various literary and historical situations. Theological concepts are learned by participating in the Bible's diverse communicative practices. We learn to think about the end of history, for example, thanks to biblical apocalyptic. For the Christian, Scripture is the school in which we learn to use terms like *God, sin,* and *justification* correctly. To the extent that we participate in this use, the Bible effectively educates our thoughts and feelings about God. It is not only narrative, but ultimately all the biblical genres that come to absorb us. The sense of the sacred page, if followed, should lead to the sanctification of the reader.[115]

3. *Reference, truth, and "sacred doctrine."* To return to Cratylus' original question: Do words give us knowledge of the world and the real? Can we talk about God truly?

(a) *Reference: to the real and to the reader.*

(i) To God. Though I have argued that meaning is not simply a matter of reference, it does not follow that language cannot refer to God truly. However, what is primarily true of God are not isolated words or concepts as representations of things or thoughts, but rather sentences and discourses that serve as larger-scale models for interpreting reality.[116] A theological concept is not a word or thought that pictures God, but rather a mental skill that makes explicit what is implicit in the way God is represented in a particular literary genre. A theological concept, in other words, is a way of thinking that is learned through an apprenticeship to biblical literature. To take a simple example: We learn the meaning of "the right arm of God" not by analyzing the etymology of the words but by becoming sensitive to the metaphorical force of the phrase and to the generic contexts in which it is used. When theological concepts are abstracted from the canonical forms of discourse that generate them, they tend to lose the specificity of their biblical meaning. It follows that our systems of theology must remain tied to the biblical texts.

To be tied to the text need not imply that "there is nothing outside of the text." To say that reference to God is always through some metaphor or genre is not to deny that such language really refers to God. If the sacred page is indeed the location of the sacred teaching, we must affirm the language of the Bible to be true. The theological view of language for which I have argued holds that language is a God-given instrument that enables interpersonal interaction *and* engages with reality. I contend, with George Steiner, that God ultimately underwrites language's ability to transcend itself, to speak of what is more than language. At the same time, we must acknowledge that what we find on the sacred page is often metaphors and other kinds of nonpropositional discourse (as well as a good number of propositions). Both metaphors and literary genres are cognitive instruments that help us to discover the real. Every genre refers and predicates, but not in the same way. Metaphors and genres are nevertheless reality-depicting.[117] The many forms of language and literature are the condition for helping us to see aspects of reality that would otherwise go unnoticed.

The biblical text is the primary location of truth for Christians; the sacred page *is* the sacred teaching. But what doctrines there are in Scripture do not always take propositional form—in some case, the story *is* the doctrine, and the task of the theologian is to render conceptually explicit the understanding that is implicit in the narrative form. There is no unmediated access to the activity of God in ancient Israel or to the activity of God in Jesus Christ. In order to have meaning and reference, we cannot go around the text, only through it. I therefore agree with Francis Watson, who argues for an "intratextual realism," which, in his words, "would understand the biblical text as referring beyond itself to extra-textual theological reality, while at the same time regarding that reality as accessible to us only in textual form."[118]

(ii) To us. There is another kind of reference that should not be overlooked. What we discover in interpreting Scripture is that the interpreter is included in the Bible's claims and references, and this in two ways. On the one hand, the world of which the Bible speaks is our world. We, like Paul, are living "between the times," in the eschatologically charged interval between the first and second comings of Jesus Christ. On the other hand, the claims that the Bible makes are often claims that impinge upon ourselves as readers. That is, the Bible is a text that demands considerable reader response: The interpreter must not only respect the author's intentions and literary conventions, but respond to the *issue* of the text as well. What is being interpreted in the process of biblical interpretation is not only the text (by the reader) but also the reader (by the text).

(b) *Understanding as discipleship: biblical truth and practical wisdom.*

(i) Canonical competence. Language, I have claimed, is a God-given capacity. Part of what it means to be in the image of God is to enjoy the capacity of verbal interaction. What Noam Chomsky attributes to an innate human capacity—the ability to generate intelligible sentences—is from a Christian perspective a gracious privilege and responsibility: the dignity of communicative agency. To be a responsible biblical interpreter is to have achieved what we might term "canonical competence"—a familiarity with the different ways in which the Bible names and speaks of God.[119] "Canonical competence" signifies the ability to relate biblical sentences vis-à-vis external reality and the social world as their authors intended: to grasp the illocutionary point of warnings as warnings, of promises as promises, of truth claims as truth claims, of histories as histories. Canonical competence refers, in short, to the reader's ability to follow the text from sense to reference. This is the first service of a theological dictionary: to help readers to become biblically literate and canonically competent.

(ii) Theological interpretation as practical wisdom. Literary styles also lead to styles of life. The forms of biblical discourse generate not only ways of seeing but also ways of *being* in the world. Following the biblical text ultimately requires of the interpreter a willingness to continue the semantic itineraries of the text: to appropriate and apply biblical meaning to oneself. Biblical interpretation, at its best, therefore yields not only theoretical knowledge but also practical wisdom. A theological dictionary provides training in how to speak, and act, biblically. Furthermore, the competent interpreter will know how to *go on speaking* about God in new contexts. The competent interpreter will know how to continue the semantic itineraries of the biblical genres and apply their ways of seeing and being in the world to the present. For instance, one who is competent in biblical narrative will know how to continue the story in to the contemporary context.

In providing definitions—guides to the use of words in particular contexts—then, dictionaries provide guidance to faith, thought, and life as well. Interpreters who allow their speech to be instructed by the communicative acts of the Scriptures will learn to continue the semantic itineraries of the biblical texts into their own times. This suggests that the ultimate function of a good theological dictionary is not only to provide mere *information*, but also to aid in the *formation* of faithful and competent disciples.

ENDNOTES

1   *The Concise Oxford Dictionary*, 8th ed., 1990, 304.
2   L. Carroll, *Through the Looking-Glass*, in *The Philosopher's Alice*, ed. Peter Heath, 1974, 193.
3   I here draw on three kinds of knowledge distinguished by Aristotle in his *Nichomachean Ethics*, Bk. VI. Biblical interpretation, I suggest, most closely resembles neither *epistēmē* (e.g., knowledge of the eternal and necessary), nor *technē* (e.g., knowledge of how to make things), but rather *phronesis* (e.g., knowledge of what to do in or make of particular situations).
4   Cratylus represents the situation after modernity: The postmodern person accepts modernity's high requirements for what counts as knowledge—namely, Cartesian certainty or foundationalism—then denies that such foundations exist.
5   The character of Socrates is something of an enigma in this dialogue. It is not entirely clear at the end with whom he agrees, nor exactly what his position is. Some Plato scholars have suggested that much of what Socrates says is satirical; he ridicules the position that one can philosophize by doing etymology.
6   *Cratylus*, in *The Dialogues of Plato*, tr. Benjamin Jowett, 1892³, 1:238.
7   Plato, *Theaetetus* 147b.
8   *Cratylus*, 372.
9   Ibid., 383.
10   Augustine, *On Christian Doctrine*, 1.8. Wittgenstein cites this passage in the opening pages of his *Philosophical Investigations* and comments that Augustine gives us a particular picture of the essence of human language. On Wittgenstein's own position, see below.
11   Augustine, *On Christian Doctrine*, 1.2.2.

12 Ibid., 2.10.15.

13 Ibid., 3.5.9.

14 Ibid., 3.10.14.

15 James Barr notes the corresponding trend in biblical studies to focus on the mind of the writers, on the authorial intentions. This eventually led to critics distinguishing between the mental representation of a series of events—the biblical accounts—on the one hand, and the results of historical reconstruction of what actually happened, on the other. See Barr, *The Bible in the Modern World*, 1973, 91-3.

16 Gottlob Frege's "On Sense and Reference," tr. Max Black, in *Translation from the Philosophical Writings of Gottlob Frege*, 1970, 56-78.

17 Cf. Barr: "We today in general do not move directly from biblical texts to external referents, but from biblical texts to the theological intentions of the writers and only from there indirectly to external referents," *The Bible in the Modern World*, 175.

18 David Kelsey calls this "biblical concept theology," in his *The Uses of Scripture in Recent Theology*, 1975, 24. See esp. ch. 1, "Doctrine and Concept."

19 Etymologies are given even in the Bible to make certain theological points, e.g., Matt 1:21 (lit.), "'and his name shall be called Emmanuel' (which means, God with us)."

20 Kelsey, *The Uses of Scripture*, 27.

21 James Barr, *The Semantics of Biblical Language*, 246.

22 Ludwig Wittgenstein, *Tractatus Logico-Philosophicus*, 1961, 2.01.

23 Ibid., 2.21.

24 See Anthony Kenny, *Wittgenstein*, 1973, ch. 4 ("The Picture Theory of a Proposition").

25 Wittgenstein, *Tractatus Logico-Philosophicus*, 3.203.

26 On logical atomism and logical positivism, see J. O. Urmson, *Philosophical Analysis: Its Development Between the Two World Wars*, 1956, and William P. Alston, *Philosophy of Language*, 1964 (ch. 4).

27 Kelsey, in his study of Warfield's use of Scripture, comments that what Warfield calls "biblical theology" is instead a kind of "biblical positivism" (*Uses of Scripture*, 23).

28 Charles Hodge, *Systematic Theology*, 1873, 1:10. For a fuller and perhaps more subtle account of the Princetonians, see David Wells, ed., *Reformed Theology in America*, 1985, chs. 2-3.

29 Benjamin B. Warfield, "The Right of Systematic Theology," in *Selected Shorter Writings of Benjamin B. Warfield*, 1970, 2:234.

30 W. Andrew Hoffecker observes that though Warfield was a persistent critic of modernity, "his own view of using 'facts'—both rational facts to demonstrate God's existence ... and biblical facts to arrive at a sound theology—sounds even more modern" ("Benjamin B. Warfield," in *Reformed Theology in America*, 79).

31 Don Cupitt (see below) associates the view that the world has a determinate extralinguistic structure that can be formulated in language with Calvinism and labels it "Protestant commonsense realism" (*The Long-Legged Fly*, 1987, 163).

32 See Erich Auerbach, *Mimesis: The Representation of Reality in Western Literature*, 1953.

33 For a recent example of this trend, see *The Postmodern Bible*, The Bible and Culture Collective, 1995.

34 I owe this particular example to Catherine Belsey, *Critical Practice*, 1980, 44.

35 François Lyotard, *The Postmodern Condition*, 1984.

36 Don Cupitt, *The Last Philosophy*, 1995, 44.

37   Cupitt, *The Long-legged Fly*, 57.

38   The British empiricists, such as John Locke and David Hume, thought of ideas as representations or impressions of experience. Words on this view represent thought or experience rather than things, as in Plato and premodernity.

39   This position is particularly associated with Michel Foucault, who argues that language, a social force, is the power of determinacy that creates the categories with which we interpret the world and human experience.

40   For another demonstration of this thesis, see Edgar V. McKnight, *Post-Modern Use of the Bible: The Emergence of Reader-Oriented Criticism*, 1988.

41   Cupitt is equally happy with "linguistic naturalism" as a description of his position (*The Last Philosophy*, 38).

42   Ibid., 44.

43   See L. Feuerbach, *The Essence of Christianity* (German edition, 1841), tr. George Eliot, 1989.

44   John Macquarrie, "Systematic Theology," *A New Handbook of Christian Theology*, 1992, 470.

45   G. R. Evans, *Old Arts and New Theology: The Beginnings of Theology as an Academic Discipline*, 1980, 108.

46   See his *Summa Theologica*, I, Q. 13.

47   Aristotle's study of the various uses of the verb "to be" (undertaken as part of his analysis of the concept "substance" in his *Metaphysics*) laid the groundwork for the medieval notion of the "analogy of being" (*analogia entis*). See Aristotle, *Metaphysics* 1016b6-10.

48   Thomas Aquinas, *Summa Theologica*, 1a. 13.2.

49   Ibid., 1a. 13.7.

50   "Ontotheology" is connected to the analogy of being insofar as it is the attempt to think the God of the Bible in terms of Greek metaphysics. See Brian D. Ingriffia's *Postmodern Theory and Biblical Theology* (CUP, 1995) for a critique of ontotheology. Ingriffia argues that ontotheology is a philosophical construction and calls instead for a return to biblical theology—not the God of abstract speculation but the God of revelation and action in history.

51   Aquinas was well aware of the discontinuities between God and his creatures as well. Some of the things we say about God we say by way of negation: for instance, God is *not* finite (infinite), *not* changeable (immutable). The idea that God cannot be understood in human categories led some patristic and medieval thinkers to do negative or apophatic theology. Pseudo-Dionysius, an anonymous writer probably dating from the sixth century, argued that God's names are only provisional: God is beyond all human names and categories.

52   For a fuller treatment of Barth's dialectical view of revelation as both a "veiling" and an "unveiling" of God by God, see Bruce McCormack, *Karl Barth's Critically Realistic Dialectical Theology: Its Genesis and Development 1909-1936*, 1995, 269-73.

53   According to G. Ward, Barth here offers a restatement of the "meaning as divine use" idea that we first saw adumbrated, and rejected, in *Cratylus*. In Barth's case, of course, revelation is a trinitarian act, involving the Son as content and the Spirit as the "Lord of the hearing" of revelation.

54   G. Ward, *Barth, Derrida and the Language of Theology*, 1995, 29.

55   McCormack, *Barth's Dialectical Theology*, 271.

56 On Ward's reading, Barth's view of language resembles Derrida's: "It is Barth's insight into the dialectical necessity of assuming that words name while also countering such an assumption that draws his theological work into the orbit of postmodern debates" (*Barth, Derrida, and the Language of Theology*, 5).

57 To be exact, Mark Taylor writes that "deconstruction is the 'hermeneutic' of the death of God" (*Erring: A Postmodern A/theology*, 1984, 6).

58 S. Burke, *The Death and Return of the Author*, 1992, 22.

59 See also M. Foucault, "What Is an Author," in *Language, Counter-Memory Practice*, 1977, and R. Barthes, "The Death of the Author," in *Image-Music-Text*, 1977.

60 D. Dawson, *Literary Theory*, 1995, 11. Dawson helpfully discusses how both Christian theology and literary theory develop the themes of spirit, body, and text.

61 Or, there is "no outside-text" (*il n'y a pas de hors-texte*); Derrida, *Of Grammatology* (tr. G. Spivak), 1976, 158.

62 Ibid., 14.

63 George Steiner, *Real Presences*, 1989, 3.

64 Ricoeur's philosophical hermeneutics similarly relies on the notion of a wager that the text mediates meaning to the reader. See, for example, his *Symbolism of Evil*, 355.

65 Steiner, *Real Presences*, 122.

66 Krister Stendahl, "Biblical Theology, Contemporary," in *IDB*, 1:418-32.

67 P. Ricoeur, *Interpretation Theory: Discourse and the Surplus of Meaning*, 1976, 8.

68 Ibid., 7.

69 Ibid., 7.

70 For a helpful study of signs and sentences in the context of communication studies, see J. Fiske, *Introduction to Communication Studies*, 2d ed. 1990. A communicative action is action oriented to achieving understanding.

71 Ibid., 2.

72 See J. L. Austin, *How to Do Things With Words*, 1961.

73 The locutionary aspect of meaning corresponds to *langue*, that is, to the range of possible sense a term could have at a given point in the history of a language.

74 Whereas Austin and Wittgenstein believed there were countless ways of using language, John Searle proposes a comprehensive fivefold typology of the basic things we do with language: "We tell people how things are, we try to get them to do things, we commit ourselves to doing things, we express our feelings and attitudes and we bring about changes through our utterances" (*Expression and Meaning: Studies in the Theory of Speech Acts*, CUP, 1979, 29). See also J. Searle, *Speech Acts: An Essay in the Philosophy of Language*, 1969.

75 Austin, *How to Do Things With Words*, 10.

76 Ben F. Meyer agrees that the object of interpretation is the intended sense of the text. Meyer, however, is more careful than E. D. Hirsch to distinguish the purpose the author may have had in writing (which lies behind the text) and the intention of the author intrinsic to or enacted in the text. See Meyer, *Critical Realism and the New Testament*, 1989, ch. 2, esp. 36-41.

77 On the significance of Dilthey for hermeneutics, see P. Ricoeur, *Hermeneutics and the Human Sciences: Essays on Language, Action and Interpretation*, 1981, chs. 2, 3.

78 For a fuller treatment of this theology and how it funds both a doctrine of Scripture and theological anthropology, see my "God's Mighty Speech Acts: The Doctrine of Scripture

Today" (in *A Pathway into the Holy Scripture* 1994, 143-97), and "Stories of the Self: Human Being, Individual and Social" (in *The Cambridge Companion to Christian Doctrine*, forthcoming).

79 C. Altieri, *Act and Quality: A Theory of Literary Meaning and Humanistic Understanding*, 1981, 10. Ricoeur, however, speaks of the "semantic autonomy" of the text, by which he means that the author's intention and the textual meaning cease to coincide. On the other hand, he is unwilling to cancel out the main features of discourse (e.g., that it is said by someone to someone about something) for fear that texts would be reduced to natural objects (*Interpretation Theory*, 29).

80 For a more complete analysis of levels of interpretive description, see my *Is There a Meaning in This Text?* ch. 6.

81 W. Jeanrond coins the phrase "text linguistics" to argue that the text should be the "basic linguistic unit." See his *Text and Interpretation as Categories of Theological Thinking*, 1988, 75.

82 For Derrida, a text is never a totality (e.g., a closed and complete whole), but is rather constitutionally open (e.g., indeterminate). An interpretation is, therefore, not so much the exposition of a system as it is an indispensable supplement to a text. On the key notion of supplement in Derrida, see his *Of Grammatology*, 141-64.

83 Westminster Confession of Faith, 1.9.

84 I owe this point to Tim Ward, one of my doctoral students.

85 Hans Frei, *The Eclipse of Biblical Narrative: A Study in Eighteenth and Nineteenth Century Hermeneutics*, 1974.

86 Frei is clear that these interpretive moves were not made in a theological vacuum. On the contrary, biblical criticism flourished in the context either of Deism or naturalism—anything but a supernaturalism that affirmed divine action in history.

87 Frei, *Eclipse*, 130.

88 In my *Is There a Meaning in This Text*, ch. 7, I explore the role of the Holy Spirit in giving interpreters ears to hear the text's voice rather than their own.

89 Several OT commentators have noted the high degree of irony and humor in the book of Jonah (see, for instance, J. C. Holbert, "'Deliverance Belongs to Yahweh!': Satire in the Book of Jonah", *JSOT* 21, 1981, 59-81). What is being ridiculed is Jonah's egocentric (read "ethnocentric") attitude with regard to the love of God. Jonah mistakenly thinks that God's love is primarily for the Jews. To his chagrin, Jonah is the only character that turns out not to have repented by the end of the book.

90 This wording is George Lindbeck's, a colleague of Frei's, but it well captures the spirit of Frei's proposal (Lindbeck, *The Nature of Doctrine*, 1984, 118).

91 Neither Frei nor Sternberg deny the historical intent of much biblical narrative, only that the Bible's historical reference should be understood in the context of modern, rather than biblical, historiography. See M. Sternberg, *The Poetics of Biblical Narrative: Ideological Literature and the Drama of Reading*, 1987.

92 Matthew highlights the parallels between Jesus' story and that of Moses (e.g., the flight into Egypt, the Law on the mountain). The other Evangelists show that Jesus is the Servant of the Lord who takes up the unfinished task of Israel and fulfills the three offices—prophet, priest, and king—that constituted Israel as the people of God.

93   B. Childs argues that the literal sense of a text is the sense it has in its canonical context (B. S. Childs, "The *Sensus Literalis* of Scripture: An Ancient and Modern Problem," in *Beiträge zur alttestamentlichen Theologie*, 1977, 80-93).

94   See B. S. Childs, *The Book of Exodus: A Critical Theological Commentary*, OTL, 1974. Childs believes that the biblical texts display a peculiar "canonical intentionality," by which he means they were intentionally shaped in such a way so as to function as normative Scripture for later generations (Childs, *Biblical Theology of the Old and New Testaments*, 1992, 70-79).

95   J. B. Gabel and C. B. Wheeler, *The Bible As Literature*, 1986, 16.

96   G. Berkouwer observes that "a serious attempt to do justice to literary types was motivated by the desire to deal correctly with the *sui ipsius interpres* ('its own interpreter')" (*Holy Scripture*, 1975, 131).

97   See J. L. Bailey, "Genre Analysis," in *Hearing the New Testament*, 1995, 197-221.

98   D. Kelsey, paraphrasing a definition given in Alistair MacIntyre's *After Virtue* (1981), in *To Understand God Truly: What's Theological About a Theological School*, 1992, 118.

99   B. Ramm, *Protestant Biblical Interpretation*, 1970, 145. Similarly, E. D. Hirsch states that verbal meaning is always genre-bound. Hirsch defines genre as the "controlling idea of the whole," an idea that governs our idea as to what a text is (*Validity in Interpretation*, 1967, 79).

100 Hirsch, *Validity in Interpretation*, 70.

101 See M. Bakhtin, "The Problem of Speech Genres," in M. Bakhtin, *Speech Genres & Other Late Essays*, tr. V. W. McGee, 1986.

102 L. Wittgenstein, *Philosophical Investigations*, 1967, I, § 11.

103 The biblical narrative maps out divine action in history; biblical law maps out God's will for human behavior; biblical prophecy maps out the privileges and responsibilities of God's covenant people; biblical wisdom maps out how persons are to fit into God's created order, etc.

104 N. T. Wright, *The New Testament and the People of God*, 1992, 37.

105 Frei, *Eclipse*, 280. See also Frei's *The Identity of Jesus Christ: The Hermeneutical Bases of Dogmatic Theology*, 1975.

106 Frei, *Eclipse*, 280.

107 Even metaphors, according to Ricoeur, are a matter not of "deviant naming" but rather of a semantic tension within sentences. For his criticism of the "names theory" of metaphor, see Ricoeur, *The Rule of Metaphor*, 1978.

108 See, for instance, Thomas Aquinas, *Summa Theologica*, Q. 1 art. 2.

109 R. Morgan, "Biblical Theology," in *A Dictionary of Biblical Interpretation*, 87.

110 I elsewhere speak of the tendency to overlook literary form in one's zeal to obtain the teaching as the "propositional heresy" ("Semantics of Biblical Literature," 72).

111 B. Ramm, *Special Revelation and the Word of God*, 1968, 68.

112 Thomas à Kempis, *Of the Imitation of Christ*, 1.1.3.

113 See Ricoeur, *Hermeneutics and the Human Sciences*, ch. 8.

114 C. S. Lewis, "Myth Became Fact," in *God in the Dock*, 1985.

115 In French, *sens* means both "meaning" and "direction." Ricoeur can thus speak of a "semantic itinerary" and call for readers to continue a text's trajectory of meaning.

116 I have elsewhere discussed the way language refers to the reality of God in terms of "rendering." See my "From Canon to Concept: 'Same' and 'Other' in the Relation Between

Biblical and Systematic Theology," *Scottish Bulletin of Evangelical Theology* 12, 1994, 96-124, esp. 123.

117 See J. M. Soskice, *Metaphor and Religious Language*, 1985, 148-61.

118 F. Watson, *Text, Church, and World*, 1994, 224-25.

119 Again, this kind of knowledge is personal—a knowledge won by acquaintance and appropriation (*connaître*). It is also practical, like Aristotle's *phronesis*—a knowledge of what to do and how to act in a particular (literary, in this case) situation.

BIBLIOGRAPHY

J. Barr, *The Semantics of Biblical Language*, 1961, 246; B. S. Childs, *Biblical Theology of the Old and New Testament*, 1991; H. Frei, *The Eclipse of Biblical Narrative: A Study in Eighteenth and Nineteenth Century Hermeneutics*, 1974; J. Green, ed., *Hearing the New Testament: Strategies for Interpretation*, 1995; W. Jeanrond, *Text and Interpretation as Categories of Theological Thinking*, 1988; G. Osborne, *The Hermeneutical Spiral: A Comprehensive Introduction to Biblical Interpretation*, 1991; P. Ricoeur, *Interpretation Theory: Discourse and the Surplus of Meaning*, 1976; M. Sternberg, *The Poetics of Biblical Narrative*, 1987; A. Thiselton, *New Horizons in Hermeneutics*, 1991; K. J. Vanhoozer, *Is There a Meaning in This Text? The Bible, the Reader, and the Morality of Literary Knowledge*, 1998; G. Ward, *Barth, Derrida and the Language of Theology*, 1995, 29; F. Watson, *Text, Church and World: Biblical Interpretation in Theological Perspective*, 1994; N. T. Wright, *The New Testament and the People of God*, 1992, 37.

Kevin Vanhoozer

PART I: THE RELIABILITY OF THE OLD TESTAMENT TEXT

Vanhoozer has argued that the "Text" is the basis for developing a view of God, one's self, and the world. Hence, the interpreter needs to know the nature of the Text that is the basis for interpretation. In this essay Bruce Waltke expertly leads the reader into the craft of the textual critic. The critic is a person who evaluates the present Hebrew text in the light of many ancient texts (Greek, Aramaic, Syriac, etc.). He also affirms that the ancient Text is reliable, in spite of the "fragility" of the process in which ancient texts have come down to us. He evaluates the scribal practices and some of the ways in which errors could have crept into the text. It is amazing that the present text is highly reliable and that the changes, proposed by a consensus of the critical students of the Bible, have little bearing on the life and practice of the church. This is more than coincidence. It is evidence of the providential work of the Spirit of God. (VanGemeren)

2. TEXTUAL CRITICISM OF THE OLD TESTAMENT AND ITS RELATION TO EXEGESIS AND THEOLOGY

A. The Task of OT Textual Criticism: Its Importance and Method

There is always a need in humanities for critics to restore original texts, be they of Homer or Shakespeare, or of Moses or Isaiah. Many texts of the OT, however, were composed over centuries, and not just by an original author, so that it is too simplistic to say that OT textual criticism aims to recover the original text of the OT. Rather, as we shall argue, "original text" in the OT refers to the text-type that lies behind the MT, the received text. The reconstruction of earlier editions of portions of the OT is the task of literary criticism, not of textual criticism.

Textual criticism is necessary because there is no error-free MS. (Even in *BHS,* the current standard representation of the MT text, printing errors can be found.) Variants occur frequently in the medieval MSS of the MT tradition, but they are minuscule compared to those found in the Dead Sea Scrolls [DSS]. In fact, the further back we go in the textual lineage the greater the textual differences. Before the text was fixed at ca. AD 100, it was copied and recopied through many centuries by scribes of varying capabilities and of different philosophies, giving rise to varying readings and recensions (i.e., distinct text types).

The restoration of the original OT text is foundational to the exegetical task and to theological reflection. For instance, whether the book of Proverbs teaches immortality depends in part on deciding between textual variants in Prov 14:32b. Basing itself on MT, the NIV renders, "even in [their] death ($b^e m\hat{o}t\hat{o}$) the righteous have a refuge," a rendering that entails the doctrine of immortality for the righteous. The NRSV, however, basing itself on the LXX, translates, "the righteous find a refuge in their integrity ($b^e tumm\hat{o}$)," a reading that does not teach that doctrine. The consonants of the MT are *bmtw,* and those of the (assumed) Vorlage (i.e., the retroverted text lying before a translator) behind the LXX were *btmw.* The slight difference due to metathesis of m and t, however, profoundly affects the exegesis of that text and the theology of the book.

48

To restore the original text the critic must know the history of its witnesses and of scribal practices, and must have exegetical competence. In this essay we will consider each of these respectively. The LXX, however, is such an important witness that we treat it separately. A knowledge of the text's history will explain the varying characteristics of the textual witnesses and why we opt for the restoring of the original text behind the MT against other literary editions of OT portions, such as the difference between the MT Pentateuch versus the Samaritan Pentateuch and of the MT Jeremiah versus the Septuagint Jeremiah. We conclude the article with reflections on the reliability of the OT text.

B. History of the Text and Its Witnesses

Because of the varying fortunes of the OT text and of our sources of information about it, its history may be analyzed into six distinct periods: (1) The determinative formative period for the production of OT texts extended from the composition of the Ten Commandments (ca. 1400 BC or ca. 1250 BC, depending on the date of the Exodus) to Nehemiah's Library (ca. 400 BC), when, according to 2 Macc 2:13, Nehemiah founded a library and "gathered together the books about the kings and prophets, and the books of David, and letters of kings about sacred gifts," or even to the late fourth century, if one opts for that date for the composition of the book of Chronicles. (2) The canon and text remained open from Nehemiah's library to when the canon was stabilized (ca. 100 BC). (3) At least two centuries elapsed between the fixing of the OT canon and the fixing of its text, now sometimes called "the Proto-MT" (ca. AD 100). (4) The labors of the Masoretes (AD 600-AD 1000), who based their work on the Proto-MT, came to a conclusion ca. AD 1000, when the Masorete, Aaron Ben Asher, produced the authoritative Masoretic text, as recognized already on the frontispiece of the Leningrad Codex (AD 1009) (see below). (5) The medieval MSS of the MT were produced between AD 1000 and the invention of printing (ca. AD 1500). (6) The Great Rabbinic Bible (ca. 1525) became the standard text of the MT until 1936, when P. Kahle got back to the Ben Asher text by basing the third edition of *BH* on the Leningrad MS B 19^a (L). Since the variants that came into the text after AD 1000 are relatively insignificant, we will not discuss the last two periods. N. Sarna ("Bible Text") superbly summarized the history of the printed Hebrew Bible.

1. *From the Ten Commandments to Nehemiah's Library.* We have virtually no external, extant data regarding the OT text during its most formative period, aside from two recently discovered silver amulets, about the size of a "cigarette butt," containing the priestly benediction (Num 6:24-26) (ca. 600 BC). From internal notices within the OT and from our knowledge of the way ancient Near Eastern literature was composed, we can infer that during this era earlier pieces of canonical literature were collected into developing books. For example, the Bible presents the Ten Commandments as the first piece of canonical literature (i.e., literature inspired by God and recognized as such by the faithful) (Exod 20:1-19; cf. Deut 5:6-27). To this original core the Book of the Covenant, mediated by Moses, was added (Exod 20:22-23:33), and to this still other pieces were added to make up the book of Exodus. We do not know how or when the book of Exodus took its final shape. In a roughly comparable way isolated hymns were collected into books, and these in turn edited to form the book of Psalms. The same dynamic processes were involved in the composition of other books of the Bible. From data within the Bible and from knowledge of ancient Near Eastern scribal prac-

tices we can infer that during the formation of the OT books, there was a tendency both to preserve and to revise earlier texts.

(a) *The tendency to preserve the text.* Elsewhere we argued (*IBHS*, 16-17:

> The very fact that the Scripture persistently survived the most deleterious conditions throughout its long history demonstrates that indefatigable scribes insisted on its preservation. The books were copied by hand for generations on highly perishable papyrus and animal skins in the relatively damp, hostile climate of Palestine....

Moreover, the prospects for the survival of texts were uncertain in a land that served as a bridge for armies in unceasing contention between the continents of Africa and Asia—a land whose people were the object of plunderers in their early history and of captors in their later history. That no other Israelite writings, such as the Book of Yashar (e.g., 2 Sam 1:18) or the Diaries of the Kings (e.g., 2 Chr 16:11), survive from this period indirectly suggests the determination of the scribes to preserve the books that became canonical. The foes of Hebrew Scripture sometimes included audiences who sought to kill its authors and destroy their works (cf. Jeremiah 36). From the time of their composition, however, they captured the hearts, minds, and loyalties of the faithful in Israel who kept them safe often at risk to themselves. Such people must have insisted on the accurate transmission of the text.

> In addition, both the Bible itself (Deut 31:9ff; Josh 24:25, 26; 1 Sam 10:25; etc.) and the literature of the ANE show that at the time of the earliest biblical compositions a mindset favoring canonicity existed. This mindset must have fostered a concern for care and accuracy in transmitting the sacred writings. For example, a Hittite treaty (of the Late Bronze Age), closely resembling parts of the Torah, contains this explicit threat: "Whoever ... breaks [this tablet] or causes anyone to change the wording of the tablet—... may the gods, the lords of the oath, blot you out." Undoubtedly this psychology was a factor in inhibiting Israelite scribes from multiplying variants of the texts.

> Moreover, scribal practices throughout the ANE reflect a conservative attitude. W. F. Albright noted, "The prolonged and intimate study of the many scores of thousands of pertinent documents from the ancient Near East proves that sacred and profane documents were copied with greater care than is true of scribal copying in Graeco-Roman times.

(b) *Tendency to revise the text.* We also argued:

> On the other hand, scribes, aiming to teach the people by disseminating an understandable text, felt free to revise the script, orthography (i.e., spelling), and grammar, according to the conventions of their own times. Albright said, "A principle which must never be lost sight of in dealing with documents of the ancient Near East is that instead of leav-

ing obvious archaisms in spelling and grammar, the scribes generally revised ancient literary and other documents periodically...." (*IBHS*)

Moreover, the many differences between synoptic portions of the OT show that authors and/or scribes, "the authorized revisers of the text" at this time, felt free to edit earlier works into new, mutually independent, literary achievements (cf. 2 Sam 22 = Ps 18; 2 Kgs 18:13-20:19 = Isa 36-39; 2 Kgs 24:18-25:30 = Jer 52; Isa 2:2-4 = Mic 4:1-3; Ps 14 = 53; 40:14-18 = 70; 57:8-12 = 108:2-6; 60:7-14 = 108:7-14; Ps 96 = 1 Chron 16:23-33; Ps 106:1, 47-48 = 1 Chron 16:34-36; and the parallels between Samuel-Kings and Chronicles). Literary critics, not textual critics, should concern themselves with the differences between these portions of the OT.

(c) *Need to emend the text.* Accidental textual errors, however, probably corrupted the text during this formative period. In cases where none of the transmitted variants satisfies exegetical expectations, text critics propose a textual emendation (a conjectured variant based on the known variants). The DSS have now validated this procedure in certain instances. F. M. Cross ("Problems of Method," 37) comments: "No headier feeling can be experienced by a humanistic scholar, perhaps, than that which comes when an original reading, won by his brilliant emendation, is subsequently confirmed in a newly-found MS." The confusion in Ezek 3:12 of the similarly formed consonants k and m in the preexilic angular script offers a good illustration of the need for emendation (Kennedy, *An Aid to the Textual Amendment*, 83-84).

All texts: *brwk kbwd-yhwh mmqwmw*
"May the glory of YHWH *be praised* in (sic!) his dwelling place" (cf. NIV).
Emendation: *brw[m] kbwd-yhwh mmqwmw*
"As the glory of YHWH *arose* from its place" (cf. NRSV).

"Be praised," *brwk*, is attested in all textual witnesses. However, the phrase is unique, awkward, and contextless. Text critics salvage the line by emending *brwk* to *brwm*, "when [it] arose." The emendation nicely satisfies exegetical expectations, Heb. syntax, and the context of the verse (cf. Ezek 10:4, 15-18).

Scholars associated with HUBP and the United Bible Societies Hebrew Old Testament Text Critical Project disallow conjectured emendations. Their stance serves as a healthy corrective away from the extremes of Duhm and the "eccentricity in the later work of Cheyne" (Jellicoe, 320). However, it is too extreme. J. M. Sprinkle (*JETS*, 28, 1985, 469) complained: "What we as students of the Hebrew Bible actually want ... is not a later stage of the text but the original."

2. *From 400 BC to 150 BC.*

(a) *An open canon.* Though we possess a good knowledge of the OT's theology, we do not know when or where the OT books were first published or precisely how they gained admission into the select group of writings we call the OT. We do know, however, that by the time of the NT the OT canon was closed (Bruce, 28). Jesus and the apostles held the same OT in hand that Protestants do today. Beckwith (165) argues convincingly that Judas Maccabeus, at a date around 164 BC, gave the OT canon its final shape. The Qumran scrolls, however, reflect a Jewish community that embraced a somewhat different canon, at least to judge from the absence of Esther among them and from the slightly different shape of 11QPs^a as compared with the MT (Sanders, *ZAW* 65, 1964, 57-75).

(b) *The DSS and the LXX*. During these two and a half centuries there was also a tendency both to preserve and to revise the text. We can now sketch the history of the text for this period on the basis of the DSS and the LXX (ca. 250 BC to 150 BC).

(i) The DSS. By the techniques of paleography, numismatics, and archaeology the DSS are dated from the middle of the third century BC to the revolt of Bar-Kochba (AD 132-35). Most MSS were found in the eleven mountain caves just west of Khirbet Qumran. These caves yielded some 800 scrolls of all the books of the HB except Esther. The other principal sites, Nahal Hever and Wadi Murabba'at, yielded texts mostly from the early second century AD. Scrolls were also found at Masada, which fell to the Romans in AD 70.

(ii) The LXX. According to the pseudepigraphic Letter of Aristeas (ca. 130 BC), the Pentateuch was translated into G at ca. 285 BC by seventy-two translators (hence its title, Septuagint). This tradition was later expanded to include all the OT books translated into G.

P. Kahle argued that a great number of independent G translations existed for all the books and that the LXX as we know it now was a creation of the church. We have argued (*EBC* 1.220-21) that studies by Margolis on Joshua and Montgomery on Daniel, as well as the realization that recensional activities to conform the OG to the Proto-MT, which had given the illusion that all these variants could not go back to one original, have led to a widening consensus that agrees with Lagarde's view that all the Greek MSS go back to one textual tradition.

It is impossible to speak generally of the character of the LXX because it is not a uniform translation. Rather, different translators with varying capabilities and philosophies of translation rendered assorted portions of the OT. Elsewhere this writer collected the conclusions of scholars about these translations:

> Swete [drew the conclusion] that the majority of the translators learned Hebrew in Egypt from imperfectly instructed teachers, and Barr ... that these translators invented vowels for the unpointed text.... Except in passages such as Genesis 49 and Deuteronomy 32, 33, the Pentateuch is on the whole a close and serviceable translation of a smoothed Hebrew recension. The Psalter is tolerably well done, though Ervin concluded that the theology of Hellenistic Judaism left its mark on it. About Isaiah, Seeligman concluded, "The great majority of the inconsistencies here discussed must be imputed to the translator's unconstrained and carefree working method, and to a conscious preference for the introduction of variations." He added, "We shall not, however, do the translator any injustice by not rating his knowledge of grammar and syntax very highly." Regarding Hosea, Nyberg found that "it is overly composed of gross misunderstandings, unfortunate readings and superficial lexical definitions which often are simply forced conformity to similar Aramaic cognates. Helplessness and arbitrary choice are the characteristic traits of this interpretation." Albrektson said of Lamentations: "LXX, then, is not a good translation in this book. But this does not mean that it is not valuable for textual criticism. On the contrary, its literal character often allows us to establish with tolerable certainty the underlying Hebrew text. It is clearly based on a text which was in all essentials identical

with the consonants of the MT; indeed the passages where it may have contained a variant are notably few." Gerleman said of Job that the translator interprets the text as well as he can, and, with the help of his imagination, attempts to give an intelligible meaning to the original, which he does not understand. He added that the many deviations between the Hebrew and the Greek translations of Job are not the result of an essential difference between the original of the LXX and our Hebrew text. They have come about in the course of translation when the translator has not mastered the difficulties of the original. Swete concluded, "The reader of the Septuagint must expect to find large number of actual blunders, due in part perhaps to a faulty archetype, but chiefly to the misreading or misunderstanding of the archetype by the translators.... ("Textual Criticism," 221-22)

Gerleman (85-86) evaluated the LXX of Zephaniah thus: "The *Vorlage* of the Greek translator was not identical with the consonantal text of the MT but close to it.... The translator is very free in his interpretation of the MT. His work points to an innumerable number of wrong vocalizations, unfortunate divisions of the text, and superficial lexical definitions.... Finally, it seems fairly clear that the capabilities of the translator were not always up to mastering certain words and expressions that are difficult to translate."

This writer (*Micah*, 1993, 597) reached independently a similar conclusion for Micah as Nyberg had for Hosea and Gerleman for Zephaniah. This is not surprising, for J. Ziegler ("Die Einheit der Septaginta") demonstrated the unity of the Septuagint in the Minor Prophets.

It is well known that the LXX translator of Proverbs was influenced by Greek ethical thought, especially Stoic, along with early Jewish midrashic tradition, and that he modified a number of proverbs and made additions (Gerleman, *OTS*, 15-27; Jellicoe, 68, 317-18). Barr (158) says of this translation: "In fact the term 'free,' as applied to a translation like the Greek Proverbs, must mean something considerably different from what we mean when we speak of 'free translation' in a modern context.... For a translator like that of Proverbs free technique meant ... that after having translated *some* elements in the text in a rather 'literal' way, he could then break loose from literality and complete the sentence with a composition so loosely related to the original that it might equally be considered as an original composition rather than a rendering...."

On the other hand, this writer also noted (*EBC*, 1:222): "The LXX of Samuel, parts of Kings, and Ezekiel is of special value because the text preserved by the Masoretes of these books suffered more than usual from corrupting influences.

With regard to the chronology from Omri to Jehu, Shenkel concluded that the OG, represented in several MSS, preserves the original chronology better than the recensional developments, represented in the majority of MSS.

(c) *Tendency to preserve the text.* Some of the oldest MSS of the DSS show a striking similarity with the MT. Their silent testimony shouts out the achievement of scribes to preserve faithfully the OT text. This text-type undoubtedly existed before the time of these scrolls. The many archaic forms within the MT confirm the inference.

The studies of M. Martin show that the DSS reveal a conservative scribal tendency to follow the exemplar both in text and form.

(d) *Tendency to revise the text.* Though the author of 1 Macc (ca. 125 BC), for example, recognized that prophecy had ceased in Israel years before his time (cf. 1 Macc 9:27), the text of the OT was still open during this period. Scribes of this era were still the authorized revisers of the text, not just copyists. They continued to expand portions of the OT and to alter it to such an extent that their productions might equally be considered as distinct literary editions rather than as copies. In addition, they continued to revise older texts philologically to make them more intelligible to later generations.

As a result of their literary achievements the line between literary criticism and textual criticism has become attenuated. The texts of some portions of the OT have come down to us in two forms, attested in both the DSS and the LXX. There is, for instance, a short form of Jeremiah preserved in 4QJer[b] and in the LXX, and a long form preserved in 4QJer[a] and the MT. In the following example the additions in the long text are noted with italics:

> This is what the *Lord Almighty, the God of Israel*, said to me: "I will break the yoke of the king of Babylon. Within two years I will bring back to this place *all* the articles of the house of the LORD *that Nebuchadnezzar king of Babylon removed from this place and took to Babylon*, and Jeconiah *son of Jehoiakim king of Judah* and *all* the exiles from Judah *who went to Babylon, I am going to bring back to this place,"* *declares the LORD* (Jer 28:1-4a; 35:1-4a).

One is reminded of the editorial comment in Jeremiah 36:32:

> So Jeremiah took another scroll and gave it to the scribe Baruch son of Neriah, and as Jeremiah dictated, Baruch wrote on it all the words of the scroll that Jehoiakim king of Judah had burned in the fire. And many similar words were added to them.

E. Tov (*Textual Criticism*, 314-49) established on the basis of the ancient texts and versions the existence of two editions of Joshua (1986), 1 Sam 16-18 (1985), Ezekiel (1986), and Proverbs (1990). The different literary editions of Daniel and Esther are well known. This scribal practice is entirely consistent with known practices of composing books in the ANE. From cuneiform texts (ca. 2000 BC) to Tatian's *Diatessaron* (ca. AD 200) one can observe that ANE literatures were composed by supplementing earlier editions of a text with later materials (see Tigay, cf. R. P. Gordon, 57-69). We drew the conclusion elsewhere (*ABD*, 5.938f.) that the major contribution of the Samaritan Pentateuch [SP] to biblical studies is to literary criticism, not of textual criticism. For example, it involves the insertion of material from Deuteronomy into Exodus and the extensive repetition of other texts.

The scribal editors not only effected literary changes, they also altered the text for both philological and theological reasons. We noted elsewhere (*IBHS*, 19):

> They modernized it by replacing archaic Hebrew forms and constructions with forms and constructions of a later age. They also smoothed out the text by replacing rare constructions with more fre-

quently occurring constructions, and they supplemented and clarified the text by the insertion of additions and the interpolation of glosses from parallel passages. In addition, they substituted euphemisms for vulgarities, altered the names of false gods, removed the phrases that refer to cursing God, and safeguarded the sacred divine name or tetragrammaton (YHWH), occasionally by substituting forms in the consonantal text.

Philological alterations were already taking place at the time of Malachi, the last representative of mainstream OT prophecy. The book of Chronicles in its synoptic parallels with the Pentateuch and Former Prophets as preserved in MT exhibits similar revisions (Kropat). Ezra-Nehemiah explicitly states that as Ezra read from the book of the Law of God, he made it clear and gave the meaning so that the people could understand what was being read (Neh 8:8).

3. *From 150 BC to AD 135*. The bulk of the DSS belong to the period between the closing of the canon and the closing of its text. During this time, the Samaritan Pentateuch (SP) began a life of its own.

(a) *Samaritan Pentateuch*. At ca. 110 BC scribes of the Samaritans, a sect similar to the Jews apart from its worship on Mount Gerizim instead of at Jerusalem (John 4:19-22), adopted and adapted a distinct recension of the text attested as early as the Chronicler to constitute the SP. They probably accepted only the Pent as their canon because OT's second division, the Prophets, and its third, the Writings, celebrate Jerusalem.

(b) *Tendency to preserve the text*. In addition to the evidence adduced above for the tendency to conserve the text, there is a Talmudic notice that the scribes attempted to keep the text "correct" (b. *Ned* 37b-38a). Moreover, the MT itself preserves the following remnants of scribal concern with preserving the text, probably from this era: (i) the fifteen extraordinary points either to condemn the Hebrew letters as spurious or to draw attention to some peculiar text feature; (ii) the four suspended letters to indicate intentional scribal change or scribal error due to a faulty distinction of gutturals; and (iii) the nine inverted *nun*s apparently to mark verses thought to have been transposed (E. Tov, *ABD*, 6:397).

(c) *Tendency to revise the text*. On the other hand, the text was not fixed, and continued to be revised. E. Tov (*Textual Criticism*, 114-17) classifies the DSS into five different text-types.

(i) There are the *Proto-Masoretic* texts, which others call "the rabbinic text," during this period. About 60 percent of the scrolls belong to this type and may reflect its authoritative status (*Textual Criticism*, 115).

(ii) The *Pre-Samaritan* text scrolls have the characteristic features of the SP, aside from the thin layer of ideological and phonological changes the Samaritans added. Basing himself on Gesenius (1815), the first to classify the variants between SP and MT in a thorough and convincing way, the present writer (*ABD* 5:936-38) hoped to demonstrate from recent philological and textual research that the SP presents a secondarily modernized, smoothed over, and expanded text. The theological changes imposed on this text, though thin, are significant. For example, the Samaritans were able to make the worship on Mount Gerizim the tenth commandment by combining the first two commandments into one and by inserting texts about Mount Gerizim (Deut

11:29a; 27:2b-3a; 28:4-7; cf. also 11:30) after Exod 20:17, numbering the material from Deut 28:4-7 and 11:30 as the tenth commandment.

(iii) About 5 percent of the DSS are *Septuagintal* in character. Some DSS scrolls, most notably Jeremiah (4QJer[b,d]), bear a strong resemblance to the LXX's *Vorlage*.

(iv) The many *non-aligned* DSS are not exclusively close to any one of the types mentioned so far. Tov (*Textual Criticism*, 116) explains: "They agree, sometimes insignificantly, with MT against the other texts, or with SP and/or LXX against the other texts, but the non-aligned texts also disagree with the other texts to the same extent. They furthermore contain readings not known from one of the other texts."

(v) Tov (*Textual Criticism*, 114) identifies a group of texts that reflect a distinctive *Qumran practice* with regard to orthography (i.e., spelling, similar to "favor" versus "favour"), morphology, and a free approach to the biblical text visible in content adaptations, in frequent errors, in numerous corrections, and sometimes in negligent script. Tov thinks that only these scrolls were produced in Qumran.

These variant recensions also find parallels in Jewish and Christian literature originating during the time in question, such as the book of Jubilees (either early or late postexilic) and, most importantly, the NT (AD 50-90). For example, Stephen's sermon (Acts 7) and Hebrews are based on the pre-Samaritan recension.

The fall of the Second Temple (ca. AD 70), the debate between Jews and Christians, and Hillel's rules of hermeneutics all contributed to producing a stable text by about AD 100. The Naḥal Hever and Mur DSS, which date between AD 100 and AD 135, attest the Proto-MT.

4. *From AD 135 to AD 1000.*

(a) *Other early versions.* From ca. AD 100 to ca. AD 500 the official Aram. Targums (Tg.), the Syriac Peshitta (Syr.), various recensions of the LXX, and the Latin Vulgate (Vg.) were produced. They all have as their common denominator the Proto-MT and so are not as useful witnesses to the early stages of the still open text as are the DSS and the LXX. We need note only here that the Syr. has been influenced both by the LXX and the Tg. Nevertheless, each of these versions sometimes contains an original (i.e., an uncorrupted) reading.

(i) Targum means specifically a translation into Aram. When knowledge of Hebrew decreased among the Jewish people during the postexilic period, targums were created orally and later committed to writing. The targum fragments found at Qumran show that both free and literal targums were made. Scholars are divided about their dates (first to fifth century AD) and their places of origin (Babylon or Palestine). These more or less paraphrastic targums are of more value for understanding the way Jewish people understood their OT than for textual criticism. For example, the Tg. of Isa 52:13 reads: "Behold, my servant, the Messiah."

(ii) Early recensions of the LXX. Some scribes deliberately revised the original LXX, known as the Old Greek (OG), according to the Proto-MT. Prior to Origen (AD 200), who brought this process to completion in his famous Hexapla, Aquila (AD 125), Symmachus (AD 180), and Theodotion (180) revised the OG and/or earlier recensions of it according to this principle. A Greek scroll of the Minor Prophets recovered at Naḥal Hever shows that this process had already begun by the middle of the first century BC. Its distinctive translation techniques enabled scholars to link it up with other texts bearing witness to an early stage of the OG. Justin Martyr in his *Dialogue* complains against the Jew Trypho about the attitude the rabbinate had taken toward the LXX in order to remove an essential arm from the Christian apologist. Barthélemy who brilliantly edited this text, showed that Justin forced himself to use this revision in order to be acceptable to his adversaries.

(iii) Vulgate. Pope Damasus I commissioned Jerome (Hieronymus, AD 345-420) to produce a uniform and reliable Latin Bible. Jerome based his original translation of the Psalms (*Psalterium Romanum*) on the *Vetus Latina*, viz., Old Latin texts based largely on the LXX. His second translation of the Psalms was based on the Hexapla (*Psalterium Gallicanum*). Dissatisfied with these translations, Jerome finally translated *The Vulgate* ("the common one") from, as he put it, "the original truth of the Hebrew text." However, the Vg. includes the Gallican Psalter.

(b) *The MT*. The Masoretes (AD 600-1000) were groups of Jewish families who produced the final form of the OT text. They added four features to the inherited Proto-MT.

(i) They "hedged in" the consonantal text with a Masorah, consisting of scribal notes in the margin with instructions to ensure its precise transmission. Scribal precision in transmitting the consonants before the Masoretes is reflected in the Talmud. R. Ishmael cautioned: "My son, be careful, because your work is the work of heaven; should you omit (even) one letter or add (even) one letter, the whole world would be destroyed" (*b. Soṭa* 2a) (cited by Tov, *Textual Criticism*, 33).

(ii) They added vowel points above and below the consonants to preserve as perfectly as possible the accompanying tradition of pronunciation. These points supplemented the early consonants (', *h*, *w*, and *y*), known as the *matres lectionis* ("mothers of reading"), which were used to mark vowels in the prevocalized stage of the text. A Talmudic anecdote illustrates an acute awareness of the importance of an accurate oral tradition. David reprimanded Joab when he killed only the men of Amalek and not the "remembrance" (*zēker*) of them. Joab defended himself, noting his teacher taught him to read: "all their males" (*zākār*). Joab subsequently drew his sword against his teacher who had taught him incorrectly (*b. Bathra* 21a-b).

A complex body of evidence indicates the MT could not, in any serious or systematic way, represent a reconstruction or faking of the vocalization. Among other things we argued (*IBHS*, 28):

> On the whole the grammar [which depends heavily on vocalization] of the MT admirably fits the framework of Semitic philology, and this fact certifies the work of the Masoretes. When in the 1930s Paul Kahle announced his theory that the Masoretes made massive innovations, Gotthelf Bergsträsser sarcastically observed that they must have read Carl Brockelmann's comparative Semitic grammar to have come up with forms so thoroughly in line with historical reconstructions.

J. Barr (*Comparative Semitic Philology and the Text of the Old Testament*, 213) demonstrates that the Masoretes were preservers of the oral tradition, not innovators like the LXX translators, by contrasting Jerome's earlier version of the Psalter, based on the LXX, and his later one, based on the Hebrew. The consonants of Ps 102:23-24a[24-25a] are:

'nh bdrk kḥw [Qere kḥy] qṣr ymy: 'mr 'ly

The LXX and the Gallican Psalter read this as:

'ānāh[û] bᵉderek kōḥô qōṣer yāmay 'ᵉmor 'ēlay

"He replied to him in the way of his force; the fewness of my days report to me" (no major Eng. version).

The MT and Psalter, "Juxta Hebraeos," however, vocalize:

'innāh badderek kōḥî qiṣṣar yāmāy: 'ōmar 'ēlî

"He broke the strength on the way, he cut short my days. I said, My God ..." (cf. Eng. versions).

(iii) The Masoretes added a system of conjunctive and disjunctive accent signs to mark the chant or music (Haik-Vantoura). These diacritical marks serve to beautify, to add dignity, to denote the stress of the word, which can be as meaningful as the difference between English "pre-sént" and "prés-ent," and, most importantly, to denote the syntactical relationship of words. It makes some difference where one places the accents in Isa 40:3:

The voice of him that crieth in the wilderness, Prepare ... (KJV).

A voice of one calling: "In the desert prepare ..." (NIV).

Here, too, the Masoretes are preservers, not innovators, unlike the LXX, whose translators seem to have been flying by the seat of their pants. Revell (181) suggests that the punctuation was the first feature after the consonantal text to become stabilized in the Jewish biblical tradition.

(iv) The Masoretes also added various paratextual elements—the verse and paragraph divisions and ancient textual corrections. Its variants known as *Kethiv* [K] (the consonants of the Proto-MT) and *Qere* [Q] (the text they read aloud) are most important among these last-named. At first the Q readings were optional corrections of the text, but by the time of the Masoretes they became obligatory. We already noted a preferred Q reading in Ps 102:23[24]. However, sometimes the K is preferred. Prov 17:27b K (+ the LXX, Syr., Vg.) reads *wᵉqar-rûaḥ*, "and cool of spirit," but Q (+ Tg.) reads *yᵉqar-rûaḥ*, "precious of spirit," which was variously and dubiously understood to mean "heavy in spirit" (Tg.), "sparing of words" (Rashi), "of worthy bearing" (Saadia) (cited by Toy, 353). Both K and Q are hapleg. K now finds support from the Egyptian side. Grollenberg (42-43) showed that the Egyptians used "hot" and "cold" in a metaphorical sense for two distinct personality types.

The title page of L, the diplomatic text of *BHK* and *BHS,* reads: "Samuel Jacob copied, vowel-pointed and Masoretically annotated this Codex of the Sacred Scripture from the correct MSS which the teacher Aaron b. Moses Ben-Asher redacted (his rest is in Paradise!) and which constitutes an exceedingly accurate Exemplar." In fact, however, L probably contains too many corrections and errors to have served as a synagogue scroll.

Conclusion. In the light of this history we can now restrict the aim of OT text criticism to that of recovering the original text that lies behind the Proto-MT recension. The witnesses show such diverse text-types for some portions of the OT, like Joshua, Proverbs, and Esther, that they are best regarded as either distinct, literary stages in the development of the text or as distinct compositions. Tov (*Textual Criticism,* 177) summarizes: "The differences between the textual witnesses show that a few books and parts of books were once circulated in different formulations representing different literary stages, as a rule one after the other, but possibly also parallel to each other." In Tov's view the text critic ought to reconstruct the edition represented in the Proto-MT. Socio-religious and historical reasons validate his view. That recension became the authoritative text both within Judaism and the church. Tov argues this case for Judaism, but he failed to note that both Origen and Jerome, the two most formative OT text critics in church history, also established the MT recension for the church. Our English versions are based on it. "This history," we said (1994, 175-76), "should not be underestimated in deciding the question, 'What is the original text?' The MT inherently commended itself to both the synagogue and the church. As the canon of the OT emerged in the historical process, so also the MT surfaced as the best text of that canon." Childs (96-97) reached a similar conclusion.

We do not agree with the theory of Ackroyd and of Sanders ("Text and Canon," 5-29) that the different recensions enjoy equal canonical status. That view is unsatisfying from both a theologian's and historian's point of view. A serious theologian will want to know whether or not the Tenth Commandment prescribes worship on Mount Gerizim, and a resolute historian needs to know whether the biblical historian recorded in Exod 12:40 that Israel spent 430 years before the Exodus in just Egypt (MT) or in Egypt and Canaan (LXX, SP). Both theology and history demand the critic decide upon an original text.

C. The Practice of Textual Criticism

Text critics traditionally distinguish between *external criticism* (i.e., the evaluation of the textual witnesses), and *internal criticism* (i.e., the transcriptional and intrinsic probability of the readings themselves). For the former critics need to know the history of the witnesses; for the latter, the kinds of errors scribes made along with a sensitivity to exegetical expectations.

1. *External criticism.* Before critics can evaluate the variants, however, they must first be collected and collated. Unfortunately the apparatus in *BHS* still swarms with errors of commission and omission. True variants, we said, are restricted to those that pertain to the editing of Proto-MT, not to the literary achievements of earlier scribes. For example, the shorter readings of Jeremiah should be passed over. This also applies to Joshua. Compare these variants of the MT and the LXX in Josh 1:1. MT reads *'ḥry mwt mšh 'bd yhwh*, "After the death of Moses servant of YHWH," but LXX read *'ḥry mwt mšh*, "After the death of Moses." The MT of Josh 1 has more than twelve additional words or phrases that are not found in the LXX, and the LXX rendering of Joshua is about 4-5 percent shorter than the MT. Plausibly the LXX reflects an earlier, shorter stage of the text and in this case should be ignored. Radically dissimilar to his NT counterpart, the OT text critic does not prefer the earlier and shorter readings! In fact, he turns them over to the literary critic.

2. *Intrinsic criticism.*

(a) *Unintentional errors.* Following are a few illustrations of some kinds of unintentional scribal errors. In each case we retrovert the LXX to its Hebrew Vorlage.

(i) Confusion of consonants. Scribes confused *b/k, b/m, b/n, g/w, g/y, d/r, h/ḥ, w/z, w/y, w/r, k/n, m/s,* and *'/ṣ.* Javan's sons are called *ddnym* ("Dodanim") in Gen 10:4 of MT and *rdnym* in Gen 10:4 of SP, LXX and in 1 Chron 1:7 of MT.

(ii) Haplography ("writing once") as a result of homoioteleuton (i.e., words with similar endings) or homoioarcton (words with similar beginnings). MT for Gen

47:16 reads: *w'tnh lkm bmqnykm,* "I will give you for your cattle" (cf. KJV), but SP and LXX read *w'tnh lkm lḥm bmqnykm,* "I will give you bread for your cattle" (cf. NIV, NRSV). The scribe may have skipped *lḥm,* bread, not only because of words with similar beginnings and endings but because of the similar sound of *k* and *ḥ.*

(iii) Metathesis (the accidental exchange or transposition of two adjacent letters within a word). The MT of Deut 31:1 reads *wylk mšh,* "and Moses went" (cf. NIV), but 4QDeut[n] and the LXX, *wykl mšh,* "and Moses finished" (cf. NRSV).

(iv) Different concepts of word and verse division. The MT of Hos 6:5 reads *wmšptyk 'wr yṣ',* "and your judgments, light goes forth" (cf. KJV, NASB), but the LXX reads *wmšpty k'wr yṣ',* "and my judgments went forth as light" (cf. NIV, NRSV).

(v) Dittography ("writing twice"). Isa 30:30 in the MT, LXX, Tg., Syr., and Vg. all read *whšmy' yhwh,* "and YHWH will cause to be heard," but 1QIs[a] reads *whšmy' hšmy' yhwh,* "and YHWH will cause to be heard, to be heard."

(vi) Doublets (conflation of two or more readings). MT of 2 Kgs 19:9 reads *wyšb wyšlḥ ml'kym,* "and he again sent messengers," and the MT of its synoptic parallel in Isa 37:9 reads *wyšm' wyšlḥ ml'kym,* "and when he heard it, he sent messengers." The LXX and 1QIs[a] of Isa 37:9 read *wyšm' wyšb wyšlḥ ml'kym,* "and when he heard it, he again sent messengers."

(b) *Intentional changes.* Following are a few illustrations of some kinds of intentional scribal changes in the text.

(i) Linguistic changes. Scribes sometimes modernized archaic features of a verse. In Num 15:35 the SP replaces the old infinitive absolute construction of the MT (*rāgōm*) for probably the imperative, *rigmu,* stone.

(ii) Contextual changes. In Gen 2:2, according to the MT, the Tg., and the Vg., God completed his work on the seventh day, but according to the SP, the LXX, and the Syr., he finished on the sixth day to avoid making it appear that God worked on the Sabbath.

(iii) Euphemistic changes. In Gen 50:3 the SP changes *'l-brky ywsp,* "upon the knees of Joseph," into *'l-bymy ywsp,* "in the days of Joseph," because it seemed improper that Joseph's grandchildren should be born upon his knees.

(iv) Theological changes. We have already noted how SP altered the Ten Commandments. Better known are the changes of early names with the theophoric element *ba'al,* lord, by the derogatory element, *bōšet,* shame (cf. 1 Chron 8:33 and 2 Sam 2:8). On the whole, however, theological changes are rare in the MT. G. R Driver (153) noted: "Theological glosses are surprisingly few, and most are enshrined in the *tiqqunê sōp^erîm,* which are corrections of the text aimed chiefly at softening anthropomorphisms and eliminating the attribution of any sort of impropriety to God."

D. Textual Criticism and Exegesis

Variants often impact the exegesis of the text and ultimately, to a greater or lesser extent, OT theology. At the same time, however, the critic must decide between them on the basis of exegetical expectations.

The basic canon for deciding between variants is: That reading is preferable which would have been more likely to give rise to the others. To say this another way: The variant that cannot be explained away is more probably the original. To apply this canon effectively demands extensive knowledge of the textual witnesses, scribal practices, exegetical factors, and also common sense. P. K. McCarter (22-24) wisely counsels the text critic to: (1) keep a clear image of the scribe in mind; (2) look first for the unconscious error; (3) know the personalities of your witnesses; (4) treat each case as if it were unique. Regarding the last he cites Housman's memorable metaphor: "A textual critic engaged upon his business is not at all like Newton investigating the motion of the planets; he is much more like a dog hunting fleas.... They require to be treated as individuals; and every problem which presents itself to the textual critic must be regarded as possibly unique."

Let us illustrate the practice of textual criticism by returning to the metathesis in Prov 14:32b: *wᵉḥōseh bᵉmôtô ṣaddîq*, "the righteous is *ḥōseh* in his death" (MT) versus *wᵉḥōseh bᵉtummô ṣaddiq*, "the righteous is *ḥōseh* in his blamelessness." The key to deciding the original text lies in a correct understanding of the q. part. of *ḥsh*. The lexeme occurs 37x and always with the meaning "to seek refuge," never "to have a refuge" (*pace* NIV) nor "to find a refuge" (*pace* NRSV). Thirty-four times, not counting Prov 14:32b, it is used with reference to taking refuge in God or under the shadow of his wings (cf. Prov 30:5). The two exceptions are Isa 14:32 and 30:2. In 14:32 the afflicted take refuge in Zion, a surrogate for God; in 30:2 Isaiah gives the expression an exceptional meaning because he uses sarcasm: *laḥsôt bᵉṣēl miṣrāyim*, "to take refuge in the shadow of Egypt!" His intended meaning is that the Jerusalemites should have sought refuge in the Lord. The q. part. of *ḥsh* or the occurrence of *ḥsh* in a relative clause denotes a devout worshiper, "one who seeks refuge in Yahweh." One other time beside Prov 14:32b the q. part. is used absolutely: "[Show the wonder of your love], O Savior of those who take refuge (*môšîa' ḥôsîm*)" (Ps 17:7). NIV here rightly glosses, "Savior of those who take refuge in you."

Gamberoni (*TDOT* 5:71) agrees that the q. part. has the same "religio-ethical" sense in Prov 14:32b as in Ps 17:7. O. Ploeger (176) and A. Meinhold (*Die Sprueche*) independently also reached the conclusion that YHWH is the unstated object of *ḥōseh* in Prov 14:32b. W. McKane (475), citing A. Barucq (*Le livre des proverbes*), recognizes this as the meaning of the MT. The LXX, NIV, NRSV, however, misunderstood the term. The unequivocal meaning of *ḥōseh*, however, nicely satisfies the exegetical expectation of "in his death," but not of "in his righteousness." McKane rejects the MT because, as he says, "I do not believe that the sentence originally asserted this [a belief in the after-life]." He follows the LXX and renders: "But he who relies on his own piety is a righteous man." His interpretation, however, violates both the lexical expectations of this word and the exegetical expectation of the book as a whole. Proverbs consistently encourages faith in the Lord (cf. 3:5; 22:19), never faith in one's own piety. In sum, the exegetical expectations of *ḥsh* and of the book favor the MT, suggesting that the corruption occurred in the LXX tradition.

In this treatment we have focused on scholarly competence. Exegetical competence also entails spiritual virtues, as we have argued elsewhere ("Exegesis and the Spiritual Life").

E. The Reliability of the OT Text

In the light of the OT text's complex history and the welter of conflicting readings in its textual witnesses, can the church still believe in an infallible OT? Can it still confess with the Westminster divines: "by His singular care and providence" the text has been "kept pure in all ages" (Westminster Confession of Faith, 1:8). We argue that in fact this history of the text and its witness and other reasons give the church good reason to continue to confess *ex animo* both the reliability of the OT text and its purity.

1. In every era there was a strong *tendency to preserve the text*, as argued above.

2. The *antiquity of the MT* can be inferred from both the DSS and from comparative Sem. grammar. There is a continuous witness to the received text-type that lies behind some of the oldest biblical MSS at Qumran and the whole versional tradition (apart from some portions of OG) that stretches from ca. AD 100 to the most modern translations into Eng. and a host of other modern languages and dialects. Moreover, the grammar of this text-type admirably fits the framework of ancient Semitic philology. In fact, it accurately preserves hapleg. such as *qar-ruaḥ*, cool of spirit, even though they were not understood later on in the text's transmission.

3. *The MT recension can be distinguished* from the scribal activity that in effect produced other literary editions of OT materials. If the church confesses that the Holy Spirit superintended the selection of books that comprise the canon of the OT, why should it not confess that the Holy Spirit also superintended the selection of the MT recension? To be sure, the NT authors exhibit the Septuagintal and pre-Samaritan recensions and unique readings, but they also had a freedom in citing noncanonical, religious literature. Even though the canon was closed, they felt free to cite noncanonical literature for theological reasons. How much more should we expect them to use texts freely before the text was finalized?

4. One needs to *keep the data in perspective*. A quick count of the textual variants in *BHS* shows that on average for every ten words there is a textual note. The humanists that produced its text-critical notes for recovering an original eclectic text imply that 90 percent of the text in hand is unquestioned. Textual criticism focuses on the problem readings, not on uncontested readings, giving a sense of disproportion to the amount of contaminated text.

5. *The significance of these variants* must be kept in view. In this essay we featured significant variants to make our points, but in truth most variants, including the 10 percent collated in *BHS,* are insignificant and do not affect doctrine. Most text-critical work is boring because the differences are inconsequential. If we restrict ourselves to the MT recension, D. Stuart (98) rightly observes: "It is fair to say that the verses, chapters, and books of the Bible would read largely the same, and would leave the same impression with the reader, even if one adopted virtually every possible *alternative* reading to those now serving as the basis for current English translations." Even if we accepted the earlier and/or other literary editions of portions of the OT, no doctrinal statement within the Protestant tradition would be affected. S. Talmon (*Textual Study of the Bible*, 326) notes regarding the variants both within and between textual traditions:

> The scope of variation within all textual traditions is relatively restricted. Major divergences which intrinsically affect the sense are extremely rare. A collation of variants extant, based on the synoptic study of the material available, either by a comparison of parallel passages within one Version, or of the major Versions with each other, results in the conclusion that the ancient authors, compilers, tradents and scribes enjoyed what may be termed a controlled freedom of textual variation.

6. Paradoxically, *the variety of texts bear witness to an original text.* Even in those portions of the OT that have been preserved in different literary editions there is still a relatively large consensus and close genetic relation among the MSS. This is best explained by a schema that commences with an Ur-text. Within the MT tradition, of course, there is a much greater agreement and closer genetic connection. The variants within this tradition point unmistakably to an original text from which they sprang. With respect to this agreement Harris (88-89) provides an apt illustration of the reliability of the text, in spite of there being no perfect witness to it. He notes how the loss or destruction of the standard yard at the Smithsonian Institution would not enormously affect the practice of measurement in the United States, for a comparison of the multitudinous copies of that yard would lead us to something very close to the original standard.

7. *The correctibility of the text* must also be kept in view. Normally an error in the transcriptional process is subject to human correction. In the same way that an average reader can normally correct errors in a book or manuscript, the text critic can correct a textual error in the OT. A good exegete can reduce the number of problematic readings considerably. Moreover, we are the heirs of the work of many competent text critics. Just as electrical engineers can remove unwanted static from a telecommunication signal, so text critics can remove scribal corruptions by their knowledge of the text's history and character and by their exegetical expectations.

8. *The variants in the NT are similar to those found in the DSS.* Our Lord and his apostles confronted OT variants qualitatively similar to the ones that confront us, yet they did not hesitate to rely on the authority of Scripture. These difference did not prevent Jesus from saying that Scripture cannot be broken (John 10:35), nor Paul from confessing that "all Scripture is God-breathed" (2 Tim 3:16). Why should the contemporary church, which is built upon Christ and his apostles, hesitate any more than they to confess the reliability and inspiration of Scripture?

9. *The variants in the DSS are not qualitatively different from those already known.* The Westminster divines knew the variants in the Samaritan Pentateuch and the ancient versions, which are qualitatively the same as those in the DSS, and yet did not hesitate to confess their conviction that the same Spirit who inspired the OT also preserved it. There are no new data to change the confession.

10. *The preserved OT achieves the work of the Holy Spirit.* Paul says: "All Scripture is God-breathed and is useful for teaching, rebuking, correcting and training in righteousness, so that the man of God may be thoroughly equipped for every good work" (2 Tim 3:16-17). The OT we have in hand does just that.

BIBLIOGRAPHY
P. R. Ackroyd, "An Authoritative Version of the Bible?" *ExpTim* 85, 1973, 374-77; A. Barucq, *Le livre des proverbes,* 1964; D. Barthélemy, "Redecouverts d'un chainon manguant de l'histoire de la LXX," *RB* 60, 1958, 18-29; J. Barr, *"B'RS-MOLIS*: Prov XI.31, 1 Pet IV.18," *JSS* 20, 1975, 149-64; R. Beckwith, *The Old Testament Canon of the New Testament Church and Its Background in Early Judaism,* 1985; E. Brotzman, *OT Textual Criticism,* 1994; F. F. Bruce, *The Canon of Scripture,* 1988; B. Childs, *Introduction to the Old Testament As Scripture,* 1979; F. M. Cross, "Problems of Method in the Textual Criticism of the Hebrew Bible," *The Critical Study of Sacred Texts,* ed. by W. D. O'Flaherty, 1979; F. M. Cross and S. Talmon, (eds.), *Qumran and the History of the Biblical Text,* 1975; F. E. Deist, *Witnesses to the Old Testament: Introducing Old*

Testament Textual Criticism, 1988; G. R. Driver, "Glosses in the Hebrew Text of the OT," L'AT et l'orient, Orientalia et Biblical Loveaniensia 1, 1957; G. Gerleman, Zephanja textkritisch und literarisch untersucht, 1942; idem, "The Septuagint Proverbs as a Hellenistic Document," OTS 8, 1950, 15-27; idem, Studies in the Septuagint, LUA NF 52, 3, 1956; R. P. Gordon, "Compositions, Conflation and the Pentateuch," JSOT 51, 1991, 57-69; L. Grollenberg, "A propos de Prov. VIII,6 et XVII,27," RB 59, 1962, 42-43; R. L. Harris, Inspiration and Canonicity of the Bible, 1957; S. Jellicoe, The Septuagint and Modern Study, 1968; J. Kennedy, An Aid to the Textual Amendment of the Old Testament, 1928; R. W. Klein, Textual Criticism of the OT: From the Septuagint to Qumran, 1974; A. Kropat, Die Syntax des Autors der Chronik verglichen mit der seiner Quellen: Ein Beitrag zur historischen Syntax des Hebräischen, BZAW 16, 1909; M. Martin, The Scribal Character of the Dead Sea Scrolls, 1958; P. Kyle McCarter, Textual Criticism: Recovering the Text of the Hebrew Bible, 1988; W. McKane, Proverbs, OTL, 1970; A. Meinhold, Die Sprueche, Zuercher Bibelkommentare, 1991; A. Millard, "In Praise of Ancient Scribes," BA 45, 1982, 143-53; R. Nicole, "The Nature of Inerrancy," Inerrancy and Common Sense [ICS], eds. R. R. Nicole & J. Ramsey Michaels, 1980, 71-95; O. Ploeger, Sprueche Salomos, BKAT, 1984; E. J. Revell, "Biblical Punctuation and Chant in the Second Temple Period," JSJ 7, 1976, 181; B. R. Roberts, The Old Testament Text and Versions, 1951; J. A. Sanders, "Text and Canon: Concepts and Methods," JBL 98, 5-29; idem, "Two Non-canonical Psalms in 11QPs^a," ZAW 65, 1964, 57-75; N. Sarna, "Bible Text," EJ 4, 1971, 831-35; J. D. Shenkel, Chronology and Recensional Development in the Greek Text of Kings, 1968; D. Stuart, "Inerrancy and Textual Criticism," ICS, 97-117; J. H. Tigay, ed., Empirical Models for Biblical Criticism, 1976; E. Tov, The Text-Critical Use of the Septuagint in Biblical Research, 1981; idem, "A Modern Textual Outlook Based on the Qumran Scrolls," HUCA, 53, 1982, 11-27; idem, "The Growth of the Book of Joshua in the Light of the Evidence of the LXX Translation," in Studies in the Bible: 1986, ScrHier 31, 1986, 321-39; idem, "The Composition of 1 Samuel 16-18 in the Light of the Septuagint Version," Empirical Models for Biblical Criticism, 1976, 97-130; idem, "Recensional Differences between the MT and LXX of Ezekiel," ETL 62, 1986, 89-101; idem, "Recensional Differences Between the Masoretic Text and the Septuagint of Proverbs," Of Scribes and Scrolls: Presented to John Strugnell, ed. by H. W. Attridge, J. J. Collins, T. H. Tobin, 1990, 43-56; idem, Textual Criticism of the Hebrew Bible, 1992; S. Haik- Vantoura, The Music of the Bible Revealed, 1991; B. K. Waltke, "Prolegomena to the Samaritan Pentateuch," Ph.D. Dis. Harvard University, 1965; idem, "The Samaritan Pentateuch and the Text of the Old Testament, in New Perspectives on the Old Testament, ed. by J. B. Payne, 1970, 212-39; idem, "The Textual Criticism of the Old Testament," EBC 1, 1979, 210-28; idem, "Aims of Textual Criticism," WTJ, 51, 1989, 93-108; idem, "Samaritan Pentateuch," ABD, 5, 1992, 932-40; idem, "Micah," The Minor Prophets, ed. by T. E. McComiskey, 2, 1993, 591-764; idem, "Exegesis and the Spiritual Life: Theology As Spiritual Formation," Crux 30, 1994, 28-35; idem, "Old Testament Textual Criticism," Foundations for Biblical Interpretation, ed. by D. S. Dockery, K. A. Mathews, R. B. Sloan, 1994, 156-86; J. Ziegler, "Die Einheit der Septuaginta zum Zwölfprophetenbuch," Verzeichnis der Vorlesungen an der Staatlichen Akademie zu Braunsberg, 1934-35, 1-16.

Bruce K. Waltke

PART II: HISTORY, THEOLOGY, AND HERMENEUTICS

The following two essays on biblical history by Eugene Merrill and V. Phillips Long are complementary. On the one hand, H. Merrill explores the theological dimension of OT texts. He raises and answers the question of how biblical history has a theological aspect. This exercise is in keeping with Vanhoozer's theological concern. The OT is relevant in that it does not just present history or a historical framework. Regrettably, this is often the way the OT is presented, as one learns a list of the kings of Israel and Judah in chronological sequence. Merrill takes the position that the historical material is presented in literary categories for the purpose of showing God's ways in human affairs. This story forms a part with the NT story as an unfolding of the history of redemption.

On the other hand, Long opens up the hermeneutical issue of how one interprets historical texts. He challenges the readers to evaluate the options and to make informed decisions on how they listen to the text. The end result is surprising. Such a reading will enhance a reimaging of Israel's sacred history that combines historical facts with a literary (imaginative) framework provided by the biblical text. (VanGemeren)

3. OLD TESTAMENT HISTORY: A THEOLOGICAL PERSPECTIVE

Students of the OT even superficially in touch with biblical theology are well aware of the sometimes uneasy coexistence of history and theology as components of that discipline. The perceptions of the relationship of the two run the gamut from an absolute bifurcation that views them as mutually exclusive to a coincidence obliterating any distinction (Deist, 23-28). Basic questions relative to this problem are: (1) Is the OT a history book? (2) Is it a theological compendium? (3) Is it perhaps somewhat a melding of the two, a history of Israel's religion? (4) Is it a *Heilsgeschichte,* an interpreted recital of Israel's faith, the underlying factual data of which may or may not be in line with the confession of what happened or even important to it? The answers to these and similar questions are essential to the resolution of the tension precipitated by the history/theology interpenetration.

A. The Nature of the OT: Theology, Not History

A confessional stance that views the OT as revelation must logically conclude that at its core it is a set of theological texts. Notwithstanding other critical and literary analyses, it presents itself as an expression of the mind and purposes of God, who, through its multifaceted witness, has spoken of himself and his works. Even those with other presuppositions as to the character of the Bible must concede that the OT's own consistent portrayal of itself is that it is the conveyor of transcendent truth. It is a word from and about God either in fact or in ancient Israel's perception.

To say this is to say nothing about the forms in which the theological message is cast, i.e., the literary garb that clothes the body of truth; or the strategy employed by the ancient authors and compilers of the texts, i.e., whether it is propositional, categorical, or (historical) narrative. Such matters must be decided on literary-critical and form-critical grounds. What is important to note here is that a theological message need not be wedded to a "theological text," if there be such a thing. Theology has to do with the content of the communication, literature and strategy with its form.

1. *The relationship of history to theology.* The objective reader of the OT comes away from the text with the overwhelming impression that he or she has been reading history. To be sure, it may be unfamiliar history and history couched in and intermingled with literary forms that seem alien to "normal" historiography, but it is history nevertheless. Those familiar with the fact that history writing can be done in almost unlimited ways have an even stronger impression that the Old Testament is professing at least to be rehearsing and interpreting historical events. However, experienced students of history are quick to sense that there is a fundamental difference between the OT as reportorial history and as ideology cast in somewhat an historiographical form. Forms resembling myth, legend, saga, aetiology, and the like offer clues to suggest that the history narrated in the OT is one that must be defined in a highly nuanced way.

The term *narrated* is perhaps the best way to characterize the overall flow of the biblical account regardless of the technical labels applied to the units forming its building blocks (Barr, 1976, 266-67). If the OT is anything, it is a story or collection of stories with discernible characters, plots, themes, crises, resolutions, and other elements familiar to this kind of literature. But specifically, it is story in the service of history or, more simply, narrated history. This is much in line with ANE and classical models, which, contrary to most modern conventions, not only do not view history and story as antithetical but rather as naturally and necessarily complementary (Millard, 47-50). If biography is the story of a single life, history is the story of many lives, even national and international in scale.

When this understanding of OT history is applied to the matter of the relationship of history to theology, it becomes clear that the OT is narrated or "historicized" theology. To refer again to the definitions of biography and history as stories of individuals and groups of individuals respectively, one might speak of theology as the story or even "history" of God. That is, God has revealed himself in creation, event, and dialogue (word) in such a way as to constitute a story, one that gives the OT such a unique historiographical shape because it is written from his perspective and designed according to his objectives. One's underlying assumptions about the OT will, of course, dictate his historiosophical conclusions about the storyline of the narrative and, indeed, the very facticity of the events purported to have occurred. Is the OT an account of history as God preordained (or at least permitted) it (theology), or is it merely the account by an ancient people of their own attempts to recover and interpret events that profoundly shaped their lives and their understanding of God (theologizing)? These questions touch upon the fundamental nature of the theological enterprise.

2. *The historical nature of biblical theology.* If history and theology are inextricable, how does this interrelationship work itself out in practical, formal terms? The response lies in recalling again that the historical framework and development of the OT message is that of narrative, the telling of stories each of which is a subset of The Story, the self-disclosure of Yahweh through his works and words. One looks in the OT, therefore, for the elements of story—for beginnings, plot, development, emphases, climax, and conclusion. But precisely because theology is the story of God—with all that implies—it is a story that leads pedagogically to decision and commitment. Its purpose is more than merely to provide information about God; it is designed also to

communicate clearly the human predicament and how that predicament can be resolved by the (re)establishment of a redemptive, divine-human relationship (VanGemeren, 31-34).

If the story as a whole is to be taken seriously as portraying facts, the persons and events to which it attests must also be taken seriously. That is, it must be seen as a true story, a narrative not only reflecting perception about events but one that recounts with accuracy and integrity the events as they actually happened. This does not mean that the "facts" lie before us unfiltered and without nuance, of course, but it does and must mean, if it is theology, that the facts conform to reality; i.e., that they are "true facts" (V. Long, 98-99, 191-93).

In many instances, however, the facts are such as to be known only to God and to be communicated only by revelation. Others are gleaned from private or personal settings, in some extreme cases only from privileged conversations or even thought. These come to be part of the story either by their being shared by the participants or by what critics call "narrator omniscience" (Alter, 157). Clues usually exist to determine when such a device is being employed so that the reader can know to what extent such scenes can be judged to reflect actuality or only a set of circumstances likely to produce the event as recorded. The theological usefulness of reconstructed events, conversation, or thoughts is, of course, a matter of some debate. But when even these are set within a theological setting that regards the whole text in some sense as being revelatory, the problems are greatly alleviated.

These theoretical and epistemological issues aside, that of the nature of the history upon which the theology is based yet remains and must be addressed, if only briefly. Following a period in the late nineteenth and early twentieth century of skeptical criticism in which the OT was divested of virtually any historical credibility, a reaction took place, especially with Gerhard von Rad, that attempted to rehabilitate the OT historically and theologically by asserting that Israel's faith was rooted and grounded in historical event (von Rad, 1984, 168-71). This retrieved a sense of the historical underpinnings of biblical theology and gave rise to a renewed appreciation of the OT as a witness to God's activity in time and space.

However, history to von Rad and his school was redefined to mean the account of the past as reconstructed and interpreted by Israel's traditionists. While appealing, therefore, to the OT as a record of God's saving acts (*Heilsgeschichte*), these scholars were suggesting that record can never be a witness to events as they actually happened but only to their meaning. That is, the ancient tradents mined from their past certain events or stories of events; reflected upon their theological implications; and then reshaped, embellished, and otherwise sacralized them as they transmitted them to later generations. The result of such a process, it was maintained, was the hammering out of a body of truth confessed in credal form but shorn of any claim to absolute historical facticity. History, then, exists in the OT at two levels; that which actually occurred (von Rad's critical minimum) and that which Israel confessed as the basis of its existence and witness (his theological maximum) (von Rad, 1962, 108).

This is not the place to enter the debate over the kind of history that constitutes the marrow of OT theology. Suffice it to say that a view of history that requires each interpreter to decide for himself what could or could not or what did or did not occur opens itself to a radical subjectivism that divests the OT of any genuine historical and theological authority.

3. *The characteristics of OT history.* Granted that the OT is fundamentally a history—albeit one designed to advance theological purposes—it is still apparent that it is history writing almost *sui generis* in its subject matter, its literary vehicles, and its unique predilections. The following list of characteristics, while not exhaustive, will help to establish the observations just made.

(a) The history of the OT is overwhelmingly *narrative* in expression. From beginning to end the dealings of God with humankind, their response to him, and their interrelationships at both individual and corporate levels appear in story form. Even so-called legal texts, paraeneses, and prophetic addresses are lodged in narrative contexts as justifications of, explanations for, or reactions to certain events of the story. The Psalms and Wisdom literature may not be so easily explained in these terms, but many Psalms titles and headings of Wisdom passages suggest a sensitivity on the part of authors and/or compilers to root these texts within some kind of historico-narrative setting. And though there are many stories, the reader of the whole OT corpus comes away with the distinct impression that they are all part of one story, one overriding message that may, indeed, be told with enormous complexity.

(b) The history of the OT is *biographical.* We have argued that the story of the OT is one related from God's viewpoint, not humanity's, and that this is one of its distinguishing characteristics as history. But ironically enough, the record is relatively absent of any story *about* God. That is, he is the principal actor—the protagonist—but he always tells the story about himself through the lives and lips of his people. One learns about God primarily as one observes God in events and persons. The theocentricity of the Bible is ultimately observable in its anthropocentricity.

This leads to the observation that the stories of the OT, i.e., its history, are essentially biographies. Nowhere is this more apparent than in Genesis, where the mighty cultures and empires of the Mesopotamian and Egyptian worlds are eclipsed by the poignant and intensely personal accounts of Abraham, Isaac, Jacob, and Joseph. To a lesser extent this focus on individuals pervades the remainder of the OT record. Even in the years of the monarchy the attention is not so much on the nations of Israel and Judah (to say nothing of those of the larger world) but on kings and prophets. A remarkable example of this is the preoccupation in the books of Kings with Elijah and Elisha, whose exploits dominate fourteen chapters out of a total of forty-seven.

(c) The history of the OT is *tendentious.* A justified criticism of all historiography is that it is inescapably biased. Any historian, no matter how resolute his determination otherwise, views the past and interprets his sources through the lenses of his own training, experiences, presuppositions, and prejudices. There is no such thing as "objective" history writing, so that there can be no such thing as a neutral portrayal of the past. The past comes to us as much as an expression of opinion or propaganda as it does a set of unsullied facts. In reality, then, there is no hope of perfectly equating historical data with the events they purport to relate.

To some extent, then, the *heilsgeschichtliche* school is correct in asserting that the OT is more an interpretation of history than a scientific attempt to reconstruct history as it actually occurred. Where this school is often wrong is in the extent to which it suggests this "mythologizing" has occurred and in the implied assertion that interpretation of event is necessarily divergent from or even contradictory to the actual facts of the event. There is no reason in principle to insist that historical occurrences cannot coincide with the way they are narrated or even understood (Goldingay, 1972, 87-91). In the case of the OT, an admittedly tendentious composition, theological concerns outweigh historical ones—but not to the point of vitiating the historical truth claims of the text. Dissonance (if any) between events and their meaning(s) is confined to matters of viewpoint, emphasis, and significance. Whether it is the viewpoint of God or only a human being that is asserted dictates the emphasis to be given to an episode and surely is decisive in determining its theological significance.

(d) The history of the OT is theocentric. The idiosyncratic approach to history in the OT derives directly from its confession that it is the Word of God, not the words of human beings, and therefore it finds its point of departure, its thematic unity, and its ultimate resolution in him. One may challenge the proposition that Scripture is in fact revelation, of course, but it is impossible to scout its unambiguous self-attestation to that effect. Regardless of any particular critical assessment, the OT reads as an outpouring of the heart of God, the benevolent Creator of all things, who, through history and word, is undertaking the mighty redemptive work of restoring all things to his dominion. The creation, especially humankind, is certainly not peripheral to the story, but neither can it usurp the narrative's own center, which is God himself.

(e) The history of the OT is selective (Halpern, 6-7). Inherent to its theocentricity is the absence in it of any other primary pole of reference. If the biblical story is indeed the story of God, events, no matter how important otherwise, that do not contribute to the central message are ignored, even those that find lavish exposure in the "press" of the ANE world. Similarly, what appear to be incidents unworthy of inclusion in any history, especially one of such brief compass as the OT, are sometimes related in painstaking detail. When either is the case, perceptive analysis of the accounts against the backdrop of the Bible's own central concerns makes crystal clear the methodological rationale: Only that which contributes to the story of God, i.e., to the theological intention of the text, is worthy of comment. Thus, whole centuries can be bypassed (e.g., the approximately 335 years between Jacob's death and Moses' birth) or long chapters can be devoted to a relatively brief period of time (e.g., the forty years covered by Exod 12 through Deut, 125 chapters!). What happened in Hyksos Egypt was of enormous significance to world history of that period but it mattered little to the salvific story. On the other hand, the Exodus deliverance, the forming of the covenant relationship at Sinai, the giving of its stipulations, and the providential care of Israel in the desert—all these, though of no concern to the empires of the world, were crucial to the working out of sacred history. Theological history speaks loud and clear, then, by what it does not recount as well as by what it does.

There are, of course, instances where the same events are attested to in both the OT and ANE texts. These provide opportunities to see not only complementary accounts at best but also clashing and contradictory ideologies at worst. One notable example is the story of Sennacherib's siege of Jerusalem in 701 BC, a siege that, according to the OT version, was lifted when Yahweh sent his angel to devastate the Assyrian army (2 Kgs 18:13-19:37). Sennacherib's scribes note only that the siege was undertaken—its outcome is not reported except for Hezekiah's payment of tribute (Luckenbill, 33-34). There is enough agreement between the two accounts to guarantee the historicity of the event but enough difference to show considerable divergence of interpretation as to causes and outcomes. The disposition of the scholar will inevitably determine the version he or she finds more credible in every such instance.

(f) OT history is professedly historiographic (Smend, 54-55). The tendentious, selective nature of a text by itself cannot preclude either its historicity or its claims to be history writing. Other disqualifications must be sought if one is interested in justifying such conclusions. The credibility of the OT as a historical account also must not rise or fall on the issue of whether it conforms to certain norms created by modern scholars as to what historiography must be or do. This is particularly the case where the Bible is disbarred from that arena of history because of its overtly theological spirit, and, more precisely, because of its inclusion of supernatural events as part of the historical fabric.

This is not the place to argue the plausibility and historical verifiability of miracles or even to address their almost routine appearance in the OT as factual data. The point is, they do appear that way, and so the question that must be asked is whether or not historiography can be compatible with the transcendent. More bluntly, can the existence of God and his supernatural interventions into human affairs qualify as the stuff of history?

Most historians will likely respond that historical accounts are reliable only to the extent that they comport with reality, that is, with experienced reality. As soon as they move into the realm of the unique, the unrepeated (or unrepeatable), especially the metaphysical, they surrender any claim to historicity (Collingwood, 135-39). While response to that line of thinking is inappropriate here, it must be stressed that there is a difference between historicity and the literary forms in which history writing is done. Whether or not the OT accounts can and must be believed, there can be no doubt whatsoever that their authors or compilers intend them to be and that they write of them according to acceptable literary standards of historiography.

(g) OT history is consistently contextual. It is the nature of most approaches to theology to be abstract and existential, but this is decidedly not true of biblical theology, which, almost by definition, is a discipline tied to historical movement and development. Such theology, then, presupposes a history in the normal sense of that form, a history that is consistent with its own set of data and that finds lodging in and reference to the larger world of its particular interest. The OT is a prime example of history writing thus understood, for its authors betray a pervasive interest in their own past and that of their forebears, as well as a constant awareness of their immediate and more remote environment.

A few examples must suffice. The deut. historian, recounting the construction of Solomon's temple, dates its commencement to Solomon's fourth year, which he further identifies as the 480th year since the Exodus (1 Kgs 6:1). By such information he not only forges theological links between the Mosaic and Davidic eras but provides a clue as to his sense of historical continuity and connectedness. The Exodus itself is said to have occurred 430 years after Jacob's descent to Egypt with his family. In fact, the author is careful to note that "at the end of the 430 years, *to the very day,* all the LORD's divisions left Egypt" (Exod 12:41, emphasis mine). In this manner he secures the Exodus as an event rooted in real time and also establishes another linkage, this between the patriarchs and the promise on the one hand, and the deliverance of the nation as fulfillment on the other (cf. Gen 15:13-14). Also, from the early period is the almost enigmatic reference to the building of Hebron "seven years before Zoan in Egypt" (Num 13:22). The identification of Zoan with Tanis, which many scholars believe was founded ca. 1730 BC, provides a rather precise date for the construction of Hebron as a city (de Vaux, 258-59). More important for the OT as history is the remarkable interest the tradition shows in places and events that were known in the ANE world, the facts of which could be validated, and the desire to embed the salvific history in the historical milieu of which it was a part.

The records of later OT history are without parallel in ANE texts in respect to their preoccupation with contextualization. From the division of the kingdom of Israel in 931 BC to the deportation of the northern kingdom in 722 BC, the historians monotonously belabor the chronological and regal interconnections between Israel and Judah. And throughout the record are references to Egypt, Assyria, and other foreign powers and their role in the history of God's own people. Such references intensify after 722 and especially after 586, the year of Jerusalem's fall and the beginning of the Babylonian exile proper. Now appear such connections as Jehoiachin's thirty-seventh year of exile and Evil-Merodach's first year as king (2 Kgs 25:27), Zedekiah's tenth year and Nebuchadnezzar's eighteenth (Jer 32:1), and the second year of Darius and the resumption of temple construction under the prophet Haggai (Hag 1:1). Clearly, Israel's history from beginning to end is marked by all the characteristics of careful, contextualized historical scholarship.

(h) OT history is interpretive. This observation is akin to the point made above that the biblical account is tendentious and selective, for a text communicates its meaning almost as much by its silence as it does by what it articulates. Here, however, the focus is on specific clues that indicate authorial assessment, reaction, or interpretation of what has happened or what has been said. Much of the Mosaic material is interlaced with this kind of material, most especially Deut with its constant paraenetic appeals and its exhortations to act on covenant expectations.

The more obviously historiographic books of Samuel, Kings, Chronicles, and Ezra-Nehemiah are replete with examples of editorial asides concerning the persons and events of history they have dutifully recorded. The author of Samuel, for example, informs his readers that in his own time, as opposed to the days of Samuel the prophet, conveyors of revelation were called "prophets," whereas earlier they were known as "seers" (1 Sam 9:9). Or he explains Israel's military difficulties in contending with the Philistines as being at least partially the superiority of the latter in the development of iron technology (13:19-22). Even the apparently laconic observation that "in the spring, at the time when kings go off to war, ... David remained in Jerusalem" (2 Sam 11:1) is fraught with overtones of theological interpretation, for the narrator is clearly standing in judgment on David's (in)action and hinting that what he did was wrong and would bring disastrous consequences.

The best-known critique is that of the so-called deut. historian, who, after looking back at Israel's history from the vantage point of her collapse in 722 BC, draws theological conclusions as to its causes and effects (2 Kgs 17). He states rather forthrightly that "the king of Assyria captured Samaria and deported the Israelites to Assyria" (v. 6) and then makes the dogmatic assertion that "all this took place because the Israelites had sinned against the LORD their God" (v. 7). There follows then a lengthy litany of specifics, which, interestingly, traces the entire history of the nation in the span of seventeen verses (vv. 7-23). These verses are more than a mere recapitulation of that 700-year period—they are a sermon reflecting on it and attempting to draw lessons from it. They form part of that inescapable thread of interpretation that is woven into the fabric of the historical story of the OT.

B. The Structure of the OT As a Historical Record

Having addressed somewhat theoretical issues about history and theology and the characteristics of OT history, it is important now to look at the record in its canonical shape in order to determine (1) what pattern, if any, informs the presentation of the narrative, and (2) what significance attaches to each section and to the whole viewed collectively.

1. *The focal point of OT history: The Plains of Moab.* An ordinary reading of the OT leads naturally to the view that the story begins with Genesis. And such a view is correct insofar as the present order of the account is concerned; but when one examines the question of the Sitz im Leben that elicited Genesis as well as the rest of the Torah (and the entire OT, for that matter), one quickly comes to a radically different conclusion. The Bible's own perspective is that Israel possessed little or no literature it considered religiously authoritative (revelatory) prior to Moses' having composed the Pentateuch, an accomplishment completed just before his death in Moab (Deut 1:1-8; 31:24-29).

Admittedly, the tradition nowhere explicitly asserts Mosaic authorship of Genesis or even Leviticus, but it does attest clearly to his having written parts or all of Exod (17:14; 24:4, 7; 34:27), Num (33:1-2), and Deut (31:9, 11). And, of course, this was the unanimous precritical opinion expressed by the remainder of the OT (Josh 1:8; 8:31; 1 Kgs 2:3; 2 Kgs 14:6; 21:8; Ezra 6:18; Neh 13:1), postbiblical Jewish tradition (*Baba bathra* 14b-15a; Josephus, *Ad Apionem* 1:8), and the NT (Matt 19:8; John 5:46-47; 7:19; Acts 3:22). The universally recognized unity of the Pentateuch from earliest times also argues presumptively for the antiquity of the Bible's own witness to the role of Moses as author/compiler of the entire collection (Dillard and Longman, 37).

Granting this construal, the occasion calling forth the inscripturation of the ancient Hebrew tradition immediately becomes clear. The audience before Moses had witnessed the mighty acts of God at Sinai, and many of the elders among them had actually participated in the most significant of all—the Exodus and the forging of the Sinai covenant relationship with Yahweh. They had all heard of the promises to their patriarchal ancestors, particularly those having to do with the land of Canaan, the very land they could see to the west, across the Jordan. How much they knew about the remote past is, of course, unknown. It is inconceivable that they were bereft of all historical resources, even written texts, but it is fruitless to speculate as to the nature and extent of these.

The immediate situation demanded certain clarifications and responses by Moses. He, Israel's theocratic leader for forty years, was denied access to the Promised Land. Under what circumstances, then, were they authorized to proceed further? Even under Joshua's command, what possible political, moral, or even theological justification did they have for crossing the river, dismantling the Canaanite fortifications, conquering the settlements, and slaughtering men, women, and children? These and other questions must have been troubling indeed.

Faced with these issues, Moses undertook to provide a fully comprehensive account of his people—who they were, whence they came, how they related to the nations of the world, and, most important, what role they were to play in the design of Yahweh their God. He had elected, redeemed, and made covenant with them—this they knew—but what did it all mean in light of a universal, overarching purpose? A canonical response is to be seen in the Torah, the massive composition that provided Israel with a raison d'être and, incidentally almost, with a context broad enough to include Creation, the Fall, the Flood, and the dispersion of the human race. It was out of these universal events and concerns that Israel had sprung precisely to address redemptively the implications of world history. It might be said, then, that the OT historical account began in Moab on the eve of the conquest of Canaan (Merrill, 21-25).

2. *Exodus-Numbers: The constitution of a nation.* From Moses' perspective the most pressing need was to provide a review of the nation's recent past, that commencing with their sojourn in Egypt and subsequent departure. Such a suggestion can by no means be based on textual data, for the record is silent as to precisely when Moses composed his history and in what order. Theologically and logically the case can be made that matters of immediate concern would first be addressed and then those more remote (Gen). Deut, it seems, would have completed the collection, serving as it did as both a summation and a prospective.

Num 33:1-4, the preface to an itinerary beginning with the Exodus and ending in the plains of Moab (vv. 5-49), states that "at the LORD's command Moses recorded the stages in their journey" (v. 2). The tradition thus asserts that either Moses kept records throughout the course of events, which he then collected into the present account (Exod 12:37-Num 33:49), or he composed the account de novo on the basis of his recollections (Ashley, 623; Budd, 351-52). The former is, of course, more likely. By "stages of the journey" is meant more than a jejune listing of sites. It is clearly a way of referring to the whole course of history associated with these places. Not to be overlooked is the reference to Aaron's death in "the fortieth year after the Israelites came out of Egypt" (Num 33:38). This presupposes that the written history as represented in the tradition was completed near the very end of Moses' life.

The beginning of the itinerary is not coterminous with the beginning of Israel's history but only with that part of it that followed the Exodus. But that was a crucial historical juncture, not just because of the unparalleled event of the Exodus deliverance itself, but because it marked the transition from Israel's being a rather loosely defined people to their being a bona fide nation. The act of national formation was the contract made at Sinai, to be sure, but Exodus redemption was essential to the process leading up to that status.

On the other hand, being merely a people did not suggest something less than a historical reality. Many (if not most) nations have a prenational stage in which various social, political, and ethnic elements coalesce for whatever reason into entities designated as kingdoms, nations, states, or the like. There was thus a clear understanding by Israel of its prenational character as a people—one in bondage to a superpower, to be sure—and even of its ancient roots in a line of patriarchal ancestors.

According to their commonly held tradition, fleshed out now by Moses in writing for perhaps the first time, Israel consisted of descendants of twelve sons of Jacob, a man whose name was changed to the eponymous surrogate Israel (Exod 1:1-7). Jacob himself sprang from Abraham, the recipient of Yahweh's elective, covenant grace and the true founder of the nation. Exod, Lev, and Num regularly refer back to this ancestral origination of the nation with the intention of demonstrating that Israel was not an ad hoc, spontaneous generation from disparate folk but rather was the national embodiment of promises made to common forefathers (Exod 2:24; 3:6, 15, 16; 4:5; 6:3, 8; 32:13; 33:1; Lev 26:42; Num 32:11).

Within the Exod-Num corpus itself, the hinge of history revolves around the Sinai covenant. All that leads up to it (Exod 1-18) is preparatory to it and all that follows it (Exod 25-Num 36) is in consequence of it. Nowhere is the theological shaping of Israel's history more clear than here, for the making of covenant, unwitnessed by the nations of earth and hence unimportant to them, became the controlling feature and factor in Israel's historical and even eschatological life. At Sinai her course was set as the servant people whose deliverance from Egypt was precisely for the purpose of entering into the privileges and responsibilities of covenant relationship. Adherence to or defection from its terms would determine Israel's future destiny as a nation, a point made most emphatically in Lev 26:3-45.

3. *Genesis: The history of Israel's origins.* Critical scholarship—even that which is open to the possibility of historical nuclei in Exod-Num—is nearly universally in opposition to the description of Gen as history. Beginning with Gunkel it has become fashionable to speak of the various elements of the book as myth, saga, legend, novella, and almost anything else but history (Coats, *passim).* It is likewise a dogma of some recent scholarship that Moses had nothing to do with the composition of Gen but that, in fact, it is primarily the product of the creative pen of Israel's great postexilic theologian, the Yahwist (Van Seters, 1992, 332).

This critical construct of the creation of Gen as literature and its historical authenticity is, of course, at variance with the Bible's own witness, the only voice to which theologians should give heed if they wish to understand Israel's own portrayal of her faith. That witness (implicitly) and later Jewish-Christian tradition (explicitly) concur that Moses was responsible for that great foundational text of the Pentateuch. We must still see how that text contributes to the theological character of OT history.

As suggested above, the OT picture is that of Moses, east of Canaan, burdened to communicate to his people in a permanent form a message by which they could understand who they were, how they originated, and what purpose they were to serve as the covenant people of Yahweh. This required a sketch of their history to that point, first as a people delivered from Egyptian bondage to become at Sinai a covenant nation, and second as descendants of a common father who found themselves in Egypt in the first place. What was required next was a narrative linkage between themselves and those ancestors of ancient times.

That narrative is Genesis. The tradition is silent as to how Moses (or any author) gained access to the events of that pre-Mosaic era, though perhaps terms such as *tôlēdôt* might suggest written texts (cf. NIV account[s]; Gen 2:4; 5:1; 6:9; 10:1; 11:10, 27; 25:12, 19; 36:1, 9; 37:2) (Harrison, 547-51). But this is not important to the Bible's viewpoint, for the real issue is how Gen functions as a prolegomenon to Israel's history. That it did so is clear from internal biblical evidence, such as the already adduced references in Exod-Num to the patriarchs and the promises made to them that constituted Israel's historical and theological underpinnings.

Another linkage is the overlapping information of the end of Gen (50:22-26) and beginning of Exod (1:1-7), especially the blunt statement "and Joseph died" (Gen 50:26; Exod 1:6). Thus one era ends ("he was placed in a coffin in Egypt") and another begins ("the Israelites were fruitful and multiplied greatly and became exceedingly numerous," Exod 1:7).

Gen as history takes the form of an alternating pattern of enlargement and constriction. It begins with the original couple, Adam and Eve, whose offspring proliferate to the point that "men began to increase in number on the earth" (Gen 6:1). The judgment of the Flood reduces this number to eight—Noah, his wife, their three sons, and their wives (7:13). Again there is expansion as the descendants of Noah's sons become "nations spread out over the earth" (10:32). The next constriction is not of a physical kind—one that reduced the human race to a biological handful—but a remnant of a theological character. Out of all the peoples and nations of the earth, a single man is called to be the progenitor of a new line, a seed that would issue into a great redemptive force designed to bless humanity by effecting reconciliation between God and his fallen creation (12:1-3). Like a new Adam or a second Noah this man, Abraham, launched once more the process of enlargement, one that in time resulted in the extravagant language of Exod 1:7: "the land [of Egypt] was filled with them."

Israel at Moab must be instructed as to this course of events, this history that accounted for who they, the "exceedingly numerous" multitude, really were. They must understand that they were not just an accident of history, one nation among many others, but that they were, in a sense, the very axis of history. The history of the pre-Abrahamic world led to him and that of the post-Abrahamic world led to them. At once an awesome privilege and an onerous responsibility, their role, Moses taught, was to be "a kingdom of priests and a holy nation" (Exod 19:6), a people whose very existence and whose claims to the land of Canaan found justification in all the elective choices that were so clearly laid out in the Gen history.

4. *Deuteronomy: The paradigm of Israel's history*. It is commonplace in modern OT scholarship to date the book of Deut in its present form to the exilic or even postexilic period, while conceding that it existed in a recension known as the "Book of the Law" somewhat earlier than the reign of King Josiah (ca. 650 BC; cf. 2 Kgs 22-23). But the view also prevails that Deut provides the ideological framework or touchstone against which the deut. history was composed. This collection, Joshua-2 Kings, is thus construed to be a history of Israel from Moses to King Jehoiachin, whose guiding editorial principle is the degree to which the nation did or did not conform to the deut. covenant mandates (Nicholson, 1967, 121-24).

A problem immediately presents itself here in that it is difficult to see how Israel could have been expected to live by deut. requirements in a time earlier than the composition of the book. Furthermore, how can the deut. history realistically portray Israel's past as one whose ebb and flow was indicative of the extent to which it conformed to as yet unwritten covenant principles? The usual resolution is to suggest (a) that the deut. tradition might greatly antedate its enshrinement in texts—even going back in nucleus to Moses himself—and (b) that the historical account of deut. history is a "theologized" version; i.e., one that is aware of the facts of Israel's history but that feels free to relate and interpret those facts so as to bring them into line with cause-and-effect nexus (Van Seters, 1983, 228, 360-61). When Israel was obedient to the Mosaic covenant stipulations, she was blessed; when she disobeyed, she experienced its curses. Further attention to the Deut-deut. history relationship follows in the next section.

Next to Leviticus, perhaps, Deut is the least overtly historiographical writing in the Pentateuch. From one perspective, it is essentially a collection of sermons and other addresses by Moses who, nearing his time of death, has an intense desire to rehearse Yahweh's covenant faithfulness to Israel in the past and to prepare them for the life to come in Canaan. The text, therefore, is peppered with warning, exhortation, praise, blame, encouragement, and threat. But modern scholarship also recognizes another way of assessing Deut: It is a massive covenant document. Without entering into the debate as to the precise cultural milieu reflected by the form and content of the book, it is safe to say that most scholars identify Deut as a composition at least loosely modeled after a suzerain-vassal treaty text. It clearly contains all the elements attested to by that genre.

Different from these models, however, are the persistent historical currents that flow through the book of Deut. This is in addition to the first four chapters, which, as a discrete element of a covenant text, may be called the "historical prologue" and therefore are patently historical in literary form. Other instances of historical reflection are found in 5:1-5, 22-33; 9:7-10:11; 23:3-8; 24:9; 25:17-19; 26:5b-9; 29:2-9; 32:6-18, 50-52. And, of course, the book concludes with the narrative of Moses' death and burial (34:1-8), an historical vignette.

The purpose of the historical references in Deut is primarily pedagogical: The Israel of the present and future should learn from the Israel of the past. The historian's selective use of historical episodes provides helpful insight into the theological appropriation of history. Thus, when Moses announces covenant renewal, he refers back to the earlier occasion of covenant-making at Sinai in order to make appropriate comparisons and contrasts (Deut 5:1-5). When he attempts to prepare the people for the Conquest (9:1-5), he reminds them of how disobedient they had been in the past, particularly in the incident of the golden calf, and what disastrous results ensued (9:7-10:11). Finally, he exhorts them to keep covenant on the basis of God's faithfulness to them in the Exodus and the desert sojourn (29:2-9). Even a static covenant relationship, then, issues from historical encounters and must be lived out in historical experience.

5. *Joshua-2 Kings: An assessment of Israel's historical and theological experience.* We noted in the previous section that the OT books of Joshua, Judges, Samuel, and Kings have come to be known as the deut. history because they appear to narrate Israel's history in terms of its conformity to or rejection of the covenant ideals of Deut. One may question the critical presuppositions that gave rise to this approach, but that these books reflect deut. concerns can hardly be doubted. In fact, such a relationship provides prima facie evidence for the Bible's own witness as to the authorship and provenance of Deut. That is, the chronological and theological priority of Deut is exactly what one would expect if indeed deut. history already posits a deut. frame of reference (McConville, 73-78).

To return to the issue at hand—the deut. history as a theological history—there are numerous references in the material suggestive of its character as such. Never is there good, objective reason for doubting the truth claims of the text, even when it rehearses the supernatural acts of Joshua, Elijah, or Elisha, but neither can one claim that it is ordinary historiography. It is historical narrative of a highly selective, tendentious, and interpretive nature, designed not merely to recount events but to explain them as part of a larger pattern of divine design and intention.

Nowhere is this seen better than in the lengthy observation by the historian as to the decline and fall of the northern kingdom Israel in 722 BC. After recounting the reign of the last king, Hoshea (2 Kgs 17:1-6), he goes on to comment on the disastrous end of this reign by linking it to the inevitable consequences of centuries of covenant infidelity (vv. 7-23). "All this [the Assyrian deportation of Israel] took place," the historian-theologian says, "because the Israelites had sinned against the LORD their God, who had brought them up out of Egypt from under the power of Pharaoh king of Egypt" (v. 7). Reaching back even before the founding of the monarchy, he speaks of Israel's worship of the gods of Canaan as the epitome of that sin against Yahweh (v. 8).

This same historian, or others like him, had to this point laboriously reviewed the details of Israel's history, but here in this summation all else is sublimated to the essential point that it was the sin of theological treason that ultimately called down the holy wrath of Yahweh. One cannot escape the impression that the entire record, then, was shaped with this central focus in view. Indeed, a close reading of the entire deuteronomistic history can lead to no other conclusion. It is history and it is to be believed, but it is history that ignores everything that does not contribute to the central idea of covenant violation as well as history that concentrates on precisely those events that illustrate that rebellion.

Careful comparison between Deut and the deuteronomistic history compels the reader to conclude that the history of Israel is the sorry recital of a systematic disregard of the covenant requirements so emphatically outlined by Moses. This could be shown throughout the corpus were space to permit, but it will be helpful to see how this summation section in 2 Kings conclusively demonstrates this assertion.

The theologian introduces his explanation for Israel's judgment by saying that Israel had "sinned against the LORD" and had "worshiped other gods" (2 Kgs 17:7) (Hobbs, 226-27). This strikes at the heart of the deut. covenant principle that "you shall have no other gods before me" (Deut 5:7). That this covenant violation is central in this indictment is clear from the statement that follows: "[Israel] followed the practices [lit. statutes] of the nations the LORD had driven out before them" (2 Kgs 17:8). Having abandoned the covenant demands of Deut, they entered into covenant with the gods of Canaan.

This was reflected by the proliferation of worship centers they installed (2 Kgs 17:9-11), contrary to the insistence that Yahweh be worshiped in one central sanctuary only (Deut 12:1-14). And the symbols of paganism they erected—sacred stones and Asherah poles (2 Kgs 17:10)—are precisely the objects that were to be demolished (Deut 12:3). These were the accouterments of idolatry, the attempt to concretize the invisible forces of nature. This was taboo to Israel (5:8-10; 7:25-26) but tragically was practiced by her throughout the course of her preexilic history.

The litany of the theological interpretation of Israel's history concludes as it began: with the observation that Israel "forsook all the commands of the LORD their God" (2 Kgs 17:16; cf. v. 7). This is illustrated by seven specific violations: (a) They made two calf idols (v. 16; cf. Exod 32:4; 1 Kgs 12:28-29); (b) they created an Asherah pole (v. 16; cf. 1 Kgs 14:15, 23); (c) they "bowed down to the starry hosts" (v. 16; cf. Deut 17:2-5); (d) they worshiped Baal (v. 16; cf. 1 Kgs 16:31); (e) they sacrificed their children in the fire (v. 17; cf. Deut 12:31; 2 Kgs 16:3); (f) they practiced divination and sorcery (v. 17; cf. Deut 18:10-12; 1 Sam 28:3-7); and (g) "they sold themselves to do evil in the eyes of the LORD" (v. 17; cf. 1 Kgs 21:20). This last statement encapsulates the whole period of the deut. history and is a fit way of interpreting the spirit of those times.

6. *Chronicles, Ezra, and Nehemiah: History from a postexilic perspective.* Spatial and chronological distance have a way of bringing refined, renewed, and perhaps even contradictory ways of perceiving persons and events. The American Revolution is understood in different ways by modern British historians on the one hand and colonial American eyewitnesses on the other. The same "facts" often yield different meanings to different persons at different times.

A superficial reading of the OT suggests that the deuteronomistic history of Israel, completed no later than 560 BC, is fundamentally dissimilar to the account of that history recorded by the Chronicler at 400 BC or a little later. The records of Ezra-Nehemiah, touching on events from ca. 540-430 BC, reflect essentially the viewpoint, concerns, and subject matter of the Chronicler for that same period of time.

That there are some factual differences cannot be denied, though they are far fewer and of lesser consequence that some scholars would make them out to be. Most of the variances between the two great histories have to do with selection of data; i.e., what is included and what is omitted (McKenzie, 71-73). It is well known that the Chronicler refrains from discussing in detail the affairs of the northern kingdom, being concerned almost exclusively with Judah as his point of departure. But even there, he overlooks events that tend to discredit the Davidic dynasty, going so far as to ignore completely David's adultery and other foibles of royal family life that play such a major role in the deut. history.

On the other hand, the Chronicler provides enormous detail concerning the Davidic covenant and its ramifications for Israel's cultus and history (see David in the Appendix). Like the deut. historian, he is careful to view history as a reflex of covenant fidelity (or lack thereof), but not with respect to the Sinai covenant. Rather, he bypasses that in the interest of focusing on the Zion theology that springs from Yahweh's election of an eternal royal house, that of David and his descendants. The books of Kings also view David favorably as the standard against whom all subsequent kings must be judged, but they lack the cultic interest of Chronicles. And it is David at worship who dominates the account. Almost summarily the Chronicler describes David's rise to power (1 Chron 11-14) so that he might present David as the builder of the place of worship and the organizer of its services and personnel (chs. 15-17, 22-29). Though he could not build the temple itself, the king made all the arrangements for Solomon to do so. The Chronicler then becomes almost totally preoccupied with the cultic aspect of Solomon's reign, just as he had with the reign of David (2 Chron 1-7; only chs. 8-9 deal with other matters).

The remainder of the history reflects the same emphases. While most of the major events attested to by the deuteronomistic historian are at least briefly cited by the Chronicler, the latter gives inordinate space to the godly reigns of Jehoshaphat ("he walked in the ways his father David had followed," 2 Chron 17:3), four chapters (chs.

17-20); of Hezekiah ("he did what was right . . . as his father David had done," 29:2), four chapters (chs. 29-32); and of Josiah ("he did what was right . . . and walked in the ways of his father David," 34:2), two chapters (chs. 34-35). In each case, the kings and their reigns are celebrated not because of political or cultural achievements but because they brought reformation and restoration to the covenant principles to which David had been called (cf. 17:3-6; 31:20-21; 34:2, 33).

From a strategic standpoint, it was important for the Chronicler to cast his historical account as he did because he (and Ezra and Nehemiah as well) composed his work long after the Davidic monarchy was a practical reality. History must henceforth be understood as a process leading to a new age, one made possible by the liberating decree of Cyrus (2 Chron 36:22-23) and the rebuilding of the ruined temple and hopes of God's people (Ezra 1:1-4; 3:8-13; 5:1-5; Neh 9). The theological *Tendenz* of such accounts of history is unmistakable.

7. *The Prophets: Interactions with history.* According to the Jewish canonical tradition, the books Joshua through Kings were known as the Former Prophets and Isaiah, Jeremiah, Ezekiel, and The Twelve, the Latter Prophets. This insightful analysis already recognized not only that prophets were important characters in the former collection, but that they were very much involved in its composition. That is, the so-called deuteronomistic history is a prophetic interpretation of Israel's past.

Whether this view of authorship is correct cannot be determined beyond a doubt. There is no doubt, however, that the canonical prophets, those whose writings are preserved in the sacred texts, were very much men of their times, who frequently shaped their messages around the historical circumstances of their own age. In doing so they themselves became historians for their interpretations of the nation's past became part of the stuff of our own understanding of Israel's history (Laato, 282-86). It is possible here to look briefly at only selected instances in which Israel's prophets demonstrate historical concern and offer theological reaction to that concern.

The great prophet Isaiah, like most of the others, links his life and ministry to the reigns of the kings with whom he was a contemporary (Isa 1:1). Like others also, he makes of the present a culminating explanation of the past, that is, its logical and theological outcome, but he also uses the present as a launching pad for the projectile of eschatological hope and expectation. Like the deuteronomistic historian and the Chronicler he rehearses Israel's past as a means of accounting for present circumstances. In parabolic language, for example, he describes Israel as a vineyard planted and tended by a loving farmer who, when he looked for grapes, found only bad fruit (Isa 5:1-3). The corruption of Israel was the inevitable outcome of her failure to match Yahweh's covenant expectations (vv. 4-7).

Jeremiah, using another metaphor, traces Israel's history back to the Exodus, From that time and all through the period of the desert and occupation of the land of milk and honey they "came and defiled my land and made my inheritance detestable" (Jer 2:7). That sordid history had become periodized in Jeremiah's time, and Yahweh described its essence as: "My people have committed two sins: They have forsaken me, the spring of living water, and have dug their own cisterns, broken cisterns that cannot hold water" (2:13). This is the great theme of the OT history of Israel: They had forgotten Yahweh and gone after other gods.

Ezekiel narrates in great detail the story of two daughters, Oholah and Oholibah, who, though harlotrous in Egypt, became the wives of Yahweh (Ezek 23:1-49). Oholah ("her tent"), says Yahweh, was Samaria, and Oholibah ("my tent is in her") was Jerusalem (v. 4). Before long Oholah revealed her true character and reverted to prostitution to the Assyrians, who, far from pandering to her, took her into bloody exile. But Oholibah turned out even worse. She plied her trade not only with Assyria but Babylonia as well. The result was the same, betrayal and deportation—a process that had already begun but that would intensify until it was complete (v. 29). The meaning of the allegory surfaces in vv. 37-38: Israel has committed adultery and has desecrated the sanctuary and Sabbath of Yahweh. This, of course, is another way of referring to covenant disloyalty, the predominant motif of the Old Testament historical record as a whole.

A final example must suffice, that in Hosea, in which Yahweh speaks, as he did in Ezekiel, of having brought his people out of Egypt in order to make a covenant with them (Hos 11:1-4; see Hosea: Theology of, in the Appendix). This time Israel is a son, a beloved (i.e., elected) one, who, though so richly endowed, violated every overture and expression of divine affection. The result would be an inevitable Assyrian conquest and dispersion (v. 5), though not with irremedial and permanent consequences (vv. 8-11). Hosea, like Isaiah, Jeremiah, Ezekiel, and many other prophets, understood the salient points of their nation's history well. But more important, he was adept at drawing from it its true significance and implication; that is, he could properly theologize it.

8. *The Writings: Interaction with Yahweh and with the historical community.* By "Writings" in this context is meant the Psalms and Wisdom literature, all of which share in common the idea of response as opposed to "normal" revelation. Though open to the criticism of being too facile or even too misleading a distinction, what is being suggested is that these texts are the expression of human feelings, worship, and philosophizings rather than vehicles of immediate divine revelation. This, we suggest, by no means diminishes their quality or character as Scripture.

Among other things this distinction connotes, it allows these writings to be perceived more clearly as theology in the abstract or systematic sense. It records the thoughtful and prayerful theological constructions of its authors as they wrestle with their own experiences with God and life as well as with whatever canonical texts existed in their times. It is in this sense that we understand them to be interactions with Yahweh and with the community of faith (Westermann, 153-74; Murphy, 125-26).

Having described these compositions as "abstract," "systematic," or "philosophizings" does not preclude their historicity. The poets and sages alike of Israel were very much in touch with the historical roots of their culture, whether or not they always verbalized it. And their theology, when properly understood as theirs, was in line with the great themes of OT theological history. More pertinent to our purpose, however, is the writings *as* history texts. How do their authors contribute to the filling out of the entire historical panorama?

The Psalms are particularly rich in this respect. In addition to information from their titles (see sec. entitled "Characteristics of OT History," p. 68), several psalms recapitulate and reinterpret brief or even rather lengthy stretches of Israel's history. David poeticizes many of the incidents of his own eventful life, some of which appear elsewhere in the historical literature (cf. Ps 18, 32, 35, 51, 55, 57, 59, 60, 63). On a grander, more sweeping scale are those that use history as a frame upon which to hang theological insights and exhortations. They may even be viewed as creedal recitations of the mighty acts of God on behalf of his people.

Ps 78 is a case in point. The poet begins with the Sinai covenant revelation (v. 5) and then reverts back to the Exodus redemption (vv. 12-13) as an event forgotten by Israel in her waywardness. He expatiates on the wilderness sojourn (vv. 14-42) and observes that again they disregarded the source of their blessings, the God who had devastated Egypt with plagues (vv. 43-53). He then traces Israel's covenant disobedience through the conquest of Canaan (vv. 54-59), the era of the judges (vv. 60-66), and the election of Judah and David (vv. 67-72).

Ps 105 goes back even further, to the times of the patriarchs and Yahweh's promise to make a nation of their descendants (vv. 6-11). Again the Exodus appears as the central event (vv. 24-38). Ps 106 harks back to the Exodus as well (vv. 6-12), but recalls more particularly Israel's rebellions in the wilderness (vv. 13-33) and their idolatry and subsequent punishment in the days of the judges (vv. 34-46). Ps 135 celebrates Yahweh's defeat of Egypt, Sihon, and Og (vv. 8-11), victories that guaranteed victory for God's people at all times (vv. 13-14). Finally, Ps 136, the great "*Hesed*-psalm," traces Yahweh's strong arm from Exodus to Conquest, all of which must be attributed not to historical accident but to his covenant love (*hesed*).

C. Conclusion

There is a history of theology and a theology of history, but neither of these is the proper subject matter of OT history as a theological enterprise. What must be understood is that the OT is both history and theology. Its theological nature does not vitiate its historical credibility or conformity to actual event nor must its historical nature be allowed to deprive it of its higher dimension of interpreted event. What exists in the record is the story of God's eternal purposes as worked out in creation, event, word, and reflection. It is not the whole story but it is the true story, one sufficient to lead to redemption and life.

BIBLIOGRAPHY
R. Alter, *The Art of Biblical Narrative*, 1981; T. R. Ashley, *The Book of Numbers*, NICOT, 1993; J. Barr, "Revelation Through History in the Old Testament and in Modern Theology," *Int* 17, 1963, 193-205; idem, "Story and History in Old Testament Theology," *Theology Digest* 24, 1976, 265-71; P. J. Budd, *Numbers*, 1984; R. E. Clements, "History and Theology in Biblical Narrative," *HBT* 4, 1982, 45-60; G. W. Coats, *Genesis, With an Introduction to Narrative Literature*, FOTL 1, 1983; R. J. Coggins, "History and Story in Old Testament Study," *JSOT* 11, 1979, 36-46; R. G. Collingwood, *The Idea of History*, 1946; R. de Vaux, *The Early History of Israel*, 1978; F. Deist, "The Problem of History in Old Testament Theology," *OTWSA* 24, 1981, 23-39; R. B. Dillard, and T. Longman III, *An Introduction to the Old Testament*, 1994; J. Goldingay, *Approaches to Old Testament Interpretation*, 1961; idem, "'That You May Know That Yahweh Is God': A Study in the Relationship Between Theology and Historical Truth in the Old Testament," *TB* 23, 1972, 58-93; B. Halpern, *The First Historians*, 1988; R. K. Harrison, *Introduction to the Old Testament*, 1969; T. R. Hobbs, *2 Kings*, WBC, 1985; D. Howard, Jr. *An Introduction to the Old Testament Historical Books*, 1993; K. Kitchen, "Ancient Orient, 'Deuteronomism,' and the Old Testament," in *New Perspectives on the Old Testament*, J. B. Payne (ed.), 1970,

19-24; A. Laato, "History and Ideology in the Old Testament Prophetic Books," *SJOT* 8, 1994, 267-97; B. O. Long, "Historical Narrative and the Fictionalizing Imagination," *VT* 35, 1985, 405-16; V. P. Long, *The Art of Biblical History*, 1994; D. Luckenbill, *The Annals of Sennacherib*, 1924; J. G. McConville, *Grace in the End: A Study in Deuteronomic Theology*, 1993; S. L. McKenzie, *The Chronicler's Use of the Deuteronomistic History*, 1984; E. H. Merrill, *Kingdom of Priests: A History of Old Testament Israel*, 1987; idem, "History," in *Cracking Old Testament Codes*, D. B. Sandy, J. R. Giese, eds., 1995, 89-112; A. R. Millard, "Story, History, and Theology," in A. R. Millard, J. K. Hoffmeier, and D. W. Baker, eds., *Faith, Tradition, and History: Old Testament Historiography in Its Ancient Near Eastern Context*, 1994, 37-64; R. E. Murphy, *The Tree of Life: An Exploration of Biblical Wisdom Literature*, 1990; E. W. Nicholson, *Deuteronomy and Tradition*, 1967; idem, "Story and History in the Old Testament," in Samuel E. Balentine and John Barton, eds., *Language, Theology, and the Bible*, 1994, 135-50; W. Pannenberg, *Revelation As History*, 1968; J. H. Sailhamer, *The Pentateuch As Narrative*, 1992; R. Smend, "Tradition and History: A Complex Relation," in *Tradition and Theology in the Old Testament*, ed. D. A. Knight, 1977, 49-68; J. Van Seters, *In Search of History*, 1983; idem, *Prologue to History: The Yahwist As Historian in Genesis*, 1992; W. VanGemeren, *The Progress of Redemption*, 1988; G. von Rad, *OTT* 1, 1962; idem, "The Beginnings of Historical Writing in Ancient Israel," in *The Problem of the Hexateuch and Other Essays*, 1984, 166-204; M. Weinfeld, *Deuteronomy and the Deuteronomistic School*, 1972; C. Westermann, *Elements of Old Testament Theology*, 1982.

Eugene H. Merrill

4. OLD TESTAMENT HISTORY: A HERMENEUTICAL PERSPECTIVE

Few areas in the landscape of contemporary OT study present such rocky terrain or are rent by such wide chasms of disagreement as is the area of the historical interpretation of the OT. So expansive is the ground that would have to be covered in order to begin to do justice to the subject, and so many are the pitfalls that would have to be avoided, that I shall have to content myself in this essay with exploring a few basic hermeneutical pathways that must be trod by any who would venture farther into the field. I will begin with some prolegomena relating to such basic questions as the relationships between OT history and the history of ancient Israel, between history and historiography, and between authority and authorship. I will then look at three requirements incumbent upon those who would involve themselves responsibly in the historical interpretation of the OT—viz., literary competence, theological comprehension, and historical criticism. Finally, I will briefly explore four basic steps that typify the work of historians as they amass and assess the available evidence and seek to synthesize their findings into a historical reconstruction that they can defend. The following may raise as many questions in the mind of the reader as it answers, but if it prompts the reader to further exploration of ancient Israelite history, then it will have succeeded, for the words of J. M. Miller written in 1985 still hold true today: "Probably there is no other area of biblical studies so obviously in need at the moment of some fresh ideas based on solid research" (1985, 23).

A. Historical Interpretation of the OT: Three Basic Relationships

1. *"OT history" and "History of ancient Israel."* It is a commonplace of contemporary biblical scholarship that a distinction must be made between "OT history" on the one hand, and "the history of ancient Israel" on the other (e.g., Tsevat; Lemche). It is assumed that the history of the people of God *as recounted in the pages of the OT* and the history or histories of ancient Israel *as reconstructed by critical historians* will differ. At one level, this assumption is unobjectionable, for it should be obvious that many different *kinds* of histories can be written—world histories, national histories, personal histories, political histories, social histories, economic histories, religious histories, medical histories, criminal histories, and the list could continue (for a more technical "checklist of historical approaches," see Stanford, 110-13; or cf. Moulton's discussion of types of history represented in the Bible, 244-52). So to say that histories can and do differ is to say nothing exceptional; they may simply approach their subject from different angles and with different interests in view. As F. Deist succinctly puts it, "The perspectivist nature of historical research is one of the reasons why history is not an accumulative science" (111).

The historiographical narratives of the OT are themselves "perspectivist." One need only recall that the section of OT text often referred to by modern scholars as the deuteronomistic history (i.e., Joshua-2 Kings) is traditionally called the Former Prophets. The perspective from which OT historiography views, selects, and reports events may rightly be described as prophetic, or simply theological. The focus is on the history of God's people, their relationship to him, and his actions and expectations for them. Commenting on "The Understanding of History in the Old Testament Prophets," H. W. Wolff once wrote: "For the prophets, history is the goal-directed conversation of the Lord of the future with Israel" (341). The same could also be said of the narrative historians of the OT. Given the theological slant of OT historiography, it should not be expected to be either exhaustive in its historical coverage or exclusive of historical treatments from other vantage points—e.g., political, economic, or whatever. (As a brief example, one thinks of the oft-noted disparity between the brief treatment given King Omri of Israel in the OT, who is mainly noted for exceeding his predecessors in doing evil, as contrasted with the much more extensive coverage of the reign of his son Ahab, though the latter was *politically* no more significant than the former.)

About such matters, there is little cause for disagreement. Where disagreements do arise, however, is over the nature and extent of the variance between OT history and the history of ancient Israel. In particular, there is disagreement as to whether one should expect the distinct histories, in the end, to be complementary or contradictory. The basic question, in other words, is whether the OT can be viewed as a worthy source, even if not an exhaustive or exclusive one, for the reconstruction of the history of ancient Israel. On this question, there is sharp disagreement among contemporary scholars. At one extreme, there are those who regard the biblical text as of little or no value for "scientific" historical reconstruction, and thus to be used with extreme caution or not at all (e.g., Garbini; Whitelam). At the other extreme, one might expect in principle to find some who view the biblical text as the *only* legitimate source for the history of ancient Israel and who regard all extrabiblical evidence as little more than unreliable distractions (in reality it is difficult to document such a view in print). The position taken in this essay falls somewhere between these two extremes. It assumes that the history of ancient Israel should be reconstructed from all the available evidence, whether literary or material. It further assumes that the OT, by virtue of its extent and authority, deserves pride of place among the literary witnesses, particularly when one's interest is in the history of the OT people of God.

2. *History and historiography.* To appreciate more fully the character of the OT's presentation of the history of Israel, we must think for a moment about what terms such as *history* and *historiography* mean. The term *history* can be employed in several senses. In informal speech, it is occasionally used simply to denote the past: e.g., "That's all history now—let's just forget it." In more technical discussions, the term may be used to describe both *significant past events* (keeping in mind that "significance" is to some degree in the eye of the beholder) and *interpretive accounts,* or *representations,* of significant past events. Thus, one may speak of both history-as-event and history-as-account (Stanford, 26-44). P. R. Davies suggests reserving the term *history* for the former, "the events of the past as a *continuum*," and the term *historiography* for the latter, "the selective telling of those events" (Rogerson and Davies, 218). This useful distinction is, unfortunately, seldom maintained in practice, though context often makes clear what is meant.

While matters of definition continue to elicit debate, it is perhaps not too far off the mark to characterize *historiography* as a kind of *verbal representational art,* analogous in significant respects to, say, portraiture, which is itself a kind of *visual* representational art (Long, 1994, 63-68 and *passim*). Neither historiography nor portraiture aims at a re-presentation that is precise, exact, and exhaustive in every respect. Both require, rather, that the "referential artist" (if I may use such a term to describe both historiographers and portraitists) first gain a vision of the subject, before beginning to write or paint. As Stanford notes, "The analogy of a work of art is appropriate partly because the past is a vision. The past does not live in potsherds and documents; it lives in the human imagination" (102). When it comes to sharing the vision with others, the verbal or visual artist must make some creative decisions: What *selection* of details will be included? From what *slant* will the subject be viewed? In what *style* will the subject be depicted? In respect to such decisions, "one simply cannot tell fictional from historical narrative" (Sternberg, 29), any more than one can distinguish the brush-strokes of a portrait from those of a "nonhistorical" painting. What distinguishes the two is not the presence or absence of artistry, but the sense of purpose of each and the constraints within which each works (for full discussions, see Sternberg, 23-35).

Historiography, then, like portraiture, is driven by an overarching aim to "paint a picture" that truly represents and interprets the significant features of its historical subject. Just as a portrait fails in its purpose if it does not "look like" its subject, so historiography fails in its purpose if it is not sufficiently cognizant of and constrained by "the facts" to offer a representation that "looks like" its historical subject, at least as viewed from one angle (on what is meant by "the facts," see Stanford, 71-74). The factual constraint does not mean, of course, that every detail must be included, or that each brushstroke of the verbal or visual artist must be rendered with photographic accuracy, or that other depictions, from different angles, would not be possible and perhaps equally illuminating.

3. *Authorship and authority.* If, then, neither historiography nor portraiture offers exact and exhaustive representations of its subjects, on what basis are they to be trusted? The authority attributed to a written history or a portrait will, to some degree at least, be a reflection of the esteem in which the creator of the work is held. A portrait by an obscure artist of mediocre talent may be undeserving of trust as a reliable guide to the appearance and character of the subject, but a portrait by a known master merits high respect (though, of course, respect in no way obviates the necessity and sometimes the difficulty of rightly interpreting the master's work).

As regards the respect to be given the OT in matters historical (assuming that historical truth claims have been rightly discerned), different scholars obviously hold different opinions. This is so because they hold different beliefs about the creator(s) of the work, about the authorial presence behind it. Some scholars believe the OT to be a body of ancient literature of unexceptional human origin, and therefore the respect they show to the OT's "pictures" of Israel's past tends, likewise, to be unexceptional; at best these scholars may see the texts as enjoying an authority ascribed to them by a community of faith, but they will not see them as possessing any inherent authority. In fact, when it comes to hard-nosed historical questions, the biblical texts are sometimes shown even less respect than other ancient documents tend to receive (Hallo, 193; Herrmann; Yamauchi, 6).

There are other scholars, however, who believe the OT texts to be of divine as well as human origin, and so they tend to accord the OT texts an authority commensurate with the respect due the texts' ultimate author (on this point generally, see Vanhoozer). Such believing scholars, while recognizing that Israel's past may certainly be explored from various vantage points and with various interests in mind, will view the biblical pictures as of highest authority and greatest significance, at least within the bounds of their particular focus—viz., Israel's (theologically) meaningful past. If they are consistent, these scholars will want to bend every effort rightly to understand and interpret the biblical material. And this in turn implies that they will need to take care to discover historical truth claims where they are present, refuse to assume them where they are absent, and remain tentative wherever the evidence is unclear (Long, 1994, 169-70).

In most of the stories of the OT, a historiographical impulse is felt. Of the "historical intentionality" of the writers of the Former Prophets (Joshua-Kings) and of Chronicles, for example, B. Halpern (1987, 115-16) writes, "Based on a survey of numerous cases, my own impression is that this was sincerely historical, authentically antiquarian: The authors were prey to bias when interpreting evidence; and they wrote the history germane to them—about Israel's relations with YHWH and how they could be repaired. But they seem to rely on sources for their data, rather than *ad hoc* concoction." Not all OT stories are histories, of course. One thinks of Nathan's parable (2 Sam 12), Jotham's fable (Judg 9), and the like; but in such cases, the text generally provides some indication that distinct genres have been introduced. Where the text offers no such clues, and where the evidence of the larger contexts and the flow of the narrative generally suggest a historiographical purpose, this should be the interpreter's working assumption (Long, 1994, 180-84). Other purposes may also be evident—e.g., theological/ideological or artistic/aesthetic—but these, as our portrait analogy has suggested, do not necessarily diminish but may actually augment the text's capacity to bear witness to the past (Geller; Halpern, 1987, 111; Sternberg, 82-83).

The above considerations begin to suggest what might be required of those who wish to do responsible historical interpretation of the OT. It is to three of these requirements that we now turn.

B. Historical Interpretation of the OT: Three Requirements of the Interpreter
   1. *Literary competence.*

> The primary influence on Wellhausen's reconstruction of Israel-
> ite history was, of course, the results and consequences of his literary
> study of the Old Testament. (Hayes, 63)

It may seem surprising to begin this section on requirements for *historical* interpretation with an emphasis on *literary* competence, but any who wish to include the OT among their sources for the history of ancient Israel or, for that matter, those who may wish to dismiss it, must at least recognize that competent literary reading of the OT with a view to discovering its truth claims (historical or otherwise) is a necessary first step (cf. Morgan, 221-22, on R. G. Moulton's view that literary study is "the prior task" to historical reconstruction, so that to ignore it "could lead to historical and exegetical mistakes"). By *literary competence* I mean a developed awareness of the conventions and workings of a given literary corpus and a consequent ability to discern what kinds of claims a given text within that corpus may be making (cf. Barton, esp. 8-19; Baron, 93). When one is learning a foreign language, one studies the grammar of that language (i.e., the linguistic principles by which it communicates) so as to increase linguistic competence and the ability rightly to interpret individual utterances. By the same token, when one's aim is to understand individual passages of a "foreign" literary corpus such as the OT (which originated at a time and place far removed from our own), it is immensely useful to learn what one can of the "grammar" of that literature (i.e., the literary principles by which it operates). Of course, given the limited number of biblical and extrabiblical texts available, consummate literary competence is an unachievable goal, but this does not mean that interpreters should despair of trying and simply read passages any way they like (cf. Sternberg, 10). Literary competence can always be improved, even if not perfected.

One of the best ways to improve one's literary competence is to read as much of the literature under consideration as possible (McCullagh, 72; Deist, 99-100 [referencing Leopold von Ranke]). For our present purposes this would mean immersing oneself first and foremost in the OT, but then also in such cognate literatures as are available from ancient Israel's neighbors (see, e.g., Younger's insightful study of Joshua 9-12 in the light of Assyrian, Hittite, and Egyptian conquest accounts). Back in 1965, M. Greenberg remarked on the "solid ground" that could be attained by "a study of their (Israel's neighbors') literary styles and habits, especially with an eye to the differences between our expectations and their performance"; he stressed that we simply "cannot have enough" of the kind of "evidence concerning the native modes of ancient writing" that such comparative studies can yield. At the time of his writing, however, Greenberg was forced to lament that "hardly a beginning [had] been made" (Greenberg, 42). Today the situation has improved, and one may benefit greatly from reading the numerous works on the poetics of biblical literature that have appeared in the last several decades. Poetics, according to A. Berlin's simple but insightful definition, is "a grammar, as it were, of literature" (15). Thus, there can be a poetics of prose as well as poetry, and indeed of any subgenres within this broad division. Since the focus of the present essay is on the historical interpretation of the OT, those works treating biblical narrative are most pertinent (see Narrative Criticism: The Theological Implications of Narrative Techniques, below). (In making this assertion I do not mean to suggest that other genres, such as psalmody and prophecy, are devoid of historiographical tendencies, but simply to recognize that the majority of OT texts in which a historiographical impulse is strongly felt happen to be narratives.)

With respect to the relationship between literary competence and historical study, the basic point is that "a literary reading of the biblical text must precede any historical reconstruction" (Younger, "Figurative Aspect," 157). This is so because "an increased appreciation of the literary mechanisms of a text—*how* a story is told—often becomes the avenue of greater insight into the theological, religious and even historical significance of the text—what the story means" (Long, 1989, 14; cf. Stanford, 137). But here a further point must be made: True literary competence can only be built on a solid base of *linguistic* competence. It is in this regard that the present, multivolume work may prove particularly useful.

Let me offer one brief example. In discussions of the definitive rejection of King Saul by Samuel in 1 Sam 15, scholars have often noted an apparent contradiction between (a) the statements in vv. 11 and 35 that Yahweh is sorry (*nhm*) that he made Saul king and (b) Samuel's insistence in v. 29 that the "Glory of Israel" does not lie or change his mind (*nhm*). On the basis of this putative contradiction and several other features of the text, a majority of scholars have concluded that 1 Sam 15 presents an internally inconsistent account and thus cannot be trusted historically. What we have, then, is a historical judgment based on a literary judgment, which, in turn, is based ultimately on a linguistic judgment. If, however, we consult the lexical entry on the root *nhm* in the present work, we discover that the several occurrences of *nhm* in 1 Sam 15 may simply be drawing on different connotations within the accepted range of meaning of the Heb. root. On the one hand, because of Saul's misdeeds God *regrets* having installed him as king. On the other hand, God does not *repent*—that is, "God does not capriciously change his intentions or ways of acting," and he will certainly not be deterred from a given course of action by human attempts to manipulate him. In the case of 1 Sam 15, then, a lexical clarification alleviates what was thought to be an internal, logical contradiction in the text and thus opens the door to a more positive literary appraisal of the story as unified and sensible and hence potentially historical, assuming that other problematic features can be successfully dealt with (this I have attempted to do elsewhere [see Long, 1993]).

   2. *Theological comprehension.*

      For ancient man the distinction of sacred from profane, of religious from secular, was unknown. (Millard, 1983, 42)

   A second requirement for those who would interpret the OT historically is theological comprehension. Again, just as it may have seemed odd in the preceding section to highlight *literary* competence as a requirement for *historical* interpretation, so it may seem odd to stress *theological* comprehension as a requirement for those who would use the OT responsibly in historical reconstruction. But the fact is that in the narratives of the OT God is a central character, not only present behind the scenes but occasionally intervening directly in the action of the story—e.g., sending plagues, parting seas and rivers, destroying city walls, appearing in visions, throwing enemies into panic, protecting his people, speaking through his prophets, fulfilling their words, and so forth. In short, the God depicted in the OT is not only transcendent but is also immanent in human (historical) affairs. As G. B. Caird succinctly puts it, "the most important item in the framework within which the people of biblical times interpreted their history was the conviction that God was the Lord of history" (217-18; cf. Westermann, 210; Wolff). But herein lies a problem. The biblical conviction that God is the Lord of *history* not only runs counter to aspects of the historical-critical method (as commonly understood) but also conflicts with the belief system, or worldview, of some modern scholars. The former issue—a methodological question—will be discussed in the next section; here we must deal with the latter—a metaphysical question.

   In this day and age, it would be the height of hermeneutical naïveté to deny or ignore the fact that one's background beliefs have a significant impact on how one processes and assesses data. "How a historian sees the past is only a part of how he or she sees the world" (Stanford, 96). For instance, to borrow an example from J. M. Miller (1976, 17), when King Mesha (in the so-called Moabite Stone inscription) attributes his subjugation to and eventual deliverance from King Omri of Israel to the divine actions of the god Chemosh, few modern scholars are likely to accept Mesha's claim at face value, for the existence of a true god Chemosh, capable of affecting the course of human history, has no place in how they see the world. Thus, in their historical reconstructions they tend to ignore Mesha's claims and seek other, usually naturalistic, explanations for Mesha's experience of subjugation and deliverance. It is worth noting, however, that most do not proceed to write off the entire inscription as historically worthless simply because of Mesha's metaphysical claims.

The OT is filled with similar claims about the divine actions of Israel's God, Yahweh. The question we must face, then, is this: Should these claims be dismissed in historical reconstructions in the same way that the claims about Chemosh were? The answer, as one might expect, will vary from scholar to scholar. For instance, scholars whose metaphysical beliefs do not include the existence of a God Yahweh will need to answer in the affirmative: *Yes, the claims of intervention by Yahweh in the historical process must be dismissed or reexplained.* Scholars of different metaphysical persuasion may see things differently. Where all scholars should be in agreement, however, is in acknowledging (a) that the ancient claims were made, whether one regards them as delusional or not, and (b) that the claims of divine intervention are not, by themselves, grounds for dismissing the entire historical import of an ancient text, biblical or otherwise. As Millard insists, "Whether or not modern readers share the belief that supernatural powers communicated with ancient leaders and others, the statements remain, and they remain as the contemporary origin or justification for many actions. The fact of the ancient belief has to be accepted, the words attributed to the divinity can be essential to any historical reconstruction" (1983, 44).

In other words, modern scholars may find themselves *metaphysically* at odds with their sources, but they must at least recognize that their misgivings arise at that level. They may not share the theological *convictions* of their sources, but, as the title of this section implies, they must at least show some theological *comprehension* of their sources. Where the biblical narratives make claims to direct divine intervention in human affairs, scholars must admit the fact of the claim itself and allow that some, then and now, believe(d) the claims to be true. If certain scholars' own metaphysical commitments force them to regard such claims as impossible and prompt them to propose alternative scenarios to those presented in the OT, they must acknowledge that their judgments reflect their fundamental beliefs and do not necessarily derive from an "objective" appraisal of the evidence. This is not to say, of course, that belief is everything and evidence is nothing, but rather that belief has much to do with how one views and interprets the evidence (Long, 1994, 171-76; Provan).

But this raises another interesting issue. Probably only a minority of *biblical* scholars would explicitly deny the existence of God, or even that God is a personal being. That is, few would wish to be characterized as non-theists or a-theists. Curiously, however, probably a majority of contemporary scholars exclude from their historical reconstructions even the possibility of divine activity. The reason for this, it seems, has more to do with methodological convention than metaphysical conviction, and so we must now turn to the question of method.

3. *Historical criticism.*

> The historian of Israel is obligated to carry out his research and
> his reconstruction according to the rules followed by any other historian.
> (Ramsey, 3)

While some readers may have been surprised to hear that two requirements for the historical interpretation of the OT are literary competence and theological comprehension, surely few will be surprised that a third requirement is historical criticism. The core story of the OT presents itself as a true story, and not just in the sense that it is "true to life." The central events of the sweep of redemptive history are presented as real events that happened in the lives of real people (cf. Arnold, 99; Halpern, 1988; Licht, 212-16). Whatever artistic traits may be present in the narratives of the OT (and they are many), it remains the case that most of these narratives present themselves as more than just art for art's sake. They present themselves not merely as realistic narratives but as referential narratives, as the verbal equivalent of portraits, not just generic paintings. Therefore, unless it can be demonstrated that this assessment of the character of the narratives is incorrect—and there are some who think so (e.g., Smelik, Thompson)—then any legitimate *literary* reading must take their *historical* truth claims seriously, whatever one may believe about the truth value of the claims.

It is necessary to acknowledge the Bible's historical truth claims not only for literary reasons, but for theological reasons as well. For "in point of fact, the Bible consistently presents theological truth as intrinsically bound to historical events" (Arnold, 99). The religious faith propagated in the OT is dependent not simply on some "story world" but on the real world about which the stories are told. As noted earlier, the God of the OT is the Lord of history, and his self-disclosure and salvific actions are accomplished in both event and word (see Long, 1994, 88-119).

Because competent literary reading of the OT and circumspect theological reflection on its message both underscore the importance of history, proper interpretation of the OT must involve *historical* criticism. But here we encounter another problem. The historical-critical method, as developed during and after the Enlightenment, seems ill-suited to deal with the biblical (hi)story. The method is commonly understood to involve three principles: *criticism* (the notion that historical judgments are to be based on a critical evaluation of evidence and should take the form of probability judgments subject to revision in the light of further evidence); *analogy* (the idea that normal, everyday experience provides the basis for judging the likelihood of claims about past events, so that claims of miraculous or unique events—that is, events without analogy—must be discounted, or at least labeled unhistorical); and *correlation* (the view that events are interrelated with one another in a nexus of cause and effect, so that events do not simply happen unprompted by their larger context). Given these three principles, especially the second, there appears to be, as Miller has noted, an "obvious conflict between the biblical claims regarding God's overt and unique actions in Israel's history on the one hand, and the presuppositions of the historical-critical method of inquiry on the other" (1976, 18).

In view of this apparent conflict, it is sometimes claimed that biblical scholars must make a choice: They can be either historians or believers, but not both (at least not at the same time). One thinks, for instance, of V. A. Harvey's book, *The Historian and the Believer: A Confrontation Between the Modern Historian's Principles of Judgment and the Christian's Will-to-Believe*, in which Harvey asserts an antithesis between the "morality of historical knowledge" and the "ethic of belief" (102-26 and *passim*). This antithesis is unnecessary, however, provided that the three principles of historical criticism are defined in a manner consistent with a theistic set of background beliefs. During and after the Enlightenment the thesis that "the absolute cause never disturbs the chain of secondary causes" (so Strauss, 88) achieved almost the status of an a priori principle, and so it remains among many practitioners of the historical-critical method today. The grounds for the view expressed at that time, however, were but vague generalizations about "the known and universal laws which govern the universe" and "all just philosophical conceptions and all credible experience" (ibid.). In the end, the principle was little more than a positivistic belief, and one that it is logical for theists to question. (For more on the deficiencies of Enlightenment thinking generally, see Westermann.)

The fact is that metaphysical commitments (and no one is without them) play a determinative role in how the principles of criticism, analogy, and correlation are understood and applied. Those who regard the Bible as a merely human document, for instance, will typically expect the Bible to err (since "to err is human"), and so the principle of criticism may be construed in terms of systematic doubt of one's sources. Those who regard the Bible as a divinely inspired human document (the historic Judeo-Christian perspective), will, if they are consistent, construe the principle of criticism in the more neutral sense described above—i.e., the notion that historical judgments are to be based on a critical (that is, thoughtful and analytical, though not necessarily negative) assessment of evidence. As for the principle of analogy, those who embrace a theistic metaphysic will find little reason to limit what is (historically) possible to that which finds analogy in common, everyday human experience. This does not mean, of course, that believing scholars will credulously accept every miracle report that they hear. Belief that "with God all things are possible" is a far cry from the assumption that all things are therefore probable. In assessing reports of unique or miraculous events, theists will always want to consider the quality and reliability of the source. And they will also want to bring to bear the third principle of the historical-critical method—viz., the principle of correlation. But again, it will be important that this principle be properly defined. While many scholars wittingly or unwittingly adopt a *material* notion of correlation that would limit the possible causes of historical change to natural forces and human beings, theistic scholars should prefer a *formal* notion of correlation in which God, as a personal being, is also allowed a role in the historical process (for full discussion of these matters, see Abraham, ch. 5 and *passim*; cf. Long, 1994, 108-16, 123-35).

In sum, then, so long as the three principles of historical criticism are defined in keeping with a theistic set of background beliefs, there is no reason to have to choose between being a historian and a believer. As W. J. Abraham succinctly puts it, "the theologian need have no fears that the historian must pronounce his commitment to divine intervention as hostile to the critical canons of the historian's trade" (188).

Many modern scholars, to be sure, will object to the above procedure. R. Morgan, for example, concedes that "stretching historical methods to make them speak of God ... is a common-sense response of any believer who does not acknowledge the limits set on historical method by the intellectual community of historians," and he admits that "there is some justification for the protest that the conventions of historical method mean that it cannot handle unique events." But Morgan nevertheless insists that these are only reasons for denying that the historical method is "the sole arbiter of truth, not for stretching and destroying the method itself." He further insists that "redefining historical method to allow it to speak of God would put theology back into the ghetto from which its use of rational methods is intended to rescue it. If believers want the benefits of using public discourse in communicating the message of their scriptures they must keep its rules" (186-87). While there is some force in Morgan's concerns, his objections raise more problems than they solve. How, for example, can theistic scholars be expected to bear the epistemological strain of embracing, on the one hand, the historical-critical assumption that God is *not* active in human affairs and, on the other hand, the biblical-theological assumption that he is? And what is the sense of insisting that believers wishing to communicate the message of their Scriptures, in which God is a major player, can only do so by first agreeing with their culture, which does not believe in God, that they will not talk about him? What message of Scripture is left?

If the historical method is to be fruitfully applied to the OT—and the OT texts seem to demand a historical approach—then the way forward must lie in first taking a step backward to consider the model of reality (including metaphysical commitments) that undergirded the earlier formulations of the method. It should then be possible to adjust the historical method in such a way that it is commensurate not only with the object under investigation, the Bible, but also with the theism that probably a majority of biblical scholars continue to profess. A-theistic biblical scholars may prefer to retain the naturalistic assumptions of the historical method as commonly practiced, but they must at least admit that their preference is a matter of faith and not of science or scholarship. And for all who regard discussion of God's role in history as irrational and irresponsible, the words of H. W. Wolff, spoken in an inaugural address in 1960, may provide a timely challenge: "It is not that belief in God supplements reason in the recognition of reality, but that it rather liberates it for an objective view of the data which are historically comparable to each other. At the same time, unbelief runs the risk of partially distorting this view and thus becoming semi-realism" (353).

4. *Conclusion: On the interrelationship of the three requirements.* It has been argued above that responsible historical interpretation of the OT requires three things of the interpreter: literary competence, theological comprehension, and historical criticism. These three requirements are in keeping with what Sternberg describes as the three chief impulses of Scripture: "aesthetics [cf. literature], ideology [cf. theology], and history" (362, see also 1-57). As Sternberg points out, however, the question of how these three interrelate is a tricky one (41).

It is common in scholarly circles to treat the literary, theological, and historical questions as separate issues. Morgan, for example, contends that "historical research and theological interpretation are in principle different tasks, done by two different interpretative communities" (184); "a historical aim or interest is naturally met by historical methods, and a literary one by methods of literary analysis. Religious and theological interests are met by theological interpretations which draw on various rational methods" (212). What is missing in such formulations, if taken at face value, is the fact that the three issues are in reality interrelated and in some sense mutually corrective (Morgan himself warns in one place of making "too sharp a division between historical and literary study" [216]). Judgments made in one area inevitably make themselves felt to a greater or lesser degree in the other areas. Often a historical judgment will depend heavily on a literary judgement, and both together may have theological implications (we need only recall Hayes's observation, quoted above, that "the primary influence on Wellhausen's reconstruction of Israelite history was, of course, the results and consequences of his literary study of the Old Testament").

In reviewing a fairly recent, major commentary on the book of 1 Sam, R. Polzin drives home this point about the interrelationship of literary and historical questions. Having noted the apparent "paucity of solid literary-historical evidence" deriving from

1 Sam, he laments that "scholars who have dealt with the complicated textual and liter-ary history of this passage generally exhibit little knowledge or awareness of how cen-tral a poetics of biblical narrative is to the recognition of, let alone the solution to, literary-historical problems." And in response to the claim that "the narratives about Samuel, Saul and David that make up (1 and 2 Samuel) have a heterogeneous appear-ance even to the untrained eye," he responds that "it may just be possible that much of the heterogeneity apparent ... 'even to the untrained eye,' appears heterogeneous *pre-cisely* to the untrained eye" (300).

Such matters will continue to be debated, but it seems fair to insist at least that because "biblical narrative emerges as a complex, because multifunctional discourse" (Sternberg, 41), those who would approach it responsibly with historical questions in mind must meet the three requirements of literary competence, theological comprehen-sion, and an appropriately conceived historical criticism.

C. Historical Interpretation of the OT: Four Steps in the Process

Having discussed three requirements of the interpreter, we may now turn our attention to four steps in the process of interpretation itself. Earlier in this essay I drew an analogy between historiography and portraiture. Here it may be helpful to adduce another oft-mentioned analogy—viz., that between history as a discipline and jurispru-dence (cf. Halpern, 1988, 13; Ramsey, 22-23; Soggin, 20). The comparison is apt, for there are many parallels between the two fields of endeavor. Both historians and jurists, for example, are concerned to reconstruct "what happened in the past"—not in any exhaustive sense, but in terms of "significant past events," with "significance" being measured in terms of the questions they are asking. Both rely on whatever verbal testimony and material evidence can be gathered. Both are concerned not only to amass all available evidence but also to assess the evidence critically and to interpret its significance with a view toward reconstructing the past. Both must strive not only to come to personal convictions about "what happened" and "what it all means" but must also seek to convince others that their reconstruction is plausible, probable, and to be preferred over rival reconstructions. In very general terms, both can be construed as involving the following steps: (1) Amass the evidence; (2) assess the evidence; (3) attempt a reconstruction; (4) advocate the reconstruction. We shall consider each of these briefly below.

1. *Amass the evidence.*

> Without evidence there can be no historical knowledge, though there can be historical guesswork. (Stanford, 56)

The first step in historical study, as in jurisprudence, is to become apprised of the evidence. In either field the evidence is generally of two types: verbal and material. During the so-called discovery period, lawyers preparing for a trial seek to collect as much pertinent verbal testimony/evidence as possible. They do this by locating and interrogating (i.e., taking a deposition from) all witnesses who may have useful infor-mation to impart. They also seek to learn of any material evidence that may have a bearing on the case (a weapon, a footprint, skid marks, etc.). Similarly, historians, dur-ing their "discovery period," seek to locate and "interrogate" potentially pertinent ver-bal (i.e., literary or epigraphic) witnesses. The verbal evidence may include biblical as well as relevant extrabiblical texts, though for some periods of Israel's history the latter are rather sparse or nonexistent (Clines, 101; Greenberg, 38; Miller, 1992, 65-66; Soggin, 36). Already at this early stage, historians' linguistic and literary competencies come into play as they "listen to" and attempt to understand the written material available to them. In one respect, however, historians are in a quite different position from lawyers, for lawyers are able to interrogate their witnesses directly, whereas historians are at best able to "listen in" on communications (of whatever genre) from a sometimes distant past. Thus, historians must often work with "unintentional" as well as "intentional evidence" in seeking to glean information relevant to the particular focus of their study (on the distinction between intentional and unintentional evidence, see Ramsey, 4).

In addition to gathering verbal evidence, historians also seek to acquaint themselves with whatever material evidence time, chance, and the efforts of archaeologists have brought to light. Today historians have the benefit not only of the kind of evidence unearthed by traditional archaeology (e.g. artifactual, architectural, stratigraphic) but also of the kind of evidence the multidisciplinary approach of the "new archaeology" produces (e.g., ecological, climatological, sociological). All of these kinds of evidence can be useful to historians seeking to reconstruct some aspect of a past event or time period. But before historians can attempt a reconstruction, there is a second step they must take.

2. *Assess the evidence.*

> Before present evidence can be used as the first link in a chain
> that leads into the past, an accurate description of that first link is essential. (In this respect, as in others, we cannot hope to be right about the
> past if we are wrong about the present.) (Stanford, 61)

Merely amassing evidence does not result, without further ado, in a historical reconstruction. Just as evidence presented in court must be carefully assessed with respect to its reliability before it can be used as part of a hypothesis about what happened, so the evidence collected by historians must be assessed, or "sifted," as Ramsey (6-10) puts it, before it can be used in historical reconstruction. It is inevitable, of course, that some evaluation of the evidence will have begun already during the discovery period, but it is important that there come a time when historians, like jurists, self-consciously review the evidence and endeavor to think critically about it.

As regards verbal evidence, two criteria stand out. In a court of law, the credibility of witnesses is judged (a) by whether their testimony is self-consistent and non-contradictory and (b) by whether they, the witnesses, are of reputable character. If a witness fails to tell a coherent story, falls into self-contradiction, or is out of accord with other testimony deemed to be reliable, then confidence in the veracity of the testimony diminishes or vanishes. But even if the witness tells a coherent story, it still may not be believed if it can be shown that the witness's character is not such as to instill confidence. If, on the other hand, the witness's character is unimpeachable, then even should the testimony seem at first confused or out of accord with other testimony, every effort will be made to come to some understanding before simply dismissing it as false or useless. In the same way, verbal (and this would include literary) evidence amassed by historians can be subjected to a two-pronged consistency/character test: (a) Is the testimony *consistent*, both internally (i.e., coherent and not self-contradictory) and externally (i.e., reconcilable with other verbal testimony deemed to be reliable)? and (b) Is the *character* of the witness such as to engender confidence in what it says?

The first test raises some questions: Just what constitutes consistency in and among ancient documents? What level of internal accuracy must each display, and what level of agreement must there be between them, in order to earn our trust? Surely no one would expect the various witnesses in a court trial to offer identical testimony—indeed, if the witnesses did, one might suspect them of conspiracy or collusion. All that one expects of truthful witnesses is that their testimony in the end be complementary, or at least not flatly contradictory. This same kind of common-sense standard should be applied to literary witnesses from antiquity, not least in the case of parallel biblical texts such as we have in the Synoptic Gospels of the NT or the synoptic histories (Samuel-Kings and Chronicles) in the OT (Long, 1994, 76-86).

But common sense alone is not enough, since what may seem sensible enough to some people living in a particular time and place may not at all seem sensible to others from a different time or place. Common sense must be augmented by sincere efforts to develop the three competencies outlined earlier in this essay. Smelik has noted, for example, that "not every literary genre will produce the same degree of historical accuracy" (5). Perhaps a better way to put this would be to say that not every literary genre attempts the same *kind* of historical accuracy. Thus the interpreter's literary competence, for example, comes into play in discovering just what kind of historical truth claims a text may be making. Only when truth claims are accurately discerned can a fair assessment of a text's truth value be made. As an illustration, consider the fact that not every visual recording of the human head attempts the same kind of representational accuracy—a portrait seeks to capture the overall outward appearance as normally perceived, whereas a CAT scan attempts something quite different. Either might be deemed "inaccurate" if judged on the standard of the other, but both may be perfectly accurate within their own intentionality. To cite a biblical example, much is sometimes made of the "inconsistent" pictures of the Israelite conquest presented in the books of Joshua and Judges. One suspects, however, that greater sensitivity to the literary and thematic emphases of the two books would go far toward resolving the perceived difficulties (Younger, 1990; Long, 1994, 165-66).

We see, then, that the first test of reliability, the consistency test, must be handled with care and circumspection; hasty judgments must be avoided. The second test, the character test, brings us ultimately back to the issue of the background beliefs of the interpreter, however these may have been formed. When approaching biblical texts, some scholars will be predisposed (perhaps, but not necessarily, because of religious conviction) to assume that they are of reputable character and are generally trustworthy—though, of course, the interpreter's *understanding* of them may prove itself in need of correction. Other scholars will be predisposed (again, perhaps because of their background beliefs) to assume that the texts are of questionable character and thus are not to be trusted in matters of history, at least not without external confirmation. To be sure, scholars sometimes change their views regarding the character of the biblical texts, but given the deep level at which religious convictions operate, changes of this sort occur only in the face of a rather large body of contrary evidence.

When it comes to material evidence, the assessment of reliability is based on somewhat different criteria. Before agreeing that material evidence of one sort or another is "admissible," both lawyers and historians must assure themselves that the evidence is genuine, that it has been rightly described, and that it was properly collected. Was this knife actually found at the scene of the crime, could it have been planted there, was it properly collected and marked? Was this potsherd actually found in an Iron I layer, was it properly collected and marked?

Once lawyers or historians have assessed the reliability of the verbal and material evidences that they amassed during the discovery period, they may begin to try to put the pieces together into a plausible reconstruction of what happened. This brings us to the next step in the process of historical interpretation.

3. *Attempt a reconstruction.*

> If history is no more than the handling of data, then it can be done by a copying clerk or a machine. But surely it is a very human activity. (Stanford, 97)

It is tempting to liken the task of historical reconstruction to the piecing together of a complex jigsaw puzzle. Each piece of evidence that has been tested and found reliable must find its place in a believable picture of what happened and why. In at least one significant respect, however, the jigsaw puzzle analogy breaks down. This is the fact that there is really only one way to put a jigsaw puzzle together, only one picture is possible, and it can be viewed from only one angle. Regardless of who is putting the puzzle together, there is only one right way to do it. Historical reconstruction, by contrast, is more complicated. As we noted earlier, historians can approach their task from various different vantage points, with various concerns in mind. Like portrait artists, to recall our earlier analogy, historians may each view their subject from a distinct perspective and under a particular light and thus paint portraits that look rather different from one another. This is not to imply that the possibilities are limitless or that just any picture will do; all good portraits must at least be compatible with one another, once the differing perspectives and styles have been taken into account.

Historians, too, may approach their subjects from different angles and under different lights, and arrive at different pictures. The primary concern of some contemporary historians is to reconstruct "history from below." Their focus is not so much on individual persons and events as it is on the general mode of life and the living conditions of a particular society or stratum of society. For their purposes, the material evidence yielded by archaeology, for example, may be more telling than literary evidence, which may speak little of the life-ways of a people in general. More traditionally, however, historians have tended to focus on specific events and individuals. For their purposes, archaeological evidence is seldom sufficient, for "although it is a good source for clarifying the material culture of times past, artifactual evidence is a very poor source of information about specific people and events" (Miller, 1987, 59). Artifacts and material remains are essentially mute. Until the archaeologist or historian begins to describe what they are, they have no voice. But in the process of description, the archaeologist is inevitably, even if unconsciously, interpreting the data. Thus, as F. Brandfon (30) has forcefully argued, it is a fallacy to assume that archaeological evidence is somehow more "objective" than other kinds of evidence. To learn about specific people and to reconstruct specific events, historians need verbal evidence.

96

It should be obvious from the above considerations that historical reconstruction is anything but automatic or mechanical. Historical reconstruction, as Stanford notes, is a "very human activity": "In all these approaches, historians employ their intentions, their hopes and fears, their beliefs, their methodological, even metaphysical, principles, their grasp and use of language and of languages, their hermeneutic capacities, and so on. All these are all relevant to the major task of seeing and understanding the past, and hence making a reasonably accurate and functioning mental model of it" (96).

This then is the situation. Historians have at their disposal both material evidence and verbal evidence. The significance that they assign to each will in large measure be a reflection of their particular interests, whether in the general life-ways of a people and period or in specific individuals and events that have catalyzed historical change. For the former, the material evidences are useful; for the latter, there must be greater dependence on the verbal (i.e., literary) evidence. These two kinds of approaches, sometimes referred to as the nomothetic and the ideographic, may peacefully coexist and even at times enrich one another. As respects OT history, for example, the generalizing information provided by nomothetic studies of material evidence can often add flesh to the skeleton provided by the ideographic information derived from literary study of the texts. Problems sometimes arise, however, when scholars, who for one reason or another dismiss the OT narratives, nevertheless proceed to propound historical reconstructions involving specific events. To do this they must consciously or unconsciously import some interpretive model—sociological, ideological, religious, or whatever. And here again one can see what a very human activity historical reconstruction is.

4. *Advocate the reconstruction.*

> At the very heart of historical activity is the point where the historian, in completing the construction of the past, begins to look to the present and the future and to consider how this new-found knowledge can be shared with other people. (Stanford, 110)

Like visual representational artists who, having caught a vision of their subject, work at their craft so as to share their vision with others, so historians work at their craft so as to share with others their understanding of what the past looked like. But more than that, historians, like lawyers, must *advocate* their reconstruction of what happened and why. The accent at this stage is on persuasion, not proof in any absolute sense, for as McCulloch observes, "historical descriptions cannot be proved true beyond all possibility of error" (4). At best they can only be shown to be probably true, or true beyond a reasonable doubt. Here again, the individual human being, with his or her own beliefs about life, the universe, and everything, intrudes him- or herself into the question of what constitutes reasonability or probability. This means that what one person finds reasonable or persuasive, another may not. In historical advocacy, there are no knock-down arguments, nor is there a particular *kind* of argument that is a distinctively historical argument. Since history, like law, is a "field-encompassing-field" (Harvey, 54-59), many kinds of arguments may be used in seeking to persuade others of a particular reconstruction. As Ramsey notes, "The element which is common to all the arguments of the lawyer or the historian (or anyone else) is the obligation to give reasons for his conclusions" (22).

Now, one may think to ask whether advocacy, that is, the construction of an argument meant to persuade, is even necessary in some contexts. What about homogeneous communities of faith (which I would regard as an apt description not only of various religious communities, but also of some secular circles whose faith consists more in what is denied than in what is affirmed)? Are the rigors of historical argumentation beneficial, or even necessary? I would contend that they are, if for no other reason than the opportunity they afford for self-correction. Has my period of discovery overlooked any vital evidence? Have I properly assessed the evidence—i.e., have I properly interpreted *both* the material evidence and the literary evidence? Are the logical steps I take in moving from evidence to historical reconstruction valid (on the nature of argumentation, see Long, 1994, 194-98)? Is my move from the available data to a conclusion supported by adequate warrants and backing? Have I considered possible rebuttals to the logical arguments upon which my historical reconstruction rests? Am I sufficiently aware of how my background beliefs affect what I am willing to consider as warrant or backing?

At all these points, the rigors of historical advocacy provide opportunities for self-correction. But this raises a larger question. While it is easy to see how I can augment my evidence base if I have overlooked something, how I can emend misinterpretations of evidence, and how I can adjust arguments if they are flawed, is there some way to correct the fundamental belief system that affects the way I see everything else? Can I do this by sheer force of will? Or must I look to some higher Author(ity)? This is a question that faces everyone interested in the historical interpretation of the OT who delves deeply enough into the hermeneutical issues involved to discover that "dominating all technical considerations of evidence, method, interpretation and construction is the individual human being" (Stanford, 96).

BIBLIOGRAPHY

W. J. Abraham, *Divine Revelation and the Limits of Historical Criticism,* 1982; B. T. Arnold, "The Quest for the Historical Israel Continued: A Review Article," *Ashland Theological Review* 24, 1992, 92-103; S. W. Baron, *The Contemporary Relevance of History: A Study of Approaches and Methods,* 1986; J. Barton, *Reading the Old Testament: Method in Biblical Study,* 1984; A. Berlin, *Poetics and Interpretation of Biblical Narrative,* 1983; F. Brandfon, "The Limits of Evidence: Archaeology and Objectivity," *Maarav* 4/1, 1987, 5-43; G. B. Caird, *The Language and Imagery of the Bible,* 1980; D. J. A. Clines, *What Does Eve Do to Help and Other Readerly Questions to the Old Testament,* 1990; F. E. Deist, "Contingency, Continuity and Integrity in Historical Understanding: An Old Testament Perspective," *Scriptura* S11, 1993, 99-115; G. Garbini, *History and Ideology in Ancient Israel,* 1988; S. A. Geller, "Through Windows and Mirrors into the Bible: History, Literature and Language in the Study of Text," in *A Sense of Text: The Art of Language in the Study of Biblical Literature,* 1983, 3-40; M. Greenberg, "Response to Roland de Vaux's 'Method in the Study of Early Hebrew History'," in *The Bible in Modern Scholarship,* 1965, 37-43; W. W. Hallo, "The Limits of Skepticism," *JAOS* 110, 1990, 187-199; B. Halpern, "Biblical or Israelite History?" in *The Future of Biblical Studies,* 1987, 103-39; idem, *The First Historians: The Hebrew Bible and History,* 1988; V. A. Harvey, *The Historian and the Believer: A Confrontation Between the Modern Historian's Principles of Judgment and the Christian's Will-to-Believe,* 1966; J. H. Hayes, "The History of the Study of Israelite and

Judaean History," in *IJH,* 1977, 1-69; S. Herrmann, "Die Abwertung des Alten Testaments als Geschichtsquelle: Bermerkungen zu einem geistesgeschichtlichen Problem," in *Sola Scriptura: VII. 1990,* 1993, 156-65; N. P. Lemche, "Is It Still Possible to Write a History of Ancient Israel?" *SJOT* 8, 1994, 165-90; J. Licht, "Biblisches Geschichtsdenken und apokalyptische Spekulation," *Judaica* 46, 1990, 208-24; V. P. Long, "Interpolation or Characterization: How Are We to Understand Saul's Two Confessions," *Presbyterion* 19, 1993, 49-53; idem, *The Art of Biblical History,* 1994; idem, *The Reign and Rejection of King Saul: A Case for Literary and Theological Coherence,* 1989; C. B. McCullagh, *Justifying Historical Descriptions,* 1984; A. R. Millard, "Story, History, and Theology," in *Faith, Tradition, and History: Old Testament Historiography in Its Near Eastern Context,* 1994, 37-64; idem, "The Old Testament and History: Some Considerations," *Faith and Thought* 110, 1983, 34-53; J. M. Miller, "Israelite History," in *The Hebrew Bible and Its Modern Interpreters,* 1985, 1-30; idem, "Old Testament History and Archaeology," *BA* 50, 1987, 55-63; idem, "Reflections on the Study of Israelite History," in *What Has Archaeology to Do With Faith?,* 1992, 60-74; idem, *The Old Testament and the Historian,* 1976; R. Morgan and J. Barton, *Biblical Interpretation,* 1988; R. G. Moulton, *The Literary Study of the Bible,* 1896; I. W. Provan, "Ideologies, Literary and Critical: Reflections on Recent Writing on the History of Israel," *JBL* 114, 1995, 586-606; G. W. Ramsey, *The Quest for the Historical Israel: Reconstructing Israel's Early History,* 1982; J. W. Rogerson and P. R. Davies, *The Old Testament World,* 1989; K. A. D. Smelik, "The Use of the Hebrew Bible as a Historical Source," in *Converting the Past,* 1992, 1-34; A. J. Soggin, *A History of Ancient Isrnel,* 1985; M. Stanford, *The Nature of Historical Knowledge,* 1986; M. Sternberg, *The Poetics of Biblical Narrative: Ideological Literature and the Drama of Reading,* 1985; T. L. Thompson, "Text, Context and Referent in Israelite Historiography," in *The Fabric of History: Text, Artifact and Israel's Past,* 1991, 65-92; M. Tsevat, "Israelite History and the Historical Books of the Old Testament," *The Meaning of the Book of Job and Other Biblical Essays,* 1980, 177-87; K. J. Vanhoozer, "The Semantics of Biblical Literature: Truth and Scripture's Diverse Literary Forms," in *Hermeneutics, Authority, and Canon,* 1986, 49-104; C. Westermann, "The Old Testament's Understanding of History in Relation to That of the Enlightenment," in *Understanding the Word: Essays in Honor of Bernhard W. Anderson,* 1985, 207-19; K. W. Whitelam, "Between History and Literature: The Social Production of Israel's Traditions of Origin," *SJOT* 2, 1991, 60-74; H. W. Wolff, "The Understanding of History in the Old Testament Prophets," in *Essays on Old Testament Interpretation,* 1963 [German orig. 1960], 336-55; E. Yamauchi, "The Current State of Old Testament Historiography," in *Faith, Tradition, and History: Old Testament Historiography in Its Near Eastern Context,* 1994, 1-36; K. L. Younger, "The Figurative Aspect and the Contextual Method in the Evaluation of the Solomonic Empire (1 Kings 1-11)," in *The Bible in Three Dimensions,* 1990, 157-75; idem, *Ancient Conquest Accounts: A Study in Ancient Near Eastern and Biblical History Writing,* 1990.

V. Philips Long

PART III: LITERATURE, INTERPRETATION, AND THEOLOGY

The next two essays explore the world of the Bible as literature. The last twenty years has seen a flurry of scholarly and popular activity dealing with literary approaches. True, many of these have perpetuated a critical attitude to biblical literature. This does not take away from the importance of understanding the approaches to the Bible as literature. Tremper Longman III traces the background behind the paradigm shift. Further, he discusses the possibilities ("promises") of and the problems ("pitfalls") with the literary approach. Finally, his constructive comments on how one interprets prose and poetry open the field of literary studies to beginning, as well as advanced, students of the Bible.

Philip E. Satterthwaite's essay is narrower in scope (narrative techniques). It penetrates the techniques involved in literary analysis of narratives. See also the previous essay by V. Philips Long, in which he argues persuasively for the engagement of literary (narrative) analysis with historical interpretation. (VanGemeren)

5. LITERARY APPROACHES AND INTERPRETATION

A. Words and Text

A dictionary is a book about words. Each entry or article in the case of the present work treats a word in a discrete and isolated way. One turns to a dictionary to find out the meaning of a word. However, we are not used to encountering words in such an artificial way. Our typical experience with words is in some kind of text, written or verbal. Words occur in sentences, paragraphs, chapters, discourses, textual wholes.

So what is the relationship between a word and a text? It is a dialectical relationship. Words are the building blocks of texts; texts are the place where words find their meaning.

What then is the relationship between a dictionary and a text; specifically, what is the relationship between a dictionary of ancient Hebrew words and a biblical text? This relationship too is dialectical.

One turns to a dictionary to get the meaning of a word. Beginning students understand the Hebrew dictionary as the source, the origin, the start of turning a mass of strange looking symbols into something real, something understandable, something readable.

But where did these meanings come from? Did they drop out of thin air? Dig under a dictionary and one will find texts. That is, scholars who write dictionaries turn to texts to discern the semantic outlines of the words they seek to define. Of course, they cite cognates from other Semitic languages when they exist, but how does one understand the meaning of the Ugaritic, the Akkadian, the Arabic cognate? We discover the meaning of these cognate words from their occurrence within texts.

Most dictionaries repress the contextual nature of their definitions because they simply list meanings and a few occurrences. There is nothing criminal in that practice, but it does give the wrong impression.Theological dictionaries such as *NIDOTTE*, because of their ambitions and scope, allow more than a list of meanings. They allow discussions of words in context. Not every context to be sure, but a substantial amount of exploration is allowed as we seek to define not just a meaning of a word, something to plug into a text, but the semantic field to which the word belongs.

So the meaning of a word is dialectically related to its literary contexts. Scholars create dictionary definitions from an examination of those contexts, and sophisticated users of dictionaries know that they must take the basic understanding given them by these scholars and reflect on them in their context, their literary context.

As we will chronicle below, biblical studies has moved from a word-focused approach to a text-oriented approach over the past few years. As we will see, this is really the reestablishment of a wholistic approach to texts that had been disrupted by forces of the Enlightenment—not a wholly new and modern idea, but, nonetheless, it feels like a novel development to us.

This new literary approach affects the way we understand the biblical texts as a whole. However, as we turn for a moment to the relatively "new" discipline of the literary approach, we will see that there are vastly different ways of conceiving the literary nature of the Bible. This article serves as a guide to the chaos of claims among competing literary approaches. It also seeks to establish general parameters and guidelines of a proper literary approach that recognizes the literary text as an act of communication between an author and an audience. (See the excellent articles by P. Satterthwaite and K. Vanhoozer in this volume, both of which complement and occasionally overlap with the present article.)

B. The Beginnings of the Modern Literary Study of the Hebrew Bible

In 1968 James Muilenburg, an established form critic, challenged the Society of Biblical Literature to move beyond the analysis of the prehistory of small units of text toward an appreciation and analysis of the literary style of larger sections of the Bible (1-18). While affirming the continuing importance of form criticism, he called for increased attention to the rhetorical strategy of OT books.

The next few years saw a smattering of books and articles devoted to the literary analysis of the OT, but nothing resembling a movement (see L. Alonso-Schokel [1963]; D. J. A. Clines [1976; 1980]; D. M. Gunn [1978; 1980]; D. Patte and J. F. Parker [1980]; S. Bar-Efrat [1980]). The effect of these first few explorations, however, was to soften the ground for a veritable explosion of interest in the literary method that began in the early 1980s and has gained momentum ever since.

The book that helped stimulate the new attention given to the literary nature of the OT was *The Art of Biblical Narrative* by Robert Alter. Alter, a professor of literature at Columbia University, described the nature of native Hebrew literary conventions in such a compelling way that many biblical scholars recognized that his approach gave promise for fruitful and interesting readings of the HB.

Indeed, we may speculate that part of the field's attraction to Alter's work was that he was able to provide meaningful readings of biblical texts, while not denying the composite nature of the material. (Note his reference to the narratives of Genesis as "composite artistry," *Art of Biblical Narrative*, 131-54.) While the results of historical critical study of the Bible grew meager and obscured the meaning of the final form of the text, Alter's approach used native literary conventions to give meaningful readings of whole texts.

In the following years, hundreds of books and thousands of articles developed and applied the literary approach. New journals, like *Semeia* and *Journal for the Study of the Old Testament*, came into existence, and most of their articles could be described as "literary." Commentaries and other reference books presented literary insights on their subject matter. R. B. Dillard and T. Longman III (*Introduction to the Old Testament*, 1994), for example, have a section entitled "Literary Analysis" for every book of the OT.

During this time period, every portion of the Hebrew canon has been subjected to a literary analysis. While this statement is true, it must also be remarked that some portions of the Bible received considerably more attention than others, particularly in the prose parts. While Lev and Num received only a few treatments (see W. G. Baroody and W. F. Gentrup, "Exodus, Leviticus, Numbers, and Deuteronomy," in *A Complete Literary Guide to the Bible*, 1993, 121-36), Gen and 1, 2 Sam, books that are rich in literary artistry, have been the subject of many studies. Alter concentrated his attention in these books in *The Art of Biblical Narrative,* as has M. Sternberg in *The Poetics of Biblical Narrative* (1985). We also make note of J. P. Fokkelman's important studies, *Narrative Art in Genesis* (1975) and *Narrative Art and Poetry in the Books of Samuel* (1981).

Alter's specific concern was to uncover and explain native literary conventions. He states this when he says ("Response to Critics"):

> every culture, even every era in a particular culture, develops distinctive and sometimes intricate codes for telling its stories, involving everything from narrative point of view, procedures of description and characterization, the management of dialogue, to the ordering of time and the organization of plot.

Alter's approach is a type of formalism, an attempt to describe the forms or conventions of ancient Hebrew literature, whether prose or poetry. He made a significant foray into the analysis of the conventions of Hebrew poetry in his *The Art of Biblical Poetry* (1985). His analysis of Hebrew literature is a "close reading" of the text, an interpretive strategy often associated with the literary school called New Criticism. New Criticism was a text-centered approach to literature that did not focus on the author or historical reference of the text. Alter agreed with historical critics that the text he was studying was the result of a historical process, but he chose to ignore the diachronic dimensions of the text. As we will see, this interpretive move has generated a controversy that continues until the present moment.

Other scholars followed in Alter's wake, many producing insightful analysis of biblical texts. Adele Berlin's *Poetics and Interpretation of Biblical Narrative* explored literary conventions like plot, characterization, and point of view to see how Hebrew literature distinctively manipulated these devices. A few years later she turned her attention to poetry in *The Dynamics of Biblical Parallelism,* continuing the work of Kugel and Alter. Kugel and Alter had earlier criticized the work of Bishop Robert Lowth, who defined Hebrew poetry with an emphasis on the synonymity of the parallel pair; they showed how the second part of a bicolon always in some sense carried forward the thought of the first part. Berlin furthered this insight on a semantic level and then showed how the grammatical structure paralleled the semantic structure of the line.

Alter and those following in his wake have initiated a new phase of literary study of the Bible. Their impact on the field has been huge. However, before examining what has followed their work, we need to step back to the past. As we do so, we will see that their work is not as novel as it first appears. Indeed, they are reestablishing an old synthesis. The literary approach is not really new, but has a history.

C. Precursors to the Literary Approach

There are ancient roots to the practice of applying literary concepts, methods, and insights to biblical narrative. Stephen Prickett has persuasively argued that the application of literary studies to the Bible is in reality a reintegration of an age-old union. At the turn of the nineteenth century there was a desire to separate theology, including biblical studies, from the more scientific study of the humanities. Specifically, Prickett cites the founding of the University of Berlin by Baron Wilhelm von Humboldt in 1809 as the moment, symbolic at least, when literary studies and biblical studies parted paths. He believes that when the biblical department was removed from the humanities, a "glacial moraine" was erected between the Bible and its literary perception.

Previous to this time it was a matter of course for the Bible to be understood in literary terms. One need only appeal to the early church fathers to illustrate this claim. Augustine and Jerome were trained in classical rhetoric and poetics. As a result, they frequently applied the principles of literature that they learned in school to the study of the Bible. They often compared biblical stories and poems with ones familiar to them in classical literature. The result was, from a modern perspective, a distortion of understanding and evaluation of the biblical texts. Jerome, for example, scanned Hebrew poems and described their poetic form in labels developed for Greek and Latin poetry (see J. Kugel, 149-56). Kugel quotes Jerome as saying (159-60):

> What is more musical than the Psalter? Which in the manner of our Flaccus or of the Greek Pindar, now flows in iambs, now rings with Alcaics, swells to a Sapphic measure or moves along with a half-foot? What is fairer than the hymns of Deuteronomy or Isaiah? What is more solemn than Solomon, what more polished than Job? All of which books, as Josephus and Origen write, flow in the original in hexameter and pentameter verses.

Jerome is just one example that can be multiplied throughout the history of the Christian and Jewish interpretation of the Bible. The literary study of the Bible in the latter part of the twentieth century is a reunion of a split that took place due to an unwarranted and unhealthy obsession with historical criticism of the OT.

D. Post-Alter Literary Approaches to the Bible

One of the earliest and most profound influences on the modern literary approach to the Bible, Alter's formalism, still practiced by biblical scholars, is just one of a number of "literary approaches" found in the pages of scholarly journals and books today. Over the past two decades biblical scholars have borrowed and applied a wide array of literary strategies to the task of interpreting biblical texts. As new theories arose for the study of literature in general, they were soon adopted by biblical scholars. We will now survey the most important of these theories: structuralism, reader-response, deconstruction, and current eclecticism.

1. *Structuralism*. Structuralism was a dominant force in the study of language, culture, and literature in the 1960s, 70s, and into the 80s (see V. S. Poythress, 221; J. Barton, 112). Today, however, structuralism as such is passé. As we will see, structuralism's quasi-scientific pretensions could not stand up to deconstruction's powerful critique. Nonetheless, since structuralist studies of biblical texts are easily found, a brief introduction to this type of thought is still important.

The origins of structuralism are often associated with the linguist Ferdinand de Saussure, who turned the attention of his field to the sign nature of language. Words are signs that have no inherent connection with their references, but rather an arbitrary one assigned by convention. J. Calloud points out that meaning is differential, that is, it is "composed of differences and opposites" (55). This "first principle" of structuralism will become important as we turn later to deconstruction's undermining of structuralism. To learn to speak a language, one learns the word-signs that habit has assigned to a thing, action, or state. In English we refer to a certain animal as a dog, whereas a German speaker would use the word *Hund* and someone who spoke French would call the animal *chien*. In typical structuralist language the word is a signifier, the animal the signified.

While structuralism as a broad cultural movement began much earlier, it was not until the 1960s that it moved specifically from linguistics to literary theory. H. Felperin dates the coming of age of literary structuralism to 1966, the year in which Roland Barthes published *Critique et verité* (H. Felperin, 74). Here Barthes proclaimed the importance of what he called the "science of literature," which is concerned not with the interpretation of particular work but with "conditions of meaning." He and others, such as Todorov, desired to describe a "grammar" of literature.

Structuralism is a quasi-scientific approach to literature. Its goal was to give literary studies a method of approaching texts that could be demonstrated and repeated. R. C. Culley summarized it by saying that structuralists "are seeking a method which is scientific in the sense that they are striving for a rigorous statement and an exacting analytical model" (R. C. Culley, "Exploring New Directions," 1985, 174).

One of the important insights that structuralism made concerning literature is that it operates by certain "conventions." Like the syntax, grammar, and lexicon of a linguistic system, the literary conventions are underlying structures that may be discerned across literature as a whole. To become competent in a language does not mean learning every word or every possible syntactical arrangement, but it does mean learning the basic rules of the language. The same is true of literature. To be literarily competent does not mean knowing the literature exhaustively, but being aware of the major conventions, or literary devices, genres, and so forth (see the discussion in J. Culler, 9).

When this is understood as simply describing the native literary conventions of a particular culture or time, then this type of analysis is not much different from the formalism practiced by Alter. However, some structuralist analysis of narrative in the Bible is quite esoteric in a way that obscures rather than illumines the meaning of a text. At an earlier point of his career, Robert Polzin was an advocate of a structuralist approach to the Hebrew Bible (see his 1977 book). Notably, he provided a structuralist analysis of the book of Job. Following the method of the famous anthropologist Claude Levi-Strauss, Polzin summarizes the message of the book of Job with the following math-like formula: $F_x(a):F^y(b)=F^x(b):F^a\text{-}1(y)$

The technical and esoteric nature of much structuralist study restricted its use and influence to a small, dedicated group of biblical scholars. But other cultural factors led to the nearly complete demise of structuralism as an intellectual framework for literary studies. This relatively optimistic method was soon to be undermined by a radical skepticism.

2. *Reader-response criticism*. Traditional literary criticism focused on the author as the locus of meaning. Formalism (New Criticism) and structuralism moved the attention of the analyst to the text itself. Not surprisingly, the next big wave of literary scholarship directed its interest to the role of the reader in the interpretive process (see, for instance, W. Iser; J. P. Tompkins).

Such a shift of attention has significant impact to the goal of interpretation. An author-centered approach will study the text in the light of the author's biography or, if the author is still living, will seek his or her validation of one's understanding of the text. If the text is ancient and anonymous, at the very least readers can set their interpretation in its original historical context. Structuralism and formalism seek understanding of the text's conventions and literary devices. Reader response focuses on the preunderstanding and ideology of the interpreter as it shapes the "meaning of the text."

We understand what is today called ideological interpretation as a species of reader-response interpretation. In particular, feminist (see J. Cheryl Exum, "Who's Afraid," 91-113), Marxist (F. Jameson; T. K. Beal), and even New Historicist (H. Aram Veeser) readings can be understood as a form of reader-response. For instance, a feminist interpreter will read a text with a specified interest in how women are treated, ignored, or oppressed and how the text has become a tool for the suppression of women. Or perhaps a text itself subverts male dominance in ways that need to be highlighted (see the description of Alice Bach's approach to Num 5, below).

Reader-response criticism runs the spectrum. Some advocate the conservative view that highlights the importance of the reader in the interpretive process, but recognizes that the text provides a limit on the reader's interpretation. E. V. McKnight puts it this way: "The relationship between reader as subject (acting upon the text) and the reader as object (being acted upon by the text), however, is not seen as an opposition but as two sides of the same coin. It is only as the reader is subject of text and language that the reader becomes object. It is as the reader becomes object that the fullness of the reader's needs and desires as subject are met" (128). No one person can exhaust the meaning of a literary text, and his or her gender, race, economic status, religion, education, and so forth will predispose that person to attend to certain aspects of a text. Others, however, encourage a more radical role of the reader. The reader actually constructs the meaning of the text. Later, when we describe today's current eclecticism, we will note that this approach is generally linked with a denial of determinate meaning all together. However, before we reach that point we must pass through the skepticism of deconstruction.

3. *Deconstruction*. Deconstruction results from a critical reaction to structuralism, so that today few structuralists can be found even in biblical studies. Structuralism's attempts at a scientific and objective grammar by which it might speak about

literature was dealt a death blow by the critique of deconstruction, a form of thought associated with the French philosopher Jacques Derrida (1976, 1978).

Structuralism focused on the relationship between a sign and that which it signified. Deconstruction questioned that relationship, noting the "slippage" between the sign and its reference, thus questioning the possibility of literary communication. At its heart, deconstruction is a form of skepticism with philosophical roots in Darwin, Nietzsche, and Freud, the so-called "masters of suspicion." (Deconstruction—Derrida in particular—is difficult to understand. Helpful sources include F. Lentricchia; J. Culler, *On Deconstruction: Theory and Criticism After Structuralism*, 1982; C. Norris; V. B. Leitch.) At the core of deconstruction is a blatant denial of any absolute signifier, anything outside of language itself that assures the process of literary communication. Nothing and no one, whether author, speaker, Platonic ideas, or God, is present out there to ground the meaning of a text. Attempts to assert such a ground are pilloried as logocentrism, asserting a false form of presence, that on further philosophical analysis is shown to be untenable.

An important result of this is that literary texts are unstable. They may seem to have a determinate and single meaning, but when studied closely the text undermines itself, revealing that it possesses no determinate meaning at all.

Indeed, perhaps not to Derrida's liking but true nonetheless, deconstructive analysis has a predictable form. A text or author is studied. The interpreter looks for an *aporia*, or basic contradiction, always present in a literary work or philosophical treatise because of the slippage between a sign and signifier. Highlighting the aporia throws doubt on the text's meaning. The intention of deconstructive interpretation, if one may use that language, is not to understand what it means, but to play with it, to enjoy it, to celebrate its indeterminacy.

This analysis has become increasingly important in biblical studies. A rather tame example is the analysis of the David and Goliath story by P. D. Miscall (47-138). He examines the traditional interpretation of 1 Sam 17, guided by the predominant narratorial voice in the text, which asserts that David was a young lad with inferior weapons and armor but a strong faith, as he stood before the Goliath, the paragon of military strength and experience. David was armed only with his faith in the divine Warrior, who would fight on his behalf and give him the victory (17:45-47).

Miscall, though, insists on an underlying tension in the text (an aporia). David was not so brave as he was sly in his approach to Goliath. After all, it would be the height of folly to approach Goliath as an equal. He thus resorted to subterfuge instead. Not wearing armor, David was mobile against this huge lout, and armed with a slingshot, David could stand at a distance not fearing Goliath's blows. The end result is not an enriched reading of the David-Goliath story, but a skepticism concerning what the text means.

E. The Current Situation

Since the 1940s the field of literary studies has passed through successive stages of new approaches to literary texts. Once the connection with authorial intention was severed, the search was on for a new locus of meaning. Starting with the text (formalism/New Criticism/structuralism), attention moved to the reader (reader-response and ideological readings) and then finally to a denial of any meaning at all. Deconstruction seemed the end of the line, even though N. Royle (*After Derrida*, 1995) attempts to read Derrida in the light of New Historicism. Where could one turn after denying meaning? Indeed, many have gone no further. Deconstruction, while suffering serious setbacks in the late 1980s and early 1990s, still lives on. It is premature to pronounce Derrida's thought passé, but it is no longer ruling the literary roost.

Some took a turn back to history. New Historicism scorns the idea that literature is totally nonreferential. It advocates the historical setting of texts; it also insists on the textual setting of history. But, at least in biblical studies, the best adjectives to use to describe current literary practice is varied and eclectic. On the one hand, all the above mentioned methods are still used by scholars today. Though the avant garde has moved far beyond formalism, some scholars still find it productive. (Many of the essays in L. Ryken and T. Longman III may be described as formalist, describing native literary conventions to understand the meaning of the biblical book under study.) Though deconstruction has been on the rapid decline in literary theory since the revelation of Paul De Man's early involvement in fascism, it too is still practiced by biblical scholars.

The cutting edge of the field, however, is not only varied in its approach to the literary study of the Bible, it is eclectic. That is, it utilizes not one but a variety of approaches at the same time. This trend in biblical studies may be illustrated by two recent collections of writings produced by some of the most active members of the guild: *The New Literary Criticism and the Hebrew Bible* and *Reading Between Texts: Intertextuality and the Hebrew Bible*.

These two works contain the writings of twenty-six scholars, who may not agree in details but share a broad consensus on what a literary approach to the text means. Foundational to their approach is the assertion that the text has no determinate meaning. This belief, of course, shapes the goal of the interpretive task. If there is no meaning to be discovered in the text, then the interpreter's job is to construct a meaning. In a postmodern world, it seems wrong, even ridiculous to believe that we can recover some hypothetical author's meaning or even believe that the text itself contains the clues to its meaning. (Of course, postmodernism's skepticism flows out of its denial of God. One would think that this would immediately invalidate it as a Christian worldview. However, T. J. Keegan [1-14] argues, unsuccessfully in our opinion, that Christian scholars can still profitably use postmodern approaches.) If anything, the reader is the one who endows the text with meaning; and since readers represent diverse cultures, religions, genders, sexual preferences, sociological, and economic backgrounds, how can any right-minded person insist on something so naive as a determinate meaning?

In line with this thinking, contemporary literary approaches to biblical interpretation rests awkwardly with its denial of the determinate meaning of a biblical text. Exum and Clines assert, and the essays in their volume illustrate, a desire to move beyond interpretation of the text to critique of the text. They call for a method of interpretation that "challenges the world views of our literature" (14). While such a challenge seems to contradict the claim that the text has no meaning, it is nonetheless true that most of the authors in their book feel it is their task to undermine the message of the text in the interests of their own pressing concerns.

Alice Bach's essay on the Sotah (Num 5) illustrates these principles well. In the first place, she practices diverse literary methods in her study, including feminist, deconstructive, and psychoanalytic approaches. Next she constructs, supposedly from the perspective of her gender, the underlying ideology of the text. In this regard, she argues that the text, a description of a ritual to be undertaken in the case of a wife suspected of adultery, is really masking male anxieties concerning their own sexuality and is exerting a divinely sanctioned control on woman's sexuality. She then moves beyond interpretation, or the construction of the text's meaning, to critique, basically pointing out how bad and unjust and ridiculous the text is.

In the light of the denial of determinate meaning, I am not quite sure how crestfallen Dr. Bach would be to be told that this is not what the text is about, but for those with ears to hear, she has constructed a fancy. The text is not about sexual anxieties as such but about the importance of paternity in the fulfillment of the promise of offspring in Gen 12:1-3. The text is also not a willful disregard for women's rights. In other words, innocent women are not being harmed as a result of male pettiness. If Professor Bach cared to enter the world of the text, she would recognize that God superintended the ritual, and innocent women would be exonerated while duplicitous women implicated. (Further, it is wrong to simply charge the Bible with a double standard. David, too, is held responsible for his adultery with Bathsheba.)

While Professor Bach's essay is illustrative of the general trends in contemporary literary studies, the most telling essay in Exum and Clines is one written by Clines himself, "A World Established on Water (Psalm 24): Reader-Response, Deconstruction and Bespoke Criticism" (79-90). In this essay, he focuses his attention on Ps 24 by subjecting it to three reading strategies listed in the subtitle to his chapter. What he does with this psalm is actually not as important or as interesting as what he seems to be advocating methodologically, especially under the name "bespoke criticism." On the basis of the lack of meaning of biblical texts and the importance of community acceptance of interpretation, he presents himself as the "bespoke interpreter," based on the analogy with the "bespoke tailor." The bespoke tailor, he reminds us, cuts the cloth according to the customer's specifications. So, he argues, since there is not determinate meaning, we should tailor our interpretations to meet the needs of the group we are addressing, those who are paying us for our wares (87).

Perhaps this is the logical route to go once one loses faith in any kind of authority of the text, any kind of determinate meaning. It is almost too easy to poke fun at such a view of interpretation, suggesting other more colorful, but less respectable analogies to someone who manipulates his or her product to bring the best price. But there are other alternatives to Clines. The first is to refuse to base one's presuppositions on the works of the masters of suspicion, Marx, Darwin, Nietzsche, and Freud, and instead consider building them on the authoritative text itself. The other is to acknowledge, as Clines does, the absence of meaning in the text, and then to resign oneself to silence. Perhaps I am being nostalgic for the 60s, but I find much more noble and honest existentialism's avowal of meaninglessness followed by despair than postmodernism's embrace of meaninglessness, followed by play and ideological manipulations of the text.

F. Pitfalls and Promise

As we surveyed the various literary approaches to biblical interpretation, the pitfalls become obvious. Before describing a constructive literary approach to the Bible, we first want to delineate a few of the ways in which a literary approach can serve, not to illuminate, but to undermine the biblical text. (This section describes only a few fundamental problems with the literary approach to the Bible. For more, please consult T. Longman III, 1987, 47-62).

1. *Pitfalls.* In part, the literary approach to the Bible was a reaction to the impasse reached by historical-critical methods. Source, form, and redaction criticism, at least in the opinion of some, had reached a dead end. The viability and importance of these studies were rarely completely rejected, but the field had grown restless and desired untouched fields to plow. As a result, many scholars moved with great enthusiasm and energy to the literary study of the Bible, applying the methods and categories developed for the study of great fiction to the Bible. One of the byproducts of this approach was a disregard, and on occasion even a disavowal, of the historical or theological significance of the text.

In any case the rupture between the literary and the referential (whether history or theology) is an axiom of modern literary theory. This rupture began with New Criticism. New Criticism developed as a reaction against a traditional biographical criticism that studied the life of the author more than the text itself. To a New Critic the text has a life of its own; the author is unimportant. Even if the author were around to question concerning the meaning of his work, he would simply be another interpreter. Furthermore, the literary work creates a world of its own. The reader must enter that world and not worry about how the work relates to the real world.

Alter, Berlin, and others who advocate this type of literary approach to the biblical text rejected or "bracketed" the questions of origin and reference as well as the ideology of a text. Typical is D. Robertson, who said, "nothing depends on the truth or falsity of [the Bible's] historical claims" (D. Robertson, "Literature, the Bible as," *IDBS,* 548). As one might expect, recognition of the literary characteristics of the Bible has led scholars to equate the Bible and literature, with the corollary that the Bible as a literary text does not refer outside of itself and, in particular, makes no reference to history. This position leads on the part of some to a complete or substantial denial of a historical approach to the text, which most often takes the form of denying or denigrating traditional historical-critical methods. Source and form criticism in particular are attacked. The following quotation is typical of such an attitude: "Above all, we must keep in mind that the narrative is a *form of representation.* Abraham in Genesis is not a real person any more than the painting of an apple is real fruit" (Berlin, 1983, 13).

The result of this approach is a turning away from historical investigation of the text as impossible or irrelevant. The traditional methods of historical criticism are abandoned, radically modified, or given secondary consideration. Concern to discover the original *Sitz im Leben* or to discuss the tradition history of a text languishes among this new breed of scholar. This attitude understandably concerns traditional critical scholarship, so that we find among recent articles ones like Leander Keck's "Will the Historical-Critical Method Survive?" (L. Keck, "Will the Historical-Critical Method Survive?" in *Orientation by Disorientation*, ed. R. A. Spencer, 1980, 115-27). While evangelicals might in some respects be glad to see the end of historical criticism, they, along with historical critics, have a high stake in the question of history.

In order to counteract this negative tendency in biblical scholarship, we must recognize that the Bible, though self-conscious about its manner of telling the story of God and his people and thus literary, is vitally interested in the content of that story.

The biblical historian is not creating a world in his mind, but is artfully relating what actually took place in space and time in the past. Recent work has shown encouraging signs of integrating a literary approach with confidence in the Bible's historical reliability. (The best such work is being done by V. Philips Long, 1989 and 1994.)

It is not only possible, it is necessary to integrate literary analysis with the study of history and the text's ideology (theology). They are all aspects of the text's act of communication. Within this understanding, an analysis of the biblical text's literary conventions is highly illuminating. Literary analysis can distort our understanding of the message of the Bible if practiced alone; it must be part of the entire interpretive practice to be effective.

Another disturbing trend is the confidence with which a number of its most able and prolific practitioners simply assume that the text has no determinate meaning. In the minds of many scholars, the author's intention in his writing is either inaccessible or irrelevant. The text is amenable to many interpretations; its meaning is not an object to be discovered. "The goal of a postmodern scholar is not to answer the question, 'What does the text mean?' but to assist the reader to arrive at ever new meanings" (T. J. Keegan, 8). In essence, this makes the text much less important than the interpreter. It really does not matter what the text means anyway; it simply becomes the vehicle for the prejudices or biases of the reader.

Such beliefs arise from a long history that casts suspicion on the possibility of competent communication. Deconstruction is the most blatant about the causes of slippage in the attempt to transform meaning from one person to another. To have such, there needs to be a Transcendental Signifier, something or someone outside of the murky sea of language who assures that adequate communication takes place. But to deconstructionists there is no such thing or being; God is dead, after all, and especially in the case of the Bible, which is supposed to be God's Word, there is no (ultimate) Author who can anchor the meaning of a text. We are thus left to the free play of signifiers; the interpreter is now god. But that is the point the Christian questions. God is not dead. There is a Transcendent Signifier, and his name is Yahweh. He created the world by virtue of his Word; language emanates from him.

That is not to say that oral or written communication is always obvious. We know it is not. It is not even to say that the interpretation of every biblical passage is clear. The history of interpretation belies that. After all, sin has clouded the picture. Nonetheless, the basic message of the Bible is adequately communicated, so that only the most mischievous reader can miss it (Sternberg, 365–440).

2. *Promise*. The form of the Bible itself insists that a literary approach is legitimate and will illuminate the text for us. Careful reading of the book, when judged according to the standards of the ANE, reveals a self-consciousness not only about what it said, but how it is said. Artful presentations of historical events, prophetic utterances, and, even more clearly, hymns of praise and lament demonstrate the need for a literary approach.

Those of us who live thousands of years after the completion of the Bible need to pay special attention to the literary approach because the literary conventions employed by the ancient Hebrew storytellers and poets are not necessarily the same as those that we are used to in our own culture. Thus, we must be self-conscious as we consider the literary aspect of the biblical text.

As we engage in literary analysis, we must be careful to avoid the pitfalls that are described above. Such an approach to the biblical text will not treat the literary approach as a new paradigm that totally replaces past approaches to the text, but rather will consider it a part of the historical-grammatical approach, to be used alongside historical and theological methods. Such an approach will study the conventions that the poets and storytellers used to relate to us God's message. It is now time to move beyond description and evaluation to a presentation of a productive literary approach.

G. Literary Conventions

1. *Genre.* Genre may well be the literary concept most important to the interpretive task. Genres are classes of texts grouped according to similarities in structure, content, mood, or setting. Authors guide their readers about the proper way to understand their message by means of genre signals. Looking at the same issue from the perspective of the reader, we observe that genre evokes certain reading strategies.

The constraints that genre places on writers and readers does not even have to occur on a conscious level. Authors want to write something like previous texts that become their model. Readers who have experience with similar sounding or looking texts know how they are intended to be understood, at least in broad terms. Thus, a text that begins "once upon a time" will trigger an association with other works that open with the same words, and the text will be understood to be a fairy tale. Fairy tales will not be understood as works of history, but will be expected to have a moral teaching of some sort. A biblical text that is introduced by the literary term "parable" will also evoke certain expectations and reading strategies on the part of the reader. All texts evoke such reactions from interpreters.

Genre, therefore, is both a literary convention as well as an important component of the literary context that must be taken into account as words are studied and dictionary meanings are derived.

As important a concept as genre is, we do not have time to develop this idea extensively. (See the insightful comments on genre in K. Vanhoozer, "Language, Literature, Hermeneutics, and Biblical Theology" in the present volume.) However, for further study the interested reader may be referred to other works by the present writer (T. Longman III, 1987, 76-83; 1991, 3-21; L. Ryken and T. Longman III, 363-66, 434-38, 463-64.)

Since genre is a fluid concept, working at different levels of abstraction or generalization from a particular text, we could proceed from this point in a variety of ways. We could, for instance, survey the genres of the Bible by looking at history, law, wisdom, prophecy, gospel, epistle, and apocalyptic, but reasons of space, we chose instead to focus on a broader level and look at two genres of biblical literature and their literary conventions: prose and poetry.

The OT presents the reader with two writing strategies that call for different interpretive approaches: prose and poetry. Poetry is a comparably more artificial language than prose, that is, artificial to everyday speech. It is more self-conscious language, which means that more thought is put into how something is said as well as what is said. Notice that the comparison between prose and poetry is couched in quantitative and not qualitative terms. Prose and poetry are not different in kind. There are no traits that are found in the one and not the other. Poetry has an intensified and heightened use of imagery, parallelism, and other literary devices. The lack of a defining trait has led Kugel to deny the distinction between poetry and prose, but we believe his reaction to be extreme.

2. *Prose and poetry*. We will now proceed to define the major conventions that characterize prose and then poetry.

(a) *OT Prose*. Prose in the Bible, as in English literature, is written in sentences, grouped in paragraphs. Most of the prose in the Bible is narrative prose. Another way to describe this is to say that the Bible is full of stories. All stories have four elements, which we will now discuss: plot, character, setting, and point of view.

(i) Plot. The plot of a literary narrative is the succession of events, usually motivated by conflict, that generates suspense and leads to a conclusion. Abrams calls it a "structure of actions" (137) and points out that plot analysis is not a simple recitation of the episodes that make up a story, but happens "only when we say how this is related to that" (ibid.). In other words, the reader must decide how each part contributes to the whole. This narrative trait of plot is so pervasive that readers will automatically attribute causation between narrative episodes even if they are not explicit in the text itself. Thus, while one is analyzing narrative in the Bible, it is illuminating to describe the plot. One way of proceeding is to identify the central plot conflict of a book and then see how the different episodes of the story fit into the progression toward the resolution of the conflict.

I will illustrate this by a brief look at the book of Jonah. The central conflict of the book of Jonah becomes obvious in the first three verses. God gives Jonah a command to preach in the city of Nineveh, and Jonah refuses by hopping on a boat that is sailing in the opposite direction. Jonah's reluctance, motivated by an intense hatred of Assyria that is rooted in his ethnocentrism, is contrasted to God's concern for his creatures in that city.

Four major scenes in the book constitute the plot and correspond roughly to the four chapters of Jonah as they are divided in the English Bible (the Hebrew differs). These are Jonah's flight from God in a boat, God's rescue of Jonah by means of a great fish, Jonah's preaching in Nineveh, and Jonah's final conflict with God after God spares Nineveh. As we will see, the four episodes are easily distinguished by means of their different settings.

The first episode heightens the conflict between God and Jonah and thus heightens the tension that the reader feels. Jonah is trying to get as far away from Nineveh as he possibly can. In so doing, he is attempting to flee from God as well, something that he soon finds impossible to do. God's long arm reaches out and causes the sailors to reluctantly throw Jonah overboard.

The second episode illustrates how impotent Jonah is as he stands against God and his purposes. God rescues Jonah from certain death by causing a large fish to swallow him. This fish provides Jonah with a safe, if admittedly uncomfortable, haven until God delivers him onto the shore. Though undignified, his arrival on the shore points him toward Nineveh, and there he resignedly goes.

The third episode shows Jonah doing God's will. The brevity of Jonah's sermon as reported in the book highlights his reluctance: "Forty more days and Nineveh will be overturned." In spite of the fact that he provides no door of hope to the Ninevites, they repent and are spared. Jonah's reaction to Nineveh's deliverance shows that the conflict with God is not resolved. Jonah fusses and fumes over God's deliverance of Nineveh, presumably because God shows compassion to a people who have oppressed and tormented Israel.

But God has the last word. The book closes with God's question to Jonah: "Should I not be concerned about that great city?" Although we never hear Jonah's response, the question is rhetorical, and thus the reader is left with the obvious conclusion that God's way of compassion and mercy is the right one, while Jonah is satirized as a narrow-minded Israelite (see below).

(ii) Characters. A second important aspect of the analysis is the examination of the characters who populate a story. The close association between plot and character may be observed in the fact that it is the characters who generate the actions that make up the plot, thus leading to the famous statement from Henry James, "What is character but the determination of incident? What is incident but the illustration of character?" (quoted in S. Chatman, 112-13).

Characters are like real people in that we can know them only partially and never exhaustively. Our knowledge of real people comes through our experience of them in their actions and conversation. We learn about the characters of a story in much the same way—by their actions and by speech (both the speeches they make and those that are made about them).

Our understanding of a character is controlled and mediated by the narrator, who may even be one of the characters. The narrator may choose to reveal much about a character, in which case the character is complex or round; or the narrator may choose to tell us very little about a character, who is therefore flat. There are even some characters about whom we learn next to nothing. They appear to perform some specialized function in the plot and are simply agents (A. Berlin, 1983, 31-32).

Other technical language that for some reason is not used as frequently in biblical studies, though it is more common in literary studies, is that of protagonist, antagonist, and foil. The protagonist is the main character of the story and the one through whose perspective we follow most of the action. The antagonist is the one who stands against the protagonist, blocking his or her desires. The foil is a character who serves as a contrast to other characters, most often the protagonist (L. Ryken, 1987, 72).

Jonah is the protagonist of the OT story. We are not sympathetic toward him, even though we may identify with him. God and the Ninevites (an unlikely pair) are Jonah's antagonists. The sailors on the boat on which Jonah tries to flee from God are a foil to Jonah, because, though they are pagans, they show respect and fear toward Jonah's God.

Jonah and God are round, complex characters, whereas the Ninevites as a whole constitute a single "corporate" flat character, and the king of Nineveh (or even the great fish for that matter) is an agent.

Since E. Auerbach (21-22) and much later Alter (1981, 114-30), the biblical narrator's reticence about such things as character development is well documented. The biblical text does little by way of direct commentary and description of its characters. When details are given, they are therefore of special significance to the story. Thus Samson's hair, Saul's height, Bathsheba's beauty, and Job's righteousness are all crucial elements of their story. Most of our knowledge of a character comes indirectly through actions and dialogue.

Biblical narrative does not speak explicitly of the characters' personality or the motivations of their actions; therefore, the reader must enter into the process and interpret the gaps of the narrative. This is not as subjective as it sounds. That David does not go out to war in the spring (2 Sam 11:1) is clearly a negative statement about the king, a fact that becomes evident because his leisurely presence in Jerusalem leads to such catastrophic consequences (chs. 11-12). Perhaps the best advice is Ryken's when he instructs Bible readers to "simply get to know the characters as thoroughly as the details allow you to" (Ryken, 1987, 75).

(iii) Setting. The setting of a story is the space in which the characters perform the actions that constitute the plot. It is important to recognize, however, that setting performs more than one function in a narrative. Much of the narrative of the Bible is highly literary prose with a historical intention. It is therefore not surprising that biblical authors give us details about a specific physical setting in biblical literature in that it imparts reality to the story. We can picture the action of the story in our minds as that action is related to well-known ancient settings. But setting contributes more to a story than providing a simple backdrop for the action. Other functions include generating the atmosphere or mood of a narrative and contributing to the story's meaning and structure. Let me illustrate these three functions of narrative with another brief look at the book of Jonah.

Although we are not told where Jonah is when he first hears the word of the Lord, we are told that he flees to the port town of Joppa. He is fleeing from Nineveh by setting sail on the Mediterranean. These locations are all historical places well known from antiquity. They are not the fabrication of the author's imagination. Their use in the narrative implies the reality of the story.

The book of Jonah further provides illustration of the other two functions of setting—generating atmosphere and contributing to the meaning of a story. God calls Jonah to go to Nineveh, and eventually he does go there. Important to the story is the fact that Nineveh was the major city of Assyria, the ruthless nation that oppressed Israel and many other small nation states for over a century. After receiving the call to go to Nineveh, Jonah flees in the opposite direction. His westward rather than eastward direction tells the reader much about Jonah's state of mind toward God without the need for direct authorial commentary.

Finally, in one of the most spectacular settings of any biblical story, Jonah speaks with God from the belly of a large fish in the depths of the sea. This setting shows God's control even over the sea and its monsters, elements that are often found, especially in poetic settings, as representative of the forces of chaos and the absence of God. By having Jonah speak to God from the belly of the fish, the biblical author makes it clear that Jonah can find no place on earth to escape God (Ps 139).

We must realize that in the historical narrative that dominates the narrative genre of the Bible, the author's choice of setting was usually restricted. Authors simply placed action where it actually occurred. Of course these authors controlled the selectivity of detail in the description of settings, requiring the reader to pay close attention to these textual signals.

(iv) Point of view. This last narrative trait is closely related to the presence of a narrative voice in the story. The narrator is the one who controls the story. His is the voice through whom we hear about the action and the people of the narrative. The narrator's point of view is the perspective through which we observe and evaluate everything connected with the story. In short, the narrator is a device used by authors to shape and guide how the reader responds to the characters and events of the story.

Literary critics make some basic distinctions in point of view, starting with first- and third-person narrative. In first-person narrative, the narrator is also a character in the story. This kind of narrative appears infrequently in the Bible, but it may be illustrated by parts of Nehemiah and the "we" passages in Acts. By far the most frequent type of narrative is that of the third-person narrator, whom Rhoad and Michie (3-4) insist does not figure in the events of the story. The narrator speaks in the third person; is not bound by time or space in the telling of the story; is an implied invisible presence in every scene, capable of being anywhere to recount the action; displays full omniscience by narrating the thoughts, feelings, or sensory experiences of many characters; often turns from the story to give direct asides to the reader, explaining a custom or translating a word or commenting on the story; and narrates the story from one overarching ideological point of view. As these and other authors have pointed out, such a narrative strategy gives the impression of an all-knowing mind standing behind the stories of the Bible—a mind that in the context of the canon must be associated with God himself.

Thus it is not surprising that the Bible knows nothing of the so-called unreliable narrator. In the words of Sternberg, "The Bible always tells the truth in that its narrator is absolutely and straightforwardly reliable" (52). As he goes on to note, the narrator, while telling the truth, often does not tell the whole truth, and this results in the characteristic brevity of biblical narration. This narrative reticence produces gaps in the story and thus both invites the reader into a participatory role in the interpretive process and protects the mystery of God and his ways in the world.

(v) Conclusion. The narratives of the Bible are thus both similar to and different from contemporary narratives. As the past few years have abundantly demonstrated, we may, as a result, benefit in our understanding of the stories of the Bible by taking a literary approach to them. In doing so, however, we must never lose sight of the other dimensions of the biblical text, notably its historical and theological significance. With this reminder, however, it is possible to bracket those functions for pedagogical purposes and to concentrate for the moment on the impressive narrative strategies of the individual books that make up the Bible.

(b) *OT poetry.*[*] While there is overlap between ancient biblical and familiar Western poetry, there are also significant discontinuities. Each culture has its own poetic code. As a result, there are strange as well as familiar features awaiting the modern reader of the poetry of the Bible.

Our discussion of these traits will be in two parts. (i) We will examine the primary traits of biblical poetry—primary because they occur consistently, almost pervasively in the poetry. (ii) The secondary traits, to be discussed in the next section, are secondary only because they occur more occasionally. The distinction between primary and secondary poetic conventions is a distinction of degree and not of kind. There is no single trait or cluster of traits that defines Hebrew poetry as over against

*This section on biblical poetry is taken from Ryken and Longman, *The Complete Literary Guide to the Bible*, 1993, 80-91.

prose. This explains why it is occasionally difficult (for instance, in some passages in Hos or Jer) to categorize a text as either prose or poetry. It used to be thought that meter was such a genre-identifying trait, but we will see how meter has proved to be an elusive category in the analysis of biblical poetry.

(i) Primary traits. The most obvious trait of Hebrew poetry is its terseness. This characteristic leaps out at even the beginning reader of the Bible by virtue of formatting conventions of English translations. With few exceptions, most English translations put a single poetic colon on a line. The result is a large amount of white space on the page.

The fundamental unit of Hebrew poetry is the line, not the sentence, as in prose. The line is composed of two or more short clauses that are often called cola (sing.: colon) by biblical scholars. The most frequent line has two cola (a bicolon), each one containing three words. Lines with one colon (monocolon) or three cola (tricolon) are not unusual, nor are cola with two or four words. It is, however, very rare to find a poetic line that consists of more than four words.

That the lines are short or terse is another way of expressing the fact that Hebrew poetry, like most poetry, is compact; it says a lot using few words. This compactness is the result of four features.

First, Hebrew poetry uses few conjunctions. Even the simple conjunction "and," the direct object marker, and the relative pronoun are only rarely used and are often suspected of being late prosaic insertions (see F. I. Andersen and D. N. Freedman, 60-66). This feature is blurred a little in English translations, which will often add a conjunction to help the reader along. For instance, in Nah 2:5, "He summons his picked troops, yet they stumble along the way," the conjunction "yet" is supplied and is not in the Hebrew text.

The second characteristic of biblical poetry that leads to terseness is parallelism, which I will describe fully below. There is a definite tendency toward a rough isosyllablism in biblical poetry that leads to terseness in parallelism. By this I mean that cola within a parallel line will normally have an equal or near equal number of syllables.

Closely related is the third source of terseness, ellipsis. Ellipsis is the tendency to drop a major element out of the second colon of a poetic line with the expectation that the reader will carry over that element from the first colon. Ellipsis (see W. G. E. Watson, 303-4) is most common with the verb and may be illustrated by Hos 5:8: "Blow the trumpet in Gibeah, the horn in Ramah."

The last source of compact expression in the poetry of the Bible, also to be discussed fully below, is imagery. Imagery stimulates the imagination by embodying multiple meanings in concise form. An image not only triggers a train of thinking about a subject but also evokes an emotional response.

The second primary trait mentioned above is parallelism. The near repetition that characterizes the poetic line in Hebrew poetry has long been observed. It was named parallelism by Robert Lowth in the eighteenth century, the term borrowed from geometry to describe what he called "a certain conformation of the sentences" in which "equals refer to equals, and opposites to opposites" (Lecture III, quoted in Berlin, 1995, 1).

116

Since Lowth, parallelism has been recognized as the most telltale feature of biblical poetry. Also since Lowth, literary and biblical scholars have emphasized the equivalence between the related cola of a poetic line. This may be illustrated by C. S. Lewis's statement about parallelism that it is "the practice of saying the same thing twice in different words" (11). While Lewis did understand the parallel line to operate according to the principle "the same in the other," his emphasis was on the coherence of the cola, and handbooks on biblical poetry presented an even less balanced statement on the relationship between the cola than he did.

Parallelism has received intense scrutiny over the past few years from biblical and literary scholars (Kugel; Alter, 1985; Berlin, 1985; M. O'Connor; S. Geller). The emerging consensus is that the parallel line is a more subtle literary device than previously thought. The new paradigm for understanding parallelism is development rather than equivalence. The biblical poet is doing more than saying the same thing twice. The second part always nuances the first part in some way. Kugel rightly refuses to replace Lowth's traditional three categories of parallelism (synonymous, antithetic, synthetic) with others. He simply argues that the second colon always contributes to the thought of the first colon, as suggested by his formula "A, what is more B."

The interpreter thus must pause and meditate on a poetic line like the well-known Ps 1:1:

Blessed is the man
who does not walk in the counsel of the wicked
or stand in the way of sinners
or sit in the seat of mockers.

Isolating the verbs in their context, we clearly see a progression of thought in the way that Kugel suggests. All three verbs figuratively relate the person to evil. As he moves from "walk" to "stand" to "sit," the psalmist imagines an ever closer relationship to evil, in other words, a more settled relation with it. In short, parallelism is based simultaneously on the logic of synonymity and the logic of progression; as we move from one line to the next, something is repeated and something is added.

Parallelism is the most frequently occurring literary device in Hebrew poetry. We must keep in mind, however, that not all poetry contains parallelism and that some prose does (e.g. Gen 21:1). Furthermore, though space does not allow a detailed description, recent studies have enlarged our understanding of parallelism beyond the semantic described above and into grammatical and even phonological dimensions (see A. Berlin, 1985; A. S. Cooper).

The fourth trait of Hebrew poetry mentioned above is imagery and figurative language. Imagery is not the exclusive province of poetry, but the frequency and intensity of imagery is heightened in discourse that we normally recognize as poetic. It is, after all, another way to write compactly as well as to increase the emotional impact of a passage.

As M. H. Abrams points out, imagery is an "ambiguous" term (78). He goes on to quote C. Day Lewis, who speaks of imagery as "a picture made out of words." Such pictures are often the result of comparison, the two most common types being metaphor and simile. Simile, on one level, is not even figurative language; it is capable of being understood on a literal level. A simile is a comparison between two things and is

117

marked by the use of "like" or "as." S of Songs 4:1b is a clear example: "Your hair is like a flock of goats descending from Mount Gilead."

Metaphor has long been considered the master image or even the essence of poetry by literary scholars since the time of Aristotle. Metaphor presents a stronger connection between the two objects of comparison and is truly figurative language, as in S of Songs 4:1a: "Your eyes behind your veil are doves." Metaphor catches our attention by the disparity between the two objects and the daring suggestion of similarity, and by so doing the reader explores multiple levels of meaning and experiences the emotional overtones of metaphor. A well-known example comes from the first line of Psalm 23: "The LORD is my shepherd, I shall not want." What does it mean to compare the Lord to a shepherd? To read the image in context, we would immediately suggest that the poem speaks of God's protection, his guidance, and his care. We would stop short, however, if we did not remember that the shepherd image was a well-used royal image in the ANE. Reading the text sympathetically, we would experience assurance and feel comfort even in the midst of danger.

Metaphor and simile do not exhaust the repertory of figurative language in Hebrew. E. W. Bullinger lists hundreds of categories of figurative language. Besides metaphor and simile, Leland Ryken treats at least four figures of speech and gives examples. The first is symbol. "A symbol is a concrete image that points to or embodies other meanings" (1984, 97). Next is hyperbole, "conscious exaggeration for the sake of effect" (Ryken, 1981, 99): "With your help I can advance against a troop; with my God I can scale a wall" (Ps 18:29). Then there is personification, which attributes personality to inanimate objects. The psalmist frequently uses this poetic device in order to demonstrate that all of creation and not just human creation is dependent upon God and owes him praise: "Let the sea resound, and everything in it, the world, and all who live in it" (Ps 98:7). Ryken notes that the poets of Israel use apostrophe in order to express strong emotion. Apostrophe "is direct address to something or someone absent as though the person were present and capable of listening" (Ryken, 1984, 98). He includes among his examples Ps 2:10: "Therefore, you kings, be wise; be warned, you rulers of the earth."

These representative figures of speech should not be taken as a mere list of categories. They are representative of the devices available to the Hebrew poet as he communicated his message with vivid freshness and concreteness. They lend richness of meaning to the poem and seek to evoke a strong emotional response from the reader.

(ii) Secondary traits. Terseness, parallelism, and imagery are the three primary traits of biblical poetry. The acrostic form is a striking example of a secondary poetic device. It stands out because it is so noticeable in the original and because its existence entails an obviously artificial form of the language. An acrostic is a poem in which the first letters of successive lines form a recognizable pattern. While in some poems from ancient times (such as some Babylonian poems) the name of a scribe who copied the text, or perhaps some hidden message, was spelled out in this way, the examples found in the OT all follow the order of the Hebrew alphabet.

There are many examples of acrostics in the Bible. The two most famous are perhaps the so-called Giant Psalm (119), which is broken up into eight-verse stanzas by the acrostic, and the book of Lamentations. In the latter, chs. 1, 2, and 4 follow a verse-by-verse acrostic whereas ch. 3 grasps the letters into three-verse stanzas, all three lines beginning with the relevant letter; ch. 4 is an extended acrostic, each verse being a four-colon stanza and beginning with the relevant letter. One of the more interesting acrostic patterns is found in the first chapter of Nahum. The acrostic covers only half the alphabet and even then skips an occasional letter. Other acrostics in Hebrew occur at Psalms 9, 10, 25, 34, 37, 111, 112, 145; Prov 31:10-31.

The purpose of acrostic form may only be guessed. On the one hand, it may help in the process of memorization. On the other hand, acrostics also communicate a sense of wholeness. As Watson points out, "By using every letter of the alphabet the poet was trying to ensure that his treatment of a particular topic was complete" (198). I would expand this to include the idea that an acrostic imparts a feeling of wholeness to a text. Nahum's first chapter confirms this. This disrupted acrostic occurs in a poem that extols God as the divine Warrior, who disrupts the normal created order. Thus, once again, form supports meaning.

A somewhat neglected secondary convention of Hebrew poetry is the use of stanzas and strophes. Most studies of biblical poetry have concentrated on the level of the parallel line. Little has been done to describe rhetorical patterns that encompass the whole poem. This neglect is due mostly to uncertainty about analysis on this level. Scholars often question if broader patterns exist in biblical poems.

There is no doubt that most poems are unified wholes, but the relationship between the parts is almost always described in terms of content. For instance, grief psalms share a similar structure, by which any individual psalm may be divided in separate parts. Thus Ps 69 may be described in the following way:

Invocation and Initial Plea to God for Help	(vs. 1a)
Complaints	(vv. 1b-4, 7-12, 19-21)
Confession of Sin	(vv. 5-6)
Further Pleas for Help	(vv. 13-18)
Imprecation	(vv. 22-28)
Hymn of Praise	(vv. 30-36)

Each of these sections is composed of at least one and usually more than one parallel line. The question arises as to whether or not it is legitimate to call these broader groupings stanzas and/or strophes. Watson (160-200) has one of the most extensive discussions of this issue, arguing that the answer to this question is affirmative as long as these terms are understood in the broad sense as "units within the poem." Furthermore, as Watson also points out, verse groupings above the level of the individual poetic line are occasionally possible by means of such devices as recurrent refrains (Ps 42-43) and acrostic patterns (Ps 119).

The significance of this discussion is to recognize that the reader can expect biblical poems to have a structure that goes beyond the individual line and encompasses the

119

whole poem. This broader structure is most easily recognized on the level of content but is occasionally supported by elements of style.

Finally, Hebrew poets often play on the sounds of language to achieve poetic effect.

H. Conclusion

One might question the appropriateness of an article on literary analysis in the introduction of a dictionary. One would be hard pressed to find a written text that is less literary, less concerned about its verbal artistry, than a dictionary. However, in the present case, that is not so obvious. This is not to say that special efforts were devoted to the actual writing of the entries. Only in rare cases, and mostly by accident, will an author of an article employ rhetorical strategies in the presentation of his material. However, this project is certainly among the first done by a group of scholars sensitive to the issues of the Bible as literature; it is impossible indeed to be a serious student of the Bible and not be affected by these new insights into the biblical text. Thus, as we studied a Hebrew word to write an entry, we studied it in its multiple *literary* contexts, taking account of the various *genres* in which it appeared. We tried to be sensitive to their use in *parallelism*, noting that parallel words were not equal in meaning, but the second somehow progressed the thought of the first. We also appreciated the *metaphorical* use of the word, when relevant. These and many other literary categories and insights stand behind the conclusions that are here presented in the articles to follow.

BIBLIOGRAPHY

M. H. Abrams, *A Glossary of Literary Terms*, 1981; L. Alonso-Schokel, *Estudios de Poetica Hebraea*, 1963; R. Alter, *The Art of Biblical Narrative*, 1981; idem, *The Art of Biblical Poetry*, 1985; idem, "A Response to Critics," *JSOT* 27, 1983, 113-17; F. I. Andersen and D. N. Freedman, *Hosea*, 1980; E. Auerbach, *Mimesis*, 1953; S. Bar-Efrat, "Some Observations on the Analysis of Structure in Biblical Narrative," *VT* 30, 1980, 154-73; J. Barton, *Reading the Old Testament*, 1984; A. Bach, "Good to the Last Drop: Viewing the Sotah (Numbers 5:11-31) As the Glass Half Empty and Wondering How to View It Half Full," *The New Literary Criticism and the Hebrew Bible*, 26-54; T. K. Beal, "Ideology and Intertextuality: Surplus of Meaning and Controlling the Means of Production," in *Reading Between the Texts: Intertextuality and the Hebrew Bible*, 1992, 27-40; A. Berlin, *Poetics and Interpretation of Biblical Narrative*, 1983; idem, *The Dynamics of Biblical Parallelism*, 1985; J. Calloud, "A Few Comments on Structural Semiotics: Brief Review of a Method and Some Explanations of Procedures," *Semeia* 15, 1979, 50-65; S. Chatman, *Story and Discourse*, 1978; D. J. A. Clines, *I, He, We, and They: A Literary Approach to Isaiah 53*, 1976; idem, "Story and Poem: The Old Testament as Literature and Scripture," *Int* 34, 1980, 115-27; A. Cooper, "Biblical Poetics: A Linguistic Approach," 1976; J. Culler, *Structuralist Poetics*, 1975; J. Derrida, *Of Grammatology*, 1976; idem, *Writings and Difference*, 1978; R. B. Dillard and T. Longman III, *Introduction to the Old Testament*, 1994; J. Cheryl Exum, "Who's Afraid of 'The Endangered Ancestress'?" in *The New Literary Criticism and the Hebrew Bible*, 1993, 91-113; idem and D. J. A. Clines (eds.), *The New Literary Criticism and the Hebrew Bible*, 1993; H. Felperin, *Beyond Deconstruction*, 1985; D. N. Fewell, *Reading Between Texts: Intertextuality and the Hebrew Bible*, 1992; J. P. Fokkelman, *Narrative Art in Genesis*, 1975; idem, *Narrative Art and Poetry in the Books of Samuel*, 1981; S. Geller, *Parallelism in Early Biblical Poetry*, 1979; D. M. Gunn, *The Story of King David: Genre and Interpretation*, 1978; idem, *The Fate of King Saul*, 1980; W. Iser, *The Implied Reader*, 1974; F. Jameson,

The Political Unconscious: Narrative As a Socially Symbolic Act, 1981; T. J. Keegan, "Biblical Criticism and the Challenge of Postmodernism," *Biblical Interpretation* 3, 1995, 1-14; J. Kugel, *The Idea of Biblical Parallelism,* 1981; V. B. Leitch, *Deconstructive Criticism: An Advanced Introduction,* 1983; F. Lentricchia, *After the New Criticism,* 1980; C. S. Lewis, *Reflections on the Psalms,* 1961; V. Philips Long, *The Reign and Rejection of King Saul: A Case for Literary and Theological Coherence,* 1989; idem, *The Art of Biblical History,* 1994; T. Longman III, *Literary Approaches to Biblical Interpretation,* 1987; idem, *Fictional Akkadian Autobiography,* 1991; E. V. McKnight, *The Bible and the Reader: An Introduction to Literary Criticism,* 1985; P. Miscall, *The Workings of Old Testament Narrative,* 1983; J. Muilenburg, "Beyond Form Criticism," *JBL,* 1969, 1-18; C. Norris, *Deconstruction: Theory and Practice,* 1982; M. O'Connor, *Hebrew Verse Structure,* 1980; D. Patte and J. F. Parker, "A Structural Exegesis of Genesis 2 and 3," *Semeia* 18, 1980, 55-75; R. Polzin, *Biblical Structuralism,* 1977; V. S. Poythress, "Structuralism and Biblical Studies," *JETS* 21, 1978, 218-31; S. Prickett, *Words and the Word: Language, Poetics and Biblical Interpretation,* 1986; D. Rhoads and D. Michie, *Mark As Story: The Introduction to the Narrative of a Gospel,* 1982; L. Ryken, *How to Read the Bible as Literature,* 1984; idem, *Words of Delight: A Literary Introduction to the Bible,* 1987; L. Ryken and T. Longman III, *A Complete Literary Guide to the Bible,* 1993; M. Shapiro, *The Sense of Grammar,* 1983; M. Sternberg, *The Poetics of Biblical Narrative,* 1985; T. Todorov, *The Fantastic: A Structural Approach to a Literary Genre,* 1981; J. P. Tompkins (ed.), *Reader Response Criticism,* 1980; H. Aram Veeser, *The New Historicism,* 1989; W. G. E. Watson, *Classical Hebrew Poetry,* 1984.

Tremper Longman III

6. Narrative Criticism: The Theological Implications Of Narrative Techniques

The literary qualities of OT narrative have long been recognized by scholars and general readers alike. In the 1980s four books were published that marked a significant advance on previous scholarly studies of OT narrative: R. Alter, *The Art of Biblical Narrative*; A. Berlin, *Poetics and Interpretation of Biblical Narrative*; M. Sternberg, *The Poetics of Biblical Narrative*; S. Bar-Efrat, *Narrative Art in the Bible*. Taken together, they provide a sophisticated and wide-ranging treatment of the workings of OT narrative. I term this approach "narrative criticism." Alter and Sternberg have since written further on this subject, and many others have followed their general approach, but I will use the four books listed above as the basis for this essay, since they provide a convenient reference point as well as being readable treatments of the topic (Sternberg's book is, however, longer and more complex than the other three).

Narrative criticism represents only one out of many literary approaches currently being applied to OT narrative. For a sampling of some others, among them reader-response criticism, deconstruction, materialist criticism, feminist criticism, intertextual approaches, see D. N. Fewell (ed.), *Reading Between Texts*; J. C. Exum and D. J. A. Clines (eds.), *The New Literary Criticism and the Hebrew Bible*; D. M. Gunn and D. N. Fewell, *Narrative in the Hebrew Bible*. Significant aspects of the work of Alter and Sternberg in particular have been criticized by scholars writing out of some of these other approaches: D. M. Gunn, "Reading Right"; B. O. Long, "The 'New' Biblical Poetics." Some of these criticisms will be picked up in what follows. Narrative criticism, however, remains full of suggestive insights, particularly in the way it links narrative techniques to a worldview or theology underlying the narrative.

The main thesis of narrative criticism is that OT narrative is in general written using certain recurrent literary techniques, which become apparent when one examines the following main features of OT narrative: its use of patterns of repetition and variation, its presentation of narrative events out of chronological sequence, and its selectivity in what the reader is told. Most narratives, ancient and modern, fictional and nonfictional, display these features to some extent: In order to create a coherent narrative, one generally has to select and reorder events, and also bring out similarities and differences between them. The claim of narrative criticism is that the writers of OT narrative exploit what were in effect the requirements of their chosen literary form resourcefully and in many ways: in order to provide interpretations and evaluations of the events narrated, to characterize the human participants in these events, to create ambiguity and suspense, and to influence the reader's response to what is described.

In what follows I will introduce these techniques more fully and then discuss their implications for OT theology. As well as working through some OT examples, I give further OT references that readers can follow up for themselves.

1. *Repetition and variation; cross-textual allusion.* An immediate impression for any reader is that OT narrative is at points repetitive. If we are at first tempted to dismiss this feature as a literary defect (arising, perhaps, from the vicissitudes of oral transmission, or accidentally created by the editorial combination of sources), closer examination suggests the reverse. For one thing, though there are many cases of exact repetition, there are as many where one of the repeated elements is given in a varied

form. And in general, in most cases of exact or varied repetition, it is possible to argue that we are dealing, not with a more or less accidental literary epiphenomenon, but with a deliberate authorial technique. Some of the uses of repetition in OT narrative are set out in what follows. See also the discussions of Alter (1980, 88-113) and Sternberg (1985, 365-440).

Repetition can take several forms. Individual words may be repeated so as to stress a key idea (e.g., the use of "sight," "vision," and "blindness" in 1 Sam 3; the use of "listen," "obey," "voice," "word" in 1 Sam 15); a series of actions or words may recur (e.g., the patterning of the days of creation in Gen 1). On a larger scale there are cases where entire incidents have a similar pattern (e.g., the account of the crossing of the Jordan in Josh 3-4 seems to be modeled on the account of the Exodus in Exod 14).

Exact or near-exact repetition can suggest such things as stability and order, inevitability, unanimity, and obedience. The patterning of the days in Gen 1 suggests God's firm control over the stages of creation. In 2 Kgs 1 the message Elijah receives to take to Ahaziah is quoted three times: as given by God to Elijah (vv. 3-4); as given by Ahaziah's messengers to Ahaziah (v. 6); as given by Elijah himself to Ahaziah (v. 16). The message is each time given in unchanged form, suggesting that for all Ahaziah's attempts to threaten Elijah, he cannot escape the death prophesied (cf. v. 17). Finally, Num 7 is perhaps the extreme case of unvaried repetition: Only the names of the tribes and their representatives change as each tribe duly brings its offering for the tabernacle.

Repetition with variation can suggest a different range of ideas: contrast or conflict, a significant development in the narrative, a climactic moment in the narrative, or an incident that in some way overturns or parodies an earlier incident. Thus, when Elisha at 2 Kgs 2:14 parts the Jordan with his cloak, as Elijah has just done before (v. 8), this suggests both continuity (God will be with him as with Elijah) and change (Elijah has gone, and Elisha is to carry on his work). In Judg 20 the different preparations for the third day's fighting against Benjamin suggest that it will end in victory, not defeat (compare vv. 18, 22-23, and 26-29; note also how the tone in which the Israelites address God becomes increasingly anguished as the fighting drags on without success, vv. 18, 23, 28). Readers may also like to study the repetitions and variations in the treatment of the successive plagues in Exod 7-11. As regards overturning and parody, large sections of Judg 17-21 (which have as their theme anarchy in premonarchic Israel) can be seen as travesties of earlier narratives: The Danite destruction of Laish is a travesty of the conquest narratives in Josh (God has not commanded the destruction, the killing of the inhabitants is portrayed as an atrocity, and the Danites institute idolatrous worship in the territory they have conquered); Judg 19:15-30 reminds the reader of Sodom and Gomorrah in Gen 19:4-13, with the difference that in Judg 19 it is the Israelites who are engaging in blatant wickedness; the ambush of Gibeah in Judg 20:29-48 reminds one of the ambush against Ai in Josh 8, except that now Israelites are fighting against Israelites. In each case, comparison between Judges and the earlier narrative underscores the theme of wickedness in Israel.

OT narrative seems at points explicitly to encourage this kind of cross-textual allusion. We may cite, for example, God's self-description in Exod as "the God of Abraham, Isaac, and Jacob" (Exod 3:6; cf. Deut 1:8). In a similar way, the recurrent "cyclical formulae" of Judg (3:7-11; 4:1-2; etc.) and "regnal formulae" of Kgs (1 Kgs

11:41-43; 14:19-20; etc.) can be seen, not as evidence of a stereotyping mentality, but as an invitation to the reader to compare and contrast the activities of earlier and later judges/kings, noting recurring themes and new developments.

Repetition with variation can take subtle forms, particularly when it involves whole episodes. Gen 37 (the selling of Joseph into Egypt) and Gen 38 (the episode of Judah and Tamar) appear to be separate narratives; but both culminate in a scene where someone is asked to identify objects linked to goats (37:22-32, 31; 38:17-18, 25-26). This similarity of plot suggests a pattern running through seemingly unconnected events: Gen 38 is clearly concerned with the survival of the line of one of Jacob's sons; but Gen 37 turns out to have been no less concerned with this theme, for it is Joseph's presence in Egypt that will make it possible for them to survive famine. God, the narrator hints, is at work in the events of Gen 37 and 38, though in a way that will only be clearly discernible later on (a point explicitly made at 45:5; 50:20). Compare also Gen 27 compared with 29:15-30, from which it emerges that Jacob suffers a deception just like that he perpetrated against his father; 1 Sam 24-6 (discussed by R. P. Gordon), in which the Nabal episode of ch. 25 turns out to develop the same themes that run through chs. 24 and 26, in particular the theme of David's vindication against a hostile kingly or king-like (see 25:36) figure.

All these uses of repetition may be termed forms of *implicit commentary:* The narrator uses repetition, variation, and patterning to emphasize points, suggests connections between events, and hints at interpretations and evaluations; but in none of the cases discussed does he explicitly state what he thinks is going on. Instead, the reader has to compare, contrast, and interpret what the narrator has no more than suggestively juxtaposed. At many points OT narrative also provides explicit interpretations and evaluations of people, actions, and events; but it may be said that one of the most fundamental features of OT narrative is an apparent reticence which, when probed, resolves itself into a sharply focused, though unstated, commentary on the events narrated. See further Bar-Efrat (23-45) for a discussion of the difference between "overt" and "covert" narrators.

The frequent reticence of OT narrative does, of course, often leave more than one interpretative option open in repetition and variation, as in other aspects of OT narrative we shall examine. While we may sometimes be confident in identifying and interpreting small- or large-scale patterns of repetition/variation (because of the number or character of similar elements, or because of other, contextual factors), on other occasions we may be more hesitant: Is there a connection between (for example) two incidents, and, if so, what does it mean? And why these two incidents in particular? Are other connections not possible? P. D. Miscall, for example, investigates Gen-2 Kgs using a deliberately loose model of "narrative analogy." According to him, all sorts of links may be made between all kinds of texts. The effect is to create so many intertextual interconnections that ultimately the procedure breaks down; all texts come to say much the same as other texts, and in this general indeterminacy of meaning, any attempt to trace focused implicit commentary is undermined (see also Fewell, for other versions of this approach). These are somewhat extreme forms of the principle of repetition and variation, partly deriving from a view according to which readers (not writers) generate any meanings a text may have and hence are at liberty to compare any

124

text with any other; on this view it is scarcely relevant whether or not the writer may have had more limited cross-textual connections in mind.

To many readers this approach will seem arbitrary. It must be acknowledged, however, that it has rightly identified a certain "open-endedness" in the surface of OT narrative; this can sometimes be resolved, but not always so. See, for example, the reference to the milk cows lowing as they bring the Lord's ark to Beth Shemesh (1 Sam 6:12). Is this simply a realistic detail? Alter (1992, 101-6) wonders whether the narrator means to produce a strange resonance with the narrative of the birth of Samuel: As the cows are unable to give their calves milk (hence their lowing), so Hannah, having weaned Samuel, has given him to the Lord's service (1:24-28), a sacrifice as costly in its own way as that which the cows endure (6:14). Does the narrator intend to suggest this train of thought? It is hard to say. The suggestive, allusive style of OT narrative does not leave every end neatly tied up.

2. *Narration and dialogue.* Dialogue is an important part of OT narrative (Alter, 1980, 63-87). A significant event in OT narrative is most usually presented in the form of a scene that contains spoken words. Judg 1:11-15 and 1 Kgs 9:10-14 are good examples of scenes that contain dialogue, though they could have been differently composed. Probably 75 percent of this dialogue is spoken by men or women (the remainder by God). It is in itself significant that so much space is given to human words (and thus feelings, motives, and views).

Dialogue in OT narrative has much in common with the patterns of repetition and variation discussed above. Implicit commentary is again involved, but here the issues raised are those of viewpoint, knowledge, and motive. The narrator juxtaposes spoken words of two or more characters, or spoken words and his own third-person discourse. As in most narratives, the narrator generally presents himself as reliable, able to tell the reader what is going on in various locations, and able to say what people, and even God, are thinking (Bar-Efrat, 17-23; Sternberg, 1985, 58-83). The spoken words of the human characters, in contrast, are not necessarily to be taken at face value: Characters may be telling the truth or lying; they may say what they think, or they may hide their feelings; they may twist facts so as to influence people; their words may be colored by a particular attitude or may reveal a misunderstanding; subsequent events may put their words in a new light. Some further evaluation of spoken words is almost always necessary (Sternberg, 1985, 129-31).

It is usually the reader who must make this evaluation, for the narrator is generally sparing in evaluative comment. Typically dialogue is introduced with nondirective formulae, such as "he said," "she answered," rather than more explicit phrases such as "he lied," "they disagreed," "she replied evasively," and "they retorted contemptuously." Falsehood, disagreement, evasion, or contempt may be present, but the reader has to deduce this by comparing spoken word with spoken word, or with the narrator's discourse. Hence dialogue can work on two or more levels, a bland-seeming surface parting to reveal more complex motives and attitudes in the characters and sharp comment on the part of the narrator (readers who wish to see how far this procedure can be taken may consult Sternberg's study of Gen 23, "Double Cave, Double Talk").

OT narrative in general appears to delight in the play between viewpoints, as if to stress the bias and limitation of human perceptions. Even third-person narration, which it might be supposed gives solely the narrator's perspective, sometimes presents events, not as they appear to the narrator, but as they are perceived by one of the characters. Such shifts of viewpoint are particularly common in descriptions of personal encounters (Exod 3:2-4; Judg 19:16-17; Ruth 3:8-9). For a discussion of this point and of the ways in which shifts of viewpoint may be marked, see Bar-Efrat, 36-39; Berlin, 59-64, 72-76. The following are examples of play between narration and dialogue. In Gen 16:4-5, Sarah's complaint to Abraham about Hagar in v. 5 is shown to be justly founded by the narrator's words in v. 4; the narrator supports Sarah's claim that Hagar has despised her (though the vehemence with which she attacks Abraham is hers alone). In 50:16-17, Joseph's brothers, fearing revenge from him, attribute to Jacob words that he is never recorded as having said, but which are at points similar to the words in which they themselves express their fear in v. 15 (v. 15, "all the wrongs we did to him"; v. 17, "the wrongs they committed in treating you so badly"). The narrator thereby suggests that they have invented the words they put into the dead Jacob's mouth. In 1 Kgs 21:2-6 Naboth's response to Ahab ("The LORD forbid that I should give you the inheritance of my fathers," v. 3, repeated by the narrator in v. 4) is polemically truncated by Ahab when he reports it to Jezebel, and it becomes "I will not give you my vineyard" (v. 6), as though Naboth had refused out of unmotivated spite (Gideon similarly twists the words of the officials of Succoth in Judg 8: cf. vv. 5-6 and v. 15). In Judg 18:7-10 the narrator stresses how remote and defenseless Laish is (v. 7), but the Danite spies give an unsympathetic description that dwells on the prosperity of Laish and the ease with which it can be conquered (vv. 9-10). The spies' viewpoint diverges yet further from the narrator's at the end of v. 10, where they confidently state that God has given them this land, a claim that the narrator nowhere validates (cf. in this regard 17:13). See also Sternberg, 1985, 390-400, and G. W. Savran.

Sternberg and Alter view the contrast noted above between reliable narrator and unreliable characters as fundamental (e.g., Sternberg, 1985, 84-99); for them the narrator's reliability suggests God's role as omniscient judge of human words and deeds (not least in the way in which, like God, the narrator often appears to withhold judgment). This view has been questioned. Gunn has drawn attention to seeming contradictions, that appear to undermine narratorial reliability (1990, 56-57). Further, is God always portrayed as omniscient in OT narrative? Some texts might suggest not (Gen 18:20-21; 22:12; cf. Long, 81-82). However, as Gunn and Fewell note (1993, 54), a scale in which information given by the narrator is usually more reliable than that given by the characters is a useful rule of thumb in reading OT narrative. In general, the suggestion that OT narrative style portrays human history as unfolding before the gaze of God seems a fruitful one.

Dialogue is also one of the chief means of characterization in OT narrative. Typically, two characters will be contrasted in what they say, how they say it, whether they speak at length or briefly, and the extent to which one of them dominates a dialogue. See, for example, the differing dynamics of the following dialogues: between Jacob and Esau in Gen 25:29-34; Jacob and Laban in 31:25-44; Micah and the Danites in Judg 18:21-26; Saul and David in 1 Sam 24:8-16; Paltiel and Abner in 2 Sam 3:13-16; Michal and David in 6:20-23; Nathan, Bathsheba, and David in 1 Kgs 1; Elijah and Obadiah in 18:8-15.

3. *Selectivity, dischronologous presentation.* As in all narrative, so in the OT the presentation of events is controlled by a narrator. Sometimes his presence is obvi-

ous: He gives information in asides (Judg 20:27b-28a; 1 Sam 9:9), gives clear explanations for events (Judg 14:4; 1 Kgs 12:15), and passes unambiguous judgments on them (Judg 17:6; 2 Sam 11:27). On other occasions he is less explicit, linking events but leaving the reader to deduce the connections between them (Gen 15:1; 2 Sam 15:1), proceeding by means of hints rather than plain statements, as in many of the examples given in the preceding sections. OT narrators are selective in what they choose to reveal: Circumstantial details are rare; topography is not described, unless important for the plot (Gen 29:2-3; 1 Sam 17:1-3); similarly with physical appearance and clothing (Gen 27:11; Judg 3:15-17; 2 Sam 13:18-19).

It is always worth asking what the narrator describes at length and what he passes over briefly: "Narrative time" (the time the narrator takes to describe each event) and "narrated time" (the length of time events are said to have taken) usually differ greatly in OT (see 2 Sam 13:23 and 38; Bar-Efrat, 141-54). An event on which the narrator dwells for a long time is generally significant. Thus in Gen 24, the meeting between Abraham's servant and Rebekah is told twice, and in full, to emphasize that God's hand can be seen in this event (see vv. 27 and 48; cf. Sternberg's treatment of the chapter, 1985, 131-52). A variation of this technique is when the narrator builds up to a significant or climactic event simply by delaying it: Judg 20:29-41 delays the moment when the Benjaminites realize they are doomed; 1 Sam 9:1-17 delays the meeting between Saul and Samuel (cf. 2 Sam 18:19-32).

Further, events are not always presented in chronological order. A piece of information relating to the past may be withheld until the point at which it is most relevant (1 Kgs 11:14-25), or when it suggests a connection between two events: In 1 Sam 23:6-14 it emerges that Abiathar brought an ephod to David after the massacre at Nob (1 Sam 22); but we only learn this when David uses it to escape from Saul, suggesting the thought that Saul's mad violence is rebounding upon him (M. Weiss, 187-88).

4. *Ambiguity; persuasion.* In connection with narratorial selectivity, Sternberg speaks of the Bible's "maneuvering between the truth and the whole truth," noting that OT narrative can vary greatly in how much the reader is told, and what questions are left unresolved (1985, 56; cf. 163-66). There is always the possibility that a later event will throw new light on earlier events.

Men and women are sometimes portrayed in a way that leaves it unclear what is going through their minds. 2 Sam 11 is thoroughly ambiguous as to how much Uriah knows or suspects about what has been going on between David and Bathsheba and how much David suspects about what Uriah knows (Sternberg, 1985, 190-213). David's motives in 1 Sam 18 are left opaque in contrast to Saul's (Alter, 1980, 115-19, part of a longer treatment of the presentation of David in 1 and 2 Sam, [115-30]). And what does Bathsheba think when she enters King David's chamber and sees Abishag ministering to him (1 Kgs 1:15)? The narrator records the detail, but does not describe Bathsheba's feelings. More generally, the behavior of human characters is not entirely predictable: After fasting for his son's life, David can accept his death with a resignation that startles his slaves (2 Sam 12:15-23); the "wise" Solomon can turn to folly (1 Kgs 11:1-8); the "righteous" Noah can get drunk (Gen 9:20-28); after a life full of strife and turmoil Jacob can reach a resigned and almost saintly old age (chs. 48-49); Moses dies with all his faculties intact (Deut 34:7); David dies a weak and indecisive old man (1 Kgs 1). Alter is correct to speak of an "abiding mystery" in the OT's depiction of human character (1980, 126).

By presenting events selectively the narrator influences the reader's responses. The same is true of the order in which he relates material facts. A fact revealed at a point when it does not seem relevant to the ongoing narrative (i.e., "too early" from the standpoint of strict chronology) can create suspense, because the reader views it as a loose end that must be tied up later on (Judg 4:11; cf. vv. 17-22). Because Amnon's motives are revealed at the beginning of 2 Sam 13 the reader fears for what will happen to Tamar and feels greater sympathy for her. On the other hand, a fact revealed "too late" may startlingly alter one's evaluation of the narrative up to this point. In Judg 20:18-28 the narrator seems deliberately to raise the question why the Israelites are defeated by the Benjaminites on the first two days of fighting. They have enquired of the Lord beforehand and have been told to join battle; yet they are defeated. Only when they enquire for the third time are they told they will win, but no explanation is given for the previous defeats. In Judg 21, however, we see that the Israelites, previously so zealous in meting out justice to the Benjaminites, resort to all manner of compromises (compare v. 5 and vv. 11-12), casuistry (v. 16 and v. 22b), and downright illegality (vv. 21 and 23) in their efforts to ensure Benjamin's survival. The reader now understands why the Israelites in Judg 20 suffered losses like the Benjaminites: They are equally corrupt; and the delayed revelation of this fact brings it home to the reader with particular force, strongly underscoring the theme of Israelite wickedness (cf. 21:25). See also Judg 8, where Gideon's hot pursuit of the defeated Midianites and his ferocity towards the inhabitants of Succoth is suddenly explained when we learn that all along he has been conducting a private vendetta on behalf of his brothers (8:18-21; Sternberg, 1985, 311-12); and Gen 34, where we learn only right at the end that the Hamorites have been holding Dinah hostage (ibid., 467-68).

There are other means by which the narrator can shape the reader's response, ranging from the direct to the highly subtle: the use of epithets (1 Sam 25:3), the use of loaded language (2 Sam 13:14), and pseudo-objective narration (Judg 17:1-5—the writer does not express his disapproval of Micah's household until v. 6). The uses of repetition and variation discussed above could also be included here (see further Sternberg, 1985, 445-75, and the list of such devices on pp. 475-81).

5. *Theological implications.*

(a) *God's purposes and human understanding.* Though OT narrative greatly condenses real life in its selectivity, it is in one respect completely true to life: People's motives and the significance of events are usually not clear at the time and only become so in the light of the subsequent narrative. The characters, and more often than not the reader, have limited knowledge in comparison to that of the narrator, who controls the presentation of events. One of the effects of reading OT narrative is a feeling of growing understanding as patterns become apparent and as new facts, words, and deeds emerge that throw light on what has happened so far. Explicit comment seems to be withheld so that the reader may experience this sensation of groping after comprehension, and thus, the limits of human understanding: "To make sense of the discourse is to gain a sense of being human" (Sternberg, 1985, 47). The other side of this is that OT narrative style leads the reader to sense behind the events narrated a God who evaluates human deeds and words and who is working out purposes that unfold only gradually; the narrator's knowledge and his control of the presentation of events seems to mirror God's omniscience and his sovereignty over history.

Some puzzles, though, are never resolved. We never learn whether Ziba or Mephibosheth is telling the truth (2 Sam 16:2-3 and 19:26-27; David's response in 19:29 is understandable). And larger enigmas remain, even on repeated reading. Why are Isaac and Jacob chosen, and Ishmael and Esau not? How is it in Judg 21 that Israel as a whole, fully as guilty as Benjamin, escapes the severe judgment that has been carried out against Benjamin? What is God's attitude to the things done in his name in 2 Sam 21? The narrative, like the God it portrays, is at points inscrutable, and sometimes the only knowledge yielded to readers is of the limits of their understanding.

(b) *Human dignity.* OT narrative, however, is not solely concerned with suggesting the power of an omniscient God. Though they are always limited in knowledge and power, the men and women of OT narrative are never reduced to pawns. Much of OT narrative is taken up with depicting human words, emotions, relationships, and actions, and these, too, play their part in, and affect the course of, the unfolding story of the OT: "God's purposes are always entrammeled in history, dependent on the acts of individual men and women for their continuing realization" (Alter, 1980, 14). Further, men and women are characterized realistically, with great subtlety and sometimes at some length. No character who features for more than a few verses in OT is simply a cardboard cutout; there is always something more to him or her than that; and brevity can be as suggestive as prolixity in this regard (Gen 4:23-24; Judg 17:2-3; 2 Sam 6:20-23). OT narrative shows a deep interest in human personality and the interactions of men and women; more than once it suggests the unpredictable, volatile, and mysterious side of human beings. Certainly there is no oversimplification here or any attempt to present humans as mere cogs in a divine plan; rather, there is a respect for human personality that it seems natural to link with statements such as those found at Gen 1:26-27 and Ps 8:4-5.

(c) *Reader involvement.* Finally, OT narrative seeks to involve the reader in three main senses. First and most obvious, it is generally told in a gripping and lively way; words are not wasted, and there is plenty in the way of interesting dialogue, characterization, and suspense. Second, the devices of implicit commentary draw the reader into the (often demanding) interpretative process; it is the reader who has to note and make sense of patterns, allusions, divergences, discontinuities, and gaps that the narrator simply allows to stand in the text, and in this sense it is the reader who interprets events. Third, and balancing the second point, the narrator often seems to lead the reader towards a particular evaluation of the events narrated by means of a variety of persuasive devices, both implicit and explicit. OT narrative style thus seeks to engage the reader's interest, requires the reader's commitment to the task of understanding the events narrated, and urges the reader towards a response, generally of faith or of ethical commitment. Though OT narrative may give the appearance of a largely neutral succession of words and events, it is, on closer examination, anything but neutral; and its neutral-seeming surface turns out to be a way of involving readers more fully and persuading them more effectively.

Conclusion

OT narrative style suggests a distinctive view of God's dealings with human beings and seeks from its readers a response to the claims of this God. It depicts the grandeur of God's purposes, underlines the worth of men and women made in God's image, and respects its readers by seeking their active engagement in the process of interpretation.

BIBLIOGRAPHY

R. Alter, *The Art of Biblical Narrative*, 1980; idem, *The World of Biblical Literature*, 1992; S. Bar-Efrat, *Narrative Art in the Bible*, 1989; A. Berlin, *Poetics and Interpretation of Biblical Narrative*, 1983; H. C. Brichto, *Towards a Grammar of Biblical Poetics*, 1992; J. C. Exum and D. J. A. Clines (eds.), *The New Literary Criticism and the Hebrew Bible*, 1993; D. N. Fewell ed., *Reading Between Texts*, 1992; R. P. Gordon, "David's Rise and Saul's Demise," *TynBul* 31, 1980, 37-64; D. M. Gunn, "Reading Right" in D. J. A. Clines, S. Fowl, S. E. Porter (eds.), *The Bible in Three Dimensions*, 1990; D. J. A. Clines and D. N. Fewell, *Narrative in the Hebrew Bible*, 1993; B. O. Long, "The 'New' Biblical Poetics of Alter and Sternberg," *JSOT* 51, 1991, 71-84; P. D. Miscall, *The Workings of OT Narrative*, 1983; G. W. Savran, *Telling and Retelling*, 1988; R. M. Schwartz (ed.), *The Book and the Text*, 1990; M. Sternberg, *The Poetics of Biblical Narrative*, 1985; idem, "Double Cave, Double Talk: The Indirections of Biblical Dialogue" in J. P. Rosenblatt and J. C. Sitterson, (eds.), *Not in Heaven*, 1991, 28-57; M. Weiss, "Weiteres über die Bauformen des Erzählens in der Bibel," *Bib* 46, 1965, 187-88.

Philip E. Satterthwaite

There has been much abuse in the interpretation of the Bible. Interpreters rival one another in setting forth their distinctive, and relative, understanding of the text. How can interpreters and readers of the text develop a common set of ground rules for interpretation? What is the nature of language and of human communication? What are the principles of understanding human speech, and how do these principles extend to understanding written communication? The authors of these next two articles (Cotterell and Walton) investigate the problems in communication and set forth clear and precise steps in determining basic steps of interpretation. Insofar as there have been so many bad interpretations, and, to our chagrin, some have abused theological dictionaries, we must develop a basic set of rules of engaging with the text and of resisting inferior approaches.

The essay by Peter Cotterell is groundbreaking work, covering the whole range of linguistics, semantics, and discourse analysis. Readers with a more pragmatic bend may want to scan this article and study carefully John Walton's article on principles for productive word study. The title of this article is a little deceiving, because it could suggest that the author favors the older word-study approach. Instead, you will find that he, too, favors the discourse meaning of a word. (VanGemeren)

7. LINGUISTICS, MEANING, SEMANTICS, AND DISCOURSE ANALYSIS

A. Linguistics and Biblical Interpretation

1. *The nature of language.* Human language is a highly sophisticated, complex, but ultimately imprecise communication system or semiotic. It has its origins in a desire, an intention, to communicate. It originates inaccessibly in a human mind. The sociolinguist H. P. Grice would insist that text originates not in a *mind* but in a *person*, reacting against the concept of a psychological other. Spoken language is primary, an attempt to express the inaccessible intention in sound. Written language is secondary, conforming to the primary spoken form in ways specific to each particular language. Written language makes use of a more-or-less arbitrary analysis of spoken language to produce a second level system of symbols, more-or-less accurately representing the features of the primary form. A speaker produces a sequence of sounds, which is then analyzed phonetically and phonemically to identify the essential sound system, grammatically to identify what are arbitrarily labeled words, roots, and affixes, and syntactically to identify complete sequences and their constituent elements.

Minimal units may then be systematically identified. Minimal units of sound are termed phonemes, minimal units of grammatical form are termed morphemes. Rather than speak of a minimal word form we speak of a *lexeme*, the arbitrary unit underlying, for example, such word forms as *sang, sing, singer, singing*. In this example, the lexeme is "sing" (see John Lyons, 101). Minimal syntactical units are syntagmemes. At these lower levels of analysis the process can claim a certain measure of objectivity. At the next, and arguably most significant level, however, the level of semantics, the identification of the minimal unit, the sememe, proves to be more difficult (Robert de Beaugrande and Wolfgang Dressler, 20). Even more difficult is the process of identifying spoken text meaning through the summation of the contributions of phonemes, morphemes, syntagmemes, and sememes present in the text.

More difficult again is the task of interpreting the corresponding written text. The text now is clearly largely robbed of its phonetic component, represented by arbitrary visual symbols but still in measure corresponding to the original spoken text. Written language, in practice, involves language with two absences: the absence of the speaker and the absence of the referents. The interpretation of a written text involves some measure of dialogue with the speaker and some attempt to identify the referents.

It is precisely these absences that precipitate the problem of polysemy—the range of possible meanings of the words used—in the written text. With the presence of the speaker there is experienced what has been termed a metaphysics of presence, but what might better be termed a metalinguistic of presence, providing its own bounds to polysemy. With the speaker and author removed, that is to say with a written text, a plurality of text meaning may be identified by the deprived, or, arguably, by the liberated, reader (see Anthony C. Thiselton, 83).

This process of interpreting written language is ultimately an art rather than a science, still less an exact science. We are dealing with a semiotic that we employ without, in general, being overtly aware of the code that lies behind it. We learn to employ hyperbole, litotes, and metaphor, to use rhetoric as individual devices or as sequential schemes: We learn to identify implicature, and even to create for a text an appropriate context, without consciously identifying the devices we employ. The meaning of what we receive or of what we transmit is encoded in a highly complex manner and is interpreted by reference to an intuitive awareness of the code, and not by a labored but precise evaluation of the speech units and the aggregation of units of meaning.

For example, a speaker generated a sequence (or an author supposed a character to have generated a sequence) that could be represented by *I am Esau your firstborn* (Gen 27:19) (or rather the Heb. equivalent, a further problem). The information recorded in this transcript is heavily edited. We do not know anything (from this text alone, although the surrounding text, the cotext, as we shall see, tells us a good deal) about the setting in which the sequence was generated, we do not know what time of day it was, and we do not know what the person addressed was wearing; we are not told whether or not the speaker bowed, held out his hand in paralinguistic gesture, or made some other gesture, nor what his facial expression was. And yet we know from our own use of language that any of this information might be important in interpreting the sequence.

Thus, in Prov 6:12-14 the worthless person is described as one who goes about "with a corrupt speech, who winks with his eyes, signals with his feet, and motions with his finger, who plots evil with deceit in his heart." Here are three gestures, and yet we cannot be sure of the meaning of any one of them. Prov 10:10 comments: "He who winks maliciously causes trouble, but he who boldly reproves makes peace." The parallel and semantically determinative phrase "he who boldly reproves" has the Septuagint as its source since the corresponding Heb. text "and a chattering fool comes to ruin" appears to be unrelated to any conceivable antithesis to the significance of winking. But this uncertainty leaves us without any sure guide to the significance of winking.

The psalmist prays, "Let not those gloat over me who are my enemies without cause; let not those who hate me without reason maliciously wink the eye" (Ps 35:19). In contrast to the significance of contemporary Western gesture, winking in the OT culture was never mere facetiousness. It is "always associated with sin"; in Semitic Ethiopian culture to wink at a woman is to invite her to have sex.

Not only are we without information on gesture in the Jacob text, but we also lack information regarding the intonation pattern employed for the sequence, the medial *loudness* of the speech, the pitch of the speaker's voice, or the place of stress within the sequence. This is, of course, typical of written text, typical of the two absences, of speaker and of referent.

We may go further: Although the import of the sequence is quite clear, that the name of the speaker is Esau, in fact we know (either from general knowledge or from reading the cotext) that his name was not Esau. We conclude, then, that the meaning of a sequence is not, after all, merely some kind of summation of the meanings of the constituent elements that comprise the sequence. We need also to know the cotext, the total text of which the sequence is a part. That in turn requires that we identify the boundaries of the text, those limits within which we may expect to locate the clues that might serve to resolve our inescapable exegetical uncertainties, before proceeding to an analysis of any part of it. In the present example, expanding the analysis of the text into its immediate cotext shows that the speaker's name was Jacob, and that he was presenting himself to his father as Esau, his elder brother.

We are confronted here by the essential difference between a *sentence* and an *utterance*, a useful distinction that will generally be maintained in this article. A sentence has no immediate cotext and no sociological context. The *sentence* rendered as "I am Esau your firstborn" does mean what it appears to mean: that the speaker is someone's firstborn son and is named Esau. The sentence may be generated by a speaker or may be written down, but there is no cotext that could bring into question the information being communicated within the limits of that sentence. An *utterance* has both context—the social milieu in which it is generated—and cotext, and the meaning of an utterance must be determined in the light of text, cotext, and context. That is to say, *the meaning of an utterance cannot be determined merely by reference to dictionary, lexicon, thesaurus, and grammar.* The possible range of meanings and the probable meaning of an ancient utterance may be ascertained through dictionary, grammar, thesaurus, lexicon, context, cotext, encyclopedia, history, geography, and a knowledge of linguistics and especially of sociolinguistics and discourse structure.

Moreover, we note that each utterance, even though it may use "the same" words as another utterance, will nonetheless have a unique singular meaning because it necessarily has a unique singular context. To make the point quite clearly, if a speaker generates the utterance "That is a horse," and someone else repeats "That is a horse," the time context of the latter utterance is different from that of the former and that will be so even if *the same speaker* repeats "the same" utterance. The meaning of the second utterance must be different from that of the first utterance precisely because it follows that first utterance. The meaning of each utterance is determined from an assessment of the linguistic elements it contains, the cotext of which it is a part, and the context within which it was generated.

Perhaps it should be added here, that this view of the process of the interpretation of a text is very different from Schleiermacher's concept of a psychological absorption into the text. We are now reasonably confident that because of our prereading of texts an objective and existential re-creation of any ancient context is denied to us. However, this does not deny to us the attempt *objectively* to re-create that context, without attempting *existentially* to experience it.

2. *Language: Barr's critique.* Biblical exegesis has suffered until comparatively recently from the manner in which academic disciplines tended to be isolated from one another. In particular theologians were largely unaware of new insights into the interpretation of texts commonplace amongst secular linguists. The end of this *jahiliya* age of ignorance was arguably signaled to theologians by the appearance of the seminal work by James Barr, later Regius Professor of Hebrew in the University of Oxford, *The Semantics of Biblical Language*, 1961. In this work Barr began by acknowledging two particular features of theological language as contrasted with the language of everyday speech. First, theological language exhibits special semantic developments; words are assigned particular and technical meanings. But at the same time Barr was aware of the danger of supposing that theological language represents a unique strand of language, exempt from those generalities observed elsewhere in language. Thus, observations made of the general phenomenon of human language can with confidence be applied also to theological language. Of course, there are those semantic specializations that have parallels in such disciplines as law and philosophy, medicine, and physics.

Second, Barr recognized that the interpretation of theological language and especially of biblical language must have a significant datum in the past. The process of exegesis involves not merely the interpretation of a text but the transculturation of meanings. This observation bears particularly on the fact that theological texts, far more than legal texts, are subject to attempts at exegesis by individuals who lack those skills that lay open to them the datum in the past and so supply the only reliable key to responsible exegesis.

It has to be said that although the Bible may well be understandable in the main by the reasonably educated individual, there can be no expectation that any *translation* can be produced that makes the meaning of the original text transparent to the ploughman. Barr went further by insisting that the study of grammar, and, more particularly, the study of words, their meanings, their etymologies, their cognates in related languages, could not lead even the best of scholars into reliable exegesis *without a profound understanding of the way in which language itself functions to communicate meaning.*

Takamitsu Muraoka, in his seminal work *Emphatic Words and Structures in Biblical Hebrew*, published in 1985 but based on his doctoral thesis of 1969-70, warns that "versional evidence and comparative Semitic parallels possess only secondary value" in determining the meaning of a particular text, and goes on to state that

> . . . before pronouncing a final judgment about the emphasizing function ascribable to a certain form or structure in a given place, the text and the wider context in which it is found must be closely examined (XVII).

The welcome caution displayed here may owe something to the earlier (p. vii) acknowledgment made to the critical reading of the manuscript by Barr. Certainly Barr would approve of the principle of cotext and context representing the primary evidence for any particular interpretation of a text, with versional evidence and the evidence of cognate languages taking a secondary place.

3. *Reading strategies.* I lived in Ethiopia for many years and was struck by the beauty of the oleander bush. It is hardy, surviving in almost waterless conditions. It is beautiful, with a brilliant waxy red flower. It is one of the few plants that is not eaten by animals, domestic or wild. However, every part of it is highly toxic. I was warned of the danger posed to my children by having this plant growing in our gardens, and to be sure of my facts I obtained a letter from the Director of the Royal Botanical Gardens in London on the dangers of the oleander. The chemical concerned was named hydrocyanic acid, and its use in some gas chambers in the USA was noted. Examples of past incidents, going back to Hannibal, in which people died from sucking a leaf or stem, were quoted. The advice was clear (to me): The plant should not be in our gardens. My neighbor was a keen gardener, with plenty of those plants in his garden. He read the letter: "It's not so bad after all, is it?" The "objective text" depends for its interpretation on the reader: He was anxious to preserve his garden while I was anxious to preserve my children, and our respective reading strategies enabled us to perceive "the same" text as we wished.

Until the second half of the twentieth century scientists were content to allow the myth of scientific objectivity to remain as the distinctive characteristic of their researches. A similar mythological epistemology could be seen in the humanities, with both ideals arguably going back to Descartes and his concept of the human observer impacting on an essentially passive and objective world. In biblical studies the supposed scientific ideal has until recently been that pursued by scholars, so that the text has only rarely been related to the real but subjectively perceived world, either the real ancient world (except in its sterilized scholarly form) or the contemporary world into which, at least for the church, it is supposed to speak. The consequences for the church have been tragic: The discoveries of the scholars have been perceived to be irrelevant, the questions asked by the scholars have not been the questions asked by the church, and the church has turned in despair away from scholarship to charismatic but often unscholarly preachers.

In Christian Bible conventions it has been customary to make use of the massacre of the Amalekites (1 Sam 15) for the sake of Samuel's apophthegm "to obey is better than sacrifice, and to heed is better than the fat of rams" (v. 22), with no reference at all to the moral problem posed by the massacre apparently commanded by Yahweh (vv. 1-3). Similarly the Esther narrative has been expounded without any real consideration of the exploitation of women, whether of Vashti or of the young women, gathered together like so many cattle, for the king's approval. As far back as 1973 Wink called for the combining of critical textual scholarship with a recognition of biblical text as that which stands over against us and questions our beliefs and practices rather than merely reinforcing them (see Walter Wink, 32).

In reading we necessarily adopt a strategy that is designed to enable us to understand the text. We make assumptions about the text—its structure and the intention of its author or editor. But these assumptions are not infrequently self-serving, aimed at ensuring that the text should confirm existing prejudices rather than challenge them. We then have a conflict between *intentio operis*, the intention of the discourse, and *intentio lectoris*, the intention of the discourse as determined by the reader's strategy. The contrast is readily seen in the oleander illustration above, but also from the account of the massacre of the Amalekites: In the interests of piety the text is not interrogated at certain points. Perhaps even more obvious is the insistence by some readers, in the interests of a teetotal conviction, that the wine produced by Jesus at Cana was unfermented wine (cf. John 2:10!).

4. *Meaning.* Semantics subsumes a subsidiary science concerned with text-meaning. In normal usage it would be expected that we could ask what the meaning of a text was and expect to find a generally acceptable answer. A little thought will show that this is an assumption and that in some literary forms there is explicitly nothing corresponding to a text-meaning. Anthony Thiselton (I think uniquely) has drawn attention to the Zen *koan*, a text-form that observes the usual grammatical and linguistic regularities but that explicitly has no text-meaning (119). The *koan* may be an apparently normal text, "Who is it that recites the name of the Buddha?" or it may be an apparently nonsensical but grammatical string, "The sound of one hand clapping." The Zen master is concerned to bring the student to the point where the *koan* is resolved not by analysis of any kind, but by intuition. The student takes the *koan* and "slowly recites the words of the question and watches it as a cat watches a mouse, trying to bore deeper and deeper into it, till he reaches the point from which it comes and intuits its meaning" (Peter Harvey, *An Introduction to Buddhism*, 1990, 274).

The postmodernist deconstructionist approach to text has clear affinities with the Zen perception of the role of language. Strings of words have apparent superficial "meanings" which, however, cloak the true function of language, which is not to communicate any intended meaning but to activate intuitive meaning. The meaning for one intuiter need have no relation whatever to that of another. In other words, the process of deconstruction as exemplified in J. D. Crossan (see *The Dark Interval: Towards a Theology of Story*, 1975), for example, starts from the denial of embodied meaning and replaces the traditional emphasis on cognitive content with a concern for *the form* of the linguistic vehicle.

This approach certainly serves to remedy the traditional concern with text as though it were no more (and no less) than a shopping list. It emphasizes the emotive force of text and the role of intuition in perceiving text as more than a mere summation of lexicon and grammar. But epistemologically the approach offers serious problems to those who assume that a text not only has cognitive content, but also has ethical imperatives and, still more, objective prophetic significance.

Deconstruction, then, serves a positive function, liberating text from a deterministic framework of abstract theory and returning it to its free function of a limited and yet indeterminate subjectivism. The problem, well perceived by many linguists, is that deconstruction linguistics tends towards nihilism, and its more radical expression in such writers as Stanley Fish and Jacques Derrida must be tempered so as to leave the reader with a text that has a real and knowable embodied meaning.

At the present time we are confronted by some measure of polarization amongst linguists, with E. D. Hirsch, H. P. Grice, and Wayne Booth defending the more traditional understanding of text-meaning, and with Jacques Derrida, Paul De Man, and Stanley Fish promoting what has been described as deconstructive nihilism or (more objectively!) as Reader-Response theory. Somewhere between the two we may place

Wolfgang Iser's Reception theory. For an introduction to this complex and fluid debate see Anthony Thiselton's magisterial *New Horizons in Hermeneutics*, ch. 2, "What Is a Text?"

With these preliminary reflections we move to the more traditional questioning of the locus of text-meaning.

B. The Source of Meaning

Amongst linguists there continues to be debate on the question of the locus of meaning in a text. There are broadly three options: that meaning lies in the text alone, that meaning lies in the intention of the author of the text, or that meaning lies in the reader of the text. It is intuitively apparent that there is a measure of truth in all three possibilities, and that alone is sufficient to warn us against any uncritical and exclusive adoption of one or other of them.

1. *The objective text.* The text is, of course, the objective reality, whether it is a written text or a spoken text. *This* is what was said or written. However, when the phrase *objective reality* is used, it applies solely and exclusively to the sounds used or the symbols written, and not at all to whatever *meaning* or *intention* might be supposed to lie behind the sounds or the symbols. Meaning and intention are always subjectively derived from objective text. And even here we must further modify our position since we never process the whole of any aurally perceived message, but subjectively filter out such elements as we assume to be irrelevant or unimportant.

It then appears that in using a term such as *objective* to describe any aspect of a text, we must disassociate it from the human interpretive sequence. But it is then arguable that we do not have a text at all, nor any communication. We have only a complex pattern of air pressures or a set of written symbols but with no receiver to decode them. However, for the present we may assume, with a mental note of caution, that a written text consists of a set of coded symbols and exists unchallenged as such. Is such a text of itself susceptible to interpretation as having a single, agreed, and identifiable meaning?

If the text includes the utterance "I am Esau your firstborn," it must certainly be distinguished from a nearby utterance, "My son ... Who is it?" But since we have already seen that the meaning of the utterance "I am Esau your firstborn" is significantly different from its apparent meaning, it is clear that reference to an utterance in isolation will not in all cases lead to a correct understanding of its meaning. Indeed the situation is sometimes made complex by the rhetorical device of ambiguity. Modern Amharic, and before it classical Ethiopic, developed an entire literary genre known as *sem inna werq*, "wax and gold," in which each word, each phrase, each sequence might be seen either as (relatively valueless) wax, an external dressing, or as significant (but indelicate or potentially politically compromising) gold, the concealed essence of word, phrase, sequence. In the cafes of Addis Ababa in the early 1960s the apparently unexceptionable "wax" toast, "Government! The government!" *Mengist! Mengistu!* was regularly heard. The "gold" was rather different: *Mengistu* Neway was recently hanged, a popular revolutionary leader of the 1960 attempt to overthrow Haile Sellassie (Donald Levine, *Wax and Gold*, 1965).

This at once raises a further point still vigorously debated by linguists: Is there such a thing as *the correct meaning* of a text? Granted that we must accept that some

137

supposed interpretations of a text are simply crass, obtuse, absurd, or even impenetrable, is it possible to assert that there is a uniquely correct meaning to be assigned to it?

Traditionally literary scholars have debated the *meanings* of their texts, separating out the "scientific," or "standard" or "normal" use of language from the "poetic" or "emotive" use of language, classifying the poetic forms, developing principles for their interpretation, and assuming that texts using "normal" language "are in no need of such interpretive tools." (See Stanley Fish, "Literature in the Reader," in his *Is There a Text in This Class?* 1980, especially his comments on Riffaterre's distinction between ordinary and poetic language, 59ff.) But the very concept of "scientific" or "normal" or even "normative" language must be challenged, first because there is no taxonomy that can delimit the normal, but second because the category "poetry" does not represent a boundaried class. All language, written or spoken, has a context, that context always involves individual speakers, and every speaker's use of language, whether sending or receiving, is idiosyncratic, always consisting of an undefined and unknowable mixture of denotation and connotation. In other words, all language may be represented as a poetical or rhetorical continuum with every particular expression of language having a place somewhere along that continuum.

It has to be said that no *extended* text (and there is no generalized means of defining the minimum level of extension required) has a single objective meaning defined by the text itself. And the reason for this is the essential imprecision of the language semiotic and its connotations, and of its function as necessarily involving multiple persons.

2. *Authorial intention.* If, surrendering the concept of the autonomy of the objective text, we locate meaning in the intention of the author, requiring the multiplicity of receivers to abandon their warring perceptions and submit to the author's intention, we are confronted by a different set of problems. Perhaps the most obvious of these, in the case of biblical text, is the fact that the authors are long since dead, and their intentions are usually not available to us. And even where the intentions *are* stated, they are stated as part of the text, not as a mind printout (cf. the prefaces to Luke and Acts, and 1 John 2:1, "I write this to you so that you will not sin").

Second, we have the problem of linguistic competence to face. The readily demonstrable fact is that we may, because of linguistic incompetence, both say and write not merely what we do not intend, but the very opposite of what we intend. Lessing's slip has become the classic example, in which Emilia's mother is made to say, "My God! If your father knew that! How angry he was already to learn that the prince had seen you *not without displeasure*" (Cotterell and Turner, 58). The cotext makes it perfectly clear that what was *intended* was that the prince had seen Emilia and been pleased by her, but a vigorous litotes has defeated the linguistic competence of the author. The celebrated statement in 1 Cor 14:22 may have a similar explanation: "Tongues, then, are a sign, not for believers but for unbelievers; prophecy, however, is for believers, not for unbelievers." The immediate cotext, however, states unequivocally that the unbeliever hearing tongues would think the speakers mad, but that unbelievers hearing prophecy would be convicted and would be led to worship God. There are too many negatives in the crucial statement, and J. B. Phillips in his paraphrase supplies what he considers to be the *discourse meaning* of the text, that glossolalia provides *a sign* for believers and prophecy *a sign* for unbelievers." (For a discussion of the significance of the omission of the second "sign for" in connection with prophecy, see D. A. Carson, *Showing the Spirit*, 1987, ch. 4.) But already the reader has intruded into the text and has made an assumption about the intention of the author.

3. *Reader-Response theory* (see Jane Tompkins [ed.], 1980). Consider the narrative relating to Mephibosheth in 2 Sam 9-19. The story is part of the longer court narrative of David and Saul. Saul has died, and David asks: "Is there anyone still left of the house of Saul to whom I can show kindness for Jonathan's sake?" (9:1). By the end of the chapter Mephibosheth has been found and is established at David's court: "He always ate at the king's table." In ch. 15 David is forced to flee from Jerusalem because of a coup mounted by Absalom. He is met by Ziba, the servant of Mephibosheth, who tells David that Mephibosheth has elected to stay in Jerusalem, hoping that the revolt will mean the restoration of the kingdom to Saul's successors. David believes Ziba and rewards him with the grant of all Mephibosheth's lands. In ch. 19 David returns to Jerusalem after the revolt. Mephibosheth meets him, and we now are told that since David left Jerusalem, he had not cared either for his person or his clothes. Ziba, he insists, had deceived him. David now decides that Mephibosheth's lands should be equally shared between the two men.

So much for the text. But how is it to be understood? What does it mean? A multitude of questions have to be considered: Was Mephibosheth being honored, or merely put into protective custody when David brought him to Jerusalem? Did Mephibosheth understand the situation? Why did he remain in Jerusalem rather than accompany David? Had he accompanied David, surely his lameness would have been a hindrance, possibly a fatal hindrance, to David. As a fellow fugitive would he, in fact, have been more of a threat to David than as a potential rival in Jerusalem? Did Ziba tell the truth, half of the truth, or a total lie? Did David believe him . . . after all, David sequestered Mephibosheth's land? During David's absence had Mephibosheth really neglected himself as the narrative says, or was this a quickly adopted subterfuge to allow him to escape from a dangerous situation? Whom did David believe? Why did he divide the land between them? Was it to save face after his earlier unjust decision? Was it because he really did not know whom to believe?

Throughout the story we are given no clue at all as to the characters of Ziba or Mephibosheth. The reader today might well be inclined to take the side of the old man Mephibosheth, to see him as a man of integrity, his infirmity exploited by Ziba, and so to assign to Ziba a sneaking, sycophantic, grasping role. But there is no more evidence in support of the one view than of the other. In other words, even given an *objective* text, the reader must *subjectively* interrogate it for its meaning, at each point in the development of the story modifying any views previously held and projecting forwards to anticipated future developments. No reader who had read as far as ch. 15 could fail to anticipate a further encounter between the three protagonists, David, Ziba, and Mephibosheth, and yet there is nothing in the *objective* text to announce such a development.

In some measure we have already brought into question the more traditional assumption that any text has a foundational meaning. Jacques Derrida's celebrated statement that a text has no meaning represents the extreme expression of antifoundational theory. Defending his own fiercely held but perhaps less extreme antifoundationalist position, Stanley Fish (1989, 29) insists that its essence is not that there are no foundations, but whatever foundations there are (and there are always some) have been established by persuasion, that is, in the course of argument and counter-argument on the basis of examples and evidence that are themselves cultural and contextual.

In other words, any conclusions we may draw with respect to the Mephibosheth narratives will be consensus conclusions, not conclusions forced upon us by the text, and the consensus will be determined by cultural factors and by the context within which the consensus is reached.

In the same compendium of his essays, Fish discusses the effect of *authority* on interpretation by reference to C. S. Lewis's well-known and, in 1942, plainly stated disapproval of the concluding books of Milton's *Paradise Lost*. Such was the scholarly stature of C. S. Lewis that for some years his view of that part of Milton's work was obediently echoed by other scholars. Today, arguably at a safe and sufficient distance from 1942, scholars are divided on the question of the literary merit of the chapters. Of course the text itself has not changed. The cultural factors and the context within which the text is discussed have changed, and it is these that have determined the interpretation of the text, not the text itself.

To take a more immediately relevant example, it has been a commonplace of NT scholarship to assign late dates to most of the books of the NT and to question their traditional authorship. In 1976 John Robinson published *Redating the New Testament*, in which he dated the whole of the NT before AD 70, and to drive home the lesson appended a letter from no less a scholar than C. H. Dodd affirming:

> You are certainly justified in questioning the whole structure of the accepted "critical" chronology of the NT writings, which avoids putting anything earlier than 70, so that none of them are available for anything like first-generation testimony. I should agree with you that much of this late dating is quite arbitrary, even wanton, the off-spring not of any argument that can be presented, but rather of the critic's prejudice that if he appears to assent to the traditional position of the early church he will be thought no better than a stick-in-the-mud. The whole business is due for radical re-examination (360).

Contemporary scholarship has yet to come to terms either with John Robinson, whose views could be dismissed, or with C. H. Dodd, whose views could not. The point is, however, that the interpretation of text is not in fact determined by an objective text alone, nor by author intention alone or with text, cotext and context, but by all of this moderated through the subjectivity of the reader and the reader's culture and context.

4. *Discourse meaning*. With the debate amongst the linguists unresolved, we must still come to some conclusions about the locus of meaning in biblical text. First of all it seems that the distinction between *meaning* and a multiplicity of *significances* is still valuable. Behind the text stands an author, an editor, a redactor, with some intention lying behind the production of the text. We have no access to that intention, although an understanding of contemporary and cognate languages and cultures, of related texts, of grammar, syntax, lexicography, and possibly some knowledge of the

author might at least indicate what the intention was *not*, and might even indicate what it was.

The clear overtones of a humanistic nihilism apparent in the more radical forms of Reader-Response theory are to be resisted. They appear to be designed not so much to explain texts as to dissolve significant meaning and to enthrone relativity in the person of the reader. As Thiselton (56) quotes Paul Ricoeur:

> Writing renders the text autonomous with respect to the intention of the author. What the text *signifies* no longer coincides with what the author meant.

The difficulty here is first that Ricoeur does not, in fact, distinguish between meaning and significance, so that he asserts a distinction between authorial intention and meaning, and second, he appears to assert that the meaning intended by an author is *necessarily* different from the meaning perceived by the reader. That the intention of an author *might* not be perceived by a reader is admitted; to suggest that it *cannot* be perceived by a reader is simply perverse. To take an entirely trite example, when the author of 2 Sam 11:17 writes: "Uriah the Hittite died" or "When Uriah's wife heard that her husband was dead, she mourned for him" (11:26), the reader does not have the meanings "Uriah died" or "Uriah's widow mourned" excluded from the interpretive process.

A *text* is *a communicative occurrence that meets seven standards of textuality* (Robert de Beaugrande and Wolfgang Dressler, 1981), and of these seven standards the first three have particular importance: They are grammatical and syntactical cohesion, semantic coherence, and intentionality. That is to say, an author produces a communicative text consisting of related strings across which there are certain constants (proforms having identifiable antecedents, for example) and with the meanings of the strings related so as to produce a topic or theme or thematic net. The reader seeks to identify the *discourse meaning* of the text.

The term *discourse meaning* is particularly important. On the one hand, we seek to avoid the notion of the semantic autonomy of the text. A text cannot carry *any* meaning, but it does carry a meaning *intended* by the original speaker or author, related to the context within which it was generated and the cotext of which it is a part. On the other hand, we avoid also the complete relativity of meaning inevitable when meaning is no more than that meaning perceived by the reader, however much that meaning might appear to others to be inimical to the objective text. In approaching a text, then, we are searching first for the *discourse meaning* and not for the *significance* of the text for us. It is certainly true that in some instances we may be forever unsure of what the intended meaning was, and we may have to admit to the possibility of several distinct meanings. But again it must be emphasized that the range of possible meanings is not infinite: Uriah was *dead*, not attending a banquet in Jerusalem.

The issue of the locus of meaning is particularly important in the case of biblical text. Rightly or wrongly, biblical text, along with other sacred texts and most didactic and historical material, is perceived as having an external, forensic, hortatory role in relation to the reader. It is expected that the text will challenge assumptions, mores, expectations, and value systems by placing them alongside an alternative system. If the relativization of Reader-Response theory is accepted then, as Thiselton has pointed out (531):

> the text can never transform us and correct us *"from outside."* There can be no prophetic address from beyond. This may still leave room for a measure of *creativity and surprise* in *literary* reading for *in such cases it does not profoundly matter whether it is ultimately the self* who brings about its own creative discoveries. But in the case of many biblical texts, theological truth claims constitute more than triggers to set self-discovery in motion (even if they are not less than this). If such concepts as "grace" or "revelation" have any currency, texts of this kind speak *not from the self,* but *from beyond the self.*

The process of seeking both meaning and significance should be expected to involve some form of hermeneutical circle. See, for example, the concise description of Gadamer's hermeneutical circle in Donald McKim (ed., 90). There is the naive approach to the text, informed by the reader's own preunderstanding of it. This should be expected to be followed by a dialogue with the text, in which the questions brought to the text and the presuppositions brought to the text are interrogated, modified, and reformed by the text, leading to a new approach to the same text. As with Zen Buddhism the text is first of all a text, then as the hermeneutical circle operates it is anything but a text, until finally if the circle is followed with perseverance, it becomes a text again. It is, in a term we have already employed, *intuited.* The process may be compared with the mathematical process of iteration, in which the solution to a problem is adduced, but with some admitted measure of imprecision, and the solution is then fed back into the problem so that a more precise solution may be found, which in its turn can be fed into the equation. The recognition of the hermeneutical circle ought not to be seen as necessarily committing the linguist to accepting the essential subjectivity of all text, but rather to an awareness of a process by which probable interpretations of text may become more probable.

5. *Speech-act theory.* Language is used to send and receive information; it is *propositional.* But the philosopher J. L. Austin has noted in a series of important books and articles (especially *How to Do Things With Words,* 1962) that while an utterance might be propositional, or *constative,* it might also be *performative.* To take the most obvious example, when ministers say, "I pronounce you man and wife," they do more than "pronounce"; new relationships are created by the utterance. The uttering of the words is clearly an *act,* and the act is termed a *locution.* But the uttering of the particular words has consequences, it is an *act* performed by the speaker in virtue of the locution, and this speech-act is termed an illocution. Illocutionary acts include promising, a judge sentencing a criminal, a jury announcing its verdict, and apologizing. Austin proposed a third category of utterances, *perlocutionary* utterances, which produce an existential response such as anger or repentance in the auditor.

From the above it is clear that speech-act theory is relevant for utterances but not for sentences, since in many cases the identification of a locution as being illocutionary depends on its context. The string, "I pronounce you man and wife" occurring in a grammar ("The words 'I pronounce you man and wife' is a sentence") is not illocutionary and only becomes so when used in an appropriate context.

142

The identification of illocutionary utterances is by no means easy, and the classification of such utterances is still more difficult because such utterances do not necessarily include a performative vb. (e.g., "I pronounce"; the utterance, "I'll see you tomorrow morning" is a promise, it commits me to being in a certain place at a certain time and is therefore illocutionary although it contains no performative vb.). Conversely, the presence of such a performative vb. is not necessarily an indication of illocution. Further, as M. Stubbs has shown, there need be no *illocutionary force indicating device* (IFID) present in the utterance at all (*Discourse Analysis*, 1983, especially ch. 8; see J. Lyons, *Semantics*, 1977, 16.1). The most readily recognized illocutionary utterances are those containing a first person, present, performative vb.

When Yahweh says to Abraham, "I will bless you; I will make your name great" (Gen 12:2), the utterance is illocutionary: An act is performed that produces a changed situation for Abraham and his descendants. Similarly, the informative statement made by Yahweh to Rebekah is illocutionary although it contains no IFID: "Two nations are in your womb, and two peoples from within you will be separated; one people will be stronger than the other, and the older will serve the younger" (25:23). In analytical terms it is the failure first of Rebekah and subsequently of Jacob to recognize the illocutionary force of these words that provides the topic holding together the subsequent Jacob discourse.

Anthony Thiselton was in the forefront of theologians who recognized the significance of speech-act theory in general and the work of J. L. Austin in particular for certain aspects of biblical exegesis (see esp. ch. 8). On the one hand was the problem posed by the covenant language of the OT, and on the other was the question of the proper understanding of the NT parables. Many utterances assigned in Scripture to God or attributed to Jesus are clearly illocutionary in form or are presented as having performed irrevocable acts (see the pathetic cry of Jacob to his son Esau: "I have blessed him—and indeed he will be blessed" (Gen 27:33). Jacob was blessed not because of some "magic" that was irreversible, not because of Isaac's superstitions, but because Isaac had no means to "unbless" Jacob (18). Thiselton also rightly recognized the importance of distinguishing between what any given speech-act necessarily produced, and what a speech-act could be shown ontologically to have produced. And again Thiselton recognized that formal illocutionary acts depend for their validity on the *authority* of their author, at the same time refuting the thesis that the "power language" of the OT merely reflected the primitive animistic worldview of the Hebrew writers.

Austin had himself identified what he termed *felicity conditions,* which must be satisfied if an illocution is to be nondefective. Felicity conditions includes sincerity in the locution, that is to say, the speaker's intention is sincere. Insincerity, while not necessarily invalidating the illocution, at least makes it defective. The same is true of commitment to the illocution from within the speaker's more general set of beliefs and practices. However, the most important of these felicity conditions is the authority condition: An illocution may be defective or even ineffective if the speaker lacks the authority required for it. The utterance "I pronounce you man and wife" has no illocutionary effect when pronounced by a child to children.

The illocutionary force of the wide range of covenant language in the OT and the *kyrios* language of the NT depends for its validity on the authority of God. This is

143

expressed first in the illocutionary language of creation: "God said, 'Let there be light'; and there was light" (Gen 1:3), second in the *exercitive* or *directive* illocution: "And the LORD God commanded the man ..." (2:16), third in the promissory Noahic illocution, precursor of the Abrahamic and Mosaic covenants, and fourth in the declaratory locution reported by Paul: Jesus was "declared with power to be the Son of God by his resurrection from the dead" (Rom 1:4). We note also Phil 2:9. It is a consequence of this fundamental illocution that "the Lord" can now judge (1 Cor 4:4) or commend (2 Cor 10:18) or save (Rom 10:9). In the OT the authority of Yahweh over his people is inculcated in them by reference to his authority over nature expressed in illocutionary language: "He spoke and stirred up a tempest that lifted high the waves.... He stilled the storm to a whisper; the waves of the sea were hushed" (Ps 107:25-29).

Thiselton demonstrates that the illocutions ascribed to Jesus by Matthew are systematically integrated with illustrations of Matthew's Christology. In one sense this is restrained since the ultimate illocution is the resurrection, and yet within the time span of the Incarnation some assertion of authority for Jesus must be given if his illocutions are to be accorded validity by the reader. Thiselton asks:

> Why should the reader be involved? The answer concerns the Christological presuppositions on the basis of which the series of illocutionary acts depicted by Matthew operate: language which brings forgiveness; language which stills the storm; language which authorizes and assigns a role. If the implicit Christology is false, the entire performative and exercitive dimension collapses and falls to the ground as nothing more than a construct of pious human imagination (288-89).

C. Lexical Semantics

Words are symbols available to an author to be given significance by being attached to a referent, an object, or an event. Of itself a word has no meaning at all. The father of modern linguistics, Ferdinand de Saussure, formalized the principle that the units of a language—sounds, words, or longer sequences—gained their meaning through their relationship to and particularly their contrast with other units in the same language system. Within this general principle de Saussure identified a word as *signe* and its referent as *signifiée*, directing attention to the primacy of *signifiée* over word and the importance of the human act of relating the two.

In fact the relation of the word stock of a language to meanings is for the most part not iconic, or physiologically or psychologically necessary, but arbitrary and conventional. Nothing about the form or sound of the word "tree" makes it particularly appropriate as a word form to denote a large woody-stemmed perennial. The G uses *dendron* or *xylon* (Rev 2:7) and Heb. uses '*ēṣ* for the same entity.

Since a dictionary is concerned with words, the secondary symbols, and the possible meanings with which those words might be associated by various individuals and across long periods of time, it is clearly important to understand their status as symbols only, to be given their significances by the respective language users. As we have seen, the task of the exegete is to determine the discourse meaning of an utterance, to which the constituent elements of the utterance make their cumulative contribution.

To take an example, Peter is represented in Acts 5:30 as saying that his hearers had hanged Jesus "on a tree," where he might perfectly well instead have employed a *stauros*-related word to express the same event. The reference to a tree, however—using G *xylon* which, unlike *dendron*, denotes both tree and gibbet—may be taken as directing the attention of a Jewish audience to Deut 21:22-23 and the assertion there that death on a tree represented the curse of God on the malefactor: Heb. *'ēṣ* also signifies both tree and gallows (Esth 5:14). Unfortunately the modern trend towards rendering denotation without connotation (hanging him on a gibbet, NEB; nailing him to a cross, GNB) serves at least to conceal the reason for Peter's (or more precisely Luke's) *not* using the terminology suggested by NEB. It is significant that here we have to hand one word in G and one in Heb. that share an element of polysemy, apparently exploited by an author, as is done with the similarly shared polysemy of the Heb. and G words for wind/spirit.

Lexemes are given meaning not only by their location within a particular syntactic structure, but also by their collocations. Thus, Heb. *zkr* (see # 2349 in the Appendix) when collocationally related to Yahweh carries a connotative meaning of encouragement (remembering past mercy) or of repentance (remembering past judgment). Indeed, the semantic domain of *zkr* is extensive, involving reflection, reasoning, meditating, submitting, committing. Remembering Yahweh's name at night means turning to him in prayerful meditation (Ps 119:55). On the negative side a time would come when it will no longer be appropriate to "remember" past events that will be transcended by new acts of Yahweh. The word may also involve perlocution, action-induced-by-word: When the butler was asked to *zkr* Joseph, the expectation was that his "remembering" would lead to action to release Joseph. Indeed, as Allen says,

> So closely is remembering associated with action that at times it functions as a synonym for action of various kinds. In Amos 1:9 Tyre's not remembering its treaty with Israel means to disregard or break it. In Ps 109:16 not to remember to show kindness to the needy connotes neglect to do so. To forget God as Savior in Isa 17:10 is to forsake him for alien gods.

Words are more than monofunctional discrete linguistic units. The incorporation of any word into an utterance and the utterance into a discourse introduces a highly subjective domain of meaning into the interpretive process, and it is from within that ill-defined domain that the exegete must find the meaning appropriate to each unique occurrence of the word.

1. *Five myths about words.* The exegetical task is made difficult by the persistence of five myths or misconceptions.

(a) *The myth of point meaning.* The first is *the myth of point meaning*—the supposition that even if a word has a range of possible meanings attested in the dictionary, there lies behind them all a single "basic" meaning.

James Barr (115) quotes Norman Snaith's formulation on this point:

> While it must be recognized that words can change their meaning in strange and unexpected ways through the centuries, yet in all languages there is a fundamental motif in a word which tends to endure, whatever other changes the years may bring. This fundamental "theme"

of a word is often curiously determinative of later meanings (quoting from Norman Snaith, "The language of the Old Testament," *The Interpreter's Bible*, 224).

A little thought will show that this thesis would be difficult to defend. In a long pericope covering twelve pages Barr deals with the vagaries attached to the elucidation of Heb. *dābār*. T. F. Torrance is quoted as finding a fundamental meaning "hinterground" in this root and goes on to write extensively of *dābār* that "on the one hand it refers to the hinterground of meaning, the inner reality of the word, but on the other hand, it refers to the dynamic event in which that inner reality becomes manifest" (Barr, 130). In other words, "every event has its *dabar* or word, so that he who understands the *dabar* of an event, understands its real meaning." The fact is that words do not function in this way in language. They are more or less effective symbols attached to referents, and each such attachment is in some sense a unique use of the word; there is no "central" or "fundamental" or "basic" meaning of a word that lies behind every usage of it.

Of course it is true that within the semantic field of any particular lexeme there will be meanings that can be related to a common theme, and the recognition of that common theme might be helpful in elucidating the meaning of a particular usage of the lexeme. The nature of the common theme, however, must not be allowed to conceal the possibility of some quite unpredictable departure from it, into a quite different and unrelated semantic field.

(b) *The etymological fallacy.* The myth of point meaning is closely related to *the etymological fallacy.* Words represent dynamic phenomena, their possible range of associated referents constantly changing, and changing unpredictably. In contemporary English the word "gay" has taken on a new meaning that is not recoverable from its etymology, and the word "presently" in most dialects of English no longer means "at once," "in the present," "now," but its logical opposite, "not-at-once," "not-now," "not-in-the-present," but "in-the-future." Although it is true that the meanings of some compound lexemes may be deduced from their constituents (G *anthrōpareskos*, man-pleaser), it is less evident why *probaton*, whose constituents suggest something that goes forward, should denote a sheep (!) (David Black, *Linguistics for Students of New Testament Greek*, 1988, 72, on a page that contains several ingenuous etymological notations).

We have already made reference to the problem posed by paralinguistic gesture and the particular problem of winking. The relevant vb. *qrṣ* is associated with the eye in Ps 35:19; Prov 10:10; 6:13, with the lips in Prov 16:30, and in Job 33:6 with clay. Its cognates carry the meaning "to cut." In Eth., for example, *qäräṣe* means incise, shear, cut, while a derived nominal is used for shears (Wolf Leslau, *Concise Dictionary of Ge'ez*, 1989, 84). We note particularly the hapleg. nominal form in Jer 46:20 is identified as some kind of stinging fly, gadfly (RSV), arguably "cutting" or "incising" creatures. The concept of "cutting" is appropriate to the passage in Job 33, and it is then tempting to interpret the association with winking in terms of a "sharp" flicker of the eyelid. But even if this process were correct, it could yield no clue at all to the meaning of the gesture, and the sharp flicker of the eyelid has no correlate in the compression of the lips. Semantic change is arbitrary, and the attempt to relate meanings to etymologies must give way to the process of relation to usage and such clues as may be provided by cotext.

Reference to the Preface to the Revised Standard Version makes this arbitrary process of change clear:

> Thus, the King James version uses the word "let" in the sense of "hinder," "prevent" to mean "precede," "allow" in the sense of "approve," "communicate" for "share," "conversation" for "conduct," "comprehend" for "overcome," "ghost" for "spirit," "wealth" for "well-being," "allege" for "prove," "demand" for "ask," "take no thought" for "be not anxious," etc.

These changes in Eng. language usage (and they are merely a few of many such changes) have taken place in some three hundred years. The process is a universally observed phenomenon and must relate to the Heb. vocabulary as well. Thus, the meaning of a word will not be revealed by consideration of its etymology but by a consideration of all possible meanings of that word known to have been available at the time the word was used (thus avoiding the diachronic fallacy), and of the text, cotext, and context within which it appears. Even then it is necessary to be aware that an individual source may make use of any available symbol in any arbitrary manner provided only that the meaning would be reasonably transparent *to the intended receivers.*

Barr makes particular reference to the supposed origin of Heb. *qahal* in the nom. form *qol*, so that the *qahal* becomes the people of Israel, "called out" by the voice of God. And the process is further confounded by associating *qahal* with G *ekklēsia,* etymologically "called-out," so that the church is the "called-out-people-of-God" (Cotterell and Turner, 113f.). In fact, the meaning of the term *qahal* must be determined at each occurrence without any necessary reference to etymology (cf. Ps 26:5, where the *qahal* is quite clearly *not* called out by God). Of course, this is not to deny the value of etymological study as such. The fact is that the etymology of a word *may* help to suggest a possible meaning in a particular text. But it is the context that is determinative and not the etymology.

(c) *The myth of aggregated meaning.* Third, there is *the myth of aggregated meaning.* Meaning is not determined by assigning meanings independently to the constituents of a text and then aggregating the constituent meanings. An example from the NT may be allowed to illustrate the point. The words used by Jesus to his mother, represented in the G as *ti emoi kai soi gynai?* (John 2:4) may be rendered as "What-to-me-and-to-you-woman." There is no particular difficulty in these individual constituents of the string, but representing the *meaning* of the string has proved to be difficult, as may be seen by reference to the various translations.

Sentences may be categorized in many ways, but may generally be divided into two classes: favorite-pattern sentences and minority-pattern sentences. The former are those within which substitutions may be allowed, and each substitution may produce a meaningful string, the meaning of which may be related to the meanings of the rest. Minority-pattern sentences cannot be modified in the same way. For example the sentence *Not on your life, boy* means something like—*Absolutely not!* but the substitution of "bed" for "life" yields a perfectly good favorite-pattern sentence *Not on your bed, boy!* the meaning of which bears no relationship to *Absolutely not!* But further substitutions in this sentence might yield *Not on my bed, boy!* or, *Not in his house, boy!* the meanings of the three favorite-pattern sentences being clearly related to one another. The string in John 2:4 is a minority pattern string, to be understood as a phrase-whole. D. A. Cruse refers to these minority patterns as *idioms* and defines them as "complex lexemes acting as a single semantic constituent" (2.7 and 2.9.).

(d) *The myth of unique denotation.* A fourth myth is *the myth of the uniqueness of denotation*, that the meaning of a word is determined once the object it denotes has been identified. But words carry also *connotations* that are primarily culturally determined, but within a culture may further be modified by individual perceptions, or *ideolects*. Considering the string in Ps 22:6, "I am a worm, and not a man," the *denotation* may readily be determined by reference to the lexicon, but it alone does not yield the meaning of the string, since no one is disputing the fact that the writer was not a worm. In some sense he *resembled* a worm, and it is assumed that it is in the sense of the worm's weakness, its *connotation*. However, this cannot simply be assumed to be the connotation; surprisingly, the connotation of *worm* in Amharic, a Semitic language, is *strong, powerful*. To the culturally determined connotation we might then add the ideolectal connotation of those individuals who suffer from a phobia, an actual terror, of worms, yielding a whole domain of connotation to the denotation.

Clearly a similar problem arises with the connotational meaning of the *fox* with which Jesus compares Herod. *The connotative meaning of a word is the subjective meaning it may carry for an individual or group through an agreed perception of the nature or character or function of the referent.* But, of course, that connotation holds for that individual or for that group, but not necessarily for any other individual or group.

Biblical interpretation has, in some measure, been impoverished as a consequence of the fact that the majority of exegetes have been male. Although this could probably be illustrated from any book of the Bible, it is, perhaps, most readily demonstrated from the S of Songs and here most particularly in the unusual *wasf* of 5:10-16, unusual in that it relates to the male form. Falk ("The *wasf*" in Athalya Brenner (ed.), *A Feminist Companion to the Song of Songs*), quotes Richard Soulen, "The *wasfs* of the Song of Songs and Hermeneutic":

> The poetic imagination at work in 5:10-16 where the maiden speaks of her lover is less sensuous and imaginative than in the *wasfs* of chs. 4 and 7. This is due in part to the limited subject matter and may even be due to the difference in erotic imagination between poet and poetess" (Falk, 231).

Falk, a feminist writer, has no difficulty in demonstrating the falsity of Soulen's judgment and tracing the fault to the reading strategy (see sec. A.3) of the author, who finds what *he* expects and intends to find.

But quite apart from the problem of gender discriminatory reading strategies we have the problem of a kind of cultural imperialism. Quoting Falk again, she notes that even Maurice Segal can dismiss the imagery of the female *wasf* in 7:1-5 as either grotesque or as comical:

> Only as playful banter can be rationally explained the grotesque description by the lover to the damsel of her neck as "like the tower of

David built for an armoury," of her nose "as the tower of Lebanon which looketh toward Damascus," and of her head like Mount Carmel . . . and similar comical comparisons of her other limbs" (Falk, 227).

Segal does indeed recognize subsequently the possibility that "our perspective radically differs from the poet's," and this is precisely the problem with all connotation: There can be no confidence that the connotative meaning *intended* by the author is even available to the reader, most especially if that reader is separated from the original location by thousands of miles and chronologically by thousands of years.

A word of caution must be added to the potential semantic anarchy invited by the concept of connotative meaning. The remarkable account in Judg 4:17-21 of the murder of the Canaanite army commander Sisera by Jael, wife of Heber, encouraged much speculation on the true nature of the event. We have a lone married woman assassinating a prominent warrior at a period of history that had thrown up a female *šôpēṭ*. It is not difficult to suppose that sexual intercourse preceded the assassination or that Jael might well have been, or at least might have temporarily adopted, the role of prostitute. However, the suggestion that the extraordinary nature of the murder was "a grim parody of the sexual act, in which the roles are reversed and Jael acts the part of the man" expects a great deal of the reader. As Barnabas Lindars comments, "Of course we cannot be sure that the people of the narrator's age would have seen it that way" (Barnabas Lindars, *Judges 1-5*, 1995, 201). Indeed, while the ingenuity of the suggested interpretation is to be admired, the phallic connotation ascribed to a tent peg is highly improbable.

(e) *The myth of totality transfer.* There is, fifth, *the myth of totality transfer*, the recognition of the polysemy of a particular word and the importation of some element of each possible meaning, the total domain of meaning, into a single occurrence of the word. Clearly a word may be employed precisely because of its particular polysemous nature, so that two or more of the potential meanings of the word may be simultaneously accessed: Heb. *rûaḥ* and G *pneuma* are obvious examples. But that is quite a different matter and within the compass of discourse meaning, in contrast to the gratuitous importation of a multiplicity of meanings not identifiable as comprising discourse meaning.

We must now ask how we are objectively to determine meaning conveyed by a string, when each symbol employed in the semiotic is potentially polysemous. At least part of the answer must lie in a determination of the syntagmatic and paradigmatic relationships of the elements of the string. The importance of the syntagmatic relationships of words flows from the recognition that the use of any one element of a string necessarily affects the subsequent generation of other units. Similarly, the importance of the paradigmatic relationships of words flows from the recognition that possible or impossible substitutions serve to identify such matters as literary genre, metaphor, and minority-pattern sentences. The fact that in the string *Not on your life, boy* the word "life" does not share paradigmatically with such words as "boat," "bed," "table" (each of which is, in terms of formal grammar, of the same word class), marks the string as not representing a favorite-pattern sequence.

Totality transfer may be seen E. Jacob's *Theology of the Old Testament*, referred to by Barr (144-47). Jacob considers the etymologies of *'adam, 'iš, ʿenoš,* and *geber* and combines his results to produce a characterization of "man": "Added together they indicate that man according to the OT is a perishable creature, who lives only as the member of a group, but that he is also a powerful being capable of choice and dominion." But as Barr points out, while *geber* is clearly related to the root *gbr*, that by no means validates the assumption that since the root carries a meaning be strong, be powerful, the nom. must carry that same meaning. And even if it once did, that is again no reason to suppose that subsequently it did not simply denote man, with no particular overtone of power.

2. *Diachrony.* To the five myths we must add the problem of diachrony. All living language is in a constant process of change; not only are new forms being created, but old forms are both gaining new meanings and losing old meanings. The Eng. word "nice" before the thirteenth century meant "simple" or "ignorant," in the thirteenth century added the meaning "foolish," "stupid," in the fourteenth century "wanton," and in the fifteenth century "coy" or "shy." Each of these is now obsolete, and even some of the sixteenth-century senses, "subtle," "precise," "minutely accurate" are only preserved in such constructions as "a nice distinction." It would thus be inappropriate to insist that when a speaker refers to a "nice" doctor, the doctor is being accused of being ignorant. This is the diachronic error.

Language may be studied either diachronically or synchronically. In a synchronic study the process of change in a language is notionally halted and the language then described in terms of its condition at that time. To demonstrate the process of change a number of synchronic studies may be compared to give a diachronic view of the language.

Changes in the semantic values of the lexical stock of a language fall into three principal categories, *shift, metaphoric,* and *metonymic.* In *shift* changes there are relatively small and even logical movements in the sense of the word—on the one hand—generalization, where "manuscript" moves from being a hand-written document to being an original document of any kind, or restriction, where "meat" moves from a general reference to food to a specific reference to flesh. Any form may become the basis for *metaphorical* extension: "spine" being applied to the back of a book, or "leaf" to an extension to a table. *Metonymy* may similarly generalize, so that a door, the element closing a doorway, becomes the doorway, or may conversely produce restriction, such as "gate," originally the gap, becoming instead the means of closing the gap. (See especially S. Ullmann, *Semantics: An Introduction to the Science of Meaning*, 1962, ch. 9; see also G. B. Caird, *The Language and Imagery of the Bible*, 1980, 62-84.) Of particular importance here are certain proper names: Moses, David, Solomon. David is at one point in Israel's history no more (and no less) than a name, but David becomes not merely king, but a king focally associated with divine covenant, founder not merely of a dynasty, but of a dynasty that expressed the eschatological expectations of a nation. Thus, "David" no longer signifies merely David, but metonymically signifies anyone of the promised ideal Davidic line.

The nominal *mal'āk* presents the exegete with particular problems since its semantic domain covers not merely the purely secular sense of "messenger" but also the sense of a divine messenger, and more than that there is reference to the *mal'ak yhwh* (see #4855 in the Appendix). The same distinct usages occur with respect to G *angelos,* but the Eng. "angel" is almost invariably reserved for the divine messenger.

D. Discourse Analysis

This article has dealt first with an indication of some developments in general linguistic and hermeneutical theory relevant to the exegesis of text, and then with the role of words in determining text meaning. Some reference must now be made to one further level of interpretation, the role of *discourse*. The meaning of a text is determined by the words from which it is constructed and the manner of their incorporation into the text syntactically and paradigmatically. But the meaning of any pericope is determined also by the larger text of which it is a part.

The Jacob discourse, which occupies some twenty-five chapters of Gen, provides an indicative model to illustrate the point. It is itself set into the larger text of Gen and the still larger pentateuchal text. It is preceded by the creation discourse, Gen 1-11, which acts as Stage, as that part of the text that states the issue addressed by the text as a whole, and then by the Abraham narrative (12:1-25:18). Gen 25:19 economically concludes the Abraham discourse and opens the new Jacob discourse. These first twenty-five chapters are given coherence through the formulaic *tôledôt,* introduced at 2:4; 5:1; 6:9; 10:1; 11:10 and 27; 25:12 and 19. These formulae may be anaphoric (as in 2:4 and 5:1), but may also be cataphoric (as in 10:1 and 11:10), with the distinction determined by the cotext.

The Jacob discourse itself is introduced by the "generations" statement at 25:19 (lit., "these are the descendants of Abraham's son Isaac"), and is punctuated by the Esau genealogy of ch. 36, itself introduced by the *tôledôt* formula at 36:1 (see Genealogy in the Old Testament in the Appendix). However there is no "generations" statement for Jacob himself. The discourse is concluded at 49:33, although followed by a sequence of post-Peak episodes recording the magnificent closure account of the burial of Jacob, one final act of deception (deception having been a major coherency theme throughout the Jacob discourse), practiced on Joseph by his brothers, and finally the death of Joseph.

While the Joseph story has its importance first in carrying forward the deception motif of the Jacob narrative and second in its broader *Heilsgeschichte* role in moving Jacob-Israel from Canaan to Egypt, it has its peak in his self-revelation to his brothers in 45:1-4, while his biography whispers to a close, the matter-of-fact account of his death and embalming in 50:26 clearly leaving that story unclosed. In Exod 13:19 Moses is depicted taking the bones of Joseph out of Egypt, while only in Josh 24:32 is the story finally concluded, with the burial of his bones at Shechem.

Gen 25-50, then, represent a coherent discourse, and we turn now briefly to a consideration of the nature of textuality and to the relevance of the identification of a text to the process of interpreting its constituent parts, illustrating the process from the Jacob discourse.

1. *The seven standards of textuality.* We have already alluded (see sec. B.4) to the fact that textuality is indicated by seven standards. There is firstly *cohesion* of grammar and syntax. Referents remain constant: Proforms in one part of the text relate to co-referring expressions elsewhere. Proforms are significant, cataphoric reference introducing a suspense feature into the semantic structure, and this in turn has the effect of transferring emphasis from one part of a text to another. In exegetical terms this means that cataphoric proforms underline a select portion of text making it more likely to be recalled. (On the use of cataphora and anaphora and their effect on learning

and recall see R. de Beaugrande and W. Dressler, 60-68.) As a general principle it may be said that any shift of emphasis produced by the reordering of words increases learning and recall at one point, but at the expense of some other point in the communicative process.

The second standard of textuality is *coherence* at the semantic level. The constituent themes of the text are meaningfully related so as to produce a thematic net. In the case of the Jacob narrative, this net is woven out of the constituent themes of divine promise and providence, human deception and human frailty.

The third standard of textuality is *intention:* There is an author who purposes a communication. The traditional monkeys, hammering randomly on typewriter, could never, in this sense, produce a text, since there could be no communicative intention behind the text. It should, perhaps, be noted that there may in any culture be specialized texts, the interpretation of which explicitly does not take account of authorial intention. In such texts it is the wording alone that carries meaning, and the possible intention of any author or drafting committee is disregarded. Legal texts frequently fall into this category.

Fourth is the standard of *acceptability*. The reader of the text accepts that the text is meaningful, that is to say, not so ungrammatical as to be incomprehensible, that it offers the possibility of a genuine dialogue leading to an intended goal, and that the special circumstances that gave rise to the text are relevant to the interpretive process. In H.P. Grice's terms a text creates cooperation.

A text is not wholly redundant, so that the fifth standard is *informativity*. This requirement of a text may be realized even where the denotative content is already familiar to the reader. Thus *Hamlet* or the account of Jacob's deception of Isaac remain texts even when denotative content has been exhausted, since their respective connotative content is in some measure determined by the unique moment of each existential dialogue with them.

Texts are more than a presentation of facts to be assimilated, and biblical texts had a didactic function in which existing ethical imperatives were either challenged or reenforced. A text is directed to a situation, and *situationality* is the sixth standard of textuality: The interpretation of the text is in some measure related to the situation which gave rise to it. The absence of an identifiable situation may be remedied in Eng. by a phrase such as "let us suppose that," or in Heb. by the employment of some term such as *māšāl* or, ambiguously in most languages, by a fictitious context, "There were two men in a certain town" (2 Sam 12:1), providing an apparent social context later revealed as *māšāl*. In this particular example, the interpretation of the text is shown to depend precisely on its situationality.

Finally is the seventh standard, *intertextuality*, the existence of a body of texts in some sense analogous to the text under consideration. The interpretation of apocalyptic literature is given some measure of credibility by the existence of an entire apocalyptic textual genre, and this may be of particular importance when interpreting apocalyptic embedded in some different text type (see Thiselton, 80-81).

The Jacob narrative clearly satisfies these seven standards of textuality.

2. *Narrative structure*. Discourse considerations suggest that the exegesis of any narrative depends not only on questions of grammar and syntax, but also on questions of textuality, and particularly on the identification of text structure and thematic

net. In any extended text, such as the Jacob narrative, the narrative consists of a sequence of contributing *topics,* which together create a network of relationships, events, and propositions. The net, which is being continuously woven as the text progresses, carries the text forward from Stage to Peak, the point at which the staged problem is resolved, the staged question answered, through a series of related Episodes. The Peak is followed by Closure, the more-or-less artistic conclusion of the text. In the Jacob narrative Stage is provided by Gen 25:23, Peak by 48:20, and Closure quite magnificently by 50:14. The verse is preceded by the spectacle of the great mass of mourners processing from Egypt into Canaan, the splendid "grievous mourning" at Abel Mizraim, and is succeeded by dispersal: Joseph and his brothers and the great company return to Egypt, leaving the central character in his lonely tomb at Machpelah.

Between Stage and Closure the narrative passes through a number of contributing pericopes (the angels at Bethel, the marriage of Jacob, Laban's household gods, the encounter with Esau), each of which must be understood not merely in its own terms but also in terms of its relationship to the total text. Even the Joseph pericope (Gen 37:2-45:28) is ultimately significant because of its contribution to the Jacob narrative. Joseph is given preeminence over his brothers and provides the two grandsons who appear in the Peak, evoking the two brothers of Stage. Within the linguistic subdiscipline of Poetics, both Jacob and Joseph are full-fledged *characters* while Joseph's brothers are *agents,* whose personalities are developed only insofar as they contribute to the narrative. Joseph's sons are mere *types*, of whom we are allowed to know very little. Development of a type into an agent, or of an agent into a character would serve only to confuse the thrust of the narrative (see Adele Berlin, *Poetics and Interpretation of Biblical Narrative*, 1983, ch. 2; of course, a *type* from a larger text may be presented as a *character* in a constituent pericope, as is Benjamin in 42:1-45:15).

Focal to the entire narrative is the onomastic element of the encounter between Jacob and the *mal'ak yhwh* at Peniel. The renaming of Jacob as Israel is itself significant, but it is arguably of greater significance that immediately afterwards (Gen 33:1) he is identified still as "Jacob," and even at Peak and Closure both names are still being used, selectively, and sometimes in typical Heb. parallelism (49:2, 24). The dual name is taken up with great linguistic skill by the so-called Second Isaiah.

3. *Peak*. Narrative moves from the staged problem or question to its resolution, the Peak. The correct identification of Peak is clearly of enormous importance, affecting the interpretation of all included pericopes. There are, in fact, generally recognized and objectively identifiable features that contribute to the identification of Peak: *concentration of participants, rhetorical underlining, locus underlining,* and *grammatical underlining.*

(a) The first of these is deliberately so placed: It appears to be the case that the bringing together of all of the *characters* and *agents* or, alternatively, the isolation of the main characters from all others, appear to be an almost universal literary device for signaling Peak. The two contrasting devices appear in the two principal Peaks of Dickens' A *Tale of Two Cities*. In the court scene, where the resemblance of Carton and Darnay is first noted, we have a concentration of participants. But at the ultimate Peak, the execution of Sydney Carton, he is left with an entirely new *type* as his only

153

companion on the journey to the guillotine, while the rest of the cast is not merely omitted from the scene, but is actually depicted as driving rapidly away from it.

In the New Testament we note on the one hand Jesus' absence from the Peak of the Cana miracle in John 2:10, when the water is found to have become wine, and on the other hand, in Matt 28 the assembling of the eleven on the unnamed mountain in Galilee, where they are joined by Jesus so that his Great Commission may form the Peak of the Gospel. We note also the confirmatory locus underlining, mountains being given a particular connotational value in the structure of the Gospel (see T. L. Donaldson, *Jesus on the Mountain*, JSNTSup 8, 1985), and the rhetorical underlining of the commission itself, with its *pasa ... panta ... panta ... pasas*. It is striking that after the account of Peter's denial of Christ the disciples are denied any further role in the crucifixion, burial, and resurrection events; they are not intended as Peak events.

(b) For *rhetorical effect* the onset of Peak may be delayed, and delayed peaking is typical of Job and Revelation. The structure of Job may well be tedious to the contemporary scholarly mind, but not at all to Semitic culture. We are warned from Job 2:11, following Stage, that we must expect speeches from Job's three friends before we are given Yahweh's explanation of Job's suffering. These three speeches take us to 11:20, with an inconclusive response from Job moving us on to 14:22, at which point Peak is further delayed by Eliphaz (ch. 15), Bildad (ch. 18) and Zophar (ch. 20). But then there is a *third* cycle involving Eliphaz (ch. 22) and Bildad (a mere six verses in ch. 25). There follows the long impassioned response of Job, taking the reader to the end of ch. 31, and precisely when we are led to suppose that we *must* now get the answer and that it must come from Yahweh, a new *agent* is introduced, Elihu, whose speech occupies no fewer than six chapters. Only then is Peak reached: The supporting cast of agents is dismissed, and Job is left confronting Yahweh.

The Peak itself is introduced by a devastating series of rhetorical questions (a device that occurs also in 1 Cor 9:1-12, signaling the episodic Peak), but the Peak is not after all provided by Yahweh, but by Job. This unexpected development forces the reader to recognize that Stage has been misunderstood. The Staged question is not "Why do the innocent suffer?" but "Can faith survive calamity?"

Rhetorical underlining may be effected in other ways. For example in repetition, as in the ten occurrences of *r'h*, see, in Ezek 1, which precede the episodic Peak "I fell facedown" (1:28c).

(c) *Change of locus* frequently signals Peak, where the new locus (as in Matt 28) has particular connotative value. We note particularly how in Exod 19:1 the change of locus to Sinai is solemnly recorded ("On the third month after the people of Israel left Egypt—on that very day—they came into the Desert of Sinai"), but then Peak is delayed as Moses repeatedly ascends Sinai and then is sent back down again by Yahweh with some warning message to the people. Only at Exod 20:1 do we reach the anticipated Peak: "God spoke."

(d) *Grammatical underlining* to mark Peak may be seen in John 2, where as the Peak approaches the present tense used for verbal acts and the aorist for nonverbal acts give way to the perfect tense, so that events now described are given particular emphasis (B. Olsson, *Structure and Meaning in the Fourth Gospel*, 1974, 182). Similarly, in the Flood narrative a great deal of paraphrase is used, and, as Longacre has pointed out, what is striking is that much of this paraphrase is presented in clauses whose verbs have the characteristic narrative tense and the word order of event-line clauses. Elsewhere event-line verbs are not used in a paraphrase of an event. Here, however, at the Peak of the story, the characteristic event-line tense is extended to supportive materials (R. E. Longacre, *The Grammar of Discourse*, 27).

4. *Deixis*. The analysis of discourse as extended text takes seriously the distinction between mere sentences and utterances. Unlike a sentence an utterance has a context and that context contributes to the meaning of the text. Within texts we find linguistic elements included that are intended by the author or redactor to enable the reader the better to visualize the events being described, These are the so-called deictic elements of language. Texts are normally speaker-oriented, so that the words used by the writers of a text or by speakers within the text place any action in spatial and temporal relationship to themselves rather than absolutely.

Deixis, then, is the encoding within an utterance of the spatio-temporal context and of the subjective experience of the encoder. Or, as John Lyons expresses it more explicitly:

> the location and identification of persons, objects, processes and activities being talked about, or referred to, in relation to the spatio-temporal context created and sustained by the act of utterance and the participation in it, typically, of a single speaker and at least one addressee (*Semantics*, 1977, 637).

Five categories of deixis are usually identified.

(a) *Personal deixis*, elements of the text that identify author, redactor, or speaker, include personal names or titles, and particularly proforms, is significant in the so-called "we" passages in Acts ("they" in Acts 16:8, "we" in 16:10 and subsequently). The change of pronoun signals the presence of the writer in the events described.

(b) *Social deixis*, which may include the use of honorifics or self-deprecating indirect modes of address, establishes the social standing of speaker and the one addressed. Thus addressing the pharaoh Joseph says: "God will give Pharaoh the answer he desires" (Gen 41:16), and "The dreams of Pharaoh are one and the same; God has revealed to Pharaoh what he is about to do" (41:25), and "the reason the dream was given to Pharaoh in two forms is that the matter has been firmly decided" (41:32).

(c) *Temporal deixis* establishes the timeline of discourse, sometimes employing nominal forms, "the third day," sometimes conjunctions, "later," "before," sometimes verbal forms, especially verbs of intention or expectation.

(d) The fourth category of deixis is *locational:* "here," "there," "at Socoh." As an example of the role of deictic elements we may note those elements that set the scene for Esther's appeal to the king in Esth 5:1:

> On the third day [pointing back to 4:16 and the requirement that the Jews of Susa fast for three days on her behalf] Esther put on her royal robes [she would be in the harem; she puts on royal robes both to

indicate her status and in recognition of the occasion, a formal audience] and stood in the inner court of the palace, in front of the king's hall. The king was sitting on his royal throne [not as though, naively, the writer supposed that he sat there each day, but because this was an audience day, and Esther knew so] in the hall, facing the entrance.

The richness of the locational deixis provided here is paralleled in the rape of Tamar pericope (2 Sam 13). The pericope is marked off by a new location, Jerusalem rather than Rabbah, by new actors, Amnon, Tamar, and Jonadab. David is reduced to a mere *type*, where he had been a full *character* in the preceding chapter. The new Stage represents a microcosm instead of the preceding macrocosm, and the literary genre changes from an epic to a classical tragedy.

The limitation of employing only grammar, lexicon, and dictionary to determine meaning is evident. Absalom is named as "David's son" (personal and social deixis), and so is Amnon, while Jonadab is identified as "son of Shimeah, David's brother" (2 Sam 13:3). These are all deictic indications that while we now have a microcosmic tragedy rather than a macrocosmic epic, the tragedy is primarily an episode within the epic.

The locational deixis is skillfully worked between the respective residences of Amnon, Tamar, and David, climaxing in the pathetic picture of the ravaged Tamar walking back to her home, ashes on her head, her torn robes clutched to her, Amnon's love turned to hate, and his door bolted behind her. No interpretation of the text that excluded the deictically determined connotational elements could possibly do justice to it.

However, for all the pathos of the Tamar tragedy, its principal purpose is to contribute to the Royal Chronicle, and to remove it from its larger cotext would provide it with a different meaning from that intended by its author or redactor.

(e) *Logical* or *discourse deixis* relates to those markers within a discourse that signal to the reader that a new phase in the developing text has been reached, or that some past phase must now be invoked to facilitate the correct understanding of the new phase. Such obviously logical lexemes as "therefore" (cf. G *oun*) may be deictic, and so also may interrogatives. Heb. *lammâ* in Eccl 2:15 is rendered unsatisfactorily in NIV by the bland "Why?" and yet the particular usage and connotative meanings of this form are far from clear (see James Barr, "'Why?' in Biblical Hebrew," *JTS* [new series] 36, 1985, 1-33). At the end of this exhaustive article Barr indicates one of the many possible connotations of *lammâ:* "A 'Why?' question may be a joyful acknowledgment, tinged with a slight reproach at the excessive kindness or consideration of another" (33). In other words, this simple lexeme cannot be so much translated as paraphrased within the larger syntactic and semantic unit. The Eccl 2 example may well represent Barr's class of *hypothetical deprecations* (19).

And so we come back to the starting point of the essay. Primary language is spoken language, an imprecise communications semiotic, demonstrating both denotations and connotations, involving text, cotext, and context, a speaker and, normally, at least one listener. The imprecision of connotation is moderated by the presence of the speaker and listener and by the existing relationship between them. Written language is secondary, an attempt to capture spoken language through an arbitrary system of signs, but compelled to do so in the absence both of the speaker and of the referents of the resultant text.

To interpret a text it is necessary to have an understanding of phonology, morphology, syntax, and lexicography. However, the imprecision of language permeates the entire semiotic: Words are polysemous, chronology brings change in the lexical stock and its usage, and even small changes in the sequencing of words may produce significant, and yet not readily definable changes in meaning. Meaning itself is distributed between denotations and connotations, these latter to be identified only with probability, never with certainty, the probability level falling steadily as the age of the text increases. We must always be aware that lexical and grammatical studies of the constituents of a text can never be simply aggregated to produce text meaning. What such studies *can* do is responsibly to contribute to what must be seen as the *art* rather than the *science* of exegesis.

BIBLIOGRAPHY
J. Barr, *The Semantics of Biblical Language*, 1961; R. de Beaugrande and W. Dressler (eds.), *Introduction to Text Linguistics*, 1981; A Brenner (ed.), *A Feminist Companion to the Song of Songs, 1993;* P. Cotterell and M. Turner, *Linguistics and Biblical Interpretation*, 1989; D. A. Cruse, *Lexical Semantics*, 1986; S. Fish, *Is There a Text in This Class?* 1980; idem, *Doing What Comes Naturally*, 1989; D. Levine, *Wax and Gold*, 1965; J. Lyons, *Language and Linguistics*, 1981; D. McKim (ed.), *A Guide to Contemporary Hermeneutics*, 1986; E. McKnight, *Meaning in Texts*, 1978; T. Muraoka, *Emphatic Words and Structures in Biblical Hebrew*, 1985; A. Thiselton, *New Horizons in Hermeneutics*, 1992; J. Tompkins (ed.), *Reader-Response Criticism*, 1980; F. Watson (ed.), *The Open Text*, 1993; W. Wink, *The Bible in Human Transformation*, 1973.

Peter Cotterell

8. PRINCIPLES FOR PRODUCTIVE WORD STUDY

Often when studying a biblical text we understand that the meaning of a passage may be heavily dependent on the meaning of a particular word or phrase. Still, all the tools in the world will avail nothing if we do not know how to use them. Any tool, instrument, weapon, or equipment is subject to the limitations of those who use them. In order to put this tool to good use, the reader needs to have an acquaintance with some of the principles of lexical and semantic analysis. These principles may be presented within the context of the science of linguistics (see the preceding article by Cotterell), or may be discussed in terms of our common, everyday use of language. This latter approach may not satisfy the linguist, but it may serve the purposes of a less technically trained student.

A. Understanding Authors' Choices

In order to understand what an author invests in the meaning of a word, we must think about what goes into the choice of a word. Biblical authors did not use some special heavenly language with mystical meanings. Like any other author, a biblical author chose a particular word because it carried precisely the meaning that he wanted to communicate. That sounds too obvious to mention, but it must be realized that there are other alternatives, and we will consider some of those others first.

1. *Considerations of form.* If an author is working within the limitations imposed by a certain form, he may choose a word not for its precision of meaning, but for its conformity to the requirements. In English a good example of this would be the choice of a word to complete a rhyme or to represent the third point in an alliterated series (persecution, penalty, p...). If form is imposing some requirements on word choice, precision of meaning may not be possible. In Hebrew this may become relevant in acrostic poems or even in parallelism. Thus, in Ps 119:105 one would not make too much of the word lamp (*nēr*; see # 5944 in the Appendix). Since all the verses between 105-12 begin with *nun*, this word was chosen to suit the form.

2. *Poetic expression.* Most languages have words available for use in poetry that would not typically be used in other types of writing. Often such expressions operate through the use of metaphor and therefore lack technical precision in terms of meaning. So when we read that "the mountains skipped like rams" (Ps 114:4), we understand that precision of meaning did not guide word choice. Likewise, when poetic terms like *tēbēl*, world, are chosen, we can credit poetic style. In these cases, we need to evaluate word choice in light of the type of literature we are dealing with.

3. *Conventional combinations.* There are some words that we choose to use in set phrases where the phrase has meaning to us even if the individual parts do not. Sometimes we use the parts always and only in the context of that phrase. In English the word "diametrically" would rarely, if ever, be used except in the phrase "diametrically opposed." Most users do not know what "diametrically" means, but the phrase has meaning. Likewise "ulterior" would not be used with anything besides "motives" and has meaning to most users only in that phrase. A third example is the word "brunt," which we would only use in the expression "to bear the brunt of . . . " and which has no independent meaning to most of its users. In BH the word *bōhû*, empty, is used only with *tōhû*, nothing, as in Gen 1:2. As interpreters, then, we must be aware

that authors at times use stock phrases, and we must learn to recognize them as such. The author is not choosing the word as much as he is choosing the phrase.

Though we can recognize the above situations as offering exceptions, the rule is that most word choices are made on the basis of the meaning of that word as the author and his intended audience understand it. The following observations can provide principles for interpretation.

(a) *Synonyms and antonyms.* In many cases the process of communication takes place as the listener/reader hears the words that the author has chosen in light of other words that could have been used. For instance, think of the different aspects that might be communicated if an author chose to use "charger" instead of "horse." What if he chose mustang, or bronco, or steed? What about stallion, mare, palfrey, or pony? In some instances he might have chosen stud or gelding. This is an example from a whole series of words in the general category of "horse." At other times the choices might involve words that refer to the same object, but raise different feelings about the object. In English one can speak of a fetus (and preserve a certain amount of objective formality) or of an unborn child (to incorporate or express one's belief of personhood). Whenever words with overlapping meaning exist, we have a right to ask: Why did the author choose this one instead of another? In the articles in these books the authors and editors have made every attempt to alert the reader to the choices that would have been available to the biblical author and to suggest what situations might lead to the choice of one alternative over another. Sometimes even if words mean nearly the same thing and can often be interchanged, there are some contexts where one would be appropriate and the other would not. For instance, in English one can almost always interchange "earth" and "ground"—but not if electricity is being discussed. Likewise, if the word were paired with heaven, ground would not be chosen.

In a similar fashion, the choice of a word is better understood by comparing words with similar meaning (synonyms) and with words of contrasting meaning (antonyms). Thus, someone who is described as running cannot be sitting, standing, or walking. Sometimes, then, words are chosen so as to differentiate between synonyms, and other times so as to contrast to antonyms.

(b) *The parts that make up a word.* When we choose to use a particular word, we are often not conscious of the parts that make up that word. For instance, we use the word "awful" without even noticing that it is a combination of awe + full. English is full of compound words, some easily recognizable, such as "understand," others not as readily noticed, such as "syllabus." Our usage of these words does not imply knowledge of the parts, nor does it intend to convey what the parts meant in their individual forms. Therefore, when we analyze the word choices of the authors of Scripture, we should not assume that the use of a compound word assumes knowledge of or carries the meaning of the parts. In Greek, where compound words are common, it is a constant temptation to the interpreter to analyze the meanings of words by their constituent parts. But a moment's thought about English usage should warn us against placing confidence in that type of approach. Our use of a word like "understand" is not at all influenced or informed by viewing it as a combination of "under" and "stand"; one cannot arrive at an interpretation of the meaning of that word by evaluating the parts.

In Hebrew the problem is not so much compound words as it is the relationship of words that share the same root. In English we understand that words that share the same root may be related and may not. The verb "exist" certainly is closely related in meaning to the noun "existence" and not many steps away from the adjective "existential." Knowing the meaning of the root, exist, can help the reader deduce the meaning of the other related parts of speech. Other examples, however, do not work so well. For instance, recognition of the root "adult" in "adultery" will not be of any use. More subtly, one can easily associate "company" and "companion," but when one gets to the verb "accompany," only partial success can be achieved. If the verb is being used to speak of joining someone on a walk, there is no problem; but if the speaker is using the more technical idiomatic sense of accompanying a soloist on the piano, the root relationship provides little assistance. Likewise in Hebrew the interpreter cannot have confidence that the words that share a common root will also share a common meaning. We must be aware, therefore, that we cannot use one to shed light on the other unless the relationship can be independently established.

Likewise the BH for angel or messenger (*mal'āk,* see # 4855 in the Appendix) certainly shares a root with the nom. work, occupation (*malā'kâ*), yet it would be a mistake to try to interpret one in light of the other. On a more popular level, it used to be common to see the Philistine god Dagon portrayed in the form of a fish. This reflected the analysis of well-meaning interpreters that *dāg* meant fish, while *ôn* was a typical nom. ending. Further discoveries have clarified that the WestSem. deity Dagon, adopted by the Philistines, was a grain deity. We cannot expect that reducing a word to its constituent parts will give reliable guidance to establishing meaning.

(c) *The history of the word.* We do not choose to employ a word based on an understanding of its history. A word's origin is called its etymology. Most speakers are entirely unaware of the etymology of the words they are using. More importantly, many words have evolved over time in such a way that their current meaning is only vaguely related to their original meaning. For example, though the English word "sinister" originally referred to being left-handed, those who use the word today are rarely aware of that history. Even if they are aware of it, they do not use the word in that connection. Linguists refer to the study of the historical development of a word as a *diachronic* approach. The alternative is to study the current usage of the word in all its possible contexts. Linguists call this a *synchronic* approach. The diachronic study of a word may help the interpreter to understand by what route a word came to mean what it does mean. A synchronic study of a word will help the interpreter know what the word means to the person who has just used it.

Though etymology or other diachronic approaches can at times provide information concerning meaning, the problem is that one cannot rely on them to do so. Since we are aware of so many cases where meaning has shifted over time, we should be uncomfortable establishing the meaning of a word on the basis of our knowledge of its history (diachronic) rather than on its usage (synchronic). An author will choose his word based on his presupposition about what his audience will understand when they hear or read that word.

A well-meaning teacher dealing with Prov 22:6 was trying to explain to his class what the text meant when it said that the properly trained child would not depart from the parent's teaching "when he was old." He informed the class that since the verb "to be old" (*zāqēn*) also contributed its root to the nom. "beard" (*zāqān*), we could understand the text to be saying that when the son was old enough to grow a beard he would not depart from the teaching. Such analysis can only mislead and distort—it contributes nothing to sound exegesis.

Given these observations concerning related words, parts of a word, and the history of a word, we can recognize that as interpreters we need to understand words in the light of what choices authors are making when they use their words. The principles that emerge are:

•A word should be understood in recognition of other related words that were not selected by the author.

•A word should not necessarily be broken down into its constituent parts or analyzed in light of its root unless it can be established independently that a relationship of meaning exists.

•Synchronic methods are to be preferred over diachronic methods.

B. Determining Meaning by the Synchronic Approach

The synchronic approach depends on the concept that the meaning of a word is established by the usage made of it by speakers and writers. Most words have a range of possible meanings, called the *semantic range,* which the interpreter should seek to define when investigating the meaning of the word in a particular context. With the help of a concordance, all of the occurrences of the word in its various forms may be located. These become the raw data of the *lexical base.* The next step, and arguably the most important, is classification of the data. In the synchronic approach one must attempt to differentiate all of the various defining aspects of how a word may be used. The following categories will provide an idea of the issues that must be considered.

1. *Author.* Different authors may use the same word in different ways. On the other hand, there are many words that may be used in the same way by many different authors. The synchronic method does not require that only usages by the same author be considered. It only requires that the interpreter be sensitive to idiosyncratic or distinctive meanings attached to certain words by certain authors. In NT studies it has long been recognized that Paul and James do not use the term *justification* with precisely the same meanings. In OT studies we are aware that the "Redeemer" motif takes on a unique role in Isa, or that the "enemy" has a distinctive sense in the Ps. In such cases the synchronic method asks us to isolate the usage of the author who has demonstrated an inclination to individualize the meaning.

2. *Genre.* The interpreter must be aware that some words may be used with distinctive meanings in certain types of literature that they would not have in other types. For instance, legal literature may use various words for law in technical ways, whereas Psalms may use the same words as virtual synonyms. It is important when classifying the data from the lexical base to be aware of the genre categories, for though the usage across the genres may be undifferentiated, the interpreter must be aware that change of meaning is possible.

In BH the term *minḥâ* refers to a particular type of sacrifice in ritual literature (Pentateuch laws) and in ritual contexts in narrative literature (e.g. Dan 9:27), but in nonritual contexts it refers to a gift in general (1 Sam 10:27; 2 Kgs 8:8) or, more technically, to tribute (2 Sam 8:2).

3. *Part of speech.* We have already discussed the fact that noms. and vbs. that share a common history at times develop very different meanings. As a result, the synchronic method must be cautious in relating various byforms to one another. In

Hebrew the noms. *miṭṭâ*, bed, and *maṭṭeh*, tribe, staff, cannot be evaluated in relation to the verbal root *nṭh*, stretch, nor in relation to one another. Verbs must be classified independent of noms. and the various nom. forms must be kept distinct unless: (a) A relationship can be established by applying the synchronic method to each form; or (b) insufficient numbers of occurrences make independent investigation impossible and contextual factors suggest a relationship.

A related distinction concerns the verbal stems. Though it is often the case that there is a level of semantic interrelation among the stems (e.g., the ni. as the passive of the q.; or the hi. as the causative of the q.), there are sufficient examples of deviation to urge us to caution. There are examples where the stems have radically departed from one another. One only has to look at the variations in the lexical listings in vbs. such as *'tq* or *pg'* to see the diffusion of meaning that is possible. More subtle are the cases where relationship between the stems remains visible but certain nuances pertain in one but not in the other. So, for instance, for the root *ṣḥq* the q. and the pi. both concern joy, laughter, and fun, but the pi. contains a more negative nuance (making fun of someone) as well as a sexual nuance (Gen 26:8, caress).

Again, then, the extent of relatedness between the verbal stems should be established by applying the synchronic method to each stem individually before the interpreter would feel free to classify all the verbal occurrences together in the semantic range.

4. *Time period.* When sorting out the lexical base it is essential to consider whether occurrences in late literature use the word in the same way as in earlier literature. We are all aware of the way in which words can shift meaning over time. It is well recognized that there was the development of what is termed late biblical Hebrew that is evident from Ezek through the postexilic books (e.g., Ezra-Neh and Chron). For example, the verb *lqḥ* develops the meaning "buy" in later times, but one would not expect that usage in earlier literature. As a result, the synchronic method cannot indiscriminately group various time periods together. Each time period should be considered independently until similarity of usage is established.

5. *Technical or idiomatic usage.* There will often be certain occurrences within the database that have a more technical sense, and these must be separated out lest they unduly influence our understanding of the meaning of the whole. The usage of the *'ēpōd* as a cult object from which oracles were obtained and as part of the linen clothing of the priest may have little to do with each other. In the theological realm, the adoption of *māšîaḥ*, *ṣemaḥ*, or *'ebed* as terms to describe a future, ideal Davidic king must be kept distinct from other nontechnical occurrences. Likewise, *śāṭān* as a general nom. must be distinguished from any technical reference to Satan.

In the idiomatic realm the interpreter must distinguish specialized uses from the other categories and deal with them separately. The fact that Hebrew uses the vb. *yd'*, know, for sexual intercourse does not suggest that such a nuance could be applied for all occurrences. A meaning that a word has in an idiomatic context cannot be applied to other occurrences of that word outside the idiomatic usage. In English it could be claimed that the word "minute" does not always apply to a period of sixty seconds, for when someone says "I'll be there in a minute," it can refer to a rather inexact and sometimes extended period of time. This would not suggest, however, that a professor could decide that the class period, consisting of 50 minutes, could be understood to last for 50 extended periods of time. The imprecise, extended aspect of the word "minute" is present only in idiomatic phrases, such as "in a minute." The synchronic approach recognizes this distinction and insists on idiomatic usages being isolated in classification of the occurrences.

Additionally, the meaning of the idiomatic phrases must be established synchronically just as individual words are. This requires that other occurrences of the idiomatic phrase be found. So the phrase *lqḥ nāšîm* in Gen 6:1 must be understood as marrying, not just having a sexual encounter. The phrase *'îš kilᵉbābô* in 1 Sam 13:14 must be understood as referring not to David's devotion, but to the fact that David conforms to God's criteria. The phrase *lqḥ nepeš* in Prov 11:30 must be understood as taking life, as in all other occurrences, rather than the traditional "saving souls" (though the interpreter must then work at figuring out why such a person would be considered wise; see the helpful discussion by D. A. Garrett, *Proverbs, Ecclesiastes, Song of Songs,* 1993, 129). R. B. Y. Scott renders the verse: "But crime takes away life" (*Proverbs and Ecclesiastes*, AB, 1985, 87).

6. *Accompanying circumstances.* When establishing categories for the lexical base the interpreter must also observe common associations for the word under study. It is of importance, for instance, to recognize that the vb. *br'*, create, has only deity as its subject, but takes a wide range of objects, including trees, humans, cities, cosmic phenomena, and abstractions (e.g., righteousness, praise); that the vb. *nṭh*, stretch out, is going to vary in meaning depending on its object (often tent, but occasionally hand, heart, peace, etc.); that the vb. *kpr*, cover, takes only items as its direct object (e.g., ark, altar) rather than people.

We will also find variations of meaning depending on the collocations in which a word is used. One common distinguishing factor in collocations is represented in the various prepositions that may accompany a vb. In English we are well aware that there is a distinct difference in meaning between saying someone "believes the President" and saying that he "believes in the President"—the collocation "believe in" has a nuance that goes far beyond the uncollocated usage. Likewise in Heb. and G, the presence of certain prepositions with the vb. can make a good deal of difference in the meaning of the vb. A synchronic study will categorize each collocation separately until it can be determined what unique nuances, if any, each one carries.

All of these factors become the basis on which the interpreter must establish categories within the lexical base. Having set up categories of author, genre, part of speech, time period, specialized usage, and accompanying circumstances, one can disregard those distinctions that show no sign of introducing different nuances. The resulting categories may then each be studied to determine from their usage what meanings they carry. Unfortunately this second step is often treacherous or seemingly impossible because of the following pitfalls.

(a) *Lack of synchronic data.* In order to establish meaning from context, as the synchronic approach seeks to do, it is necessary to have a number of clear and precise contexts. This is often a problem in BH. If occurrences are few or contexts do not provide the information necessary for nuancing, the synchronic method cannot produce reliable results. For the former consider the plight of the interpreter trying to determine the meaning of the "desire" of woman in Gen 3:16. There are only two other occurrences of this word (Gen 4:7; S of Songs 7:10), and the three together simply do not provide the necessary information to arrive confidently at an understanding of meaning. As an example of lack of contextual information consider the difficulty in arriving at the meaning of the *kappōret*, mercy seat(?). Its twenty-six occurrences (all in Exod, Lev, and Num + 1 in Chron) are all so much the same that they give little information and no explanation sufficient to understand it.

In these sorts of cases, since the synchronic approach is incapable of providing reliable solutions, interpreters are often forced into the shoals of the diachronic method in the hope of improving our understanding of the word. Resorts would include many of those aspects that we have previously separated out: A nom. may find help from its verbal root; etymology may suggest some possibilities. Additionally, Heb. can at times turn to comparative Semitics to supply hints. We must understand, however, that comparative Semitics must usually be identified as a diachronic approach. That a particular word has a certain meaning in Arab., Ugar., Akk., Sumerian, or Aram. does not mean that it will have the same meaning or nuance in Heb. Nonetheless, when synchronic information is lacking or when context gives some reason to suspect the value of comparative Semitics, it can be a valuable tool.

Examples of comparative Semitic assistance can be found in the following situations:

> *kpr* occurs in the q. only in the Flood story (Gen 6:14) and means to cover with pitch. It is known from Akk. *kupru* and the context makes the connection clear.
>
> *mkr* occurs only in 2 Kgs 12:6, 8 in the account of Joash's financing of the temple restoration. Again, context suggests the connection with Akk. *makkuru,* which refers to temple or palace assets or estate (cf. *CAD* M1:133-37) or to Ugar. *mkr,* merchant (cf. NIV and *HALAT* 551). Here the guesses of translators have tried to make connection to supposed verbal roots (e.g., *nkr,* thus, "acquaintances," NASB).
>
> *melek Yareb* occurs in Hos 5:13 and, rather than a proper name, has now been understood as *malki rab,* the Hebrew equivalent of the well-known Assyrian title, *šarrū rābū,* the great king. Here the cognate relationship can easily be accepted because Hosea is referring specifically to the Assyrian king, so it is appropriate that he use the native title.

(b) *Determining the degree of unity in the semantic range.* A second pitfall is that interpreters are left to their lexical art and dexterity to determine when categories share a relationship in a base meaning and when they do not. As the synchronic approach proceeds to delineating the semantic range of a word (that is, all the possible meanings and the conditions under which each meaning applies), there is the temptation to establish relatedness to all the parts. It is often assumed that there is some individual core meaning to which all aspects of meaning and nuance can be connected. Again, however, this can easily reflect a diachronic mentality. The history that exists in the background of the word should not dictate our nuancing of the word, because it is an element that the users are only subconsciously aware of at best.

As an example we might consider the Heb. vb. *hgh.* The q. occurs 24x with a variety of meanings, differentiated by collocations with prepositions. In combination with *b* it takes God or his law as object and means to meditate; with *k* it refers to animal sounds; with *l* it means desire or yearning; and with no preposition it refers to pondered action, either positive or negative. Each of these meanings can be established with confidence by the synchronic approach. While the interpreter might be inclined to seek out some common denominator to these collocations, such as "private articulation of base instincts," such an endeavor is diachronic in nature and is unnecessary, unhelpful, and potentially damaging to semantic study if we allow it to regulate nuancing. Since this proposed core meaning is not a level of semantics of which the users of the collocations would have been consciously aware, it should be considered tangential to the interpreter's task.

But here we have a fine line. Though we desire to avoid diachronic influence, it is also true that attention to the patterns of meaning may help the interpreter to nuance the aspects of the semantic range in a more accurate way. The best way to decide whether to seek common ground or not is on the basis of the amount of data available. Where various aspects of the semantic range are well established on synchronic grounds, there is no need to seek out common ground in order to establish nuance. If, however, the synchronic data are limited, one might use the assumption of cohesiveness within the semantic range as a guide to possible nuances.

For an example we might return to the case of $t^e\check{s}\hat{u}q\hat{a}$, desire, in Gen 3:16. Interpreters who opt for a sexually oriented interpretation tend to emphasize the usage of S of Songs 7:10 to the neglect of Gen 4:7. Those who favor the domineering interpretation exalt Gen 4:7 (contextually nearer) to the neglect of S of Songs 7:10. In this situation where synchronic data is so limited, it is preferable to try to find resolution assuming semantic cohesiveness: that all three occurrences should be able to be accounted for in the nuance suggested. Such a search would commend consideration of a more general nuance (necessary to encompass all three) along the lines of "desire to fulfill one's most basic instincts" (whatever they may be). Thus, among the woman's most basic instincts would be reproduction (a topic under discussion in the context of 3:16); in 4:7 the basic instinct would be to deprave; and in S of Songs 7:10 the male sexual drive would be aptly defined as a basic instinct. This approach seeks to use the concept of core meaning as a means of establishing nuances of individual occurrences only when synchronic and contextual data are so limited or ambiguous. While such a conclusion would not offer the confidence that synchronic data would provide, its ability to account for each item in the lexical base could be offered as support.

Even when there are more extensive occurrences to deal with, there are times when an assumption of cohesiveness might offer a slightly different nuance than purely synchronic investigation has suggested. An example can be seen in the vb. *nṭh*. As mentioned earlier it most often occurs with "tent" as its object and is usually translated as "stretch." But several other direct objects also occur. With most of these other objects, the translation "extend" works much better (e.g., extending the hand, the heart, or peace). Working with the principle of semantic cohesiveness might suggest considering the concept of extending the tent, in the sense of extending the space under the tent, i.e., raising the tent (a more appropriate description of how tents are pitched). This would appear to be a trivial distinction until we get to the passage where the distinction is necessary for proper interpretation. In Ps 18:9[10] the NIV translates "He parted (*nṭh*) the heavens and came down." In other passages Yahweh is portrayed as pitching the heavens as a tent (e.g., Job 9:8), but here that is not the metaphor. Instead, with the newly established nuance, we can understand Yahweh as raising up the tent of heaven (i.e., lifting the canopy) and slipping under it.

Another function of the assumption of cohesiveness is in accommodating all of the necessary elements in the lexical base. For instance, as one examines the nom. $b^e tûlâ$ (see # 1435 in the Appendix). one must seek a nuance that accounts for all of the contexts, unless some can be set aside on the basis of criteria such as we have previously discussed. That not being the case, it is the assumption of cohesiveness that protects us from arbitrarily discounting any occurrence that undermines our preconceived notions of the meaning. We cannot just say that it means something different in those passages. In the case of this word, the hypothesis that the meaning is "virgin" is severely damaged by usage in Esth 2:17-19; Job 31:1; and Joel 1:8, and another meaning must be sought that will account for all the occurrences.

Our conclusion then is that while we cannot assume a common core meaning to exist across the semantic range, there are situations when an assumption of cohesiveness is preferable, profitable, or even necessary.

(c) *Lack of synchronic and diachronic data.* If the synchronic data are insufficient to achieve confident nuancing, and if diachronic approaches are likewise unable to resolve the ambiguity, the interpreter must be content to accept a vague translation and avoid building any exegetical or theological case on that translation. There are a number of places where it must be concluded that data are simply too sparse. For example, Zech 12:3 uses the adj. $ma^{\,a}māsâ$ to describe a stone that metaphorically represents Jerusalem. Though this is the only occurrence of the substantive, the vb. '*ms* occurs 9x with the meaning of load or carry. Since synchronic information is limited to what can be derived from the context of Zech 12, we can only resort to the vb. to help establish meaning. We find, however, that even then we are left without a definitive nuance. Thus, the traditional translation, heavy, is only a creative suggestion. Other equally creative (and equally unverifiable) suggestions could be offered (e.g., a loaded stone, such as one used for leverage or ballast). Nevertheless the interpreter must conclude that even though guesses can be proffered, we do not know the precise nuance of the word and must settle for something vague. For another good example see the root *śrṭ* in the same verse.

C. Applying the Semantic Range to Individual Occurrences

Once the interpreter has categorized the lexical base and established the semantic range, he is now faced with the task of deciding where any particular occurrence fits within the semantic range. Many occurrences will be already placed by their circumstances (e.g., their collocations, vb. stems, idiomatic phrases), but there will still be many decisions to be made. Whenever there are decisions to be made, there are errors to be avoided.

1. *Avoid the "cafeteria" approach.* In a cafeteria the diner moves through the line choosing whatever food he likes. In a similar fashion some interpreters feel that it is their free choice to decide which aspect of the semantic range to associate with a particular occurrence of a word. Sometimes this is done to the neglect of categories established in the semantic range. For instance, the claim is often made that the word *yôm*, day, can mean a period of undetermined length. However, most, if not all, of the occurrences where such flexibility can be demonstrated are related to idiomatic phrases. The

aspects of the semantic range connected to idiomatic phrases cannot be extended to nonidiomatic occurrences.

At other times the cafeteria approach may involve the issue of a theological meaning as opposed to a general or secular meaning. Words like "redeem" and "salvation" are capable of carrying theological baggage. When we encounter these words, however, we must ask: (a) whether a synchronic study would include the theological meaning in the semantic range (e.g., does the OT ever demonstrably use *yš'* or its derivatives for salvation from sin?); and (b) whether the author intended to use the word with that meaning in the particular context under investigation.

Another variation of this problem occurs when an element from the semantic range of an Eng. word is applied to the corresponding Hebrew word that itself has a more limited semantic range. In a classic example the Eng. word "glory" has in its semantic range the meaning "heaven" (e.g., "gloryland"). The Heb. word *kābôd*, though properly translated "glory," does not have "heaven" in its semantic range. The lay Eng. reader then might be excused for making the mistake of interpreting Ps 73:24 as a reference to heaven, but linguistically informed interpreters are without excuse. Likewise the understanding of the "circle of the earth" in Isa 40:22 is often understood in light of the semantic range of Eng. (circle can include sphere) rather than in Heb., where *ḥûg* is used to describe the curvature of the horizon (see Prov 8:27). These are cases of Eng. semantic ranges being imposed on Heb. semantic ranges.

In all of these cases the way to avoid the arbitrary subjectivity of the cafeteria method is to appeal to the author's intention. The fact that a word can have a particular meaning does not prove that it does have that meaning. What was the author trying to communicate? What aspect of the semantic range was he making use of? Though these questions cannot always be answered with absolute confidence, the very asking of them will help the interpreter retain balance in the exegetical and lexical process. The Amplified Bible approach, where all the choices are before us and we are free to choose the one we like, can easily lead to distortion and misunderstanding.

2. *Individual occurrences of a word generally do not carry all of the different elements found in the semantic range.* Just as we are not free to choose the one meaning that appeals to us most, we are not free to assume that multiple meanings can be associated with the choice of a word. In Heb. the word *rûaḥ* has both wind and spirit in its semantic range. It would not be acceptable to try to incorporate two distinct concepts of wind and spirit into a context using this noun. At a more sophisticated level, however, one could also question whether a cultural difference might be revealed in this lexical information. Is it possible that the use of *rûaḥ* for both wind and spirit suggests that in the Heb. mind the two were more closely associated and perhaps less distinguishable than we are inclined to consider them? These are the sorts of issues that emerge from thoughtful and careful word study.

3. *We must distinguish carefully between the lexical sense and the contextual sense.* The lexical sense refers to those elements of meaning that the word will automatically carry into any of the contexts in which it is used. If there is even one occurrence (in the same category of the semantic range) that does not carry that element of meaning, then that element must be excluded from the lexical sense. So, for instance, one could not include "creation out of nothing" in the lexical sense of *br'* because there are a number of occurrences that clearly do not involve creation out of nothing (e.g.,

Gen 5:1-2). On the other hand, there is no reason why this verb could not express creation out of nothing, but it is up to the context to establish that nuance. Such a restricted meaning could be part of the contextual sense of the verb, but it is not a meaning inherent in the very nature of the word.

D. Conclusion

We will be better interpreters when we understand words and their usage. Authors make choices in the communication process, and it is our task to understand the choices they have made. Our goal is to be on their wavelength. We need to learn about words, including the lexical base and the categories they can be divided into. It is also important to know the delineation of semantic ranges and the application of semantic ranges to individual passages. Though all of this information is important and necessary to the exegetical task, it must be understood that it is only the beginning. Word study is a step in the process of exegesis; it does not comprise the whole of the process. The authority of the Scriptures is not found in the words, though each word has an important role to play; rather, the authority is embodied in the message—that tapestry for which words serve but as threads that derive their significance from being viewed within the tapestry rather than being explored on the skein.

BIBLIOGRAPHY
J. Barr, *The Semantics of Biblical Language*, 1961; idem, *Comparative Philology and the Text of the Old Testament*, 1987; P. Cotterell and M. Turner, *Linguistics and Biblical Interpretation*, 1989; W. Klein, C. Blomberg, and R. Hubbard, *Introduction to Biblical Interpretation*, 1993; G. Osborne, *The Hermeneutical Spiral*, 1991, 64-92; M. Silva, *Biblical Words and Their Meaning*, 1993.

John H. Walton

The last two articles bring these methodological essays to a close. The hermeneutic approach to the biblical text produces a theological synsthesis—a synthesis that includes hermeneutics, the text (textual criticism), biblical history, literary genres, and a strategy for understanding words in relation to each other (semantics). This synthesis embraces also the connection of meaning (what the text *meant*) and significance (what the text *means*). As Elmer A. Martens demonstrates, this basic postulate has received much critical attention in the last two hundred years. As the critical walls are crumbling from a lack of consensus, new voices for studying the text's canonical dimension are being raised. Richard Schultz's essay on the canonical study of the text is another attempt at such synthesis. He argues that good exegesis is theological in nature and that, consequently, it leads to understanding texts in their holistic relationships. The texts are a part of a discourse, which in turn are a part of a book. The books are related to each other as parts of larger collections (Pentateuch, OT), and the OT must be heard in relation to the NT. This exegetical and theological endeavor is threatening for many, because it embraces so many components (hermeneutics; textual criticism; historical, literary, linguistic studies; and theological and canonical connections) and because it challenges our basic fear of uncertainty. Positively, interpretation of this magnitude presents us with a God who is marvelous, awesome, and holy. Moreover, the interpreter who so finds God learns to deny self, to walk by faith, and to worship God in Spirit. (VanGemeren)

9. THE FLOWERING AND FLOUNDERING OF OLD TESTAMENT THEOLOGY

Like a nation's economy, which has its downturns and upturns, so the discipline of OT theology has in the last two hundred years seen both good and bad days. Especially in the twentieth century, OT theology has by turns been riding the crest or has plunged, about to disappear, into the proverbial watery trough. Even the term, "Old Testament Theology" is under attack; a substitute designation is "Theology of the Hebrew Scriptures" (for discussions and assessments cf. Sanders, 1987; Hasel, "The Future of Old Testament Theology," 373-83; Moberly, 159-66; Smith, 64-69). The purpose of this essay, however, is not to chronicle the history of OT theology. Such overviews have been written (cf. Hayes and Pruessner, *OTT*; Hasel, *OTT*, 10-27; Høgenhaven, 13-27; Ollenburger, "From Timeless Ideas to the Essence of Religion," 3-19; Reventlow, 1985; Smith, *OTT*, 21-24). The purpose instead is to sketch the dynamic that accounts for the oscillation of this discipline's fortunes, a dynamic inherent in the issues surrounding it. Specifically, disagreements have persisted about goal, orientation, and methodology.

Biblical theology provides a theological synopsis of the biblical material. Or, as I have elaborated elsewhere:

> (Biblical theology is) that approach to Scripture which attempts
> to see Biblical material holistically and to describe this wholeness or

synthesis in Biblical categories. Biblical theology attempts to embrace the message of the Bible and to arrive at an intelligible coherence of the whole despite the great diversity of the parts. Or, put another way: Biblical theology investigates the themes presented in Scripture and defines their inter-relationships. Biblical theology is an attempt to get to the theological heart of the Bible (Martens, 1977, 123).

Other definitions have been proffered (cf. Dentan, 122; Ebeling, 84; Scobie, 50). Biblical theology is a capsule description of the Bible theologically; it summarizes the exegetical results so as to help the faith community in its self-understanding.

In the early decades of the twentieth century Otto Eissfeldt (20-29) questioned the legitimacy of biblical theology as a scientific discipline. At mid-century Brevard Childs wrote *Biblical Theology in Crisis*. Critics such as James Barr (1988), British scholar R. N. Whybray (1987), and other detractors have pronounced the enterprise misguided and floundering. These sniper attacks were augmented by an armored attack by H. Räisänen (*Beyond New Testament Theology*). However, Scobie rightly remarks, "For many the whole concept of Biblical Theology is dead; but it is just possible that in true biblical fashion it will rise again" (61).

A. Divergent Objectives

If there is some disarray to the discipline at the end of the twentieth century, it is because the goals of the discipline have varied over the past two hundred years. Concise treatments of the discipline are offered by Stendahl, Barr (1976), Hanson (1985), and Zimmerli (426-55).

1. *Goal: A "pure" theology.* Johann P. Gabler gave a lecture in 1787 at the University of Altdorf, near Erlangen, on the distinction between biblical and dogmatic theology. Even if Gabler's address is too simplistically hailed as the beginning of the discipline of biblical theology, it is nevertheless a helpful starting point for a discussion of its objectives. Gabler was dissatisfied with a church dogmatics too much overlaid with church tradition. A true son of the Enlightenment, he intended to return to the roots by examining the source book, the Bible, and suggested a two-step process. First, material on a subject should be gathered from the Bible, noting and comparing the historical settings. From this historical interpretation would emerge a *true* (read, accurate) biblical theology. Second, these results should be subjected to a sorting process at the bar of reason, thereby establishing a *pure* or universal theology. This pure theology, with the particularist nuances of an Israelite history removed, would become the grist for a dogmatic theology.

It was in the form of presenting a historical interpretation that the first OT theology (as distinct from a full-blown biblical theology) was produced by Bauer (*Theologie des Alten Testaments*) in 1796, subtitled *A Summary of the Religious Concepts of the Hebrews*. Such a work corresponded to the first step of Gabler's program, namely, establishing the *true* biblical theology. Some years later (1835) Vatke provided an extended philosophical preface to his treatment of OT theology. The filter for a purified biblical theology in the mid-nineteenth century was the reigning philosophy of Hegel with its notion of development and progress. Vatke, while mindful of the OT's historical character, was also attentive to the philosophical dimensions. Not so subsequent scholars. They were enamored of the historical character of the Bible and left largely neglected Gabler's second philosophical-related step toward a pure theology.

2. *Goal: A scientific "critical" theology.* Vatke himself made a contribution to the historical reconstruction of Israel's history by hypothesizing that the legislation found in the Pentateuch came after and not before the prophets. Once the "criticisms" (source, comparative, textual) were entrenched as the acceptable procedure for biblical research and once the development of Israel's religion was reconstructed, two results for biblical theology followed. First, Israel's faith development was compared with that of her neighbors. Biblical theology went into eclipse. In the latter part of the nineteenth century scholars focused almost exclusively on the history of religions—Israel's and those of surrounding peoples. A second result of the burgeoning of the criticisms was to put into question whether a biblical theology could at all operate within a scientific critical method.

This second issue came to a head in the 1920s with the debate between Eissfeldt and Eichrodt. Eissfeldt distinguished between knowledge and faith, and hence between the history of religion and OT theology. In Eissfeldt's view the history of religion can be objectively researched and therefore established as knowledge. However, statements of faith, which deal with what is timeless, while legitimate for theologians, are largely determined by confessional (denominational) perspectives. Faith assertions, being of a subjective nature, are not amenable to rigorous "scientific" research.

Eichrodt disagreed, arguing that the tools of historical criticism are indeed germane to biblical theology. Through scientific investigation one can penetrate to the essence of a religion. By defining the essence of religion as the deepest meaning of the religious thought world that historical research can recover, Eichrodt can be credited, whether for good or ill, with keeping OT theology within the sphere of historical scholarship. The goal now became, not the determination of a pure theology, as Gabler had proposed, but the formulation of the essence of Israel's religion, as Ollenburger (1992) has explained.

Debate on whether a biblical theology can be formulated on the basis of historical criticism continues. Collins (1-17) is of the opinion that confessional perspectives have too much influenced the work of biblical theologians such as von Rad, Wright, and Childs. He affirms the "hermeneutic of suspicion." Function rather than fact is paramount. For Collins, a biblical theology critically derived is possible, but the resultant theology is a functional construct in which God-talk helps to regulate religious piety, which is the heart of religion. Collins signals a change in the objective of the discipline—a functional tool informing conduct—rather than an attempt, as earlier, to delineate a structure of faith, or, somewhat later, to define the essence of a religion. There continues to be a difference of opinion about the intended outcome for a biblical theology.

3. *Goal: A "Christian" theology.* One of the recurring questions has been whether the aim of the discipline is to set forth the faith structure of the OT independent of the NT or in connection with it. Is the goal of an OT theology to situate it within the Christian faith? Already in Eichrodt's formulation of an OT theology (*TOT*), one of the aims was to show how the OT bridged to the NT. At issue, in part, was the nature of the unity of the OT. If that unity consisted in the concept of covenant, then the connection with the NT was readily made. Von Rad (*OTT*) had a similar agenda in

mind, though he did not assume a conceptual unity within the OT. Both viewed OT theology as closely linked with the Christian faith, much as their predecessors (e.g., von Hofmann) had done.

That the function of an OT theology is folded within the Christian faith was also assumed by others. Jacob (12) asserted that a theology grounded in the OT as a whole "can only be a Christology, for what was revealed under the old covenant, through a long and varied history, in events, persons and institutions is, in Christ, gathered together and brought to perfection." Vriezen wrote at length on the appropriation of the OT by the Christian church. Baker has summarized approaches taken to relate the two Testaments (cf. Oeming).

Moreover, some attempts were made at a comprehensive theology that included both OT and NT. The list includes Burrows (1946), Vos (1948), Lehman (1971, 1974), Terrien (1978), VanGemeren (1988/1995), and Childs (1986 and 1992).

But not all have been of the mind to write an OT theology so as to connect it with the NT. McKenzie wrote as though the NT did not exist. Others argued for a free-standing OT theology since the rabbinic writings represent a sequel to the OT (cf. the nomenclature, "Theology of Hebrew Scriptures"). Eichrodt (*TOT*) and von Rad (*OTT*) were criticized for their "anti-Judaism" bias (Hayes and Prussner, 276). Clements acknowledged the place of law in the OT and so validates the emphasis found in Judaism, but he also sketches the promise motif, a motif elaborated in the NT. Jewish scholars, while traditionally disinterested in an OT theology, are now entering the field (cf. the works of Jon Levenson, e.g., *Sinai and Zion*).

The on-again, off-again fortunes of the discipline are due, indirectly, to a debate on whether one of the goals is to treat the OT as free-standing or to see it theologically within a framework that includes the NT. For most Christians, the answer is the latter, often in the form of a biblical theology (cf. Hasel, 1994). The debate then soon turns to the methodology by which the two Testaments are best related, e.g., by typology, the promise-fulfillment schema, or tradition history (cf. discussion in Hasel, *Old Testament Theology*).

4. *Goal: Descriptive or normative discipline?* A question not yet resolved is whether biblical theology is merely descriptive or whether its results are to be normative. Gabler argued for normativity. A biblical theology, though initially describing the belief system of ancient Israel, has for its ultimate goal a definition of what the faith community should now embrace theologically.

On the other hand, a strong case for limiting the task to description only was made at mid-twentieth century by Stendahl, who distinguished two steps in treating a biblical text. First, interpreters must establish what the biblical text *meant* (in the past). The second step, not within the mandate of biblical theologians, is to explain what the biblical text *means* (now). Biblical theology's occupation is only with the first step, to describe what ancient Israel believed. For Barr (1988, 11) biblical theology is a descriptive and not normative or prescriptive task. Knierim (38) asserted: "As soon as we ask the legitimate question of its meaning 'for our time,' we are no longer dealing with Old Testament Theology but with Old Testament Hermeneutics." Knierim (16), however, envisions the function of an OT theology as adjudicating theologies found in the OT.

Stendahl's position has been challenged, partly because it assumes that the scholar can rather objectively define what the text meant (e.g., Ollenburger, "What Krister Stendahl 'Meant'"). Hanson (1985, 1062) has insisted that biblical theology cannot be reduced to "a strictly descriptive discipline or to an attempt to proceed in a positivistic manner." Brueggemann (1977, x) as an editor in the OBT states that "the yearning and expectation of believers will not let biblical theology rest with the descriptive task alone."

Traditionally it is systematic theology that has offered a "normative" under-standing of the faith. Those who view the task of OT theology as going beyond the descriptive to the constructive (and so invade the "space" of systematic theology) have offered a variety of suggestions. Hasel ("The Relationship Between Biblical Theology and Systematic Theology") describes a "historical-theological" approach, which, while acknowledging the historical particularities, will nevertheless advocate a norma-tive-like theology. Scobie refers to biblical theology as an "intermediate" discipline. Perhaps both biblical and systematic theology have reason to orient themselves to the biblical text as well as to the current agenda. Granted, each discipline will do so with different concentrations (cf. Martens, 1991; Ollenburger, 1991; and other essays in Ollenburger, ed., 1991; also Ollenburger, 1995).

The question is, "Is a biblical theology normative for the current believing com-munity?" Leaving aside quibbles about definition, the answers range from a categori-cal "No," to a guarded affirmative, to an assured "Yes."

B. Shifting Orientations

Perspectives with which scholars work often depend on the reigning cultural paradigm. If, as in the nineteenth century, the governing lens was history, then the biblical material was interrogated for scientific precision, stages of development, and theology arising from event. Over the decades, fresh angles of vision have sometimes either stimulated the discipline or brought near gridlock to the enterprise.

1. *The historical angle of vision.* For centuries, it seems, a helpful and virtually dominant way of study and analysis was via the grid of history. In 1828 Baumgar-ten-Crusius noted (as quoted in Ollenburger, *FOTT*, 4), "The idea and the execution of biblical theology are joined essentially with historical interpretation, and each of them has developed in recent times in relation to the other." Vatke (1835), though keenly cognizant of historical dimensions, infused his presentation of theology with a healthy dose of Hegelian philosophy. Von Hoffman (1841-44) and the Erlangen school, more dubious about the place of philosophy in the whole enterprise, stressed strongly the historical character of the OT. That history, under God's superintendency, was aimed at redemption; hence the telling term, *Heilsgeschichte* (salvation history).

Writing a century later, G. E. Wright, an archaeologist as well as a theologian, held that OT theology is best constructed through the prism of history. Wright not only captured a major biblical emphasis, but served to reassure a religiously disillusioned post-war America about God's ways. While there remained ambiguity about the way such a theology was to be appropriated by the contemporary church, the inspiration brought by Wright's version of OT theology was considerable. F. Hesse, on the other hand, is one of a few who has categorically dismissed *Heilsgeschichte* as a legitimate notion.

The question of how a theology is to be derived from narrative is a vexing one. The debate heated up around the question: How is a theology to be fashioned from historical accounts? In what ways are events revelatory? R. Rendtorff (1968) gave large significance to the event itself. Zimmerli's study of the recognition formula in Ezekiel, "They (you) will know that I am the LORD" was a significant tributary that fed into the larger discussion. Zimmerli emphasized that "knowledge" of God comes through "event-interpreted-through-word"—events in and of themselves are not the carrier of revelation. Summaries of the debate are given by Robinson (1967) and Childs (1992, 196-207). Some biblical theologians, such as Wright, have attended maximally to the rubric of history; others, such as Clements, have largely downplayed the category of history (cf. Perdue for discussions about the role of history; cf. Adam; Hasel, *OTT* ch. 3; Martens, 1994).

Von Rad (*OTT*) shared Wright's view on the importance of Israel's faith as being rooted in Yahweh's acts in history—but with a twist. Since Israel's confessed history differed from the critic's reconstructed history, he was faced with a choice. He remained with Israel's confessed history—a decision for which he has been both censured and lauded—but emphasized the transmission of traditions (patriarchal, Exodus, settlement traditions) as well as their appropriation through time (cf. Eichrodt, *TOT* 2:512-20). Gese (*Essays on Biblical Theology*) has capitalized on this approach by following the trajectories of traditions into the NT.

Another twist, still history related, has to do more broadly with the history of religions, especially that of Israel's neighbors. With archaeological discoveries in Mesopotamia and Egypt in the late nineteenth century, scholars became intent on sorting out the development of religious ideas. But describing the unfolding of a religion and setting out a theology are not the same thing. For more than a quarter of a century, fascination with writing Israel's religious history eclipsed work on biblical theology. That scenario is somewhat echoed at the end of the twentieth century with fresh attempts to write the history of ancient Israel. Albertz (16) commenting on OT theology, says, "I cannot disguise the fact that in the present situation I regard the history of religion as the more meaningful comprehensive Old Testament discipline." It may well be, then, that the relationship between the history of Israelite religion and a theology of the OT will again become an agenda.

2. *The sociological angle of vision. Contextualization* is a term that sociologists and anthropologists relish. The lens of sociology complements the lens of history more than replaces it. In the social scientific paradigm the OT is subjected to a fresh barrage of questions. Now various social dynamics are said to account for the shape of the material. Gottwald, using the conflict model of social theory, contends that ideologies were in the service of those in power. So, for example, the conflict in Jeremiah's time between the "autonomy party," and the "coexistence party" was an ideological struggle. Jeremiah, as part of the "autonomy party" looked for theological grounding to the intertribal traditions of the God of the Exodus who had entered into covenant with Israel and brought them to the land of Canaan. The "co-existence" party, by contrast, was rooted in the David-Zion complex of traditions (cf. discussion by Perdue, 97-98).

An example of an OT theology sensitive to social dynamics is Hanson's *The People Called*. Hanson asks in what way the Israelite community was distinguished from other communities and answers via the triadic notion, viz., that Israel was a people of God differentiated from others in their attention to worship, righteousness, and compassion. Hanson's work generally illustrates an agenda shift. One need only compare the work of G. E. Wright in the 1950s with Hanson's: For Wright the angle of vision on theology is via history, while for Hanson it is sociology.

The emphasis on sociology and related disciplines extends into the doing of theology in still another way. The focus on social location and dynamic is important not only for the ancients, but for the contemporary theologian. True, the shape of a theology will arise from the nature of the material. But increasingly it is recognized that the shape of any theology will be heavily influenced by the "spin" put on the material as a result of the social context of the theologian. Perdue (32) is of the opinion that John Bright's interpretation of Jeremiah, not as an "ethical preacher and religious innovator in the style of old liberalism" but as a neoorthodox preacher who proclaimed the acts of Yahweh and applied normative tradition to current events, has been shaped by John Bright's own position in the community as a theologian in the neoorthodox tradition. Bright (1953) stressed history as an avenue of revelation, the importance of historical criticism, the unity of the Bible in Christ, and the authority of Scripture—all elements of neoorthodoxy. It should not be surprising, the argument goes, to learn that Eichrodt (*TOT*), of the Reformed tradition, latched on to covenant, or that W. Kaiser, in the evangelical tradition, should concentrate on promise. It is congruent with this perspective that feminist and liberation theologians each offer distinctive angles of vision on the OT.

If, then, the shape of biblical theology differs from theologian to theologian, even were the methods identical, their respective social locations and hence their underlying agendas would significantly affect the result. The privileged position of the social sciences in doing OT theology has both recast the results and disclosed the bias in arriving at the results.

3. *The literary/linguistic angle of vision.* The shift from an historical to a social-scientific paradigm is continuing with a further shift to the literary/linguistic paradigm. The historical paradigm had focused on the events behind the text and the social-scientific paradigm on the community and text interplay; the literary/linguistic paradigm now focuses more singularly on the text as text. This angle of vision follows three streams. One stream is that of the narrow literary or linguistic approach; a second is the canonical construal of the literary text; and a third is to invoke features of literature, namely, story and metaphor.

(a) A venerable, though also controversial, approach was quite strictly *linguistic.* Theological elaborations centered on Heb. and G vocabulary and word studies. Word studies have included research into etymology, cognates, semantic fields, and statistics of usage. E. Jacob treated the understanding of God, for example, by explicating the Heb. terms employed for the attributes of God. The heyday of the word-study approach was represented in the multivolume theological dictionary (*TDNT*) and those in its genre, *TWAT*; *THAT*; *TDOT*; *TWOT*. The word-study approach as theologically productive has been properly challenged by pointing, for example, to some fallacies of assumptions about etymology and the limitations of an exclusive linguistic approach (e.g., Barr, 1961; for a recent approach, see Cotterell's essay "Linguistics, Meaning, Semantics, and Discourse Analysis" in this volume).

(b) A second literary-related stream highlighted not the constituent terms of a text but the *canonical framework* (see the essay by Richard Schultz, "Integrating Old Testament Theology and Exegesis: Literary, Thematic, and Canonical Issues" in this volume). Sanders pinpointed the importance of the literary development of a biblical text in its interplay with community dynamics. Childs, known for his canonical approach, spearheaded a move to focus on the canonical text (rather than on events or on social dynamics) as a locus for biblical theology. At issue for Childs was not the stages by which the biblical text was formed, but the way in which the present text, in its arrangement, contributes to an articulation of theology. Parts of the canon are regarded as in dialogue with other parts. An individual text is to be interpreted in the context, not so much of history, but of the canon (cf. the exposition of Childs' approach by Perdue, 155-75, and the critical but sympathetic appraisal by Brett; cf. also Rendtorff [1993]; Sailhamer). An example of this canonical angle of vision is the proposal that a key to the theology of the Psalms lies in its first two Psalms. The Psalms have a didactic intent (Ps 1) and an eschatological perspective (Ps 2). Compatible with the canonical approach is the emerging method of intertextuality.

(c) Toward the end of the twentieth century, the literary angle of vision diverged into a third stream that highlighted the importance of metaphor and story. This interest in the "new literary criticism" may be due to several reasons: disenchantment with historical criticism, a shift away from the paradigm of history, a pervasive Zeitgeist, and a postmodern interpretation of reality as language-based (cf. the writings of Stanley Fish, Jacques Derrida; see esp. Jean-Francois Lyotard). Whatever the reason, doing biblical theology largely by means of metaphor is increasingly championed and practiced. The fascination with narrative, metaphor, and symbol has been fueled through the writings of scholars such as Hans Frei, Paul Ricoeur, and Phillip Wheelwright (cf. pertinent works by R. Alter, F. Kermode, and T. Longman). Attention is on the artistry of the text but especially on symbolism (cf. L. Perdue, chs. 6, 8, 9, on metaphor, story, and imagination). While traditional descriptions of God have been largely cast in patriarchal language (God is suzerain, lord, king, father), feminine writers point out that religious language is metaphorical in content and includes female imagery (e.g., Trible, McFague). But exploration of metaphor extends beyond the work of feminine scholars. Longman and Reid, who incorporate both OT and NT, are but one example among increasing presentations.

The shift to the literary paradigm in doing OT theology gives rise to a series of questions. If the literary approach complements the historical, what weight is to be assigned to the rooting of the Christian faith in history? Does the literary approach necessarily invalidate the focus on history? How are historical, sociological, and literary perspectives on biblical material to be integrated? Answers are in short supply. Meanwhile, the dominant paradigms or angles of vision infuse the discipline with vigor, though admittedly also with some confusion. Proposals for proceeding follow different routes (e.g., Perdue; Sailhamer; Knierim; Hasel; and Hubbard). In this situation it is not easy to determine whether OT theology is cresting or waning.

C. Ambiguity About Method

To some extent much of what has been said about goal and orientation impinges on the method of formulating a biblical theology. Some specifics on method, most of which relate to structuring an OT theology, can be identified. Davidson, working in the early part of the twentieth century, organized his research around the traditional dogmatic scheme of God, humanity, and salvation. A similar scheme was followed by the Catholic theologians Paul Heinisch and Paul van Imschoot. Few, however, have followed that schematic; it seemed too confining. Nor did it greatly aid in understanding the essence of biblical faith. Suggestions for structuring an OT theology have taken other turns.

1. *Diachronic or synchronic.* It was argued by some, especially when the category of history had a privileged position, that an OT theology must take account of eras or periods of Israelite history. Whether one spoke the language of progressive revelation or that of an evolution of theological insights, there were significant distinctions to be made between the early and later stages. Examples of OT theologies organized chronologically are those by von Rad (*OTT*), W. Kaiser, and W. VanGemeren.

A different viewpoint is that one should proceed synchronically, namely, by arranging the material thematically perhaps around an idea or set of ideas (cf. discussion on diachronic and synchronic in Sailhamer, 184-94). Eichrodt (*TOT*) presented his work under the three rubrics: (a) God and People; (b) God and World; and (c) God and Man. He described his method as a "cross-cut" method. He asked what fundamental understanding governed the OT, irrespective of time period. His answer was that the fundamental understanding was the establishment of the kingdom of God, a code word for which was "covenant." Others who have proceeded synchronically in order to display the essence of OT faith are Vriezen, Clements, and Childs (1986) (cf. *God's Design*, where I intend to combine the diachronic with the synthetic).

2. *Centered or non-centered.* A vexed question for biblical theologians has been: Does the OT have a center? For the NT the answer is not really debatable: The center is Jesus Christ. One could say that God is the central figure in the OT, but that helps little in getting a handle on the material. The question of center is important, of course, for the structuring of an OT theology. But the question has a larger significance, for behind the question lies another: Is there unity in the OT, and if so, does it cohere around a theological center? Methodologically the question is whether the search for a theological center is legitimate, and if so, by what process?

A significant number of theologians have identified a center, but because the centers vary, the problem is not resolved but sharpened. Is the assumption that the OT has a center legitimate (cf. Hasel, 1991, 139-71)? Eichrodt (*TOT*) maintained that covenant was the center. Other proposals have been promise (Kaiser), the covenant formula, "Yahweh the God of Israel, Israel the people of Yahweh" (Smend), or the book of Deuteronomy (Hermann). For Preuss, election and obligation come together as a center.

The roster of those who questioned the possibility of a center begins with von Rad (*OTT*), who held that a series of traditions reappropriated through the centuries and not any one center accounts for the unity inherent in the thirty-nine books of the OT. McKenzie, skeptical of a center, organized his book around several themes such as cult, history, and nature. Hasel (1991) concluded that a search for a center was futile. His own proposal, advanced but never implemented by him because of his untimely death, was to consider a multiplex approach. Poythress proposed a multiperspectival approach.

Fohrer (1968; cf. 1972, ch. 4) suggested that, much like an audio cassette, the OT be viewed as an ellipse and so be construed as having a double center. The two centers he proposed were the rule of God and the communion of God with humankind. Roughly in the same camp are those who have proposed a dialectical approach. Westermann proposed an emphasis on salvation (interventionist activity) and blessing (sustaining activity). Terrien's portrayal of a God both present and absent is likewise dialectical, as is Brueggemann's structure legitimation and embrace of pain.

With this plethora of proposals, it is not surprising that some feel that the discipline is in some disarray and is floundering rather than flowering. But another reading of the situation is that the discipline, while seeking stabilization as to methodology, has churned up a cornucopia of insights. The community of faith is the richer for struggling with answers to questions of methodology and center, and is the richer also for the additional dimensions of faith suggested by different starting points.

3. *Scientific or artistic.* The ambiguity about method has continually plagued attempts to set out an OT theology. Can one clearly define procedural steps, as is customary in a science? Or is the task more akin to that of an artist dependent on imagination and intuition? The answer is not strictly one or the other, but both.

If one begins in a more limited way with the task of setting out the theology of a biblical book, one can follow some basic steps. The formal structure of a book needs first to be established and carefully pondered. The format of the book, including attention to the weight of component parts or climactic sections, can be expected to point to a theological substructure. It is helpful to ask and to answer the question, "What drives the book?" Perhaps the agenda is stated in the book itself. Attention to dominant metaphors employed may be a clue to the latent theology present in the book. A checklist of procedures is set out by Martens ("Accessing the Theological Readings").

But just as great literature cannot be circumscribed or explained via recipes, so the Bible, and especially its theology, cannot be reduced to recipe-like procedures. At work in formulating the theology of a book or a block of books such as the OT is a factor identified by Kelsey as "imaginative construal." When a biblical scholar is thoroughly conversant with a body of material and wishes to recast it in summary fashion, he or she must be open to—and even await—the so-called "aha experience." Quite inexplicably, meditation and probing reflection may yield a *Gestalt* by which to explicate biblical material. The theologian is both scientist and artist.

D. Conclusion

One way of analyzing the "fortunes" of biblical theology is to note stages of differentiation in its history. Biblical theology originated as a discipline when it became unhooked from dogmatic theology. Another burst of activity came when it was liberated from the history of religion. Still another significant chapter opened with some options beyond the historical paradigm: sociology and literature. The current fascination with the latter, while temporarily stimulating, may need to be superseded by a further detachment. In this new stage, one may envision biblical theology to be more clearly a branch of *theology,* not of historical, sociological, or literary criticism.

Considering the vigor and rigor of research that this discipline has engendered, it would be shortsighted to write off the efforts of biblical theologians as unprofitable. Discussions between Christians and Jews, clarity regarding the relationship of OT and NT, a better understanding of the limits and the contributions of philosophical theology, a sense of identity for the Christian community of faith, and a curiosity and inquisitiveness about biblical faith have all been facilitated by this discussion. One could wish that more of the uncertainties surrounding the discipline could be resolved, but in the meanwhile the enterprise is making a substantial contribution and is better characterized as flowering than as floundering.

BIBLIOGRAPHY

A. K. M. Adam, "Biblical Theology and the Problem of Modernity: Von Wredestrasse zu Sackgasse," *HBT* 12/1, 1990, 1-18; R. Albertz, *A History of Israelite Religion in the Old Testament Period*, 1: *From the Beginnings to the End of the Monarchy*, tr. by John Bowden, 1994; D. L. Baker, *Two Testaments, One Bible: A Study of Some Modern Solutions to the Theological Problem of the Relationship Between the Old and New Testaments*, 1976, 1991; J. Barr, "Biblical Theology," *IDBS*, 1976, 104-11; idem, *The Semantics of Biblical Language*, 1961; idem, "The Theological Case Against Biblical Theology" in *Canon, Theology, and Old Testament Interpretation: Essays in Honor of Brevard S. Childs*, ed. by G. M. Tucker, David L. Petersen, and Robert R. Wilson, 1988, 3-19; G. L. Bauer, *Theologie des Alten Testaments; oder, Abriss der religiösen Begriffe der alten Hebräer von den altesten Zeiten bis auf den Anfang der christlichen Epoche: Zum Gebrauch akademischer Vorlesungen*, 1796; M. G. Brett, *Biblical Criticism in Crisis? The Impact of the Canonical Approach on Old Testament Studies*, 1991; J. Bright, *The Kingdom of God: The Biblical Concept and Meaning for the Church*, 1953; idem, *Covenant and Promise: The Prophetic Understanding of the Future in Preexilic Israel*, 1976; W. Brueggemann, "A Shape for Old Testament Theology, 1: Structure Legitimation," *CBQ* 47, 1985, 28-46; idem, "A Shape for Old Testament Theology, 2: Embrace of Pain" *CBQ* 47, 1985, 395-415 (reprinted in *Old Testament Theology: Essays on Structure, Theme, and Text*, ed. P. D. Miller, 1992, 1-21, 22-44); idem, *The Land: Place As Gift, Promise, and Challenge in Biblical Faith*. OBT 1, 1977; M. Burrows, *An Outline of Biblical Theology*, 1946; B. S. Childs, *Biblical Theology in Crisis*, 1970; idem, *Biblical Theology of the Old and New Testaments*, 1992; idem, *Old Testament Theology in a Canonical Context*, 1986; R. E. Clements, *Old Testament Theology: A Fresh Approach*, New Foundations Theological Library, 1978; J. J. Collins, "Is a Critical Biblical Theology Possible?" in *The Hebrew Bible and Its Interpreters*, ed. W. H. Propp, B. Halpern, D. N. Freedman, Biblical and Judaic Studies from the University of California 1, 1990, 1-17; A. B. Davidson, *The Theology of the Old Testament*, 1904; R. C. Dentan, *Preface to Old Testament Theology*, 1950, rev. ed., 1963; G. Ebeling, "The Meaning of 'Biblical Theology'" in *Word and Faith*, 1963, 79-97; O. Eissfeldt, "The History of Israelite-Jewish Religion and Old Testament Theology," *FOTT*, [1926] 1992, 20-29; W. Eichrodt, "Does Old Testament Theology Still Have Independent Significance Within Old Testament Scholarship?" *FOTT*, [1929] 1992, 30-39; idem, *Theology of the Old Testament*, 2 vols., 1961, 1967; G. Fohrer, "Der Mittelpunkt einer Theologie des Alten Testaments," *TZ* 24, 1968, 161-72; idem, *Theologische Grundstruckuren des Alten Testaments*, 1972; H. Frei, *The Eclipse of Biblical Narrative: A Study in Eighteenth and Nineteenth Century Hermeneutics*, 1974; J. P. Gabler, "On the Proper Distinction Between Biblical and Dogmatic Theology and the Specific Objectives of Each," *SJT* 33, 1980, 133-44, reprinted in *FOTT*, 492-502; H. Gese, *Essays on Biblical Theology*, 1981, excerpt in *FOTT*, 387-405; N. Gottwald, *The Tribes of Yahweh*, 1979; P. D. Hanson, *The People Called: The Growth of the Community in the Bible*, 1986; idem, "Theology, Old Testament" in *HBD*, 1985, 1057-62; G. F. Hasel, "The Future Of Old Testament Theology: Prospects and Trends," in *FOTT*, 373-83; idem, *Old Testament Theology: Basic Issues in the Current Debate*, 4th edition, 1991; idem, "The Problem of History in OT Theology," *AUSS* 8, 1970, 23-50; idem, "The Relationship

179

Between Biblical Theology and Systematic Theology," *Trinity Journal*, n. s. 5, 113-27; idem, "The Nature of Biblical Theology: Recent Trends and Issues," *AUSS* 32/3, 1994, 203-15; J. H. Hayes and F. C. Prussner, *Old Testament Theology: Its History and Development*, 1985; P. Heinisch, *Theology of the Old Testament*, 1950; S. Hermann, "Die konstruktive Restauration: Das Deuteronomium als Mitte biblischer Theologie," in *Probleme biblischer Theologie: Gerhard von Rad zum 70. Geburtstag*, ed. by H. S. Wolff, 1970, 155-70; F. Hesse, *Abschied von der Heilsgeschichte*, ThST 108, 1971; J. C. K. von Hofmann, *Interpreting the Bible*, 1959, 1972; J. Høgenhaven, *Problems and Prospects of Old Testament Theology*, Biblical Seminar 6, 1988; R. L. Hubbard, "Doing Old Testament Theology Today," in *Studies in Old Testament Theology*, ed. by R. L. Hubbard, R. K. Johnston, and R. P. Meye, 1992, 31-46; P. van Imschoot, *Theology of the Old Testament*, Vol. I: *God*, 1965; E. Jacob, *Theology of the Old Testament*, 1958; W. C. Kaiser, Jr., *Toward an Old Testament Theology*, 1978; D. H. Kelsey, *The Use of Scripture in Recent Theology*, 1975; R. Knierim, *The Task of Old Testament Theology*, 1995; S. J. Kraftchick, C. D. Myers, Jr., and B. C. Ollenburger (eds.), *Biblical Theology: Problems and Perspectives*, 1995; C. K. Lehman, *Biblical Theology*, 2 vols., 1971, 1974; W. E. Lemke, "Is Old Testament Theology an Essentially Christian Theological Discipline?" *HBT* 11, 1989, 59-69; J. Levenson, *Sinai and Zion: An Entry into the Jewish Bible*, 1985; excerpt in *FOTT*, 437-44; T. Longman and Daniel G. Reid, *God Is a Warrior*, SOTBT 1995; J.-F. Lyotard, *The Postmodern Condition: A Report on Knowledge, Theory and History of Literature*, trans. by G. Bennington and B. Massumi, 1984; S. McFague, *Metaphorical Theology*, 1982; J. L. McKenzie, *A Theology of the Old Testament*, 1974; E. A. Martens, "Biblical Theology and Normativity," in *So Wide a Sea: Essays on Biblical and Systematic Theology*, ed. B. C. Ollenburger, IMS Text Reader 4, 1991, 19-35; idem, "Accessing the Theological Readings of a Biblical Book," *AUSS* 34/2, 1996, 233-49; idem, *God's Design: A Focus on Old Testament Theology*, 1981, 1994[2], excerpt in *FOTT*, 300-320; idem, "Tackling Old Testament Theology" *JETS* 20, 1977, 123-32; idem, "The Oscillating Fortunes of 'History' in Old Testament Theology," in *Faith, Tradition and History: OT Historiography in Its Near Eastern Context*, ed. by A. Millard, J. Hoffmeier, and D. Baker, 1994, 313-40; idem, *Old Testament Theology*, IBR Bibliographies No. 13, 1997; J. W. Miller, *The Origins of the Bible: Rethinking Canon History*, 1994; R. W. L. Moberly, *The Old Testament of the Old Testament*, OBT, 1992, 159-66; M. Oeming, *Gesamtbiblische Theologien der Gegenwort: Das Verhältnis von AT und NT in der hermeneutischen Diskussion seit Gerhard von Rad*, 1985; B. C. Ollenburger, "Biblical and Systematic Theology: Constructing a Relation" in *So Wide a Sea: Essays on Biblical and Systematic Theology*, ed. B. C. Ollenburger, IMS Text Reader 4, 1991, 111-45; idem, "From Timeless Ideas to the Essence of Religion: Method in Old Testament Theology before 1930" in *FOTT*, 3-19; idem, E. A. Martens and Gerhard F. Hasel (eds.), *The Flowering of Old Testament Theology [FOTT]*, Sources for Biblical and Theological Study, Vol. 1, 1992; idem, "Old Testament Theology: A Discourse on Method," in *Problems and Perspectives*, ed. S. J. Kraftcheck, et al., 1995; idem, ed., *So Wide a Sea: Essays on Biblical and Systematic Theology*, IMS Text Reader 4, 1991; idem, "What Krister Stendahl 'Meant' —A Normative Critique of 'Descriptive Biblical Theology,'" *HBT*, 8, 1986, 61-98; L. G. Perdue, *The Collapse of History: Reconstructing Old Testament Theology*, OBT, 1994; V. S. Poythress, *Symphonic Theology*, 1987; H. D. Preuss, *Old Testament Theology*, 2 vols., 1995; G. von Rad, *Old Testament Theology*, 1962, 1965; H. Räisänen, *Beyond New Testament Theology: A Story and a Programme*, 1990; R. Rendtorff, *Canon and Theology: Overtures to an Old Testament Theology*, OBT, 1993; idem, "Die Offenbarungsvorstellungen im Alten Israel," Eng. tr. in W. Pannenberg, R. Rendtorff, T. Rendtorff, and U. Wilkens, *Revelation As History*, 1968, 23-53; H. G. Reventlow, *Problems of Old Testament Theology in the Twentieth Century*, tr. by J. Bowden, 1985; P. Ricoeur, "The Metaphorical Process," *Semeia* 4, 1975, 75-106; idem, *The Rule of Metaphor*, 1977; J. M. Robinson, "Revelation As Word and As History," in *Theology as History: New Frontiers in Theology*, 1967, 42-62; J. H. Sailhamer, *Introduction to Old Testament Theology: A Canonical Approach*, 1995; J. A. Sanders, *Canon and Community: A Guide to Canonical Criticism*, 1984; idem, "First Testament and Second," *BTB* 17, 1987, 47-49; W. H. Schmidt, "The Problem of the 'Centre' of the Old Testament in the Perspective of the Relationship Between History of Religion and Theology," in *Old Testament Essays* 4, 1986, 46-64; R. Smend, *Die Mitte des Alten Testaments*, Theologische Studien 101, 1970; C. H. H. Scobie, "The Challenge of Biblical Theology," *TB* 42/1, 1991, 31-61; R. L. Smith, *Old Testament Theology: Its History, Method and Message*, 1993; D. G. Spriggs, *Two Old Testament Theologies: A Comparative Evaluation of the Contributions of Eichrodt and von Rad to our Understanding of the Nature of Old Testament Theology*, SBT 2/30, 1974; K. Stendahl, "Biblical Theology, Contemporary" *IDB* 1:418-32, = "Biblical Theology: A Program," *Meanings: The Bible as Document and Guide*, 1984, 11-44; S. L. Terrien, *The Elusive Presence: Toward a New Biblical Theology*, Religious Perspectives 26, 1978; P. Trible, *God and the Rhetoric of Sexuality*, OBT 2, 1978; W. A. VanGemeren, *The Progress of Redemption*, 1988/1995; J. K. W. Vatke, *Die biblische Theologie wissenschaftlich dargestellt*, Vol 1: *Die Religion des Alten Testaments nach dem kanonischen Büchern entwickelt*, 1835; G. Vos, *Biblical Theology: Old and New Testaments*, 1948; Th. C. Vriezen, *An Outline of Old Testament Theology*, 2d ed., 1970; C. Westermann, *Elements of Old Testament Theology*, 1982; P. Wheelwright, *Metaphor and Reality*, 1962; G. E. Wright, *God Who Acts: Biblical Theology As Recital*, SBT 8, 1952; R. N. Whybray, "OT Theology—A Nonexistent Beast?" in *Scripture: Meaning and Method. Essays Presented to Anthony Tyrrell Hanson for His Seventieth Birthday*, 1987, 168-80; W. Zimmerli, "Biblische Theologie," *TRE* 6, 426-55; idem, "Knowledge of God According to the Book of Ezekiel," in *I Am Yahweh*, 1982, 29-98.

Elmer A. Martens

10. Integrating Old Testament Theology And Exegesis: Literary, Thematic, And Canonical Issues

If the OT is approached not simply as a human religious document but as sacred Scripture, then exegesis involves ascertaining not only its *meaning* but also its *message*. In other words, determining the theology of a given text is an essential part of the exegetical process. However, this raises the difficult problem of methodology in biblical theology: If scholars cannot agree on a method for construing OT theology as a whole (cf. E. A. Martens' essay in this volume and the survey and proposals of G. Hasel, *Old Testament Theology*), what can be stated definitively about the theological dimensions of an individual text? To be sure, some might decry any attempt to analyze and synthesize the theological content of various pericopes as theologizing, i.e., thinly veiled homiletizing, or as employing simplistic shortcuts, i.e., "What does this text say about God, about sin...?"

In this essay one foundational methodological principle will have to suffice: Just as in *literary* analysis, "the intended meaning of any passage is the meaning that is consistent with the sense of the literary context in which it occurs" (Klein, et al. *Introduction to Biblical Interpretation*, 157), so in *theological* analysis, the intended theology of any passage is the theology that is consistent with the sense of the theological context in which it occurs. The theology of each passage must be viewed in the light of its larger theological context, including both the theology of the biblical book in which it is found as well as the larger concentric circles of theological context (i.e., the theology of the major divisions or genres of the OT, the theology of the OT as a whole, and of the entire Bible).

The preceding essays have addressed a number of crucial issues in OT theology and hermeneutics, thoroughly expounding and critiquing various theories and judiciously weighing various methodological options. This essay presupposes and builds on their insights; it seeks to be practical and illustrative. Stated simply, our purpose is to answer the question: How does one do responsible, theologically rich exegesis of the OT text by being sensitive to (1) its words, some of which are more theologically significant than others, (2) its literary features, (3) its historical framework, and (4) the relationship between the text and other canonical texts?

A. The Theology of OT Books

1. Methodological options: inadequate models. A crucial step in determining the theology of a text is discovering the theology of the book of which it is a part. However, this raises a further methodological problem: How does one analyze and synthesize the theology of a book? Although little has been written addressing this issue (but cf. Martens, 1996), there are many examples one can examine in order to discover which principles and procedures were followed. The introductions to most commentaries contain a section summarizing the "theology," "message," or "key themes" of a book, as do also the treatments of the individual OT books in Bible reference works and some OT surveys and introductions. Furthermore, there are series that focus on theological themes, such as Word Publishing's *Understanding the Basic Themes of...*, individual volumes on Old Testament theology that employ a book-by-book approach (cf. Childs, *Biblical Theology*, Part 3; Dumbrell, *The Faith of Israel*; Sitarz, ed., *Höre, Israel! Jahwe ist einzig*; Zuck, ed., *A Biblical Theology of the Old Testament*), and numerous essays expounding the theology of individual books (including those regularly published in journals such as *Biblical Theology Bulletin* and *Interpretation*; see also specific examples below). An examination of these efforts reveals several methodologically-flawed models, but this is not to say that publications that follow these models do not contain many valuable theological insights.

(a) *Systematic categories: God/Man, Sin/Salvation.* One of the earliest and persistent models for presenting OT theology is that of adopting the categories of systematic theology, e.g., God and man, sin and salvation, history and eschatology (cf. Hasel, who labels this the "dogmatic-didactic method," 39-42). The attractiveness of this approach is readily apparent: The same categories can be applied to every book and the results easily synthesized. This approach is applied fairly rigidly by Wolf in his introduction to Isaiah (*Interpreting Isaiah*, Part III: "Theological Emphases: Christology, Eschatology) and more loosely in the volume edited by Zuck (cf. Merrill, "A Theology of Chronicles," which employs the following headings: "The God of the Kingdom," "The People of the Kingdom," "The Charter of the Kingdom" [covenant and salvation], and "The Course of the Kingdom" [history and eschatology]; and "A Theology of Ezra-Nehemiah and Esther," which focuses on "The Person and Actions of God," "The People of God").

The problem with this approach is that it tends to flatten the unique shape of the individual canonical books and obsure their dynamic theology. Something is lost by focusing only on those statements that contribute to one of the predetermined categories rather than on the interrelations among major theological themes.

(b) *Historical-critical reconstructions.* A second inadequate model is that of deriving theology only from the reconstructed "original" book or its redactional layers, as determined by historical-critical methodologies. For example, in the volume edited by Sitarz, Frank-Lothar Hossfeld distinguishes the theologies of the Jahwist, Elohist, the "Jehowist," the Deuteronomist, and the Priestly writer. Similarly, Hans Wildberger presents the theology of Isaiah under two rubrics: "Isaiah's Theology," and "Toward a Theology of the Non-Isaianic Sections" (within Isa 1-39), limiting his discussion to the "book" of "First Isaiah" (*Jesaja*, 1634-84). Aarre Lauha summarizes the message of Qoheleth only after removing nearly all references to God, judgment, and the enjoyment of life as orthodox redactional additions, resulting in an unorthodox theology of a cynical pessimist whose God is a distant unknowable despot (*Kohelet*, 5: "Die theologische Problematik"). The continuing debate over Martin Noth's posited deuteronomistic and Chronicler's histories also affects how one conceives of the theology of the individual historical books, e.g., whether or not to seek a theology common to both 1-2 Chronicles and Ezra-Nehemiah (see the summary of the discussion in Williamson, *1 and 2 Chronicles*, 5-11). Here one could also include those approaches that understand theology more in terms of ideology (N. Gottwald), history of religions (R. Albertz), or history of traditions (G. von Rad; H. Gese).

The problems with such approaches are twofold: First, the theology presented in this model is not that of the canonical book but only that of a part or preliminary edition of the book. Seldom is there any attempt made to demonstrate that this "layer" is theologically more significant or authoritative than any earlier or later layer (cf. Sanders, *Canon and Community*, ch. 2: "Canonical Process"). Second, since historical-critical research is unable to reach a consensus regarding the extent of a particular source, redactional layer, or edition, each reconstruction will have slightly different theological contours.

(c) *History-based approaches*. A third inadequate model views the historical background or foreground of the book as the key to determining its theology. There are three types of history-based approaches. (i) Some scholars focus on the theological significance of the book's date and purpose. For example, how one understands the basic message of Judges depends on whether one dates it in the early monarchy, as a polemic for the monarchy, or in the postexilic period, as a plea for theocracy (cf. Cundall, "Judges—An Apology for the Monarchy?"; Dumbrell, "The Purpose of the Book of Judges Reconsidered," 23-33). Similarly, the debate over Jonah's "missionary message" is closely tied to how one conceives of its purpose (cf. Childs' summary and critique of this approach in "The Canonical Shape of the Book of Jonah"). Others, however, *use* the theology of a book or a section thereof to determine its date, e.g., the mention of Satan in Job, "apocalyptic" in Joel and Isaiah, or the references to the resurrection in Daniel or personal piety in the Psalms.

(ii) Some scholars focus on "the mighty acts of God" as theology (cf. G. E. Wright, 13, for whom the theology of a book is "the confessional recital of the redemptive acts of God in a particular history").

(iii) Some, such as W. C. Kaiser (1978), present OT theology within the framework of history as portrayed in the OT. Thus Kaiser summarizes the theology of the "prepatriarchal" and "patriarchal" eras rather than developing a theology of Genesis within the framework of the Pentateuch ("Mosaic theology" might be a more appropriate designation, see discussion below), and discusses Wisdom literature as stemming from the "sapiential," i.e., Solomonic, era (chs. 5-6, 10).

The problems with the above-mentioned approaches can be summarized only briefly. The first approach is in danger of forgetting that the OT is primarily *divine revelation* rather than *political propaganda*, and it is the former that is central for theology. The second approach may be dependent on an understanding of history as reconstructed by historical-critical approaches and is unable to deal adequately with books in which *Heilsgeschichte* is less prominent (e.g., Wisdom literature). Furthermore, theology must be *text-centered* (e.g., on the portrayal of God in the biblical accounts) rather than *event-centered* (cf. Sailhamer, *Introduction to Old Testament Theology*, ch. 3). The third approach tends to fix its attention on those aspects that reflect the progressive revelation of the divine plan and loses sight of significant theological motifs that are more distant from this "theological Autobahn."

2. Literary approaches. It should be apparent from the preceding section that if the theology of an OT book is to be the primary theological context for the theological assessment of an individual text, another model must be sought for analyzing and synthesizing the former. Fortunately, that which has been emerging for several decades under the rubric of "literary approaches" to the Bible (cf. the essays by Longman and Long in this volume) offers a model for a more comprehensive, synthetic, and text-based approach. From these studies two hermeneutical guidelines emerge. These will be illustrated on the book and on the pericope level: (1) Just as a text must be interpreted in light of its placement within the book as a whole, so its theology must be assessed as it partakes in and contributes to (a dynamic relationship) to the theology of the book as a whole. (2) The theology of a text must be assessed in the light of its literary genre (that is, of the individual text and of the book as a whole), taking into consideration that genre's characteristic elements, style, and function.

(a) *The structure of books.*

(i) The theological significance of book structure. One of the observations that has emerged from literary studies of the Bible (as well as from some of the redaction- or composition-critical studies of the OT (e.g., Rendtorff, "The Composition of the Book of Isaiah") is that the structure of individual books does not result from the haphazard collection of transmitted materials or from strictly following chronological ordering principles but reflects a hermeneutically significant design, regardless of whether that design stems from an author or an editor (cf. Licht, *Storytelling in the Bible*, ch. 6; Pratt, *He Gave Us Stories*, ch. 9). The selection and ordering of material in *all* OT books has been determined, at least in part, by the message that was to be communicated. Even in the book of Proverbs, in which the proverbs of chs. 10ff. traditionally have been understood as "card file" collections, compositional patterns are apparent (cf. Whybray, *The Composition of the Book of Proverbs*). Thus it is crucial to understand the structure of a book in order to understand how its theology is unfolded in the course of a book. Dumbrell's stated goal in *The Faith of Israel* is "to present the theological movement of each book, endeavoring, where possible, to indicate how the flow of content in each book contributes to the concept of that book's purpose" (1988, 11).

(ii) Book structure: objective or arbitrary? Here one must distinguish clearly between book outline as "table of contents" (e.g., Whybray claims that no integrative structure is to be found in the book of Ecclesiastes, and simply lists thirty-four sections (*Ecclesiastes*, 17, 30-31) or as "integrative structure." A structure-based theology is as prone to subjectivity as are the other models we have rejected. Some of the complex chiastic book structures that have been "discovered" surpass any reader's "competence," whether ancient or modern, though we are suggesting that such a structure *must be* identified in order for the book's message to be assessed properly (note the examples cited in J. Welch, *Chiasmus in Antiquity*, 1981; for a brief but persuasive critique of "chiasmania" see Kugel, "On the Bible and Literary Criticism"). Furthermore, multiple outlines of various books have been suggested. Dennis Olson found among the forty-six commentaries on Numbers he surveyed twenty-four substantially different proposals for the outline or structure of the book (*The Death of the Old and the Birth of the New*, 31-37), and Hendrik Koorevaar found thirty-one different outlines of Joshua (*De Opbouw van het Boek Jozua*, 95-102).

However, many of these outlines were derived by focusing on major geographical, historical, or content transitions within the respective books and fail to indicate how the major divisions are integrally related to one another or to the structure of the book as a whole. If it can be demonstrated that the suggested structure is simple and obvious (i.e., easily identifiable and supported by internal thematic and content patterns) as well as hermeneutically significant (i.e., contributing to exegesis and theological analysis), it cannot be dismissed as arbitrary.

(iii) Examples of book structure as theological outline. The book of Exodus, for example, can be understood as an extended exposition of the tripartite formula that expresses a central theological theme of the Bible: "I will be your God, you will be my people, and I will dwell in your midst" (cf. Lev 26:11-13; note the NT development in John 1:14 and Rev 21:3), each of the major sections of the book developing one of the clauses: In Exod 1-18 the deity identifies himself as Yahweh, the covenant-keeping God of Abraham, Isaac, and Jacob, who will bring his people out of Egypt (6:2-8), beginning with fulfillment of the patriarchal promise of multiplied seed and concluding with Jethro's praise of Yahweh as greater than all the gods (1:7; 18:10-11); in chs. 19-24 Israel becomes Yahweh's people through the covenant ratification ceremony (24:3-8), the section being framed by two theophanies (19:16-19; 24:9-11, 15-18); and in chs. 25-40 a tabernacle is constructed so that God can dwell in Israel's midst (25:8-9; 29:45-46; 40:34-35), two parallel sections recording God's instructions and their execution by Israel (25-31, 35-40), framing a section describing Israel's apostate worship using the golden calf, whereby they almost forfeited their status as God's people (32:9-10) until the issue was resolved through a covenant renewal (34:10). Uniting these three sections are God's three self-revelations to Moses (3:1-6; 19:3-6; 34:5-7). This three-part outline was suggested by Ramm (1974) and followed by Kaiser, *Exodus*, both of whom used the headings: Divine Redemption, Divine Morality, Divine Worship.

An awareness of this theological development can help the exegete to note that the call of Moses (ch. 3) is part of covenant fulfillment, that prior to the covenant ratification ceremony God does not punish the people's complaining (ch. 16-17; in contrast to the rebellions in Numbers), that the giving of the Ten Commandments (ch. 20) already presupposes the redemption of Israel from slavery, and that detailed typological treatments of the tabernacle may well miss the actual theology of the text.

Olson (1985) has demonstrated that the central theme of Numbers is the comparison of two generations of God's people, represented by the two censuses in chs. 1 and 26 (125). The Exodus generation, which obediently prepares to leave Sinai (1-10) but then as a result of rebellion and apostasy is sentenced to die in the wilderness (11-25), is succeeded by the new generation, which obediently prepares for the Conquest (chs. 26-36; the chs. following the second census are framed by the narratives concerning Zelophehad's daughters, 27:1-11; 36:1-12). The book is open-ended: Will the second generation succeed where the first has failed? In Olson's words (183): "The concern of the book is to establish a model or paradigm which will invite every generation to place itself in the place of the new generation."

Understanding this structure not only undercuts Martin Noth's contention that Numbers represents a poorly ordered hodge podge of narrative and cultic material, an unfortunate and secondary breaking up of the Sinai tradition complex, but also supplies a theological framework for interpreting individual texts. Following the condemnation of the Exodus generation in ch. 14, 15:1-21, a legal text that mandates offerings to be brought "after you enter the land I am giving you" (v. 1) ... "for (throughout) the generations to come" (vv. 14, 21), takes on an added theological dimension that is promissory in nature (cf. Olson, 170-74). Accordingly, this pericope on supplementary offerings has a different theological content than other similar cultic texts in Exodus, Leviticus, or Deuteronomy. Moreover, 15:37-41, which discusses the tassels of garments and immediately precedes Korah's rebellion, should be understood as providing the theological foundation (15:40-41) for the rebels' assertion that "the whole community is holy, every one of them, and the LORD is with them" (16:3). The rebellion text concerning the poisonous serpents is not simply a typological precursor of the crucifixion (John 3:14-15), but marks the climactic rebellion text, the last of seven in the book of Numbers, which are arranged in symmetrical order with regard to the cause of the murmuring (A. 11:1-3: general difficulties; B. 11:4-34: monotonous food; C. 12: leadership; D. 13-14: enemies in the land; C^1. 16-17: leadership; B^1. 20:1-13: lack of water; A^1. 21:4-9: general difficulties). The first and seventh texts are not only the briefest but both also conclude with Moses' intercessory prayer (11:2; 21:7, the only occurrences of the vb. *pll* [hitp.] in the book; cf. R. Schultz, "Numeri/4. Buch Mose"). The primary theological contribution of the Balaam narrative (chs. 22-24) is not to demonstrate that "God can use anyone," though the pagan curser Balaam is as least as well suited to be a divine spokesman as his donkey! Instead, the Balaam oracles confirm that the patriarchal promises remain intact (24:9) despite Israel's sins (cf. Allen, "The Theology of the Balaam Oracles").

According to Hendrik Koorevaar the book of Joshua consists of four symmetrically arranged sections (cf. the summary in McConville, *Grace in the End*, 101-2): A. 1:1-5:12: going over (*'br*); B. 5:13-12:24: taking (*lqh*); B^1. 13:1-21:45: dividing (*hlq*); A^1. 22:1-24:33: worshiping (*'bd*), with each section containing a spiritual highpoint (Gilgal: 5:1-12; Ebal and Gerizim: 8:30-35; Shiloh: 18:1-19:51; Shechem: 24:1-28). Adopting Koorevaar's analysis helps one to see the key battles (Jericho, Ai, Gibeon) as theologically paradigmatic demonstrations of God's covenant fulfillment and the consequences of Israel's obedience and disobedience (cf. 21:45; 23:14). Even the seemingly mundane conclusion of the book, which reports three funerals (24:29-33), contributes a final example of the fulfillment of the divine promises to Abraham (Gen 15:13-14; 50:24-25): Joseph's mummy is finally home! The book of Joshua clearly contains more than a mere history of the Conquest.

Even in a book like Proverbs, in which a detailed structure is not readily apparent, the prologue (chs. 1-9) and the epilogue (chs. 30-31), which emphasize both the vertical/religious (the fear of the Lord: 1:7; 9:10; 31:30; and the knowledge of the Holy One: 9:10; 30:3) and the horizontal/moral dimensions of wisdom and folly (what is right, just, and fair: 1:3; 2:9; cf. 31:8, 20), and which equate the authority of proverbial wisdom with that of the Mosaic law (calling it *tôrâ*—1:8; 3:1; 4:2; 6:29, 23; 7:2; compare 30:5-6 with Ps 18:30[31] and Deut 4:2), supply the theological framework for interpreting the proverbial collections in chs. 10-29. This invalidates any attempt to reduce folly to intellectual weakness rather than associating it with moral perversity: The wise man is righteous, the fool is wicked. Wisdom is personified by Lady Wisdom (1:20-33; 3:15-18; 8; 9:1-12) and exemplified by the capable and virtuous wife of 31:10-31 (cf. Childs, 1979, 551-56; Camp, 1985, ch. 6). In addition, various theological themes are also developed within the individual collections (e.g., divine sovereignty and human responsibility in 16:1-9).

The length and scope of the book of Isaiah, as well the form-critical analysis focusing on individual prophetic oracles and the redaction-critical break-up of the book into various smaller sections, might give the impression that it has no unifying theme or structure. This, however, is not the case. Chapter 1 serves to introduce the major theological movements within the book: rebellion, judgment, the call to repentance, and the offer of deliverance or further judgment. Following an initial contrast between Zion's present and future condition (chs. 1-5), the prophet is purged, thus forming the core of the faithful remnant, and commissioned to be spokesman to an unseeing, unhearing people (ch. 6). In three groups of texts the king and the people are challenged to trust God in the midst of a political crisis, and God's deliverance is promised: Chs. 7-11 present King Ahaz who fails, chs. 28-33 present an unnamed king who is tempted to rely on Egypt, and chs. 36-39 present Hezekiah who "passes the test." The intervening sections announce God's universal sovereignty, which will be demonstrated in the immediate and distant future (chs. 13-23, 24-27, 34-35). Chapter 39 concludes with the announcement of the Babylonian exile, but ch. 40 proclaims God's return to a people in need. Isa 40-48 portrays Yahweh's political deliverer, Cyrus, while his spiritual deliverer, the Suffering Servant, introduced in 42:1-7, emerges in chs. 49-57 as the only solution for a recalcitrant people. Only then can Zion be glorified by God and the nations (cf. Webb, 65-84; Seitz, 1988, 105-26). However, the book does not end on a positive note: The first and final words of Isaiah concern the fate of those who rebel (*pš'*) against God (1:2 and 66:24). Thus, Isaiah concludes as it begins, by describing those who will not heed the divine warning.

The exegesis of any pericope should take into consideration its placement within the book as a whole: The portrayal of Zion's future exaltation in Isa 2:1-5 is not primarily contributing to OT eschatology (Will Mount Zion replace Mount Everest as the mountaineer's goal?) but is intended as a contrast to Zion's present corruption (1:21-22) and imminent purging through judgment (1:25-27) and to show that the transformation does not depend on Israel's faithfulness. The announcement of the coming of an eschatological king (9:6-7[5-6]) certainly contributes to the growing messianic expectation of Israel but, in context, offers the divine solution to the problem of Israel's faithless kings.

(b) *Theological implications of genre approaches to books and texts.* A second insight from the literary approaches to the Bible that has theological implications is the significance of genre for interpretation. Longman has defined genre as "a group of texts that bear one or more traits in common with each other" (e.g., content, structure, phraseology, function, style, and/or mood, Longman and Dillard, 30). Genre theory in its application to the OT not only helps to overcome many of the flaws of classic form criticism but is beginning to make a major contribution to OT interpretation. (Especially helpful in this regard are Sandy and Giese, eds., and Fee and Stuart.) Although all of the major OT genres have parallels among ANE texts, it is evident that, if dependent on literary conventions, these genres have not merely been "Yahwehized" but also theologically enriched (cf. Walton, 1989, ch. 10).

(i) Distinctive vocabulary and genre identification. There are a number of respects in which theological and genre concerns intersect. For example, the occurrence of several of the characteristic terms of wisdom literature in various psalms is considered to be a primary criterion for the identification of the sub-genre "wisdom psalm," to which scholars have assigned twenty or more psalms. Approximately twenty psalms are labeled as such by several scholars (cf. Kuntz for a listing of these terms and a discussion of other criteria). If a psalm is clearly identifiable as "wisdom," then its primary context for theological assessment is the larger collection of wisdom psalms, secondarily the wisdom books. The discussion of suffering, injustice, the wicked, and the threat of death (such are found in Ps 49), though quite common in individual lament psalms (e.g., Ps 6), when found in wisdom psalms represents a different theological emphasis, for the psalmist is not only wrestling with his own experienced sufferings but also with the larger issue of theodicy. Thus Ps 49 should be grouped with Ps 37 and 73 when analyzing its theological response. In resolving the question of whether "take" (*lqḥ*) in 49:15[16] refers to life after death as the psalmist's resolution to the problem, after examining the immediate context of the word within Ps 49, one should look first to the use of the same term in a similar context in Ps 73:24 (cf. Kuntz, 1977, 231-32; also Gen 5:24; 2 Kgs 2:10). Similarly, the awareness that nearly all of the so-called "imprecations" in the psalms are found in lament psalms (a possible exception is 139:19-21, although its genre is disputed) cautions one against hastily deriving a "theology of revenge" from such psalms. Instead, their precise placement and function of this element within the laments must be analyzed before drawing any theological conclusions.

(ii) The importance of genre for semantics. A knowledge of genre categories and features is also helpful for semantic studies. In studying a word like righteous (*ṣaddîq*), not only is it illegitimate to read NT dimensions into the OT occurrences, but it is also important to determine whether the term is used identically in different genres. In narrative contexts there are not many references to "righteous" people; *ṣaddîq* is used primarily as a relative term (e.g., morally outstanding or more righteous than) or it designates the innocent pary in interpersonal disputes (Gen 6:9; 7:1; 18:23-26, 28; 20:4; 1 Sam 24:17[18]; 2 Sam 4:11; 1 Kgs 2:32; 8:32 ‖ 2 Chron 6:23; 2 Kgs 10:9). In legal texts the word "righteous" also seldom occurs (Exod 23:7-8; Deut 16:19; 25:1 = "innocent," almost a technical term). In wisdom literature, however, especially Proverbs, it becomes a ubiquitous category, which is virtually coreferential with "wise" (*ḥākām*) (Prov 10:3, 6, 7, 11, 16, 20, 21, 24, 25, 28, 30, 31, 32; cf. Eccl 9:1-2). The wisdom psalms employ "righteous" similarly (e.g., Ps 37:12, 16, 17, 21, 25, 29, 30, 32, 39); elsewhere in the Psalter it is applied frequently to God (Ps 7:11[12]; 119:137; 129:4; 145:8), who, by virtue of this trait, is the rewarder and deliverer of the righteous (Ps 5:12[13]; 7:9[10]; 32:11; 34:14, 19, 21[16, 20, 22]). The usage in the prophets is similar but not identical.

Another common OT phrase that has different theological nuances in different genres is "the fear of the LORD" or "fearing the LORD" (employing *yr'/yir'â* in verbal, adjectival, and genitival constructions; the most thorough treatment of this phrase is by J. Becker. "The fear of the LORD," which could be described as the OT equivalent of faith (*pistis*) in the NT, occurs frequently in all OT genres. However, in narrative contexts it is used to describe exclusive, even radical, trust in or worship of God and basic morality (Gen 20:11; 22:12; 42:18; Exod 1:21; 14:31; Josh 4:24; 24:14; 1 Sam 12:14, 24; 1 Kgs 18:12); in legal contexts it usually is expressed in obedience to the law (Exod 20:20; Lev 19:14, 32; 25:17; Deut 5:29; 6:2, 24; 8:6; 10:12-13); in wisdom books, especially Proverbs, it expresses a fundamental attitude toward God that leads to wise behavior and the avoidance of every form of evil (Prov 1:7, 19; 2:5; 8:13; 9:10; 10:27; 14:26-27; 15:16, 33; 16:6; 19:23; 22:4; 23:17; 31:30; cf. Job 1:1, 8; 2:3; 28:28; Eccl 5:7[6]; 8:12-13). The lexical sense of *yr'/yir'â* may remain constant throughout the OT, but its discourse sense varies (e.g., its behaviorial expression) in ways that apparently correspond to the characteristic thematic emphases and concerns of the basic OT genres.

The usage of a theologically significant phrase also may differ within various genres. For example, in narrative and prophetic contexts the expression, "servant of God the LORD" is used mostly to describe those rare individuals who were distinguished by their divine election to carry out a unique task or by exceptional obedience or faithfulness (Abraham, Moses, David, Joshua, the nation of Israel, the agent of salvation in the Isaianic "Servant Songs"; cf. also Job), while in the Psalms the expression primarily occurs as a self-designation employed in describing the pious in calls to praise or in providing the basis for the appeal to God in the laments (Ps 27:9; 31:16[17]; 34:22[23]; 69:17[18]; 79:2, 10; 86:2, 4, 16; 90:13, 16; 102:14, 28[15, 29]; 113:1; 134:1; 135:1; 143:2, 12). In this case, the person using the designation (God or an individual) is clearly more important than the genre of the text that contains it. However, since these two distinct usages may involve polysemy, the former reflecting the high honor of being called the (divine) king's servant and the latter deriving from the (court) convention of humbly designating oneself the servant of another upon whose favor one depends, these two categories must not be confused in determining their theological significance: To call oneself "God's servant" is *not* to compare oneself with Moses or David!

Furthermore, in analyzing some terms, it should be noted that some vocabulary may be genre- or even book-specific; thus the rarity of more common synonyms in a given book, and possibly even the presence of a rarer term, may not be theologically significant. For example, the preferred lexeme by the author of Chronicles for sin is *m'l*, be unfaithful, unfaithfulness (17x; 48x in the rest of the OT, in Ezek 13x). The term abomination, *tô'ēbâ*, is most frequent in Deuteronomy (17x), Proverbs (21x), and Ezekiel (43x, 37x in the rest of the OT). How these various books portray sin is more important than the specific word they use to designate it.

The characteristic language of both faith and folly also can be genre- or book-specific. In narrative and prophetic texts the verb *'mn*, believe, predominates, referring primarily to individual acts or demonstrations of faith (cf. Gen 15:6; Exod 4:8; Num 20:12; 2 Chron 20:20; Isa 7:9; 28:16). The verbal form of *'mn* is used 42x outside of Psalms and Proverbs, but only 9x in Psalms and Proverbs, three of which are in historical psalms. Psalms and Proverbs prefer *bṭḥ*, trust, a term referring primarily to a basic attitude toward God (cf. Ps 25:2; 26:1; 28:7; 31:6, 14[7, 15]; Prov 16:20; 28:25); *bṭḥ* occurs 56x in Psalms and Proverbs, but only 64x in the rest of the OT. Although the word "fool" is commonly found throughout the Wisdom literature, each wisdom book does not utilize precisely the same terms (cf. Donald). Furthermore, one of the strongest Heb. word roots for designating folly, *nbl*, familiar from its use in Ps 14:1 and 53:1[2], "The fool says in his heart, 'There is no God,'" occurs 38x in the OT (e.g., Gen 34:7; Josh 7:15; Judg 19:23-24; 20:6, 10), only seven of which are in wisdom books.

Thus, the assessment of theologically significant terms as a part of the exegetical process must take into consideration possible generic influences and constraints on usage and discourse meaning. When exploring the theological dimensions of a given term, one cannot simply consult a concordance, arbitrarily drawing on any passages that contain the same term. (For additional examples of genre-specific semantics, cf. H.-P. Müller, 282.)

(iii) Genre and theological diversity. One of the features of OT literature that contributes to its theological richness is the way in which various themes are developed differently in different books. Such theological diversity is not necessarily contradictory (cf. Goldingay, ch. 1; McConville, 1987), nor does it force one to speak of OT theologies. However, it does warn against simplistic or harmonizing attempts to synthesize the unique voices of the various canonical witnesses.

One of factors that produces theological diversity is the treatment of the same theme within different genres. For example, the development of the creation theme in Genesis, wisdom, and prophecy each emphasizes various dimensions that are genuinely complementary. In Gen 1:1-2:3, emphases include the sovereign authority of a God whose commands are instantly obeyed, the establishment of order within creation, the universal blessing, and the setting apart of the Sabbath, all themes that will be developed further in the books of the law. Gen 2:4-25, on the other hand, presents an immanent God who is intimately involved with humanity, one who will reveal himself repeatedly to the patriarchs. This relationship is reenforced by the incorporation of this account within the framework of the ten-part *tôledôt* ("these are the generations of....") structure, indicating an unbroken progression from the creation to the beginnings of a covenant people (see Genealogy in the Old Testament in the Appendix). Thus Gen 2 shares many of the genre features of the post-Eden Genesis narrative, despite its context of origins that scholars often label as myth.

However, in other genres both the style and the emphases are quite different: poetic rather than prose, amply utilizing images that are familiar from ANE creation myths, combining creation and redemption, emphasizing God's wisdom (especially wisdom books), power (especially prophets), and glory and uniqueness (especially psalms) as revealed through and reflected by creation (Job 26:5-14; 38-41; Ps 8; 19:1-6[2-7]; 89:9-13[10-14]; 104:5-9; Prov 3:19-20; 8:22-31; Isa 40:12-17, 26, 28; 44:24; 51:9-10, 13, 16; Amos 4:13; 5:8; 9:5-6). An exegesis of any of these texts should be cognizant of the genre-appropriate theological emphases it contains, compare a given text with other texts of the same genre that present this same theme, and be wary of the dangers involved in deriving theology from poetry (see B. W. Anderson, 1984; Dassmann & Sternberger, eds., "Schöpfung und Neuschöpfung," *JBTh* 5, 1990).

3. Thematic emphases. However, as valuable as analyses of book structure and genre may be in helping one to assess the theological contribution of an individual text, another complementary approach must be added: the study of themes. Whereas the exegete seeks to identify the dominant structure and most precise genre category for a given book or section thereof, several divergent themes may be identified in the same text. For example, although Peter Miscall views the book of Isaiah as "The Labyrinth of Images," and there are only a few major themes that are developed throughout the book and that serve to connect its various sections.

(a) *Definition and scope of themes.* Here we are defining *theme* as used in tradition criticism. Georg Fohrer (99-109) distinguishes between a motif (humankind like a fading flower, God like a rock) and the related theme (the brevity of life; the trustworthiness of God). In studying a theological theme such as sin within a given book, it is not sufficient simply to examine all the occurrences of the key synonyms for sin, such as missing the mark (*ḥṭ'*), rebellion (*pešaʻ*), and iniquity (*ʻāwōn*; the most comprehensive treatment of the subject is by Rolf Knierim); one must also include all terms for sins and all descriptions and images of sinfulness. For example, in Isa 1 alone, all of the following belong to the theological theme of sin (and some additional phrases could be included):

"children ... have rebelled against me"(2);

"sinful nation, a people loaded with guilt, a brood of evildoers, children given to corruption! They have forsaken the LORD; they have spurned the Holy One of Israel and turned their backs on him" (4);

"persist in rebellion" (5);

"you rulers of Sodom ... you people of Gomorrah" (10);

"Your hands are full of blood" (15);

"Take your evil deeds out of my sight! Stop doing wrong" (16);

"Though your sins are like scarlet" (18);

"if you resist and rebel" (20);

"a harlot ... now murderers"(21);

"your silver has become dross" (22);

"Your rulers are rebels, companions of thieves; they all love bribes and chase after gifts" (23);

"my foes ... my enemies" (24);

"your dross ... all your impurities" (25);

"rebels and sinners ... those who forsake the LORD" (28).

Similarly, in studying the theological theme of wisdom, it is insufficient to limit oneself to the basic lexemes for wisdom which von Rad describes as "stereometric" (*Wisdom in Israel*, 13 n. 10; see the more detailed study by M. Fox, "Words for Wisdom"): Prov 1:1-5 includes the terms byn/bînâ, da'at I, ḥokmâ, leqaḥ, mᵉzimmâ, mûsar, 'ormâ, śkl, and taḥbulôt, which refer to complementary aspects of wisdom. Other terms that belong to the semantic field of wisdom, including antonyms, such as the terms for folly, and positive terms associated with wisdom, such as righteousness and diligence, as well as descriptions and illustrations of wise and foolish behavior, also contribute to the development of the wisdom theme.

(b) *Themes and rhemes.* Having discussed the macro components of textual exegesis—the structure of books, the genre categories that group together books or individual texts, and themes that weave their way through entire books, encompassing numerous words and related phrases and descriptions—we must return to the micro components—those fundamental building blocks of the text: the words. Certainly there have been many abuses of the word-study approach in the history of biblical theology (cf. the survey by Cotterell and Turner, ch. 4; Louw). However, despite the dangers associated with overvaluing individual words, the accurate identification, understanding, and comparison of theologically significant words within a text can make a substantial contribution to the theological assessment of a text.

Several factors must be taken into account to help guard against such abuses. First of all, one must shift one's attention from the sentence level to the discourse level as the primary context for interpretation. Decisions regarding word usage are not made simply on the sentence level, dictated by syntactical rules, but more often are made on the discourse level. In Isa 28, Wildberger (1078) eliminates verse 19 as a later "actualizing" addition, partly because verse 19b ("The understanding of this message [hābîn šᵉmû'â] will bring sheer terror") repeats and, in his opinion, misunderstands the similar phrase in verse 9 ("To whom is he explaining his message?" [yābîn šᵉmû'â]). However, this explanation overlooks the technique of the author who repeats various words and phrases in this section (vv. 7-23) to make a contrast between the false security of foreign alliances and the rejected offer of divine security, resulting in disappointment and divine judgment (cf. v. 9 ‖ v. 19; v. 10 ‖ v. 13; v. 14 ‖ v. 22; v. 15 ‖ v. 18). The shift in nuance from verse 9, "to understand the prophetic message," to verse 19, "to understand the news" of the inescapable disaster, is made by the repetition of the "hear" root (*šmʿ*) in verse 12, "but they would not listen." Refusing to hear the prophetic message regarding the divinely offered "resting place" (v. 12), they would be forced to hear a terrifying message, perhaps "delivered" by the invading foreign troops (v. 11). They had chosen their bed, and now they must lie in it! (v. 20). From a discourse standpoint, the reuse and meaning shift of the phrase from verse 9 is logically understandable and rhetorically effective.

This example illustrates a second caution in word study: One must understand the difference between theme ("the starting point, the given") and rheme ("the new element in what is being communicated," Jeanrond, 85). Linguists have emphasized the importance of distinguishing between a general motif (topic) and its nuancing in a particular context (comment). Wildberger, for example, is unwilling to allow the prophet Isaiah to give a familiar topic a unique twist or comment in order to make a point. In the book of Isaiah (cf. "hearing" and "not hearing" or "hearing but not understanding") deafness is a major motif that is introduced early and developed throughout the book, but especially in the section Isa chs. 28-33 (1:19; 6:9; 29:18; 30:9; 33:15; 40:28; 42:18-20; 65:12; cf. Aitken, "Hearing and Seeing"). In ch. 28, the prophet is highlighting two types of messages that can be "heard" by giving similar phrases different nuances.

To cite another example from Isaiah, in chs. 40-55 "God's servant" becomes a major theme (Oswalt even claims that "servanthood" is the overarching theme of the entire book [54]; cf. "*Book of Isaiah*"). The servant theme is introduced in 41:8-9 using terms that emphasize his election. This passage is sandwiched between two divine announcements of a conqueror coming from the east and the north, presumably Cyrus (vv. 2-4, 25-27), who will make the islands tremble (v. 5). In 42:1, however, a servant is presented who, in contrast to Cyrus, will give the islands reason for hope (v. 4). Who is this servant? As the portrait develops, each occurrence of the theme adds a new "comment" to the "topic," and gradually two different pictures emerge: a corporate servant Israel and an individual servant who ministers on behalf of the other (compare 44:21 with 49:6).

Essentially, no two occurrences of the same word, even within the same book as part of the same larger theme, have precisely the same nuance. For example, several essays suggest that the prophetic author in Isa 42 and 59 is repeating and playing with the various nuances of *mišpāṭ*, judgment, justice in the respective contexts (cf. Beuken; Jeremias; Kendall, 59). Despite the value of lexical entries that attempt to categorize accurately the various usages a word can have in the OT, the exegete must attempt to determine the specific emphasis a word is being given in a given text, for a sudden shift in its discourse meaning may underline the major point the author is making.

There are several additional aspects of themes that should be noted, especially as they are developed through key words. In many cases, themes are paired, either as a fixed linguistic expression (a syntagmatic collocation) or in their usage in a given book. The two terms, *mišpāṭ ûṣᵉdāqâ*, judgment/justice and righteousness, are probably best understood as a hendiadys, that is, two terms that can be translated as "righteous judgment" or "social justice" (cf. M. Weinfeld, 1995, 1). Either word can occur first in this combination, and the two also occur as word pairs in poetic parallelism. Whenever one of the two terms is thus used in close proximity to the other, it is appropriate to understand them in terms of the combined concept rather than sharply distinguishing between the two (Ps 99:4—combined; Isa 28:17—poetic parallelism; → Judgment/Justice). Another frequently occurring word pair is *ḥesed we'emet*, covenant loyalty and faithfulness or, as more commonly translated, love and truth (Prov 3:3; 14:22; 16:6; 20:28—word pair; Ps 26:3; 57:10[11]; 69:13[14]; Isa 16:5—in poetic parallelism), better understood as "reliable goodness" or "loyal love."

Other terms or themes are combined in particular books. In Isaiah, the words "salvation" (*ye šû'â*) and "righteousness" (*ṣe dāqâ*) occur together in Isa 33:5-6; 51:6, 8; 56:1; 59:17; 60:17-18. This should alert the exegete to the need to examine the relationship between the reference of these two words within the theology of Isaiah. In some books, it may be fruitful to map out the relationship between a whole series of terms. In Chronicles there are at least eight theologically significant terms that are characteristic of the book and clearly interrelated. The primary theme is the need to seek God (*drš*: 1 Chron 10:13, 14; 13:3; 15:13; 16:11; 21:30; 22:19; 26:31; 28:8, 9; 2 Chron 1:5; 12:14; 14:3, 6; 15:2, 12, 13; 16:12; 17:3, 4; 18:4, 6, 7; 19:3; 20:3; 22:9; 24:6, 22; 25:15, 20; 26:5; 30:19; 31:9, 21; 32:31; 34:3, 21, 26; + *bqš*, 8x), both in a cultic sense and in seeking to do God's will "with a whole heart" (1 Chron 22:19; 28:9; 2 Chron 12:14; 15:12; 19:3; 22:9; 30:19; 31:21; 32:31). Then one will "have success" (*ṣlḥ*, 11x) because God will be "with" that person (*'im*, 22x). However, if one "abandons" God (*'zb*, 15x) and is "unfaithful" (*ma'al*, 17x), one will experience the divine wrath (*qeṣep*, 7x) until one humbles oneself again (*kn'*, 15x). In exegeting a text that contains one or more of these terms, one must determine how this particular situation illustrates what it means to seek or abandon God and what consequences ensue, as an illustration of divine retribution.

(c) *Theology as a book's key themes.* It is evident, then, that when one seeks to exegete a text in terms of its theological context, one must note how the theology that emerges from the book's structure intersects with the theology borne by its themes. In some books, the themes bear the primary theological freight.

In Isaiah, several theological themes can be discerned, some related to Israel's present and future state, others more related to appropriate responses that any reader can make. A major theme is Zion's immediate and ultimate future (Isa 1:27; 2:3; 4:5; 8:18; 14:32; 24:23; 28:16; 33:5; 35:10; 46:13; 52:8; 64:10; 66:8; cf. Seitz; Webb) in the light of the present guilt of the people (primarily idolatry and social injustice: 1:2; 5:18; 22:14; 27:8; 30:13; 33:24; 40:2; 59:2-3, 12, 20; 54:4-8), which initially will evoke the judgment of the Holy One of Israel but ultimately will lead to his salvific initiatives, beginning with the formation of a remnant (10:20-22; 11:11, 16; 17:6; 28:5; 37:4, 31-32, cf. 35:10; 48:10; 51:10).

These initiatives are a manifestation of God's plan (*'ēṣâ*; 5:19; 16:17; 25:1; 28:29; 30:1; 44:26; 46:10-11) and involve not only his intervention as divine warrior (42:13; 51:9; 63:1-6) but also through his agent, the eschatological Davidic king (Isa 9, 11, 32) and servant (42, 49, 50, 52-53, 61, who can be identified with the king; cf. Schultz, 1995, 154-59), as well as the anointed political deliverer, Cyrus. This divine intervention will encompass not only Israel but also the nations (42:6-7; 49:6; 51:5-6;

52:10), a clear demonstration of God's superiority over the gods (2:8, 18, 20; 10:10, 11; 19:1; 21:9; 30:22; 31:7; 40:19-20; 42:8, 17; 44:9, 10, 15, 17; 45:20; 48:5). God will judge the proud and lofty and reward the humble (especially 4:2; 24:4; 29:19; 38:15; 54:4; 58:3, 5; 60:15; 66:2) and desires that his people fear him and not human powers (esp. 7:4; 8:12, 13), and believe in him unreservedly (2:22; 7:9; 8:17; 12:2; 26:2, 4; 28:12, 16; 30:15; 31:1; 36:15; 42:17; 43:10; 50:10; 53:1; 57:13; 60:9). In examining these theological themes as they are reintroduced and developed in the course of the book, it is evident that there is not only a close relationship among the various themes but also between the ancient witness and the contemporary application.

Ecclesiastes is a very different book, but its themes are also dominant over structure in conveying its theology and are closely interrelated. Qoheleth views humankind as God's creation (12:1, 7) and as originally upright (7:29). He views God as the giver of all that is good, including joy, wisdom, riches, honor, and life itself (2:24, 26; 3:13; 5:18-19[17-18]; 6:2; 8:15; 9:9) but his work is unfathomable (3:11; 7:13-14; 8:17; 11:5). However, sin has cast the shadow of temporality (*hebel*) over the world, filling it with injustice (3:16; 4:1; 5:8[7]; 7:7; 8:11; 9:2) and death (3:2; 7:2; 9:6, 10) and turning work into toil (*'amāl*, 1:13). In such a world all gain is relative, though wisdom is advantageous (2:13; 7:11-12). God expects people to fear him (3:14; 5:7[6]; 7:18, 26; 8:12-13; 12:13), to accept their portion (2:10; 3:22; 5:18-19[17-18]; 9:9), and to enjoy life (2:24-25; 3:12-13; 5:19-20[18-19]; 8:15; 9:7-8; 11:8-10), while keeping in mind the coming judgment (3:15, 17; 11:9; 12:14), for in the midst of temporality there is also an eternal dimension (3:11, 14). Otherwise, all human efforts are merely "chasing after wind" (1:14, 17).

To summarize, exegesis is incomplete if it does not lay bare the theological thrust of a text, seeking to identify words, phrases, motifs, images, and even structural elements that reveal aspects of God's will and work in the world as it places demands on or otherwise affects Israel, the nations, and/or all humankind. These elements should be analyzed in terms of their function within a given text and synthesized in terms of their participation in and contribution to the theological emphases of the book as a whole, whether structural or thematic in nature. Theological exegesis must be sensitive to the larger theological context of the text, to generic factors that affect both word usage and thematic development, and to semantic issues such as discourse and theme/rheme considerations. Moreover, an exegesis that is consciously theological will also result in greater clarity regarding the contemporary implications and application of a given text.

B. Canon and Theology

However, as important as the book context is for the exegete, it is not the only context that must be taken into consideration. In recent decades, the importance of canon for OT theology has received greater attention, largely through the work of Brevard Childs. Although biblical theology has always claimed to take the entire biblical canon seriously, Childs' "canonical approach" has resulted in some new emphases in OT theology. This is not the place to debate all of the complex issues regarding the formation of the biblical canon, the determination of which church's canon should be made the basis for biblical theology, or the strengths and weaknesses of Childs' proposal. (For a thorough discussion of these and other related issues, see Brett; Noble; and Sailhamer, 1995.) Our goal in the following is more modest: to explore and illustrate some of the implications of taking the canon seriously as one of the theological contexts for exegesis.

1. The importance of canon for OT theology. The canonical approach conceives of the canon not simply as a loose collection of diverse literary works but rather as a carefully conceived and integrated whole, which, accordingly, must constitute the context that enriches the interpretation of all of its constituent parts. According to Childs (*OT Theology in a Canonical Context*, 6-15), a canonical approach to OT theology (a) is essentially a Christian discipline; (b) consists of reflection on the canonical Heb. Scriptures, despite the fact that the NT church generally used its Greek form; (c) sees the OT as functioning as a witness to Jesus precisely in pre-Christian form; (d) reflects theologically on the text as it has been received and shaped; and (e) combines both descriptive and constructive features. Manfred Oeming, in a review of Childs' OT theology, characterizes his approach as more text-based, more objective, more useful for the church, more sensitive to history, and more theological than other contemporary models ("Text-Kontext-Kanon," 242-but Oeming rejects Childs' approach!).

Such an approach has implications for the way one conducts exegesis in the theological context of canon. First of all, if the canon is a carefully composed whole, there may be hermeneutical significance even to the order of the individual books. Whereas the Greek canonical ordering places Ruth after Judges as an example of how God was working in the midst of this period among those who were obedient to the law (gleaning, levirate marriage, kinsman-redeemer) to bring about the birth of the great King David, who finally would be for Israel a leader after God's own heart, Sailhamer (1995, 214) understands the "semantic effect" of the Hebrew ordering in which Ruth follows Proverbs as presenting Ruth as the "virtuous woman" of Prov 31:10-31, "who is to be praised in the gates" (cf. Ruth 3:11; 4:11). More clearly, the Hebrew designation of the Minor Prophets as the Book of the Twelve leads the interpreter to seek aspects of thematic development and connecting sutures between the individual books (cf. the proposal of House; the use of Exod 34:6-7 in Jon 4:2; Mic 7:18; and Nah 1:3; also the examples cited by Nogalski).

Second, if canon is the context for OT theology, one can legitimately compare a theological theme, such as creation, with analogous presentations *anywhere* in the canonical OT Scriptures, not simply in what one considers to be chronologically *antecedent* texts (contra Kaiser, 1981, 16, 18).

Third, theological syntheses must take the entire canonical text of a book in its final form into account, neither bracketing out any parts as "later additions" or ignoring them as theologically insignificant. All books and passages should be viewed as contributing theologically to the whole. Even though some contain fewer theological "calories" per pericope, they are still legitimate objects of theological analysis.

Finally, positing canon as a carefully composed whole suggests that it is legitimate to assume—and to seek—a fundamental unity in OT theology rather than contradictory theologies in the midst of literary diversity.

2. The theology of blocks of books. Such a unity should be sought within the major divisions or generic groupings of books. John Goldingay writes (1994, 132): "In the scriptures themselves the individual books do not appear in isolation but within complexes with varying degrees of interlinking." In the Pentateuch, the dominance of source- and tradition-critical models have effectively kept most scholars, even those who defended an *authorial* unity, from seeking an underlying *theological* unity. Clines' examination of *The Theme of the Pentateuch* has convincingly demonstrated the centrality of the provisions of the patriarchal covenant in their partial fulfillment and nonfulfillment in Exod through Deut as the major theological link between Gen and the "books of the law" (cf. also T. W. Mann, *The Book of the Torah*). In addition, as Torah, Gen teems with "pre-Sinai" allusions to the law: Sabbath, freewill offerings, capital punishment, the tithe, an awareness of the wrongness of adultery, even the claim that Abraham obeyed God's commands, decrees, and laws (Gen 26:5). An exegete handling any of these texts must realize that its theological context is larger than just the book in view.

Furthermore, Sailhamer (1987, 1991) has noted the eschatological horizon of the Pentateuch, something often lost amidst the law collections ("in the last days"—Gen 49:1; Num 24:14; Deut 31:29; cf. 32:20, 29; here one might note also the covenant blessings and curses as laid down in Lev 26 and Deut 28) and the emphasis on the faith of Abraham and in Moses' day (Gen 15:6; Exod 4:1, 5, 8, 9, 31; 14:31; 19:9; Num 14:11; 20:12; Deut 1:32; 9:32).

The fact that the deut. presentation of covenantal law is foundational for the historical books of Josh through Kgs has been used to bolster Noth's theory of the "Deuteronomistic Historian" but less frequently has enriched the interpretation of these books theologically (but see Wenham and the introductory synthesis of McConville, 1993). Though addressing the subject from a variety of perspectives, these books present a powerful theology of leadership, i.e., kingship, under the kingship of God.

The prophetic literature, though reflecting the diverse circumstances and personalities of the prophets, contains a core of theological themes that each prophet consciously drew upon and contributed to, to a lesser or greater extent. W. VanGemeren lists these "prophetic motifs" as the day of the Lord, the kingdom of God in creation, the Messiah and the messianic kingdom, the Spirit of restoration, the new people of God, and Israel and the nations (1990, 212-44; for a discussion of the evidence that the prophets quoted their predecessors, see Schultz, *The Search for Quotation*, forthcoming). The so-called messianic prophecies are not merely isolated highlights of an otherwise mundane prophetic career, but are a deliberate building up of a concrete expectation (cf. K.-D. Schunk). For the prophets of Judah, the consequences of the election of Zion is a significant theme. For Isaiah this issued in a call to trust in the God who elected Zion as his dwelling rather than in political alliances; for Jeremiah this theme involved rejecting the Jerusalemites' false assurance that nothing could touch them as God's chosen city (Isa 14:32; 31:8-9; 37:35; contrast Jer 9:7-15; 26:1-6). The interpreter of prophetic literature needs to ascertain (a) which of these major theological themes is/are central to a given text; and (b) how the prophet develops the theme(s) in a given text, both in the context of the major themes of the prophet as a whole and in the context of the development of the theme(s) in the larger prophetic corpus. (For a discussion of common theological structures within the prophetic corpus as a result of conscious canonical shaping, cf. Clements, 1977.)

Recently several major efforts to synthesize the theology of the wisdom books as a whole have been published, rather than simply analyzing the theology of the individual books (R. E. Clements, 1992; R. E. Murphy; L. G. Perdue), although the prevailing approach still involves contrasting the earlier optimistic proverbial wisdom

(Proverbs) with the later pessimistic "critical" wisdom (Job, Ecclesiastes; but see Schultz, "Unity or Diversity in Wisdom Theology? A Covenantal and Canonical Perspective," *TynBul* 42, 1997, 271-306). The growing consensus that wisdom's theological contribution is essentially "creation theology" (cf. Perdue) provides a common basis for interpreting the wisdom books, even though each develops the creation theme in a different manner (Proverbs: creation order; Ecclesiastes: creation gifts; Job: the sovereign power and inscrutable ways of the Creator).

3. The theological relationship among blocks of books. The interpreter should take into account not only the theology of the blocks of books but also the complementary emphases and theological relationship among these major blocks. Goldingay (1994, 132-35) describes these emphases:

> The narrative from Genesis to Kings has magnificent highpoints in the time of Moses and Joshua and that of David and Solomon, but it has an ultimately tragic shape.... The prophets begin with forebodings of disaster but promise blessing and hope.... The relationship between Torah and Prophets can also be portrayed as one between order and freedom. The former establishes the norms that are vital to identity, and the latter prevents order from becoming institutionalized and fossilized.... The Writings as a whole are books produced "between the times" and designed for people living between the times.... They reflect a hermeneutical dialogue between the accepted canonical text of the Torah and the Prophets and the Second Temple community seeking to live its everyday life with God. (Cf. also Sailhamer, 1995, 239-43, re "canonical redaction" of the entire OT.)

If this is the case, then von Rad's conception of the traditions of confessional salvation history, the prophets, and wisdom as independent theological streams was seriously flawed. The theological significance of Torah for the rest of the canon cannot be overemphasized. Joshua's primary charge is to study and obey the Torah (Josh 1:7-8); similarly, the first psalm describes the one who meditates on the Torah as truly blessed (Ps 1:2). Thus both the "Prophets" and the "Writings," the second and third divisions of the Hebrew canon, begin with the call to turn to the Torah for orientation in one's life and work. The close relationship between proverbial wisdom and the OT law cannot be overlooked (Weinfeld, 244-74; Gese, ch. 3), although the dominant view that wisdom influenced Torah rather than vice versa is by no means certain (cf. McConville, 1993, ch. 3; Craigie, 24-29, 79-83, regarding the date of Deut's composition). Furthermore, Douglas Stuart has demonstrated convincingly the prophetic dependence on the pentateuchal covenantal blessing and curse texts (Lev 26; Deut 28-32; Stuart, 1988, xxxi-xlii), texts that are also of fundamental importance for understanding the course of Israelite history.

In the context of the OT canon, the interpreter also must take into account the progressive growth of OT theology. Although the scholarly "dating game" may never be over, exegesis cannot be carried out in the theological context of the OT canon without taking into account what Robert Girdlestone termed *The Building Up of the Old Testament* (1912), but more recently has been described as "canon consciousness." The exegete must seek to discover the antecedent theology that the biblical author was assuming (Kaiser, 1981, 134-40), laying bare the underlying theology that informs each text (Bright, 143, 170), and to determine to what extent the author was reinterpreting earlier theological traditions (see the magisterial study of Fishbane; for an approach to intertextuality that seeks to circumvent the chronological disputes over the dating of the biblical literature, see Eslinger, 47-58).

The covenant between God and his creation—first with all humankind (Gen 9) and then with Israel—may not be the center of OT theology, but it certainly is foundational to Israel's understanding of its relationship to God and to the unfolding of its history. It also involves a theological concept that progressively developed. John Walton has argued that there was only *one* covenant between God and his people that was modified and amplified in the course of Israel's history: the covenant with the patriarchs (Gen 12, 15, 17), which later led to the covenant with the entire nation at Sinai (Exod 19-24), which later was mediated through the Davidic king (2 Sam 7 ‖ 1 Chron 17), and which is to be renewed and transformed through the new covenant (Jer 31), a covenant, through which all the nations were to be blessed (Gen 12:3; cf. Ps 72:17; Walton, ch. 3; cf. also Dumbrell, 1984). Exegesis constantly must relate the theological statements in a given text regarding divine blessing and human obligation to that stage in the unfolding of the covenantal relationship that that text reflects (cf. examples below).

4. OT theology and biblical theology. However, since God's covenant certainly is not foreign to a church that was established through the "new covenant in my [Jesus'] blood" (Luke 22:20), a canonical approach to OT exegesis cannot limit itself to an exclusively OT perspective but must seek to reflect the relationship between the two Testaments within the larger context of biblical theology. According to Childs (1985, 8-9), it is wrong both to "force the entire Old Testament within a fixed schema of prophecy and fulfillment" and to "read the Old Testament as if [one] were living before the coming of Christ."

As noted above with regard to the OT, the exegete must be aware of the progress of redemption and revelation as one crosses the threshold from the OT into the NT (cf. VanGemeren, 1988). Christian theological reflection on the OT must not address issues from an exclusively "BC" framework, but it must also not read NT developments into OT theological themes (cf. Bruce). For example, David's plea to God not to remove the Holy Spirit from him (Ps 51:11[13]) must be understood within the OT context, when the divine Spirit was given in order to equip individuals, sometimes temporarily, for a specific task or service. David had personally witnessed how Saul, following his disobedience to God's commands, had been cast away from the divine presence and "lost" the Spirit, a fate that David greatly feared (cf. 1 Sam 15:35; 16:14; 28:6).

The temptation is great to read a NT understanding of salvation into various OT terms, which, in their OT contexts, primarily refer to temporary, often corporate, deliverance from death or the enemy. Lev 18:5 ("Keep my decrees and laws, for the man who obeys them will live by them. I am the LORD") is no promise of eternal life through adherence to the law (cf. Kaiser, 1971). Nevertheless, the theological development of the theme of salvation in the OT is certainly analogous to that in the NT. The OT assures the Israelite of forgiveness for sins through its sacrificial system (Lev 4:21, 26, 31, 35), just as certainly as the NT does on the basis of Jesus' sacrificial death, so that its sacrifices cannot be viewed simply as a typological preparation for the crucifixion. The prayers and praise of the psalmist cannot be viewed as simply the well-worn formulas of an institutionalized religion but rather as reflecting a genuine personal faith and confidence in God that is comparable to that expressed by NT believers. (On OT soteriology, cf. J. S. Feinberg, Part 4; and Farris.)

It already has been noted that an eschatological perspective is evident even in the Pentateuch. Though 1 Pet 1:10-12 states that the OT prophets knew that they there were serving *us* when they spoke of future things, both ancient Israel and the contemporary church find themselves "between the times" of prophecy and fulfillment. However, the Christian exegete cannot simply mine the prophets seeking eschatological details to fill out his or her chart of the last days. The strongly covenantal and national emphasis of OT eschatology with its abundance of rich imagery must not be flattened and spiritualized as now occurring in the church. The larger context of the new covenant passage (Jer 30-33) primarily describes the promised restoration of covenant blessings to Israel through the transformation of the people to guarantee obedience and through the raising up of a righteous (messianic) leader to rule over them (cf. Walton's chart of the subjects covered in "aftermath oracles," 1994, 135; also see Dumbrell, 1994). Both OT Israel and the church look forward to the coming of the Messiah.

As a result of the renewed interest in the relationship between the Testaments, the interpreter has been provided with helpful discussions and syntheses to aid in the responsible interpretation of the OT text within the context of biblical theology (cf. Childs, 1992; Fuller). Nevertheless, one of the most helpful tools is to study how the NT interprets and applies specific OT texts in profoundly theological, though sometimes confusing ways (cf. Beale). As the interpreter diligently seeks to integrate OT theology and exegesis, he or she can be assured that this is not simply an academic exercise but an essential step toward personally appropriating its message, for "everything that was written in the past was written to teach us, so that through endurance and the encouragement of the Scriptures we might have hope" (Rom 15:4).

BIBLIOGRAPHY

K. T. Aitken, "Hearing and Seeing: Metamorphoses of a Motif in Isaiah 1-39," in *Among the Prophets, Language, Image and Structure in the Prophetic Writings*, JSOTSup 144, 1993, 12-41; R. B. Allen, "The Theology of the Balaam Oracles" in *Tradition and Testament* [Feinberg FS], 1981, 79-119; B. W. Anderson, ed., *Creation in the Old Testament*, 1984; G. K. Beale, ed., *The Right Doctrine From the Wrong Texts? Essays on the Use of the Old Testament in the New*, 1994; J. Becker, *Gottesfurcht im Alten Testament*, 1965; W. A. M. Beuken, *"Mišpāṭ:* The First Servant Song and Its Context," *VT* 22, 1972, 1-30; M. G. Brett, *Biblical Criticism in Crisis? The Impact of the Canonical Approach on Old Testament Studies*, 1991; J. Bright, *The Authority of the Old Testament*, 1975; F. F. Bruce, *New Testament Development of Old Testament Themes*, 1968; C. V. Camp, *Wisdom and the Feminine in the Book of Proverbs*, 1985; B. S. Childs, *Biblical Theology of the Old and New Testaments. Theological Reflections on the Christian Bible*, 1992; idem, "The Canonical Shape of the Book of Jonah," in *Biblical and Near Eastern Studies* [LaSor FS], 1978, 122-28; idem, *Introduction to the Old Testament As Scripture*, 1979; idem, *Old Testament Theology in Canonical Context*, 1985; R. E. Clements, "Patterns in the Prophetic Canon," in *Canon and Authority*, 1977, 42-55; idem, *Wisdom in Theology*, 1992; D. J. A. Clines, *The Theme of the Pentateuch*, 1978; P. Cotterell and M. Turner, *Linguistics & Biblical Interpretation*, 1989; P. C. Craigie, *The Book of Deuteronomy*, NICOT, 1976; A. Cundall, "Judges—An Apology for the Monarchy?" *ExpT* 82, 1970, 178-81; E. Dassmann and G. Stemberger, eds.,

JBTh 5: Schöpfung und Neuschöpfung, 1990; T. Donald, "The Semantic Field of 'Folly,'" *VT* 13, 1963, 285-92; W. J. Dumbrell, *Covenant & Creation: An Old Testament Covenantal Theology*, 1984; idem, *The Faith of Israel: Its Expression in the Books of the Old Testament*, 1988; idem, "'In Those Days There Was No King in Israel; Every Man Did What Was Right in His Own Eyes.' The Purpose of the Book of Judges," *JSOT* 25, 1983, 23-33; idem, *The Search for Order: Biblical Eschatology in Focus*, 1994; L. M. Eslinger, "Inner-Biblical Exegesis and Inner-Biblical Allusion: The Question of Category," *VT* 42, 1992, 47-58; T. V. Farris, *Mighty to Save: A Study in Old Testament Soteriology*, 1993; G. D. Fee and D. Stuart, *How to Read the Bible for All Its Worth: A Guide to Understanding the Bible*, 1993; J. S. Feinberg, ed., *Continuity and Disconti- nuity: Perspectives on the Relationship Between the Old and New Testaments*, 1988; M. Fish- bane, *Biblical Interpretation in Ancient Israel*, 1985; G. Fohrer, et al., *Exegese des Alten Testamentes*, 1979, 99-109; M. Fox, "Words for Wisdom," *ZAh* 6, 1993, 149-69; D. P. Fuller, *The Unity of the Bible: Unfolding God's Plan for Humanity*, 1992; H. Gese, *Essays on Biblical Theology*, 1981; R. Girdlestone, *The Building Up of the Old Testament*, 1912; J. Goldingay, *Models for Interpretation of Scripture*, 1994; idem, *Theological Diversity and the Authority of the Old Testament*, 1987; G. Hasel, *Old Testament Theology: Basic Issues in the Current Debate*, 1991; P. R. House, *The Unity of the Twelve*, 1990; W. G. Jeanrond, *Text and Interpretation As Categories of Theological Thinking*, 1988; J. Jeremias, "מִשְׁפָּט im ersten Gottesknechtslied," *VT* 22, 1972, 31-42; W. C. Kaiser, *Exodus*, EBC 2, 1990; idem, "Leviticus and Paul: 'Do This and You Shall Live' (Eternally?)," *JETS* 14, 1971, 19-28; idem, *Toward an Exegetical Theology*, 1981; idem, *Toward an Old Testament Theology*, 1978; D. Kendall, "The Use of *Mišpāṭ* in Isaiah 59," *ZAW* 96, 1984, 391-405; W. W. Klein, C. L. Blomberg, R. L. Hubbard, Jr., *Introduction to Biblical Interpretation*, 1993; R. Knierim, *Die Hauptbegriffe für Sünde im AT*, 1965; H. J. Koor- evaar, *De Opbouw van het Boek Jozua*, 1990; J. Kugel, "On the Bible and Literary Criticism," *Prooftexts* 1, 1981, 99-104; J. K. Kuntz, "The Canonical Wisdom Psalms of Ancient Israel: Their Rhetorical, Thematic, and Formal Dimensions," in *Rhetorical Criticism* [Muilenburg FS], 1974, 186-222; idem, "The Retribution Motif in Psalmic Wisdom," *ZAW* 89, 1977, 223-33; A. Lauha, *Kohelet*, BKAT XIX, 1978; J. Licht, *Storytelling in the Bible*, 1978; T. Longman III and R. B. Dillard, *An Introduction to the Old Testament*, 1994; J. P. Louw, "How Do Words Mean—If They Do?" *Filologia Neotestamentaria* 4, 1991, 125-42; T. W. Mann, *The Book of the Torah: The Narrative Integrity of the Pentateuch*, 1988; E. A. Martens, "Accessing the Theological Readings of a Biblical Book," *AUSS* 34, 1996, forthcoming; J. G. McConville, *Grace in the End: A Study in Deuteronomic Theology*, 1993; idem, "Using Scripture for Theology: Unity and Diversity in Old Testament Theology," *Scottish Bulletin of Evangelical Theology* 5, 1987, 39-57; P. Miscall, "Isaiah: The Labyrinth of Images," *Sem* 54, 1991, 103-21; H.-P Müller, "Formge- schichte/Formenkritik I," *TRE* 11:271-85; R. E. Murphy, *The Tree of Life: An Exploration of Biblical Wisdom Literature*, 1990; P. R. Noble, *The Canonical Approach: A Critical Reconstruc- tion of the Hermeneutics of Brevard S. Childs*, 1995; J. Nogalski, *Literary Precursors to the Book of the Twelve*, BZAW 217, 1993; M. Oeming, "Text-Kontext-Kanon: Ein neuer Weg alttesta- mentlicher Theologie?" *JBTh 3: Zum Problem des biblischen Kanons*, 1988, 240-45; D. Olson, *The Death of the Old and the Birth of the New: The Framework of the Book of Numbers and the Pentateuch*, BJS 71, 1985; J. Oswalt, *The Book of Isaiah, Chapter 1-39*, NICOT, 1986; L. G. Perdue, *Wisdom & Creation: The Theology of Wisdom Literature*, 1994; R. L. Pratt, Jr., *He Gave Us Stories*, 1990; G. von Rad, *Wisdom in Israel*, 1972; B. L. Ramm, *His Way Out: A Fresh Look at Exodus*, 1974; R. Rendtorff, "The Composition of the Book of Isaiah," *Canon and Theology*, 1993, 146-69; J. H. Sailhamer, "The Canonical Approach to the Old Testament: Its Effect on

Understanding Prophecy," *JETS* 30, 1987, 307-15; idem, *Introduction to Old Testament Theology: A Canonical Approach*, 1995; idem, "The Mosaic Law and the Theology of the Pentateuch," *WTJ* 53, 1991, 241-61; J. A. Sanders, *Canon and Community: A Guide to Canonical Criticism*, 1984; D. B. Sandy & R. L. Giese, eds., *Cracking Old Testament Codes: A Guide to Interpreting the Literary Genres of the Old Testament*, 1995; R. L. Schultz, "The King in the Book of Isaiah," in P. E. Satterthwaite, et al., eds., *The Lord's Anointed: Interpretation of Old Testament Messianic Texts*, 1995, 141-65; idem, "Numeri/4. Buch Mose," *Das grosse Bibellexikon*, 1988, 2:1068-72; idem, *The Search for Quotation: Verbal Parallels in the Prophets*, JSOT-Sup forthcoming; idem, "Unity or Diversity in Wisdom Theology? A Covenantal and Canonical Perspective," *TynB*, forthcoming; K.-D. Schunk, "Die Attribute des eschatologischen Messias: Strukturlinien in der Ausprägung des alttestamentlichen Messiasbildes," *ThLZ* 111, 1986, 541-52; C. R. Seitz, "Isaiah 1-66: Making Sense of the Whole," in *Reading and Preaching the Book of Isaiah*, 1988, 105-26; idem, *Zion's Final Destiny: The Development of the Book of Isaiah: A Reassessment of Isaiah 36-39*, 1991; E. Sitarz, ed., *Höre, Israel! Jahwe ist einzig. Bausteine für eine Theologie des Alten Testamentes*, 1987; D. K. Stuart, *Hosea-Jonah*, WBC 31, 1988; W. VanGemeren, *Interpreting the Prophetic Word*, 1990; idem, *The Progress of Redemption: The Story of Salvation from Creation to the New Jerusalem*, 1988; J. H. Walton, *Ancient Israelite Literature in Its Cultural Context: A Survey of Parallels Between Biblical and Ancient Near Eastern Texts*, 1989; idem, *Covenant: God's Purpose, God's Plan*, 1994; B. G. Webb, "Zion in Transformation: A Literary Approach to Isaiah," in *The Bible in Three Dimensions*, 1990, 65-84; M. Weinfeld, *Deuteronomy and the Deuteronomic School*, 1972, 244-74; idem, *Social Justice in Ancient Israel and in the Ancient Near East*, 1995; J. Welch, *Chiasmus in Antiquity*, 1981; G. J. Wenham, "The Deuteronomic Theology of the Book of Joshua," *JBL* 90, 1971, 140-48; R. N. Whybray, *The Composition of the Book of Proverbs*, JSOTSup 168, 1994; idem, *Ecclesiastes*, NCB, 1989; H. Wildberger, *Jesaja*, BKAT X, 1982; H. G. M. Williamson, *1 and 2 Chronicles*, NCB, 1982; H. M. Wolf, *Interpreting Isaiah: The Suffering and Glory of the Messiah*, 1985; G. E. Wright, *God Who Acts: Biblical Theology As Recital*, SBT 1/8, 1952; R. B. Zuck, ed., *A Biblical Theology of the Old Testament*, 1991.

Richard Schultz

APPENDIX

בְּתוּלָה (bᵉtûlâ), girl under the guardianship of her father (# 1435); בְּתוּלִים (bᵉtûlîm), adolescence (# 1436).

ANE   Akk. m. batūlu, young man; f. batultu, adolescent, nubile girl (CAD, B, 173a; in neo-Babylonian marriage contracts the word takes on the more specialized connotation of virgin, ibid, 174a.); Ugar. btlt, used most often as an epithet of Anat, the wife of Baal; Aram. bᵉtûltāʾ, young girl. More specifically, "In an Aramaic text from Nippur, a spell by a barren wife seeking children, there occurs the phrase, btwltʾ dymḥblʾ wlʾ yldʾ, 'a "virgin" travailing and not bearing'" (Wenham, 326-27). It is Wenham's conclusion that the cognate occurrences consistently refer to a girl of marriageable age (326-29).

OT   Turning to the OT material, Wenham maintains that the lexical profile is identical to that of the cognates. One of the principal arguments supporting this conclusion is the fact that in their respective legal materials, Assyr. and Heb. law share nearly identical formulations of certain laws each using this cognate. If the laws are the same and the cognates are used, Wenham argues that the meanings of the cognates must be the same (330). Additional reasons he lists are as follows:
   1. In Esther bᵉtûlâ is applied to the new members of the harem both before and after they have spent their night with the king (Esth 2:17-19).
   2. bāḥûr (young man) and bᵉtûlâ often occur as a fixed pair, and the former shows no evidence of referring to sexual status.
   3. In Joel 1:8 the bᵉtûlâ has a baʿal, presumably a husband.
   4. Job 31:1 is much more easily understood if the bᵉtûlâ he is referring to is married; otherwise it would be difficult to understand why this would be an offense in a polygamous society.
   On the other hand, 2 Sam 13:18 speaks of Tamar tearing the garment indicative of her bᵉtûlâ status after she had been raped by Amnon. If, as argued by Wenham, this is nothing more than tearing one's clothing in grief, the text would not have needed to go into detail concerning the significance of the garment. Rather, it is likely that Amnon's act has caused her to lose her status as a bᵉtûlâ. Even so, however, that does not mean that bᵉtûlâ means virgin.
   Another difficulty with Wenham's theory is that neither the girls in Esth 2:17 nor the woman in Joel 1:8 could still be called marriageable, in that they are officially spoken for. If availability for marriage was the criterion for the designation bᵉtûlâ, one would think the term would cease to be applicable when a marriage arrangement was made. If the term did not cease to be applicable until the consummation of the marriage, then sexual status again becomes an issue. In reality it appears that Wenham is suggesting "teenager," though a specifically female one. Given passages such as 2 Sam 13:18, however, one must wonder if that is all that there is to it.

Perhaps responsible for some of these lexical difficulties is our unwarranted assumption that categories classifying individuals in any society are definable by a single feature rather than being multifaceted. So, for instance, "spinster" in English has elements of age, marital status, and, less definably, sexual status all as criteria. In a similar way we suggest that b*e*tûlâ has age, marital status, *and* sexual status as criteria.

Age. There is every indication that a b*e*tûlâ is young. This is supported by the many passages that contrast the term with those who are old (Deut 32:25; 2 Chron 36:17; Ps 148:12).

Marital status. It appears that a young woman may be betrothed and still be in the category of b*e*tûlâ, but the evidence concerning whether a married woman can be in this category is inconclusive. In Judg 21:11-12 a contrast is drawn between nāšîm (wives) who had had sexual relations and b*e*tûlôt who had not. One might then infer that a young girl who becomes an 'iššâ (wife) ceases to be a b*e*tûlâ.

Sexual status. It is likely that a young girl is not considered a b*e*tûlâ until she reaches puberty (see the discussion of b*e*tûlîm below). Then, as mentioned above, at least certain types of sexual activity preclude one's being considered a b*e*tûlâ (e.g., Tamar). Nevertheless, it is not clear that any sexual activity disqualifies one from this category. Esth 2:19, Ezek 23:3-8 are the primary mitigating contexts, with the cognate material contributing to the uncertainty. Perhaps one's sexual reputation is more at issue. In such a case rape or prostitution eliminate the possibility of a girl being considered a b*e*tûlâ. Consequently, it is preferable to speak of the girl as being reputable. This would assume no wanton behavior.

Given these categories, our conclusion is that b*e*tûlâ should be identified as a social status, defining someone as "an ostensibly reputable young girl who is past puberty and is, by default at least, still in the household of her father." In Joel 1:8 we assume that the marriage has not been consummated and the woman is therefore still technically in her father's household (cf. H. W. Wolff, *Joel and Amos,* tr. W. Janzen et al., Hermeneia, 1977, 30). Likewise, the young women in Esther do not cease to be b*e*tûlôt until they are officially given a place within the king's harem. Job's claim that he has not looked upon a b*e*tûlâ is maintaining that he has never considered any action that would ruin a girl's reputable status. Even the Aram. spell of the barren wife may suggest that she has not achieved secure or permanent status in her husband's household until she has borne a child. Overall, the cognate usage is in close agreement with this description, which is substantiated by the details of Middle Assyrian Law A55: "(If someone) took by force and dishonored a man's (daughter), a *batultu,* (who was dwelling in her father's house), whose (body?) had not been soiled, who had not been (forcibly?) deflowered and not married (betrothed). . . (Wenham, 329; *ANET,* 185).

Epithetical usage. Epithets, by their very nature, must be considered in isolation from the rest of the semantic field. Epithets tend to represent frozen forms and may, as such, fail to offer a reliable guide to the current usage of the word. Additionally they may be applied in an honorary, idealist, or even patronizing spirit. The Canaanite goddess Anat is most frequently given the epithet btlt in the Ugar. texts. Though she is the consort of Baal, she is also his sister and so is still technically within the household of her father, El. She is a goddess of war, whose bloodshed is wanton but whose sexual conduct is not addressed in the literature. Anat is poorly attested in the literature. For more information see A. Kapelrud, *The Violent Goddess: Anat in the Ras Shamra Texts* (1969), and U. Cassuto, *The Goddess Anath* (1971).

There are allusions to the beauty and fertility of Anat, but no preserved text clearly depicts her as giving birth to offspring. However, Anat can be viewed as a fertility goddess in this sense: she is Baal's partner, zealous for his cause, aiding him, and by her defeat of Mot, enables Baal to come back to life (W. A. Maier III, "Anath," *ABD* 1:226). Consequently, the Ugar. epithets cannot serve to inform the details of our study.

The use of *bᵉtûlâ* as an epithet for a city is understandable within the general framework of the definition offered above. A city that is politically reputable and under the guardianship of its people or gods could be so described. So Israel's status as a *bᵉtûlâ* is compromised by her unfaithfulness to Yahweh (Jer 18:13-14; 31:21).

The lexical relationship between *bᵉtûlâ* and *'almâ* is that the former is a social status indicating that a young girl is under the guardianship of her father, with all the age and sexual inferences that accompany that status. The latter is to be understood with regard to fertility and childbearing potential. Obviously there are many occasions where both terms apply to the same girl. A girl ceases to be a *bᵉtûlâ* when she becomes a wife; she ceases to be an *'almâ* when she becomes a mother.

In the theological discussion it has at times been suggested that if Isa 7:14 intended to make reference to a virgin, the prophet would have used the word *bᵉtûlâ*. However, if the woman is already pregnant (Walton, 290-91) or is one of the women from Ahaz's harem, the term *bᵉtûlâ* would hardly be suitable.

The m. pl. form, *bᵉtûlîm* typically occurs as the nom. abstraction for the social status detailed above (Lev 21:13; Judg 11:37-38). "Adolescence" is inadequate as a translation, but is closer than the other Eng. alternatives. In a context such as Judg 11, "virginity" is certainly to the point, but that is a contextual decision, not a lexical mandate. Further clarification is necessary for Deut 22:14-20. The use of the pl. abs. form in the husband's accusations could certainly be understood as nom. abstractions. But the const. pl. forms used by the parents (vv. 15, 17, also the construction in v. 20) refers to material evidence of her status as a *bᵉtûlâ,* which v. 17 identifies as a garment (*śimlâ*). Wenham's interpretation that this is a garment worn recently by the girl showing menstrual stains, thus proving that she was not pregnant, is plausible (334-36; but see P. C. Craigie, *Deuteronomy*, NICOT, 1976, 292-93).

BIBLIOGRAPHY
TDOT 2:338-43; T. Wadsworth, "Is There a Hebrew Word for Virgin?" *ResQ* 23, 1980, 161-71; J. Walton, "Isa 7:14—What's in a Name," *JETS* 30, 1987, 289-306; G. J. Wenham, "Bᵉtulah 'A Girl of Marriageable Age'" *VT* 22, 1972, 326-48.

John H. Walton

2349	זכר

זכר (*zkr* I), q. remember, reflect on, commemorate; ni. be remembered, invoked; hi. mention, invoke, praise, give evidence, bring a memorial offering (# 2349); אַזְכָּרָה (*'azkārâ*), nom. offering over which God's name was invoked (# 260); זָכוּר (*zākûr*), remembrance

(# 2345); זֵכֶר (*zēker*), nom. remembrance, proclamation, name (# 2352); זִכָּרוֹן (*zikkārôn*), nom. remembrance, memorial (# 2355); מַזְכִּיר (*mazkîr*), secretary, recorder (# 4654).

ANE The vb. is well attested. Phoen. *zkr* and *skr*, Aram. *zkr* and *dkr*, and Eth. *zakara* all mean "remember." Akk. *zakāru is* a vb. of speaking, signifying "declare, mention, invoke, swear." Old South Arab. and Arab. *dkr* means both "remember" and "mention." In Ugar. the root occurs only in personal names.

OT   1. The root and its derivatives have crucial roles in the OT. On the human level, the words embrace reflection, especially on what is in the past. Such reflection may lead to regret or relief, or more actively appreciation and commitment. God's remembering has to do with his attention and intervention, whether in grace or in judgment. Religious worship is the context where human and divine usage come together, in the fellowship of praise and blessing.

    Remembering can refer to worrying or consoling reflection or to reasoning. The rich person does not "reflect" on the brevity of life (Eccl 5:20[19]). Thinking about the wicked prospering is disturbing (Job 21:6). Remembering present affliction means being engrossed by it (Lam 3:19-20). On the other hand, the exiles are exhorted to remember Yahweh (Jer 51:50; cf. Zech 10:9). The young in their pleasures are to remember their Creator and so to take him into account (Eccl 11:9-12:1). Job is urged to "consider" that the innocent are never punished (Job 4:7) and to remember to praise God's work rather than criticize him (36:24). Remembering God's past dealings with Israel suggested that the present rupture in the covenant relationship was Israel's fault, not his (Mic 6:4-5). It also showed his sovereignty over history and so leads to a monotheistic conclusion (Isa 46:9). Remembering God's laws brings encouragement (Ps 119:52). Remembering his name at night means turning to him in prayerful meditation (Ps 119:55; cf. 63:6[7]). To remember God's greatness is an antidote to fear (Neh 4:14[8]; cf. Deut 7:18). To remember Zion (Ps 137:6) is to be committed to the city of God and appreciate all it stands for. The vb. is even applied to the future, in the sense of bearing in mind the predictable consequences of sin ("reflect on," Isa 47:7; "consider," Lam 1:7).

    2. In many of the cases with human subjects, changes of life situation stir up memories of relief or nostalgia. Thus, Zophar assured Job that, if he repented, he would recall his present troubles "as waters gone by" (Job 11:16). On the other hand, Israel complained in the desert about its lack of the varied diet that they remembered eating in Egypt (Num 11:5). The exiles missed worshiping in Jerusalem and engaged in a sort of funeral lament (Ps 137:6; cf. 42:4[5]). In the lament of Ps 77 the initial reaction to Israel's downfall is one of frustration: God's earlier salvation was now a missing element (Ps 77:3[4], 5[6]; see NRSV). The death of an individual or community carries with it the fate of being forgotten (Job 24:20; cf. Ps 83:4[5]; Jer 11:19; Ezek 21:32[37]; 25:10; Zech 13:2).

    3. Eschatological promises speak of past or present phenomena or experiences being transcended and no longer remembered. The ark would be superseded and not missed (Jer 3:16). The exiles were not to dwell on God's past saving acts, which would be eclipsed by his new work of redemption (Isa 43:18). Jerusalem, personified as a

bride, was to remember no more the humiliation of her exilic widowhood (54:4). In the new heavens and earth the former things that brought sorrow will be forgotten (65:17).

4. Remembering can connote gratitude. Abigail urged David to remember her in his future time of blessing, after she had brought food and wine to him and his men (1 Sam 25:31). Not remembering someone's former benefits is condemned in the OT as an act of ingratitude. Joash forgot Jehoiada's former help when he killed his son (2 Chron 24:22). Nobody remembered the poor wise man who saved his city (Eccl 9:15). At the divine level, Israel in the desert forgot the power of God displayed in the Exodus (Ps 78:42; 106:7; cf. Judg 8:34; Neh 9:17; Isa 57:11). Unfaithful Jerusalem failed to remember the ignominious origins from which God had rescued it (Ezek 16:22, 43). After sinning against God, Israel is urged to remember and appreciate his past grace: "Is this the way you repay the LORD?" (Deut 32:5-7).

5. Rather than denoting simply a mental process, remembering frequently induces present action, like tying a knot in a handkerchief. In fact, the tassels on the Israelites' garments were to remind them of God's commands and so to obey them (Num 15:39-40). The purpose of Joseph's appeal to the chief butler to remember him was that he would get him released from prison (Gen 40:14). To remember God's precepts leads to obeying them (Ps 103:18). Keeping the leprosy regulations was motivated by the reminder of God's striking Miriam with leprosy (Deut 24:9; cf. Num 12:10). Challenging Israel to remember God's past saving deeds was tantamount to a call to praise (Ps 105:5; 1 Chron 16:12). In Deut memory plays a major role as a positive constraint. The Israelites' historical experience of being slaves in Egypt is urged as a reason to include their slaves in the Sabbath rest and in the Feast of Weeks (Deut 5:15; 16:12), to release their slaves in the seventh year (15:15), to leave part of their crops for the underprivileged (24:22), and generally to respect their right to justice (24:18). Further, in 8:2 God's dealings in the desert are meant to stimulate Israel to obedience, while in 8:18 the reflection that Israel's prosperity is God's gift is an incentive to obey and stay loyal to him, rather than worshiping other gods. In 9:7 the exhortation to remember Israel's continual rebellion in the desert introduces a long narrative of sin and grace, which culminates in a passionate call for obedience (10:12-13). In the book of Ezekiel remembering past sin is a powerful impetus for good. The exiles were to remember how they had personally grieved God in their preexilic history and so come to a true sense of God's will (Ezek 6:9). Moreover, their resettlement in the land was to be marked by remorse for their bad lifestyle when they were there before, the act of remembrance serving as an incentive to new loyalty (16:61, 63; 20:43; 36:31).

6. Remembering God is often a dynamic phenomenon that leads to the situation of the believer or the believing community being transformed, especially in the Psalms. Recalling God's past saving work becomes a bridge from a grim present to a blessed future. In Ps 77:11[12] his saving activity at the Exodus is seen to be relevant to Israel's disastrous situation and an implicit promise that the God who saved them will save again. In 143:5 the recollection of God's past salvation changes despair into hope and prayer. Jonah, at death's door, remembered God and turned to him in a prayer for rescue (Jon 2:7[8]). In Ps 78:35 seeking God in repentance is triggered by memories of God as Savior. Similarly, in Isa 63:11, after sinning and being punished, Israel is represented as recalling the Exodus and turning back to God, while in Zech 10:9 those of Israel still in exile were to remember God and turn to him again in faith, as a prelude to

their return to the land. Many of these examples focus on the Exodus not simply as an event in history but as a window through which to glimpse God's redemptive will for his people and individual believers in every generation. To this end the Exodus was to be personally remembered in the Feast of Unleavened Bread (Exod 13:3; Deut 16:3).

7. So closely is remembering associated with action that at times it functions as a synonym for action of various kinds. In Amos 1:9 Tyre's not remembering its treaty with Israel means to disregard or break it. In Ps 109:16 not to remember to show kindness to the needy connotes neglect to do so. To forget God as Savior in Isa 17:10 is to forsake him for alien gods. For the Transjordan tribes remembering Moses' command to fight alongside the other tribes until the whole land was won (Josh 1:13; cf. Deut 3:18-20) connotes obedience. Similarly, to remember the Torah is to obey it (Mal 4:4[3:22]; cf. Isa 64:5[4]). To remember the Sabbath day (Exod 20:8; cf. "observe," Deut 5:12) is to observe it by abstaining from work. The remembering of the Feast of Purim (Esth 9:28) refers to its celebration.

8. All the preceding examples relate to human recollection. The vb. often has God as subject, especially in prayers. Samson so prayed in his helplessness, asking for renewed strength (Judg 16:28). Hannah, praying for a son, asked God to remember her (1 Sam 1:11). Nehemiah, in a series of prayers that punctuate his memoirs, requested that his work might stand as a memorial to his service for God and his fellow Jews. Evidently he had enemies who gave him no credit for his dedicated labors and sought to undo them. So he committed to God both his own work (Neh 5:19; 13:14, 22, 31) and the opposition he had encountered (6:14; 13:29) (see H. G. M. Williamson, *Ezra, Nehemiah*, xxv-xxviii). In intercessory prayer for Israel's survival Moses reminded God of his promises to the patriarchs (Exod 32:13; Deut 9:27). In Ps 132:1-10 (cf. 2 Chron 6:42) the reigning king prayed for blessing on his reign for David's sake and was given a favorable reply in vv. 17-18.

9. An appeal to remember frequently features in lament petitions. In Ps 106:4-5 the psalm leader interrupts a communal lament, praying to be included in Israel's coming salvation. Specific appeals are made to God's commitment to the covenant (25:6-7; 74:2; Jer 14:21), to the dishonor God is suffering (Ps 74:18, 22; 89:50-51[51-52]), to his compassion for human frailty (89:47[48]; Job 7:7), to sympathy for human affliction (Lam 5:1-20) or to his mercy (Hab 3:2), to God's previous personal care (Job 10:9), and to his scriptural promises (Neh 1:8, with reference to Deut 30:2-4; Ps 119:49). Past loyalty to God is sometimes pleaded in individual laments (2 Kgs 20:3 = Isa 38:3; Jer 18:20). God is reminded of injustice Judah has suffered in Ps 137:7 (cf. Jer 15:15). In Ps 88:5[6] the lamenter compares his low level of life with being dead and so outside God's remembering care. In Job 14:13 Job quaintly asks God to let him shelter in Sheol, out of reach of his anger, and remember him when the danger was past.

10. Narratives record God's favorable response to crises and/or to petitions associated with it (Gen 8:1; 19:29; Exod 2:24); childlessness is reversed in Gen 30:22; 1 Sam 1:19. Hymns celebrate his active remembering, whether motivated by the covenant (Ps 98:3; 105:8, 42; 106:45; 111:5; cf. 9:12[13]; 115:12) or compassion (78:39; 103:14; 136:23). God's mindfulness in blessing humanity is praised in 8:4[5].

11. In promises God's faithfulness to his covenant is affirmed (Gen 9:15; Lev 26:42, 45; Ezek 16:60; cf. Exod 6:5; Num 10:9; Jer 31:20).

12. Divine remembering can have negative overtones of accusation or punishment. God laments Israel's short-lived devotion in Jer 2:2. Sinners are warned that God remembers their sins, storing them up for judgment (14:10; Hos 7:2; 8:13; 9:9), or are urged to interpret disaster in this way (Jer 44:21). A curse urges that punishment of the family's earlier sins should be inherited (Ps 109:14). In a communal lament this very fate is deprecated (79:8). Petitions that an individual's or the community's own sin be not remembered are offered in Ps 25:7; Isa 64:9[8]. In Ezekiel assurances are given that the previous sins of repenting sinners will not be remembered against them (Ezek 18:22; 33:16), and warnings are given that earlier good behavior of backsliders will not count to their credit (3:20; 18:24; 33:13). God promises to forgive and forget his people's sins in Isa 43:25; Jer 31:34.

13. The hi. or causative form of the vb. occasionally relates to memory. In 2 Sam 18:18 Absalom is said to have no son to carry on his memory. In 1 Kgs 17:18 fear is expressed that the prophet in God's name will "bring" hidden sins "to light" (REB) and exact punishment for them. In Ps 87:4 God promises to "record" foreign nations on the register of his people. However, the normal meaning of the hi. is to mention in speech (e.g., Gen 40:14; 1 Sam 4:18; Isa 19:17), especially the name of God or other gods (Exod 23:13; Josh 23:7; Isa 62:6; Amos 6:10; cf. the ni. in Hos 2:17[19]). The servant in Isa 49:1 describes God's commission in terms of his mentioning his name (cf. Acts 9:10-11). It often refers to invoking God in worship (e.g., in Isa 26:13 [REB]; 48:1). God causes his name "to be invoked" at the sanctuary (Exod 20:24, REB). The task of the Levites was to "invoke" God (1 Chron 16:4, NRSV), whether in praise or in "petition" (NIV), and the term reappears in the headings to Ps 38 and 70. Thus, it also means to praise the beloved in a love song (S of Songs 1:4) or to cause a king's name to be celebrated (45:17[18], NRSV). Ps 20:7[8] affirms that "we boast" (REB) of Yahweh's name, instead of chariots or horses. In Ps 71:16; Isa 12:4; 63:7 God's attributes are proclaimed in praise.

14. The hi. also has two special meanings. First, in Isa 66:3 it is used of bringing incense as a memorial offering ('azkārâ: see below). Second, it can have a forensic flavor. In 43:26 God challenges the exiles to "cite" him "to appear" (REB) or to "accuse" him (NRSV). In Ezek 21:23[28] Nebuchadnezzar's divination shows Jerusalem's guilt as legal proof (W. Zimmerli, *Ezekiel*, 1:438, 445), while in Ezek 21:24[29] Judah by its sins had also presented such evidence. In 29:16 Egypt's role was to attest Judah's guilt. Similarly, in Num 5:15 the purpose of the grain offering used in the ordeal of the wife accused of adultery was to expose or "draw attention" to her guilt.

15. The nom. *zēker* refers to remembrance when it is associated with death. Evildoers and Israel's enemies suffer the fate of not being remembered at the time of death (Exod 17:14; Deut 25:19; 32:26; Ps 9:6[7]; 34:16[17]; 109:15; Isa 26:14). On the other hand, wisdom teaching promises that the righteous will always be remembered (Ps 112:6; Prov 10:7). Ecclesiastes provocatively asserts that not even the righteous have lasting remembrance after their death (Eccl 9:5). Like the Akk. *zikru*, the term is also used in human contexts as a parallel and synonym of "name" or "fame" (Prov 10:7; Hos 14:7[8]).

16. When used of God, this latter meaning also applies (Exod 3:15; Ps 30:5; 97:12; 102:12[13]; NRSV "name"; 135:13; Isa 26:8; Hos 12:5[6]). This usage is developed from a basic meaning of invocation or proclamation and corresponds to the hi. of

the vb. In Ps 6:5[6] the parallelism indicates that the meaning is not remembrance but praise (Childs, 71; Schottroff, 294-95). In Esth 9:28 recounting the message of Purim seems to be in view (Childs, 72). To "celebrate" God's goodness in Ps 145:7 is to engage in proclaiming it in worship. Similarly, in Ps 111:4 the *zēker* that God established for his wonders denotes proclamation of the Exodus (Childs, 22; Schottroff, 193).

17. The nom. *zikkārôn* has at least three meanings. First, like *zēker*, it can mean remembrance: Eccl 1:11; 2:16 denies that the dead are remembered. Second, it is a memorandum, record, or "something to be remembered" in itself (Exod 17:14), such as the scroll (*sēper*, → # 6219b) of remembrance in which God lists his true people's names (Mal 3:16). The most common sense is a memorial or reminder of something else. It is applied to religious objects, even to pagan symbols in Isa 57:8. The twelve stones at the Jordan (Josh 4:7) were a monument to God's bringing Israel's twelve tribes into the land. The two onyx stones and twelve gems on the high priest's ephod and breastpiece (Exod 28:12, 29; 39:7) were a means of bringing the names of the twelve tribes into God's presence for his blessing. The bronze censers used by Korah and his followers were hammered into an overlay for the altar as a reminder to Israel that only Aaron's family could be priests (Num 16:40[17:5]). The gold looted from the Midianites was put in the sanctuary as a permanent thank offering for the victory (Num 31:54; cf. also Zech 6:14). The term is also applied to festivals and rites of worship. The Passover was a memorial or commemoration of the Exodus (Exod 12:14), keeping its memory green for each generation. However, in Num 10:10 the trumpets at festivals and sacrifices were a reminder for God, calling on him to graciously accept his people's offerings (cf. Exod 30:16). The trumpet calls that signaled the autumn celebration of Lev 23:24 (cf. Num 29:1-6) probably likewise requested that God should take note of Israel. In Exod 13:9 the Feast of Unleavened Bread is said to function in the same way as phylacteries, reminding God's people to obey his Torah. The "reminder offering" in Num 5:15, 18 is explained in the text as a reminder or way of establishing the guilt or innocence of the wife suspected of adultery. In Neh 2:20 the meaning of *zikkārôn* is uncertain. It is best taken as an invocation or proclamation, like *zēker*. Sanballat and his fellow leaders had no right to engage in worship in Jerusalem.

18. The nom. *'azkārâ* (NIV "memorial portion, memorial offering") is used of certain offerings. In form it is an Aram. aphel inf. used as a nom. Like the Heb. hi. vb., it seems to refer to the invoking of God's name, in this case, over the part of an offering that was burned in sacrifice as distinct from the rest that was given to the priests (Schottroff, 334-38). It is used of different types of grain offering in Lev 2:2, 9, 16; 5:12; 6:15[8]; Num 5:26. In Lev 24:7 it is applied to the frankincense placed beside the showbread and later, representing the bread, burned on the altar as an offering (cf. Isa 66:3).

P-B   In the Qumran writings there are three interesting uses. As in the Ps, in 1QH 4:35 remembering God (in this case, "the might of your hand and the greatness of your compassion") gives the individual believer new confidence. The blowing of trumpets in battle so that God might remember and rescue in Num 10:9 is quoted in 1QM 10:7 and applied to the eschatological war. The cultic trumpets of Num 10:10 are also applied thus: one set of trumpets was to be inscribed "reminder of vengeance in God's appointed time" (1QM 3:7; 7:13; 16:4; 18:14). In 1QS 10:5, however, Num 10:10 is echoed with reference to the festivals and holy days. The promise that God will remember the covenant with Israel's ancestors in Lev 26:45 is claimed by the community in CD 1:4; 6:2 (= 6QD 3:5).

NT   → *NIDNTT* 3:230-47.

BIBLIOGRAPHY
TDOT 4:64-82; *TWAT* 2:571-93; P. A. H. de Boer, *Gedenken und Gedächtnis in der Welt des Alten Testaments,* 1962; B. S. Childs, *Memory and Tradition in Israel,* 1962; W. Schottroff, *'Gedenken' im Alten Orient und im Alten Testament,* 2d ed., 1967.

Leslie C. Allen

4855	מַלְאָךְ

מַלְאָךְ (*mal'āk*), nom. messenger, angel (# 4855); מַלְאָכוּת (*mal'ākût*), nom. message (hapleg. in Hag 1:13; # 4857).

ANE   The *mār šipri* in Akk. and *mal'āk* in WestSem. sources denote a mediator of communication in business and political affairs (cf. Heb. *mᵉlā'kâ,* business). The messenger delivered an oral message, along with documentation, explaining and defending his master's word. A god might also send a messenger or vizier (*sukkallu*) on business.

OT   1. Human leaders frequently send *mal'ākîm* on business or diplomacy (Gen 32:3-6). These human messengers are fully equated with their senders (Judg 11:13; 2 Sam 3:12, 13; 1 Kgs 20:2-40). God can send prophetic or priestly messengers (Hag 1:13; Mal 2:7). The prophetic commissioning and messenger formula ("Thus says Yahweh") reflect the image of diplomatic protocol (Ross, 99-102). It was sometimes difficult to distinguish between human and angelic messengers (Judg 13:20; Mal 3:1).

2. Angels serve as messengers of revelation, for example, in the role of the *angelus interpres* of Zech 1:14; 2:3. Most striking is the figure of the *mal'ak yhwh*, like human messengers, who speaks in God's name and occasionally appears as Yahweh himself (e.g., Gen 16:7-14). Of the three "men" who appear to Abraham and Sarah, one speaks in Yahweh's name (Gen 18:22; cf. Dan 12:5), and the other two are called *mal'ākîm* (19:1). Manoah's wife describes the "man of God" as looking like "an angel of God" (Judg 13:6), but Manoah later learns that he is the *mal'ak yhwh,* who is closely identified with God himself. While it may be anachronistic to speak of the *mal'ak yhwh* as a hypostasis of God, he does provide a provocative image of divine agency and hence a proleptic type for NT Christology (Hurtado, 71-92).

3. God's angel is instrumental in the saving events of Exodus, Sinai, and Conquest (Exod 14:19; 23:20; Josh 2:1-4; cf. Hos 12:14). Angels can also threaten the wicked with destruction and death (Exod 12:23; 1 Chron 21:12; Ps 78:49; Prov 16:14), and they are associated with eschatological judgment (Ezek 9:1-8; Dan 7:9-14).

4. There are no named angels in preexilic writings. In Isa 14:12, the traditional "Lucifer" glosses *hêlēl ben-šāhar,* bearer of light ("morning star," "son of the dawn" [→ # 2122]), and is an incomplete metaphor for the "king of Babylon" (cf. Isa 14:4). Angelic names are usually theophorous: Gabriel = *geber 'ēl* (man of God, Dan 8:15-16; cf. Judg 13:6, 8). Whereas Michael (# 4776) is represented in Daniel as a military *śar,*

211

Gabriel (# 1508) is more of a priestly figure (Dan 9:21-24; 12:6-7). This distinction holds true in the NT (cf. Luke 1:26; Rev 12:7).

5. The association of angels with God's holiness is found occasionally in the OT. While entitled *qᵉdôšîm*, they cannot be compared with Yahweh himself (Exod 15:11 [LXX, Q]; Job 15:15). The elect of Israel are found in close communion with these holy ones (Dan 7:18, 27; see Brekelmans; Collins, 123-52).

6. A related lexeme is found in Daniel. *'îr*, watcher [Aram.], in the idiom: *'îr wᵉqaddîš*, holy watcher (# 10541). *'îr wᵉqaddîš* suggests the role of angelic temple guardian found only in postexilic literature, and canonically only in Dan 4:13-23[4:10-20]. The "decree" of the watchers (4:14) may suggest a scribal function for priestly angels, keeping the heavenly books (Ezek 9:2; Dan 7:9).

P-B In pseudepigraphical lists of archangels, both Michael and Gabriel appear, with Michael taking precedence. In the Enoch tradition *'îr* may refer to a good or a fallen angel, whereas *'îr wᵉqaddîš* refers to holy angels (1 En 13:10; 93:2 [Aram.]).

BIBLIOGRAPHY
H. Bietenhard, *Die himmlische Welt im Urchristentum und Spätjudentum*, WUNT 2, 1951; C. H. W. Brekelmans, "The Saints of the Most High and Their Kingdom," *OTS* 14, 1965, 305-29; J. J. Collins, *The Apocalyptic Vision of the Book of Daniel*, 1977; W. Eichrodt, *Theology of the Old Testament*, 2:15-228; N. Forsyth, *The Old Enemy: Satan and the Combat Myth*, 1987; C. H. Gordon, "History of Religion in Psalm 82," in G. A. Tuttle (ed.), *Biblical and Near Eastern Studies*, FS W. S. LaSor, 1978, 129-31; M. Greenberg, *Ezekiel 1-20*, AB, 1983, 37-59, 164-206; I. Gruenwald, *Apocalyptic and Merkavah Mysticism*, AGJU 14, 1980; L. W. Hurtado, *One God, One Lord*, 1988; P. J. Kobelski, *Melchizedek and Melchiresha*, CBQMS 10, 1981; S. A. Meier, *The Messenger in the Ancient Semitic World*, HSM 45, 1988; P. D. Miller, *The Divine Warrior in Early Israel*, HSM 5, 1973; C. Newsom, *Songs of the Sabbath Sacrifice*, 1985; J. F. Ross, "The Prophet as Yahweh's Messenger," *Israel's Prophetic Heritage*, FS J. Muilenburg, 1962, 98-107; C. C. Rowland, *The Open Heaven: A Study of Apocalyptic in Judaism and Early Christianity*, 1982; J. de Savignac, "Les 'Seraphim,'" *VT* 22, 1972, 320-25; W. A. VanGemeren, "The Sons of God in Genesis 6:1-4," *WTJ* 43, 1981, 320-48; R. de Vaux, "Les chérubins et l'arche d'alliance," FS A. Robert, 1967, 231-59.

Stephen F. Noll

5944	נֵר

נֵר (*nēr* I), nom. lamp, light (# 5944); נִיר (*nîr* I), nom. lamp (# 5775).

ANE Cognate with Akk. *nūru*, nom. light, fire, lamp, frequently used as a divine epithet, especially of the sun god Shamash. Compare also the Old Aram. divine name *nr* (Sefire), the Ugar. divine epithet *nyr* (also Ugar. *nr*, lamp), and a Punic personal name (*b'lnr*, Ba'al is a lamp).

OT 1. As a familiar symbol of domestic and working life (Jer 25:10), the lamp (*nēr*) is a natural metaphor for life. It is used primarily as a symbol for the quality and length of life. The recurring phrase "the lamp (of the wicked) goes out," which occurs several times in the Wisdom literature (e.g., Job 18:5; Prov 13:9; 20:20), appears to mean that life for the wicked is shortened and unfulfilled. This is suggested by Prov 24:20, which affirms that the wicked have no future (Heb. *'aḥᵃrît*; # 344).

2. Although the comparable phrase "the lamp of the righteous" does occur (Prov 13:9; Heb. *'ôr*, # 240), the OT seems to assume that without God human lives are in darkness and that even the righteous have no lamp of their own. Only Yahweh can give light to a person's lamp, that is, his life (Ps 18:28[29]; the parallel verse says simply "You are my lamp, O LORD" (2 Sam 22:29). Yahweh, in fact, gives light to human beings through his own lamp. This idea is applied both to the guidance given by God's word (Ps 119:105) and to the spiritual and physical growth resulting from the gift of Yahweh's life or breath (Prov 20:27, "The lamp of the LORD searches the spirit [breath] of a man"; cf. Gen 2:7).

3. The separate metaphor of a lamp shining in darkness gives rise to two further distinctive concepts. First, the lamps on the tabernacle or temple lampstand were to be kept burning all night (Exod 30:7-8; Lev 24:3-4; contrast 2 Chron 29:7). As with the lampstand, the lamps probably represent the light of God's continuing presence. Second, specific representatives of the Davidic line are described as a lamp (2 Sam 21:17; 1 Kgs 11:36; Ps 132:17; in this sense always *nîr* (II) in Kgs and Chron). The context usually refers to some potentially fatal threat (2 Sam 21:17), notably through David's own family (2 Kgs 8:18-19 ‖ 2 Chron 21:4-7). The meaning here is neither life nor "yoke, dominion" (Hanson), but a guarantee that David's house will survive even the darkest days because of God's covenant promise.

P-B   *nēr* is generally used for the lights on the candlestick in the temple. The expression "God's lamp" may refer either to the candlestick or to the Law, and "lamp of Israel" is often used to describe a great scholar or teacher.

NT   Though Jesus is once called a lamp (Rev 21:23), as is John the Baptist (John 5:35), the NT mainly refers to a lamp to encourage believers not to hide God's light but give it maximum exposure (Matt 5:15; Mark 4:21; Luke 8:16). The eye as the lamp of the body enables others to see a person's inner light (Matt 6:22-23; Luke 11:34-36). The lampstand is used mainly in Revelation as a symbol for individual churches (Rev 1:12-20). However, churches are only light-bearers, for the true light of the Messiah, and their lampstand, may be removed if they do not repent (Rev 2:5).

BIBLIOGRAPHY
NIDNTT 2:484-96; *TDNT* 4:16-28, 324-27; *TWOT* 2:565-66; P. D. Hanson, "The Song of Heshbon and David's *Nir*," *HTR* 61, 1968, 297-320.

Martin J. Selman

| David | David (דָּוִד [*dāwid*], # 1858). |

David, the youngest son of Jesse of Bethlehem, became the second king of Israel and the founder of a short-lived empire and a much longer-lived dynasty that ruled in Judah until the Babylonian exile. His rule was remembered as one of special prosperity for the united kingdom of Israel and was cherished as an ideal to be realized again when the Davidic monarchy reached its full potential. The main OT sources for the presentation of David and the Davidic monarchical ideal are 1-2 Sam, 1 Chron, and the book of Psalms, as well as certain sections within the Prophets. References to

David as the dynastic founder and the exemplar for monarchical rule in Judah are also beaded through 1-2 Kings.

1. *David in Samuel.* The account of David in 1-2 Sam is commonly divided into two main narrative segments, the "History of David's Rise" (1 Sam 16-2 Sam 5[7]) and the "Succession Narrative" or "Court History of David" (2 Sam 7[9]-20; [1 Kgs 1-2]), which may or may not represent separate literary sources dealing respectively with David's early career and then his rule in Jerusalem. The earlier narrative functions as a kind of *Bildungsroman,* which tells how the young hero emerged from his lowly family origins to become a warrior of renown, a member of Saul's court, and then the victim of the king's excessive envy. Whereas Saul was impressed by his physical appearance (1 Sam 9:2; 10:23-24), the choice of David was based on a more profound evaluation (16:7). And whereas Saul's election had been in response to the original demand of the people expressed through their tribal elders (8:4-5), David is described as "a man after his [God's] own heart" (13:14), where "heart" signifies "will" or "choice" (see McCarter [1980], Gordon [1986]). The story of David and Goliath in 1 Sam 17, usually read as a tale of derring-do, presents the young man David as a model of faith in God: "You come against me with sword and spear and javelin, but I come against you in the name of the LORD Almighty, the God of the armies of Israel, whom you have defied" (v. 45). The ensuing defeat of Goliath in the Valley of Elah brought David into the closest possible relationship with Saul and his family through his friendship with Jonathan (18:1-4), with whom he entered into a covenant of loyalty (20:16-17), and also through his becoming Saul's son-in-law (18:20-27). Jonathan's initial reaction after the victory over Goliath was to present David with the symbols of his own princely status (18:4), in an act that may fairly be seen as a "virtual abdication" in favor of David (cf. Jobling). The commitment to David's cause on the part of both Jonathan and Michal (cf. 19:11-17) contributes significantly to the apologetic function of the (so-called) "History of David's Rise" in that it undermines, from within Saul's own family, the case for the king's distrust of his rival. But while Saul has no compunction about trying to kill David (18:10-11, 17, 20-21, 25), a great deal is made in the narrative of the latter's unwillingness to harm Saul inasmuch as he was "the LORD's anointed" (e.g., 24:6; 26:9).

It is evident that disaffected elements under the Davidic monarchy viewed the dynast as a usurper who had achieved his position at the cost of the lives of some of those who stood between him and the throne. This surfaces in the taunting of David by the Benjaminite Shimei when the king was forced to evacuate his capital at the beginning of Absalom's rebellion. Shimei claimed that David's misfortunes at the hand of Absalom were God's punishment for his murderous treatment of the family of Saul, "in whose place you have reigned" (2 Sam 16:7-8). The "History of David's Rise" has, then, the defense of David against such charges as one of its primary aims. At various points David is seen as, almost ostentatiously, avoiding even the appearance of ill-will towards Saul and his house, perhaps most conspicuously in the double sparing of the king when it would have been possible to end his life (1 Sam 24; 26). Some explicit theologizing of the motif is given in Abigail's speech in 1 Sam 25: "When the LORD has done for my master every good thing he promised concerning him and has appointed him leader over Israel, my master will not have on his conscience the staggering burden of needless bloodshed or of having avenged himself" (vv. 30-31).

The circumstances in which David was neither in the service of the Philistines nor yet available to help his own people on the day of Israel's defeat and Saul's death in the hill country of Gilboa are carefully detailed in 1 Sam 29-31. His reaction to the news of Saul's death (2 Sam 1:15-16), as to the murders of Abner and Eshbaal (2 Sam 3:28-39; 4:9-12), makes the same kind of point: David did not shed Saulide blood, nor was he implicated in others' shedding of Saulide blood on his way to the throne. It is perhaps more of a modern scholarly conceit that sees the theme of "the LORD's anointed" in these chapters as conveying a message about how people should view *David's* kingship: If he acted so honorably towards the rejected figure of Saul, how much more deserving of respect, not to say sacrosanctity, was David (or, for that matter, his successors) as "the LORD's anointed"! On the other hand, in that the chapters corresponding to the "History of David's Rise" deal in "royal messianism," in which the anointed status of the king betokens his special position in relation to God and the nation, the dignifying of Saul by the term "the LORD's anointed" is a datum to be included in any consideration of Davidic messianism in the OT.

The account of David's tenure of the throne in Jerusalem begins in 2 Sam 5 with the capture of Jerusalem from its Jebusite inhabitants. The transference thither of the ark of the covenant was the first step in the city's becoming the religious as well as the political capital of Israel (ch. 6). In a side glance in the narrative that describes this development, the possibility of Israel being ruled by descendants of a Davidic-Saulide union is excluded following a disagreement between David and Michal over the king's exuberant celebration of the ark's arrival in the capital (6:20-23). Following upon the report of this domestic altercation is the comment that Michal, daughter of Saul, "had no children to the day of her death" (v. 23).

The military exploits of David as king are summarized briefly enough in 2 Sam 8, with his victories being attributed directly to God's involvement on his behalf (vv. 6, 14). After the account of how David fulfilled his oath to Jonathan (cf. 1 Sam 20:14-17) by granting special favors to his son Mephibosheth (2 Sam 9), there is a longer report of military encounters with the Ammonites and their Aramean allies, but this extended coverage is partly because the Ammonite wars provide the context for David's adultery with Bathsheba, the killing by proxy of Uriah her husband, and the series of domestic tragedies in chs. 13-19, in which the judgment announced by Nathan was worked out ("the sword will never depart from your house, because you despised me and took the wife of Uriah the Hittite to be your own," 12:10).

The most serious development, because it was the most dangerous for David and his kingdom, was the rebellion by his son Absalom, who played upon certain administrative weaknesses of his father and was so successful in his wooing of disgruntled elements in the kingdom as to force David to flee Jerusalem and withdraw to Transjordan. The David of these chapters is a pitiable, contrite character (cf. 2 Sam 16:11-12), bearing the weight of his own punishment and in some respects more akin to the fugitive figure described in the second half of 1 Sam. When David returns to his capital after the collapse of the rebellion, he is magnanimous towards those who had opportunistically abused him or whose allegiance had been called in question (2 Sam 19:15-30)—which contrasts strikingly with the vindictive death-bed advice that is given to Solomon in 1 Kgs 2:1-12, in the so-called "David's Testament," and that apparently is contradicted within divine speech in 1 Kgs 3:11, in the account of Solomon's dream at Gibeon.

Further modification of the portrayal of David as a man of power and military achievement is offered in the "Samuel Appendix" in 2 Sam 21-24. Two narratives dealing with famine and plague, in chs 21 and 24 respectively, show David having to engage in remedial action for the good of the kingdom, even though in the first case the blame is attached to the name of Saul for his unlawful killing of Gibeonites during his reign (21:1, 5). The vulnerability of David and his dependence on divine help, not least in battle, are also brought to attention in the central sections of the Appendix, in which David is shown as in danger of his life and is rescued only by the intervention of one of his men ("But Abishai son of Zeruiah came to David's rescue," 21:17) and then, as the speaker in the psalm in ch. 22 (= Ps 18), attributes his successes against his enemies to the delivering acts of God on his behalf.

2. *The Davidic covenant.* A special place in the Davidic traditions of 1-2 Sam is enjoyed by 2 Sam 7, where God announces through the prophet Nathan that David's son and successor will build a temple in his honor and, more significant still, that God would "establish the throne of his (sc. Solomon's) kingdom forever" (v. 13). Though the actual word "covenant" (*bᵉrît*; # 1382) does not occur in the chapter, the content nevertheless shows this undertaking to be the same as the "everlasting covenant" mentioned in the "last words of David" in 23:5. Moreover, it is represented in the primary text in 2 Sam 7 as an unconditional commitment on God's part in favor of David and his dynasty. In the inevitable event of failure on the part of David's successor(s)—v. 14 refers specifically to Solomon—the misdemeanor would result in discipline but not in the ending of the relationship now to be established (vv. 15-16). Comparisons may be made with the Abrahamic covenant of Gen 15, which is also expressed as an unconditional undertaking by God to Abraham's descendants, as also with the broader Abrahamic tradition in Genesis (compare Gen 12:2 with 2 Sam 7:9). The covenant with David evidently occupied a central place in the official theology and worship of the Jerusalem temple before the Exile (cf. Ps 2:7-12; 89:19[20]-37[38]; 132:11-18). The problem of the historically experienced conditionality of the theoretically unconditional Davidic covenant is addressed directly, and under the pain of the Babylonian exile, in Ps 89:38[39]-51[52]. The friability of the concept of the unconditional covenant is already evident in 1 Kgs 9:6-9, where keeping faith with Yahweh becomes a prerequisite for the continuation of the covenant (cf. also 1 Sam 2:30 in this respect).

The Davidic covenant as expressed in the Nathan oracle of 2 Sam 7 represents a perspective on David that is determinative for the evaluation of his successors in 1-2 Kings. David is the model ruler in this part of the (so-called) deuteronomistic history (→), and from time to time his successors are compared with him, whether to their advantage or (often) disadvantage. For the former see 1 Kgs 15:11 (Asa) and 2 Kgs 18:3 (Hezekiah). On the other hand, Solomon's heart "was not fully devoted to the LORD his God, as the heart of David his father had been" (1 Kgs 11:4); similar judgments are made on Abijah (1 Kgs 15:3), Amaziah (2 Kgs 14:3), and Ahaz (2 Kgs 16:2) (cf. G. von Rad, *Studies in Deuteronomy,* 1953, 86-88). But in spite of God's displeasure with Solomon there was no immediate retribution, on account of David: "Nevertheless, for the sake of David your father, I will not do it during your lifetime. I will tear it (sc. the kingdom) out of the hand of your son. Yet I will not tear the whole kingdom from him, but will give him one tribe for the sake of David my servant and for the sake of Jerusalem, which I have chosen" (1 Kgs 11:12-13). The same sentiment is expressed in relation to the failure of Jehoram, who "walked in the ways of the kings of Israel" (2 Kgs 8:18-19). This positive estimation of David is aptly summed up in von Rad's description of him as "the king after the heart of the Deuteronomist" (88). This David is manifestly not the character of 2 Sam 9-20, weak and vacillating at home though victorious in battle; now he is a figure of proto-messianic proportions, and his reign has become the standard of comparison for all his successors. But this lauding by the biblical historian is possible because it is *cultic* loyalty to Yahweh that the Deuteronomistic writer prizes, and in that respect the David of tradition was more exemplary than was even Solomon.

3. *David in Chronicles.* The idealization of David, as also of Solomon, is still more pronounced in 1-2 Chronicles. Here large sections of the story of David as recounted in Samuel and as was probably known to the Chronicler (cf. the implications of 1 Chron 20:1-3) are omitted, especially insofar as they relate to the "negatives" in David's life, whether the fraught circumstances in which he succeeded Saul as king or the Bathsheba affair and all that 2 Sam associates with it by way of judgment on David and his family. Again, whereas the biblical tradition testifies univocally that Solomon built the temple of God in Jerusalem, and the Chronicler is no exception in this respect, in Chronicles it is David who makes all the preparations for the building, despite his exclusion from the actual construction. The reason for his disqualification is given in 1 Chron 22:8 and repeated in 28:3: "But this word of the LORD came to me: 'You have shed much blood and have fought many wars. You are not to build a house for my Name, because you have shed much blood on the earth in my sight'" (22:8). Thus, in this speech of David to Solomon, the dynastic oracle of 2 Sam 7 is amplified beyond the mere statement that it would be David's son who would build the temple. This disqualification notwithstanding, in Chronicles David plays a crucial role in the making of Israel's temple, collecting the building material and organizing the levitical personnel in advance of its actual building. In this connection, the story of the census, the plague, and the purchase of Araunah's threshing floor assumes an importance that it does not explicitly have in 2 Sam 24. There the threshing floor is simply the place where David rears an altar and offers sacrifice in order to avert the plague that has followed his ill-advised census-taking. 1 Chron 21-22 says this much, but adds that David, seeing that his sacrifices were efficacious, announced: "The house of the LORD God is to be here, and also the altar of burnt offering for Israel" (22:1).

1 Chron 22:2-26:32 records the steps David took thereafter because "my son Solomon is young and inexperienced" (22:5). "Aliens" were set to prepare the stones, and large amounts of metal and timber were stored in readiness. Perhaps even more significant for the depiction of David as temple-planner are the lists of temple officials that take up a large part of 1 Chron 23-26. Temple praise, and temple organization in general, are the work of David, who implements the relevant laws and statutes of the Mosaic code. According to one interpretation this concentration on David as temple planner and organizer represents the "Davidic hope" of the Chronicler and of his generation, in all probability: "Whatever his hopes for the future were, he does not express them. For the fulfillment of history is not envisioned in an event of the future which would supersede and even negate past history, but is recognized in the present order"

(P. D. Hanson, *The Dawn of Apocalyptic,* 1975, 276-77). The dates given for the composition of Chronicles range from ca. 516 to ca. 350 BC and, though this is "a matter of the greatest delicacy" (Williamson, 121), the evidence favors a later rather than an earlier date. This would mean that, by the time of the Chronicler, the reconstituted state of Judah/Israel had existed for perhaps several generations without the restoration of its monarchy. In such circumstances the relevance and validity of the Davidic promise would have come into question. If, even after restoration to the land, there was no sign of a Davidide to sit on David's throne, was it possible that the old traditions were finding fulfillment, not in a Davidide, but in the Davidic institutions that were still in place? However, it is not as simple as that, since, in the first instance, the Davidic genealogy in 1 Chron 3 comes down well into the fourth century and, whether original or supplementary, is evidence of a lingering interest in the Davidic house, as if all hope of fulfillment of the dynastic oracle had not yet been abandoned.

There are other features of Chronicles that suggest that the Davidic hope retained its vitality as far as the Chronicler was concerned. It is noticeable, for instance, that the version of the Nathan oracle given in 1 Chron 17:14 relates it directly to Solomon ("I will set *him* over my house and my kingdom forever; *his* throne will be established forever"; compare 1 Chron 22:9-10 and contrast 2 Sam 7:16). 1 Chron 28:7 ("I will establish his kingdom forever if he is unswerving ... as is being done at this time") pins everything on Solomon's obedience to the commands and ordinances of God, and the Chronicler's undoubted judgment is that Solomon complied. And since Solomon is held to have fulfilled his contractual obligations, most conspicuously in the building of the temple, there is no question of the Davidic promise ever having been revoked. Thus Abijah of Judah may claim in 2 Chron 13:5 that God had given the kingship of Israel to the house of David "forever by a covenant of salt," and the Chronicler himself may append the following comment to his reference to the evil ways of Jehoram: "Nevertheless, because of the covenant the LORD had made with David, the LORD was not willing to destroy the house of David. He had promised to maintain a lamp for him and his descendants forever" (2 Chron 21:7). Comparison with the Chronicler's *Vorlage* in 2 Kgs 8:19 shows that the Chronicler has introduced a couple of significant changes, for, whereas Kings talks about the destruction of Judah, Chronicles is concerned with the house of David, and where Kings explains that the withholding of judgment is "for the sake of David his servant," Chronicles introduces its reference to the covenant with David. On this reading of these texts it would therefore look as if, perhaps even late in the fourth century, the hope of a restoration of the Davidic monarchy was cherished by the Chronicler and those likeminded.

4. *David in the Psalter and the Prophets.* The tradition of David the musician and psalmist (cf. 1 Sam 16:18, 23; 18:10; 2 Sam 23:1[?]; Amos 6:5) is deeply ingrained in the OT, and nowhere more deeply than in the Psalter, where seventy-two psalms are associated with his name, with a subgroup specifically related by their superscriptions to experiences in David's life. Since the expression *lᵉdāwid* does not necessarily imply authorship (though see Waltke, 586), the extent of the relationship must remain a subject of debate. It is, however, possible to make a few uncontentious observations on the David of the Psalter. In the first place, the association of David with a large number of psalms by means of superscriptions that are probably later additions to the psalms parallels the enhanced "temple reputation" of David in 1 Chron and

may even have originated in the same general period. Second, the majority of the historical superscriptions relate to the difficulties in David's life, whether in his fugitive days during Saul's reign or when he himself was king. Third, and as a consequence of the previous point, David becomes a "type" of the righteous sufferer who, in the psalms of lament, seeks from God redress for wrongs experienced from personal or other enemies. Though there are other superscriptions that, with the accompanying psalms, celebrate the achievements and special status of David, this identification of him with suffering and complaint runs counter to popular estimations of him as the acclaimed ruler of Israel and rampant victor in his various Near Eastern military campaigns. But it does square with the balance of the David tradition in 1-2 Sam, which, as we have observed, makes proportionately less of his triumphs and rather more of his trials.

The messianic—in its qualified OT sense—significance of David is especially apparent in the prophetic books, where the longer-term future of Judah/Israel is portrayed in terms of a restored and enhanced rule by a Davidic scion. The eighth-century prophets Isaiah and Micah express this expectation against the background of the failure of the contemporary ruling Davidides to live up to the expectations encouraged by, for example, the royal Davidic ideology fostered within the cultic setting of the Jerusalem temple and probably expressed at the accession of each new king in language akin to that of Isa 9:1-7. In that case, a different type of Davidide from what has been on offer is required: The hoped-for ruler will be "a shoot from the stump of Jesse" (Isa 11:1); it is "back to Bethlehem" for a fresh beginning to the Davidic story and for a new Davidic ruler (Mic 5:2). The "Davidic hope" is articulated in other prophetic books of the OT (e.g., Jer 33:15, 21-22, 25-26; Ezek 34:23-24; 37:24-25; Hos 1:11; 3:5; Amos 9:11-15; Hag 2:23). Although Ezekiel, from the advantaged perspective of the Babylonian exile, has reason to question the value of monarchy as an institution in a properly constituted polity—witness his preference for the limiting term "prince" in reference to the envisaged ruler (e.g., Ezek 44:3; 46:8)—he does have a place for a David *redivivus,* who would feed his people as their shepherd-ruler (34:23). But alongside this unsurrendered expectation of a Davidic ruler, despite the disaster of the Exile, there is also, in a notable text from that period, a "democratizing" of the Davidic covenant when, in Isa 55:3, the "sure mercies of David" ("my faithful love promised to David," NIV) are extended to all those who would respond to the divine mercy and so enjoy the privileges once vested in the highly favored but historically failed dynastic line of David.

5. *Beyond the Old Testament.* Later tradition embellished David's reputation in various ways. The number of his psalms and other compositions is given as 4050 in a Qumran text (11Q5, col. 27 [*DJD* IV 48 (text), 91-93 (translation and discussion)]). In the LXX additional psalms are attributed to him (e.g., Ps 95; cf. Heb 4:7), while the Babylonian Talmud speaks of him as the general editor of the psalter (see Baba Bathra 14b-15a). The "lionizing" extends to other aspects of David's career: "He played with lions as though they were young goats, and with bears as though they were lambs of the flock" (Sir 47:3, NRSV). But in the same section Ben Sira also pays tribute to his devotedness to God, whom he praised with all his heart (v. 8). He was also remembered as merciful (1 Macc 2:57) and as an intercessor (2 Esdr 7:108)—the prayer of 2 Sam 24 (see vv. 10, 17, 25) being cited as an example of the righteous praying for the

ungodly (v. 111). The victory over Goliath in the valley of Elah remained as an inspiration for later generations faced by military invasion (1 Macc 4:30).

In the NT David is called a prophet (Acts 2:30), in keeping with the postbiblical tendency to extend the currency of the term (though see 2 Sam 23:2). Preeminently, however, it is as ancestor of Jesus, the Christian Messiah, that he features in the NT. Davidic genealogies of Christ are given in both Matthew (1:1-16) and Luke (3:23-38), and his Davidic descent is presented as a significant element of the Christian *kerygma* (Rom 1:3; 2 Tim 2:8). The designation "Son of David" evidently had strong messianic associations and was commonly applied to Christ (e.g., Matt 12:23; Luke 18:38-39), but its limitations from a NT Christological point of view are indicated in Matt 22:41-45, while in the preceding chapter a notable contrast is made between the warlike David, whose conquest of Jerusalem is associated in 2 Sam 5:8 with a saying about the barring of the blind and the lame from "the house" (= temple?), and the irenic "Son of David" who, when he came to the city on Palm Sunday, made a point of receiving the blind and the lame in the temple and healing them (Matt 21:14).

BIBLIOGRAPHY
L. C. Allen, *Psalms* (Word Biblical Themes), 1987, 122-25; R. C. Bailey, *David in Love and War: The Pursuit of Power in 2 Samuel 10-12,* 1990; W. Brueggemann, "David and His Theologian," *CBQ* 30, 1968, 156-81; idem, *In Man We Trust,* 1972, 29-47; B. S. Childs, *Introduction to the Old Testament as Scripture,* 1979, 520-22; R. E. Clements, *Abraham and David: Genesis 15 and Its Meaning for Israelite Tradition,* 1967, 47-60; J. P. Floss, *David und Jerusalem,* 1987; S. Gelander, *David and His God,* 1991; R. P. Gordon, "David's Rise and Saul's Demise: Narrative Analogy in 1 Samuel 24-26," *TynBul* 31, 1980, 37-64; idem, *I and II Samuel: A Commentary,* 1986; J. H. Grønbaek, *Die Geschichte vom Aufstieg Davids (1. Sam. 15-2. Sam. 5),* 1971; D. M. Gunn, *The Story of King David: Genre and Interpretation,* 1978; D. Jobling, *The Sense of Biblical Narrative,* 1978, 4-25; G. H. Jones, *The Nathan Narratives,* 1990; J. D. Levenson, "1 Samuel 25 as Literature and as History," *CBQ* 40, 1978, 11-28; idem, "The Davidic Covenant and Its Modern Interpreters," *CBQ* 41, 1979, 205-19; P. K. McCarter, *I Samuel,* 1980; idem, *II Samuel,* 1984; D. J. McCarthy, "II Samuel 7 and the Structure of the Deuteronomic History," *JBL* 84, 1965, 131-38; T. N. D. Mettinger, *King and Messiah,* 1976; R. Polzin, *David and the Deuteronomist,* 1993; L. Rost, *The Succession to the Throne of David* (ET), 1982; J.-P. Sternberger, "David est-il parmi les prophètes? La mention du nom de David dans les oracles des prophètes postérieurs," *Etudes théologiques et religieuses* 69, 1994, 53-61; T. Veijola, *Die ewige Dynastie,* 1975; idem, *David: Gesammelte Studien zu den Davidüberlieferungen des Alten Testaments,* 1990; B. K. Waltke, "Superscripts, Postscripts, or Both," *JBL* 110, 1991, 583-96; R. N. Whybray, *The Succession Narrative,* 1968; H. G. M. Williamson, "Eschatology in Chronicles," *TynBul* 28, 1977, 115-54.

Robert P. Gordon

Genealogy in the Old Testament

A genealogy, according to the often-quoted definition of R. R. Wilson, is "a written or oral expression of the descent of a person or persons from an ancestor or ancestors" (*Genealogy and History,* 9). Two main types of genealogy may be distinguished: *linear* genealogies, in which only one line of descent from an ancestor is traced; and *segmented* genealogies, in which more than one line is traced from an ancestor, and which therefore branch into two or more distinct lines at some point.

1. *OT genealogical data.* The main genealogical materials in the OT are as follows:

Gen 4:17-22: the line of Cain through seven generations;

Gen 5:1-32, cf. 4:25-6: the line of Adam through Seth, going down to Noah's sons, Shem, Ham and Japheth;

Gen 10:1-32: the descendants of Noah's sons, also known as the Table of Nations;

Gen 11:10-26: the line from Shem to Abram; Gen 11:27 extends the list to Abram's nephew Lot;

Gen 19:37-38: Lot's sons, Moab and Ben-Ammi, from whom the Moabites and Ammonites are descended;

Gen 22:20-24: Nahor's sons;

Gen 25:1-4: sons of Abram, now named Abraham (cf. 17:5), by Keturah;

Gen 25:12-18: sons of Ishmael;

Gen 35:23-26: Jacob's sons by Leah, Rachel, Bilhah, and Zilpah;

Gen 36:1-43: Esau's descendants; this includes a list of tribal chiefs descended from Esau (vv. 15-30), a list of kings of Edom (vv. 31-39), and a list of chiefs descended from Esau "according to their clans and regions" (vv. 40-43);

Gen 46:8-25: Israel's (= Jacob's) sons and grandsons;

Exod 6:14-25: descendants of Reuben, Simeon, seemingly listed merely as a preamble to a more extensive listing of sons of Levi, which traces all his descendants down to the second generation, and focuses then on the descendants of Levi's grandson Kohath, especially on the descendants of Aaron and Korah;

Num 3:17-20: descendants of Levi to the second generation, giving the division into Gershonite, Kohathite, and Merarite clans, which forms the basis of the allocation of duties relating to the tabernacle and sanctuary in vv. 21-38;

Num 26:41-60: list of fighting men of the twelve tribes of Israel (vv. 5-51), followed by list of Levites (vv. 57-60); this list also functions as the basis for the division of the land of Canaan among the tribes;

Ruth 4:18-22: the genealogy of David, traced from Perez through seven generations;

2 Sam 3:2-5: the sons born to David in Hebron;

1 Chron 1-9: an extensive collection of genealogical material stretching from Adam down to the postexilic period. Some of this material seems to be a summary of other parts of the OT (compare 1 Chron 1:5-23 with Gen 10, 1 Chron 1:29-31 and 32-33 with Gen 25:12-18 and 25:1-4), whereas other material is found only here (1 Chron 4:39-43; 5:19-22; 7:20-27). The material falls into three sections: 1 Chron 1 covers the period from Adam to Israel; 1 Chron 2-8 covers the fortunes of the sons of Israel and their descendants in the preexilic period; and 1 Chron 9 relates to the postexilic period.

The OT material includes linear genealogies (e.g., Gen 5:1-32; Ruth 4:18-22) and segmented genealogies (Gen 10; Num 3:17-20). Genealogies describing the origins of nations or smaller ethnic groupings include both personal names, names that in other parts of the OT feature as place names, and gentilic names (e.g., Gen 10:4 lists among the sons of Javan "Elishah, Tarshish, the Kittim and the Rodanim"). The genealogies occur mainly in texts relating to the early and late periods of Israel's history. We may have here a phenomenon similar to that found in Old Babylonian texts, where segmented genealogies are important in the premonarchic period (because they reflect political/tribal realities) but are subsequently replaced by linear genealogies, describing the ancestry of kings (see below concerning the regnal formulae in 1 and 2 Kgs).

Various other OT texts are also relevant here, because like many of the OT genealogies they deal with issues relating to the composition or the internal organization of the Israelite people: censuses of the Israelites (e.g., Num 1:19-43; 4:34-49); the disposition of the twelve tribes (each with a tribal elder) around the tabernacle (2:1-34); the list of tribal offerings for the tabernacle (7:12-83); lists of tribal territories (Josh 15:1-21:42); lists of priests and temple functionaries (1 Chron 15:5-24; 23-26); lists of men chosen from the tribes for various purposes, to aid Moses in the census (Num 1:5-15), to spy out Canaan (13:4-15), to help in the allocation of the Promised Land (34:19-28), to see to the provisions for Solomon's household (1 Kgs 4:8-19); lists of David's soldiers (2 Sam 23:8-39) and officials (1 Chron 27:25-34); lists of individuals and families in the postexilic community at the time of Zerubbabel (Ezra 2:3-63; Neh 7:7-63); those who accompanied Ezra on his journey to Jerusalem (Ezra 8:2-14); those who rebuilt the walls of Jerusalem (Neh 3:1-32); and those found to have married foreign women (Ezra 10:18-43). In Ezra and Neh the point at issue is often the purity of the postexilic community. The regnal formulae in the books of Kings (1 Kgs 2:10-12; 11:41-43; 14:19-20, etc.) form a distinctive category. These short texts note which king succeeded which in both the southern and the northern kingdoms, and in effect trace the line of the southern kings, but not that of the kings of the north, where there was more than one royal dynasty.

2. *The functions of OT genealogies.* OT genealogies serve important functions in the books Gen-Neh. They give a sense of continuity between generations and provide a framework (at least in part) for a series of narratives that stretch from creation to the period after the Exile. However striking the individual narratives may seem, the recurring genealogies remind us that the narratives are part of a larger story. Other aspects of the interplay between narrative and genealogy are noted in the discussion of Gen and 2 Chron (below).

In general terms the genealogies have two main purposes: to describe the descent of the nations of the known world from Adam via Noah (see esp. Gen 10:1-32 and parts of 1 Chron 1); and to trace a "line of promise" that reaches from Seth through Abraham to Jacob/Israel, whose descendants become the nation Israel, God's chosen people. Genealogies, therefore, give concise expression to the unfolding of God's purposes in the bringing of Israel into being; they define the bounds of this chosen people and are thus closely linked to the themes of election and promise, and of Israel's inheritance of Canaan. They are a clear expression of Israel's identity. Within the Israelite genealogies, the genealogies of Levi's descendants mark out the Levites as a distinct group within Israel, whose sphere of ministry is to be God's tabernacle; different groups of Levi's descendants have different roles. As noted in the following section, one function of genealogies both in the OT and elsewhere in the ANE seems to have been the legitimization of functionaries.

Even some of the genealogies that do not describe the line of promise or even refer to Israelites seem to be organized with the promised line or the nation Israel in view. A. P. Ross has noted how the arrangement of the peoples in Gen 10 seems to be centered around the future land of Israel ("The Table of Nations," 22-34): The descendants of Japhet spread from east to west across the northern border; the descendants of Ham surround the land from south to west; the sons of Shem follow a line from east to south around the land. In particular, the mention of the Canaanite nations (10:15-18) suggests that the writer is focusing on the land God intends to give Israel.

In a similar way, though on a different scale, the listing of Nahor's offspring (Gen 22:20-24) introduces Rebekah, who will become Isaac's wife. Sometimes divergent genealogical lines seem to be traced in detail to mark a contrast with the line of promise. The lines of both Ishmael, Abraham's son by Hagar, and Esau, Jacob's twin brother, give the appearance of "shadow lines of promise": Ishmael is explicitly said to have fathered twelve "tribal rulers" (Gen 25:16), suggesting that he is, so to speak, a "shadow Israel"; and among Esau's descendants are a line of kings (36:31-39), described as having "reigned ... before any Israelite king reigned" (v. 31), which again suggests a contrast with Jacob's descendants. The narrator deliberately traces parallels between the rejected brother and the one who carries the line of promise, as though to emphasize the theme of God's sovereign choice by suggesting the thought "so near and yet so far."

3. *Comparison of OT and ANE genealogical material.* The ANE provides a variety of comparative material (helpfully discussed by R. R. Wilson, who devotes particular attention to Sumerian, Akkadian, Assyrian and Babylonian materials [*Genealogy and History*, 56-136]; see also M. Chavalas ["Genealogical History as 'Charter'," 103-28]). King lists predominate in these materials, but there are also priestly and scribal genealogies.

This material contains some features potentially relevant to OT genealogies. For example, genealogies can combine material of varying dates (e.g., the Assyrian King List, *ANET*, 564-66); genealogies extant in more than one version sometimes diverge at points, perhaps because they are upholding rival inheritance claims (Chavalas, "Genealogical History as 'Charter'," 114-23, compares the Assyrian King List and the Genealogy of the Hammurabi Dynasty in this regard); and genealogies may telescope several generations. Further, ANE genealogies are almost always concerned with legitimation, establishing the claims of an individual to rule or fulfil an official function by virtue of his descent.

An example of the legitimizing function of genealogy is the Sumerian King List (see *ANET*, 265-66), which has some similarities with the genealogies in Gen 1-11. The list is extant in a number of versions (to be dated between 2100 and 1950 BC), one of which is connected with the dynasty of the Sumerian city of Isin (ca. 1950 BC onwards). It is a list of kings who reigned in Sumer and the cities from which they reigned. The list distinguishes reigns before and after the Flood. The figures given for the reigns are enormous: Before the Flood eight kings are said to have ruled for 241,000 years, followed by twenty-three kings who are said to have ruled for 24,510 years (the longevity implied by these figures is one of the points of comparison with Gen 1-11). Chavalas ("Genealogical History as 'Charter'," 110-13) argues that at least in the Isin version the list was designed to support the claims of the Isin dynasty to rule Sumer; it glosses over the fact that the Isin dynasty could not claim a legitimate descent from previous rulers, but suggests that since various cities had each ruled Sumer in turn, there was nothing untoward in Isin now becoming the center of rule.

Legitimation appears to be the point at issue in those OT genealogies that trace levitical descent, in the regnal formulae, and also in the lists of members of the postexilic community in Ezra and Neh. These materials address questions such as: Who may serve as priest? Who is of genuine royal descent? Who truly belongs to Israel? The same could be said of the genealogies of the descendants of Israel in the Pent. and 1 Chron 2-8. Once we try to go beyond the general rubric of legitimation, however, the ANE material, though of value in suggesting possible approaches to the OT genealogies, is less helpful in interpreting their details.

Comparisons have customarily been drawn between Gen 1-11 and various ANE materials. However, R. S. Hess ("The Genealogies of Genesis 1-11," 241-54, esp. 247-50) notes the following important differences between ANE genealogies and Gen 1-11: (a) The ANE material contains nothing of the scope of the Table of Nations in Gen 10. (b) Legitimacy is not generally the point at issue in the genealogies of Gen 1-11. (c) The figures in the Sumerian King List (with which comparisons to Gen 1-11 have often been made) seem to have different functions from those in Gen 4-5 and 11. In Gen the focus is on the lifespan of the individual, whereas in the Sumerian King List the figures describe solely the years each king reigned. (d) In Gen 4-5 and 11 the genealogies are forward-looking, moving from father to son; in ANE king lists the movement is usually backward, moving from the last descendant to his forebears. Detailed comparisons between ANE and OT genealogies have value. However, the OT genealogies seem to have distinctive purposes that the ANE material can elucidate only in a limited way.

4. *OT genealogies and historical reconstruction*. Some of the problems in using OT genealogies for historical reconstruction have already been noted. Two main issues may be mentioned (cf. Wilson, *Genealogy and History,* 137-98, and "The Old Testament Genealogies," 169-89).

(a) There are cases where genealogical data seem to conflict. The sons of Eliphaz are reported as Teman, Omar, Zepho, Gatam, and Kenaz (Gen 36:11), whereas the name Korah is elsewhere inserted between Gatam and Kenaz (36:15). The materials relating to Caleb (or should it be two Calebs?) in 1 Chron 2:18-24, 42-50 seem contradictory (cf. the different approaches of R. Braun [*1 Chronicles*, 1986, ad loc.] and M. J. Selman [*1 Chronicles*, 1994, ad loc.]). The genealogy of Samuel puts him at an impossible distance of nineteen generations from Levi at 1 Chron 6:33-38[18-23] and is also difficult in that he was of Ephraimite descent (1 Sam 1:1). Errors of transmission were likely to occur in material of this sort, and no doubt some of these (and similar) conflicts can be explained as arising from scribal slips. The fact that names tend to recur in family lines is a particular source of difficulty; an example of this (and of the confusion that may result) can be found by comparing the lists of high priests given at Ezra 7:1-5; 1 Chron 6:1-15[5:29-41]; 6:50-53[35-38].

One should not, of course, simply focus on inconsistencies. G. A. Rendsburg has recently presented a case for the general accuracy and consistency of the genealogies in Exod-Josh ("The Internal Consistency," 185-206). Piecing together the genealogical information in these books and also the relevant material in 1 Chron and Ruth 4, he concludes that for every individual in Exod-Josh whose genealogy can be traced, there is a distance of three to six generations between him and one of Jacob's sons (this sort of variation is not problematic, as Rendsburg demonstrates by means of a comparison with the English royal family). The one exception to this pattern is that Joshua's genealogy in 1 Chron 7:20-27 puts him at ten generations' distance from Joseph (he also discusses Samuel's genealogy at 6:33-38[18-23], 195-96). This is an impressively consistent picture, particularly given that the OT genealogical data may come from more than one source.

(b) Related to this are the various possible ways of understanding some of the OT genealogies; it may be that they operate according to conventions foreign to us. For example, some of the key genealogical terms ("father," "son," "brother") are on occasion used loosely in OT: Achan is described as "son of Carmi, the son of Zimri, the son of Zerah" at Josh 7:1 and 18, but as "son of Zerah" in 7:24; Abraham describes himself and Lot as "brothers" at Gen 13:8 (i.e., allies, bound by kinship ties), when Lot is more precisely his nephew (14:12). Could it be, to extrapolate, that sometimes the language of family relation was used to express political affiliation?

Rendsburg, for instance, has suggested that the description of the birth of Jacob's sons in Gen 29-30 is a representation in familial terms of the early history of the Israelite tribes ("The Internal Inconsistencies," 201-4). According to him, the six sons who are born early to Leah or Rachel, that is, Reuben, Simeon, Levi, Judah, Joseph, and Benjamin (who are the only sons who play any individual role in Gen 30-50) were indeed Jacob's sons, who became the eponymous ancestors of six of the tribes. The six remaining sons, Dan, Naphtali, Gad, Asher, Issachar, and Zebulun, are either born late to Leah or are born to the handmaidens Bilhah and Zilpah. These tribes, suggests Rendsburg, had no family ties with Jacob, but gradually joined the first six tribes so that by the period of the Judges there were twelve tribes.

According to this view, the description of all twelve tribes as descended from Jacob partly expresses reality, but also partly uses the language of family ties to describe tribal alliances in which no family ties were involved, the distinction being marked by the description of the second six sons as having been born either late or to the handmaidens. Various objections could be raised against this view, which Rendsburg himself acknowledges is speculative. My purpose here is simply to show that the language of genealogies can be interpreted in more than one way. Both Rendsburg's view and the traditional view that the twelve tribal heads were all Jacob's natural sons accept that Gen 29-30 (and the genealogies listing Jacob's sons, e.g., 35:23-26; 46:8-25) express historical reality; the point of disagreement concerns the reality expressed and the way in which genealogical language is used to express it (cf. the way in which, in the Sumerian King List, the language of physical descent is used to express a particular view of political reality). We may disagree with Rendsburg, but his interpretation of genealogical language in Gen 29-50 has at the very least a surface plausibility. The question, in essence, is one of genre.

225

One further example relating to the issue of genealogical literary conventions may be mentioned. The figures given in Gen 5 for the lifespans of those who lived before the Flood range between 365 years (Enoch, Gen 5:23) and 969 years (Methuselah, 5:27). (Thereafter the figures gradually decrease, so that, for example, Abraham dies at age 175, 25:7, and Jacob at age 147, 47:28.) The figures in Gen 5 (which are given in significantly different forms in LXX and Sam.), as well as seeming extraordinarily high, also, when other data are taken into account, give the date of the creation of the world as 4004 BC, a figure greatly at odds with the findings of geology. Many approaches to these figures have been suggested (see G. J. Wenham, *Genesis 1-15*, 1987, 130-34 for a survey). For example, the high numbers may be a polemic against the kind of figures in the Sumerian King List, challenging the idea that semidivine men whose lives spanned thousands of years, ever walked the earth. Or the large figures suggest a human history that goes an inconceivable number of years back into the past; the fact that each human being is given a precise figure would, according to this view, balance this point by emphasizing that these distant persons were nonetheless real, mortal people. J. Hughes treats the figures in Gen 5 as part of a much larger priestly chronology, covering the period from creation down to the Exile and beyond (*Secrets*, 4-54). None of the suggestions made, however, has secured widespread acceptance. We seem to be dealing with a literary convention that we can no longer interpret with certainty.

5. *OT genealogies in context: Genesis and Chronicles*. Though the OT genealogies stand out from their narrative context, it is wrong to study them in isolation from that context, as they often contribute to the unfolding narrative. Thus, for example, the brief list of David's sons in 2 Sam 3:2-5 underlines the point made in v. 1 that "David grew stronger and stronger, while the house of Saul grew weaker and weaker." In a similar way, the Levite genealogy at Exod 6:14-25 focuses on Aaron and Korah and their sons (vv. 20-25); it is as though the writer is preparing for subsequent narratives in which they will play an important part (e.g., Lev 9-10; Num 16). More elaborate connections occur between genealogy and narrative in Gen and in the (in some ways different) case of the relationship between 1 Chron 1-9 and the rest of 1 and 2 Chron.

(a) *Genesis*. As noted earlier, the genealogies in Gen both trace the origins of the nations of the world and mark out a line of promise among these nations. The genealogies marking out the line of promise are regularly introduced by the formula, "These are the generations (*tôlēdôt*, # 9352) of ..." (RSV, 5:1; 6:9; 11:10, 27; 25:19; 37:2). This recurring formula gives a clear structure to the narratives of Abraham, Isaac, Jacob, and Joseph (see B. Renaud, "Les généalogies," 5-30). These narratives, of course, also have as their main theme the emergence of the line of promise among the nations of the world. However, as R. R. Robinson ("Literary Functions," 595-608) has noted, the very different styles of genealogy and narrative create a significant tension in Gen. Genealogies are by nature dry, unemotional summaries, which focus on one crucial fact, the progress of a family line generation by generation. They do not hint at the problems along the way. By contrast, in the narratives of Abraham's line, as Robinson puts it, "Genesis pursues virtually every imaginable threat to a linear genealogy": Sarah's barrenness; the possibility that Pharaoh or Abimelech will take Sarah from Abraham (Gen 12 and 20); the command to sacrifice Isaac (Gen 22); and sibling rivalry between Esau and Jacob (Gen 25), which flares up yet more fiercely between

Jacob's sons in the next generation (Gen 37), all detailed with great vividness. The two ways of tracing the line of promise seem to suggest two perspectives: that of God, before whose gaze generation irresistibly follows generation (has he not promised and it will be so?), and that of the individual members of the line, faced by threats to the promise in each generation, to whom it is anything but certain that the promise will be fulfilled (and yet it is).

Other, smaller-scale connections between genealogy and narrative can be noted. Gen 5:1-2 introduces Adam's genealogy with a reference to the creation of humankind in God's image (cf. 1:26-27). The clear implication is that succeeding generations continue to bear the image of God. Here a brief narrative insert significantly affects our reading of the genealogy. The opposite phenomenon may be observed in the repeated phrase "and he died" in Gen 5: Though formally unnecessary, it has the effect of stressing that, with the exception of Enoch (5:24), none of Adam's line escaped death. Here the genealogy develops a narrative theme first introduced at 2:17 (cf. 3:19).

R. S. Hess, in an etymological study of Gen 1-11, has argued that the names in the genealogies have their own story to tell by means of wordplays (*Studies in the Personal Names of Genesis 1-11*, 1993, esp. 111-62): they provide an "'onomastic commentary' parallel to the events within the narratives" (158). The names in Cain's line (4:17-24), for example, seem to be related to words that suggest urban culture (Irad), religion (Mehujael, Methusael), art and music (Adah, Zillah, Naamah), and religious processions (Jabal, Jubal, Tubal-Cain). But none of this culture and religion can prevent the murderous passion of Cain recurring in a yet more lethal form in Lamech, seven generations later (4:23-24). By contrast, the line of Adam through Seth (Gen 5:1-32) contains names that suggest the thoughts of substitution (Seth; cf. 4:25), the renewal and reestablishment of humankind (Enosh, Kenan), praise (Mahalalel), prayer for God to come down and aid (Jared), and rest from labor (Noah). Note how in both these genealogies, the "commentary" provided by the names is reinforced by brief narrative inserts that make the same points: 4:17, 20-22; 5:24, 29 (on these two genealogies, see also D. J. A. Clines, *Theme of the Pentateuch*, 66-68). Lastly, after the account of the tower of Babel (11:1-9), whose builders attempt to "make a name" for themselves" (v. 4), the genealogy of Shem (= "name") in vv. 10-26, part of the continuing line of promise, suggests an ironic commentary: Humans in their pride may oppose God, but only God can give their lives significance.

(b) *1 Chronicles 1-9*. In 1 and 2 Chron the genealogies are not interwoven with the narrative as in Gen, but occur in a block in the first nine chapters of 1 Chron. It might not appear that such dense lists of names could articulate anything of theological significance, but on closer examination these chapters turn out to adumbrate many of the themes that run through the rest of 1 and 2 Chron; hence seem to be integrally connected with the rest of the two books (for much of what follows, see H. G. M. Williamson, *1 and 2 Chronicles*, 38-92, and M. Oeming, *Das wahre Israel*, 1990, esp. 206-18).

First, the tripartite division of 1 Chron 1-9 into time periods (from Adam to the sons of Israel [1:1-2:2], the sons of Israel in the preexilic period [2:3-9:1], and the postexilic period [9:2-34]) sets the account of Israel in the context of a wider world history. In the first section the line of promise is marked by always being presented last (1:17-27, 34; 2:2). This first section is in effect a drastically stripped-down version of the book of Gen, which similarly sets the account of Abraham's line (Gen 12-50) in the context of an account of the origins of humankind (Gen 1-11).

Second, in the central section the three tribes treated at greatest length are Judah (2:3-4:23), Levi (6:1-81), and Benjamin (8:1-40); they are also positioned so as to form the beginning, middle and end of the Israelite genealogies. This has the effect that the three tribes whom the Chronicler held to have been faithful to the Davidic monarchy and temple before the Exile become the frame into which all the remaining tribes are fitted. It seems that this structure implicitly advocates an "inclusive ideal" of Israel (all may belong to Israel if they "fit in with" Judah, Levi, and Benjamin), which accords with the positive attitude later expressed towards the northern Israelite tribes (cf. 2 Chron 13:4-12; 30:1-12; both these texts express the view that the northern tribes may return to God if they acknowledge David's royal line and Jerusalem as the rightful place of worship).

A similar point may be made by the brief note at 1 Chron 5:1-2, which introduces Reuben's genealogy. Though "Judah was the strongest of his brothers and a ruler came from him" (v. 1), this statement is followed by the further assertion that Reuben's birthright passed not to Judah, but to the sons of Joseph (v. 2, a tradition not found elsewhere in the OT). As Williamson puts it: "The Chronicler has gone out of his way here to safeguard the highly honoured place of 'the sons of Joseph,' the core of the old northern kingdom, within the whole family of Israel" (*1 and 2 Chronicles*, 63).

Third, much of the material relating to Judah deals with David's descendants (1 Chron 3:1-24, going down even beyond the Exile), who occupy a central position in the Judahite genealogies (H. G. M. Williamson, "Sources and Redaction," 351-59). All this is fully in line with the emphasis in 1 and 2 Chron on David's line as God's chosen royal dynasty. In a similar way, the Levite genealogies have service in the temple particularly in view (1 Chron 6:31-32[16-17], 48-49), reflecting the Chronicler's pervasive interest in the role of the Levites in worship (1 Chron 15; 2 Chron 5, 35). The reference to David and Solomon in 1 Chron 6:31-32[16-17]) anticipates the Chronicler's description of the work of David and Solomon in organizing the Levites (1 Chron 23-26) and seeing to the building of the Jerusalem temple (1 Chron 28- 2 Chron 7).

Fourth, 1 Chron 9:2-34, listing people in Jerusalem who returned from exile in Babylon, especially priests, Levites and other temple functionaries (vv. 2, 13-34), suggests that though the postexilic community is a shadow of its former self, yet, in its internal organization and particularly in the fact that it is centered on the "house of God" (vv. 13, 26-27), it stands in recognizable continuity with former generations of Israel and may again display some of Israel's former glory. The same point about continuity (and possible hope for the future?) is made by extending the list of David's descendants into the postexilic period (3:17-24).

Occasional narrative inserts in 1 Chron 1-9 also seem to have a similar purpose. They are on two topics: the conquest of territory by the tribes (4:39-43; 5:10; 7:21-24; this material, as noted above, is peculiar to the Chronicler) and the Exile (5:6, 25-26, in reference to the northern tribes; 6:15[5:41] in reference to Judah; cf. 9:1). On the one hand, the Chronicler squarely attributes the exile of both kingdoms to their unfaithfulness (5:25; 9:1) and to God's judgment on this unfaithfulness (5:26; 6:15[5:41]), thereby introducing the theme of retribution, a theme that runs through all 1 and

2 Chron (1 Chron 10:13-14; 2 Chron 7:1, etc.). On the other hand, the mention of tribal territories at a time when the community occupied a tiny area shows the Chronicler's continuing interest in the land that had been promised to Abraham and that had belonged to the Davidic kingdom. He seems at least to hint at the possibility that this land will again belong to Israel (even if only through small-scale initiatives such as described in these inserts); and we may note that the Chronicler's theology of retribution is balanced by an equally strong emphasis that repentance and restoration are possible in every generation (2 Chron 7:14).

OT genealogies, then, share many theological themes with the narratives in which they stand. If the majority of OT genealogies underline Israel's status as a chosen people, then the fact that all nations of the world trace their ancestry back to Adam through Noah also reminds us of what Israel has in common with these nations: All nations bear the image of God (cf. Gen 1:26-27) and are dependent on his mercy and blessing for their continued existence (cf. 8:21-9:1). Further, those genealogies that trace the descent of the nations of the world make it plain that Israel's role is defined with reference to God's purposes for all nations (cf. 12:1-3). One could say that the OT genealogies find their logical conclusion in the genealogies of Jesus in Matt 1 and Luke 3, which set before us a Savior of Israelite descent, who brings salvation for all humankind.

→ Old Testament History: A Theological Perspective (pp. 65-82, above)

→ Old Testament History: A Hermeneutical Perspective (pp. 83-99, above)

BIBLIOGRAPHY
M. Chavalas, "Genealogical History as 'Charter'," in A. R. Millard et al., *Faith, Tradition and History*, 1994, 103-28, esp. 114-23; D. J. A. Clines, *The Theme of the Pentateuch*, 1978; R. S. Hess, "The Genealogies of Genesis 1-11 and Comparative Literature," *Bib* 70, 1989, 241-54; J. Hughes, *Secrets of the Times*, 1990; M. D. Johnson, *The Purpose of the Biblical Genealogies*, 1988[2]; B. Renaud, "Les généalogies et la structure de l'histoire sacerdotale dans le livre de la Génèse," *RB* 97, 1990, 5-30; G. A. Rendsburg, "The Internal Consistency and Historical Reliability of the Biblical Genealogies," *VT* 40, 1990, 185-206; R. R. Robinson, "Literary Functions of the Genealogies of Genesis," *CBQ* 48, 1986, 595-608; A. P. Ross, "The Table of Nations in Genesis 10—Its Contents," *BSac* 138, 1981, 22-34; H. G. M. Williamson, "Sources and Redaction in the Chronicler's Genealogy of Judah," *JBL* 98, 1979, 351-59; R. R. Wilson, *Genealogy and History in the Biblical World*, 1977; idem, "The Old Testament Genealogies in Recent Research," *JBL* 94, 1975, 169-89.

Philip E. Satterthwaite

Hosea: Theology of

A. Historical Context
The introduction of the book of Hosea presents us with the following historical setting of the prophetic proclamation: "The word of the LORD that came to Hosea son of Beeri during the reigns of Uzziah, Jotham, Ahaz and Hezekiah, kings of Judah, and during the reign of Jeroboam son of Jehoash king of Israel" (1:1). Noteworthy is the preference given to the Davidic dynasty in the super-

scription of a book of an Israelite writing prophet—in fact, the only one who lived and worked in the northern kingdom. This is a clear indication that this book received its final character in Judean circles; Jeroboam II is the only Israelite king mentioned here. Bearing in mind the fact that his reign stretched over a period of forty years (787-747 BC), it then becomes evident why it is impossible to pinpoint the beginning of Hosea's ministry. Most scholars are, however, agree that the sayings in ch. 2 concerning economic prosperity and those in chs. 4-5 on the flourishing cult mirror the politically stable period of the last years of Jeroboam II. If that is the situation, the beginning of Hosea's career could be dated somewhere around 755/50.

For the rest of the sayings in the book it is difficult to establish exact dates, for it is not evident that they are chronologically arranged. Alt's claim (*Kleine Schriften*, 1953, 2:163-87) that Hos 5:8ff. refers to events around the Syro-Ephraimite war (733/2) has been widely accepted. Hos 8:7-10 could reflect the outcome of these events when the Syro-Ephraimite coalition collapsed and the territories of Galilee and Gilead were cut off by Tiglath-Pileser III and transformed into Assyrian provinces (Donner, 56). Perhaps 5:13 is to be connected with the aftermath of this war, when King Hoshea (731-723), the murderer of Pekah (who was a member of the Syro-Ephraimite coalition), surrendered to the Assyrians and paid a heavy tribute (cf. 2 Kgs 17:3). The sayings in Hos 9-12 are most intelligible when they are fitted into the quiet period following Shalmaneser V's accession to the throne in 727 (Wolff, xxi). Shortly afterwards (ca. 724), however, Hoshea, who was not content to remain loyal to the Assyrian throne, decided to revolt. He then tried to establish diplomatic ties with the Egyptian king (2 Kgs 17:4). Quite probably 9:3 and 12:1[2] presuppose those overtures to Egypt. In 13:16[14:1] we may possibly hear the punitive measures that resulted from this revolt. The fall of Samaria (722) is not reflected in this book, and we can therefore assume that Hosea's prophetic activity in Israel came to an end shortly before the final destruction of the northern Kingdom.

B. Literary Structure

1. *Chapters 1-3*. The book of Hosea consists of two distinctly different parts, viz. chs. 1-3 and chs. 4-14. Chs. 1-3 have as their general theme the marriage of Hosea and its symbolic significance. Each of these chapters concentrates on an aspect of this relationship: 1:1-9 records the constitution of the marriage bond and the birth of the children with their symbolic names; 2:2-15[4-17] centers on the adulterous conduct of Israel as Yahweh's wife and on Yahweh's measures to win her back, while ch. 3 records the commencement of a new marriage relationship between Hosea and his wife. Each of these units is concluded with a message of hope: 1:10-2:1[2:1-3]; 2:16-23[18-25]; 3:5.

In chs. 1-3 two types of literary presentation can be distinguished: Ch. 1 is biographical, while ch. 3 is autobiographical. The first two chapters most probably originate with the prophet's disciples or close followers. Ch. 3 reflects a later stage in the prophetic oracles since it presupposes the earlier accounts in chs. 1 and 2. It could be surmised that chs. 1-3, with their dominant marriage theme, were originally transmitted separately and were added to the second block (chs. 4-14) only at a later stage.

As a transmission complex chs. 1-3 constitute a structured whole. Andersen and Freedman (122-41) have convincingly pointed out that in these chapters interlocking patterns of introversion unify extended stretches of text. There is a kind of organic growth. As each theme is worked out, new themes develop from it, and there are no abrupt transitions to new material. There is little in chs. 1-3 that could stand on its own and that has no structural counterpart elsewhere within these chapters. Words and phrases that have already been used are taken up again and integrated into a unified composition. The correspondence of words and phrases between chs. 1 and 2 clearly illustrates that a definite architecture underlies this literary piece of art. The different ideas in 2:2-12[4-14] and 2:14-23[16-25] are, furthermore, arranged in such a manner that they correspond in reverse order, with v. 15 constituting the axis (D. Lys, "J'ai deux amours ou l'amant jugé," *ETR* 51, 1976, 59-77).

Another prominent stylistic feature in ch. 2 is the effective use of the first person (as verbal form or as pronominal suffix) to portray the deeds of Yahweh, in contrast with the third person that describes Israel's response. Compare the frequent employment of "I" and "my" when Yahweh is the speaker, over against "her" (her husband, her face, her breasts, her children, her lovers, etc.) when the reference is to Israel. By adopting this style the misdeeds of Israel seem even more serious when compared with Yahweh's goodwill. This stylistic device is used to heighten emotion and to accentuate contrast. It possibly derives from the idea of Yahweh's self-deliberation in advance of announcing his decision as regards Israel within the "divine council."

Although chs. 1 and 3 are part and parcel of the marriage metaphor, they also belong to the literary category of prophetic symbolic acts, with the following three distinctive elements: (a) the instruction to carry out the symbolic act (1:2; 3:1), (b) the carrying out of the act(s) (1:3; 3:2), and (c) the explanation of its meaning (1:4-6; 3:4). Ch. 2 cannot be properly understood without 1:2-9. In the latter passage the consummation of the marriage bond, as well as the birth of the children, is described. In ch. 2 divorce is presupposed (2:2[4]), but the soliloquy quickly moves beyond the circumstances of Hosea's own marriage to a consideration of Yahweh's plans to bring Israel, his marriage partner, back to himself. Chs. 1-3, therefore, represent a unique combination of symbolic acts and a metaphorical description. They constitute an artistically structured composition which makes it almost impossible to separate off distinct literary units.

2. *Chapters 4-14.* A second larger transmission complex (Hos 4-14) is introduced by the summons in 4:1 and concluded by the prophetic formula in 11:11. This second part presents a series of individual oracles. The internal structural coherence is difficult to describe since there is a conspicuous absence of the typical prophetic formula: "This is what the LORD says." In view of this it is understandable that so many scholars in the past have deemed chs. 4-14 to be an amorphous mass of material. J. Jeremias ("Hosea 4-7: Beobachtungen zur Komposition des Buches Hosea," *FS Würthwein*, 1979, 47-58) has demonstrated, however, that a certain underlying principle was in operation in the structuring of chs. 4-7, viz., a progressive linking up with words and ideas mentioned earlier. As is the case in the first complex, chs. 4-11 are also concluded with words of hope (11:10-11).

Chs. 12-14 belong to another transmission complex, as is clear from its transmission history. The expression "the LORD your God," for instance, which may reflect liturgical traditions, occurs only in this complex (Wolff, xxxi). It has been suggested that Hos 14:1-8[2-9] was not originally part of chs. 12-13, but should be attributed to a later (postexilic?) worshiping community, which adjusted the prophetic oracles for use in the cultic sphere (P. A. Kruger, "Yahweh's Generous Love," 1:27-48). The wisdom saying in 14:9[10] stems from the final redactor who, perhaps mindful of the difficult symbolic-metaphoric nature of the prophetic oracles, commends the book as wisdom that requires serious reflection (cf. Sheppard, 129-36).

C. Theological Themes

1. *Chapters 1-3.* The dominant subject of these chapters is the symbolic marriage of the prophet. Chapter 1 records the consummation of the marriage, the birth of the children, and the explanation of their symbolic names (Jezreel, Lo-Ruhamah, Lo-Ammi). Hos 2:2-13[4-15] opens with a divorce lawsuit. The children, who were the main actors in ch. 1, occupy in this chapter a secondary position; they are mentioned only in vv. 2[4], 4[6], 5[7]. The extent and motivation of the wife's (Israel's) promiscuity are set forth in the narrative material in vv. 5b-13[7b-15]. She is accused of regarding Baal rather than Yahweh as the dispenser of the fertility of the land. In vv. 14-23[16-25] a radical change in the conduct of Yahweh towards his wife is observed. Whereas vv. 2-13[4-15] are full of threats, the tone in these verses is conciliatory and constructive. D. J. A. Clines has commented on ch. 2 as setting out the options considered by Yahweh as he decides what to do with his wayward spouse. Each of these is juridical in tone, introduced by the transitional "therefore" (*lākēn*, vv. 6[8], 9[11], 14[16]); but it is only the third that Yahweh actually decides to implement, and it is a judgment that is actually a decision to deal graciously with the offender (*Studia Biblica* 1, 1978, 83-103). Ch. 3 describes a renewed command from Yahweh to the prophet to go and show his love to a wife (who is most probably his own unfaithful Gomer) once again (v. 1).

2. *Chapters 4-14.* The second part of the book deals with Israel's moral, cultic, and political sins. The first few introductory verses of ch. 4 pinpoint the actual sickness of which these offenses are only the symptoms: "There is no faithfulness, no love, no acknowledgment of God in the land" (v. 1). This sad state of affairs was due to the negligence of the priests, who were in the first instance responsible for the passing on of religious knowledge (4:4-10).

The next feature that comes under the barrage of the prophetic condemnation is Israel's political life: Internally there were the palace revolts, and externally there was strife between Israel and Judah (5:8-15), while expedient calls, now to Egypt and now to Assyria, marked Israelite international diplomacy (7:8-8:10).

From 9:10 onwards it is Israel's historical traditions that stand in the foreground—the desert period (9:10), the conquest of the Promised Land (10:1), the Exodus from Egypt (ch. 11)—and there is even reference to patriarchal traditions (ch. 12). The prophet uses these retrospections to illustrate the long history of Israel's sinning in contrast to Yahweh's continuously gracious deeds in the past.

3. *Polemic against Canaanite religion.* Throughout the book the cult and mythology of the god Baal are the target of most of the prophetic sayings (Mays, 8). The approach involves a twofold strategy: (a) It attacks Baalism with its own weapons, and (b) it accommodates certain Canaanite ideas to describe Yahwism in a fascinating new way. In this approach the prophet engages in a process of reinterpretation so as to make it clear that the Yahwistic religion was not concerned with mythological ideas but with historical realities (Kinet, 218ff.). To this end Hosea creates the marriage metaphor as the mould into which he casts his ideas. One of the primary contributory reasons for the creation of this image was probably the fact that the idolatrous Canaanite

practices, owing to their peculiar sexual-orgiastic nature, were already, in the time of Hosea, known by the abusive description "adultery" or "prostitution" ($z^e n\hat{u}n\hat{i}m$, Hos 1:2; see, for instance, Jehu's words to Joram in 2 Kgs 9:22, where the same Hebrew word is used).

Hosea's own marriage with its symbolic significance, however, rendered the necessary depth and emotion to this sexual metaphor. In contrast to the prevailing view in Hosea's day that the role of a god in the god-man relationship was to be understood in a cultic-sacral sense, in Hos 2 the point of contact is that of the juridical principles that governed the marriage institution. The marriage metaphor in this chapter operates on two different, but skillfully integrated levels, viz., the juridical and cultic-religious. Viewed superficially, it describes the unhappy marriage between Yahweh and his wife, Israel, and the juridical consequences. If, however, the context of the image is studied, it becomes clear that the prophet is in fact attacking fundamental beliefs in the Canaanite fertility cult. The themes of looking and finding (2:7[9]), which were so fundamental to the fertility myths of the ANE (W. H. Schmidt, "Baals Tod und Auferstehung," *ZRGG*, 15, 1963, 1-13), are especially prominent here.

4. *Israel's sin*. Right from the beginning of the book, great stress is laid on the deep-rootedness and gravity of Israel's apostasy. It had a long history. It was not a phenomenon that came into existence after the Conquest (Hos 10:1), or in the desert period (9:10), or even in Egypt (11:1). It is traced still further back. Already in the deceitful conduct of their ancestor Jacob the guilt of the nation became evident (12:2-6).

A variety of descriptions and images is used to depict the people's backsliding. They are first and foremost accused of harlotrous (*znh*) behavior. This figure was especially popular to portray Israel's general malpractices (there are twenty-two occurrences of the root *znh* in the book). Even in the political sphere the idea of harlotry is used: "Ephraim has sold herself (for a prostitute's fee) to lovers" (8:9). Further descriptions of Israel's sinful deeds are that she "forgot" (2:13[15]; 4:6; 8:14; 13:6), "deserted the LORD" (4:10), "(went) after her lovers" (2:5[7], 13[15]), "strayed from" Yahweh (7:13), "rebelled against" him (7:13; 8:1), was "unfaithful to the LORD" (5:7; 6:7), was "stubborn" (4:16; 9:15), and "practiced deceit" (7:1; 10:2) and "lies" (7:3; 10:13; 11:12[12:1]; see Wolff, xxviii).

Although Hosea uses the term $b^e r\hat{i}t$, covenant (# 1382), in a theological sense only once (8:1), some of these descriptions just mentioned (e.g., to go after, rebels against, to be unfaithful to the Lord, and prostitute themselves) can only be adequately understood against the background of the covenant idea. The prophet selects the marriage image as a vehicle to highlight certain key aspects of the covenant relationship. Throughout the OT marriage is of a juridical nature. Certain obligations are expected and certain privileges granted to each partner in a mutual deal. It was exactly these characteristics that made this life-form so supremely suitable to express what Yahweh had bestowed on Israel and also what he was entitled to demand from her. M. Weinfeld ("$B^e r\hat{i}t$—Covenant vs. Obligation," *Bib* 56, 1975, 120-28) maintains that the ANE marriage formula ("I will be your husband; you will be my wife") stands in fact behind the "Bundesformel," "I will be your God and you be my people" (Exod 6:2-7; Lev 26:9-12; Deut 29:12-13[11-12]). In this regard the announcement in Hos 1:9—"You are not my people, and I am not your God"—is clearly a direct negation of this formula. In

2:23[25], however, this broken relationship is healed again when God promises: "'You are my people; and they will say, 'You are my God.'"

To depict Israel's political promiscuity among the nations powerful images are employed: "Ephraim mixes with the nations" as the ingredients of bread are mixed together (7:8); "Ephraim is a flat cake not turned over" (7:8); "Ephraim is like a dove, easily deceived" (7:11). Yahweh could not, however, allow his people to act in such a wayward manner. In a shockingly bold and unrivaled imagery, God is represented "like a moth to Ephraim, like rot to the people of Judah" (5:12). So Yahweh responds: "I will come upon them like a lion ... like a bear robbed of her cubs" (13:7-8).

The political crisis in Israel was the direct consequence of the religious crisis (Utzschneider, 86ff.). In both these areas Yahweh did not receive his rightful place. The close relationship between politics and religion is clearly illustrated in 8:4: "They set up kings without my consent; they choose princes without my approval." It deals with the uncharismatic way in which the succession of kings was decided on in Israel. This passage cannot, however, be separated from all the others that also criticize the monarchy: 7:3-7; 10:3; 13:10 (Gelston, *OTS* 19, 1974, 71-85). Two serious objections are especially raised against this institution: its legitimacy and its inability to save the people in time of distress.

5. *Yahweh's love*. Notwithstanding the gravity of Israel's sin, there is no other OT prophetic book where the intensity of the divine love is demonstrated more clearly than in this book. God could simply not tear himself loose from his apostate people. A demonstration of the endlessness and graciousness of this divine love can be found in the marriage metaphor of ch. 2. In vv. 2-13[4-15] the theme is the promiscuity of the wife Israel, but vv. 14-23[16-25] portray an unexpected and radical change in Yahweh's conduct towards his people.

Despite Israel's backsliding the marriage relationship will start all over again: a new courtship (2:14[16]), a new bridal price (v. 15[17]), and a new engagement (vv. 19-20[21-22]). The desert, the place where the helpless Israel was abandoned to die of thirst (v. 3[5]), becomes the place from where Yahweh's new future deeds are conducted (v. 14[16]). Wild animals, which in the past unrestrictedly endangered the lives of men (v. 12[14]), are also objects of a covenant (v. 18[20]), so that the land can live in peace. The barley and wine that must be suspended, owing to the promiscuous behavior of Israel (v. 9[11]), are kindly granted to Israel once again (v. 22[24]). The valley of Achor, which literally means "valley of misfortune" (Josh 7:25-26), will become "a door of hope" (v. 15[17]).

In this new age the desert period (2:14[16]; see also 9:10; 11:3; 12:10, 14; 13:5) plays a central role and correctly so, because it constitutes a decisive point in the history of Israel: It lies halfway between the great salvation deeds of the Exodus and the entry into the Promised Land. Whereas the threshold of the land of Canaan is the symbol of Israel's apostasy (9:10; 10:13; 11:2), the desert signifies the time of undisturbed harmony between God and his people.

To portray the magnitude of the divine compassion and discipline, the father-son metaphor (ch. 11) is chosen. God had elected the people of Israel (v. 1a), and he had led them and cared for them (vv. 3-4); but they had responded negatively to these gracious acts (v. 2) and had, therefore, to bend under the divine judgment (vv. 5-6). But God could not bring himself to destroy his own people. Verse 8 records what happens in God's heart when there is conflict between the divine love and wrath. Instead of his overturning Israel like the cities of Admah and Zeboiim of old as they deserved, God's heart is changed within himself (his heart is overturned) and his compassion is aroused. The divine love is always stronger than the divine wrath.

D. Canonical Context

This book, like all the other OT prophetic books, was "heard, shaped and preserved" (Childs, *IOTS*, 377) by successive communities of faith. It seems that its literary development went through the following major canonical shapings:

1. The core and most of the material of the book originated with Hosea or his immediate followers and is directed at the people of Israel. Probably the different parts (1-3; 4-11; 12-13:16[14:1]) were already assembled into a larger compilation when they found their way to Judah after the destruction of Samaria, there to be reshaped for a new audience (Jeremias, 18).

2. Indication of an early Judean redaction that supplements the original words to meet their new historical context is possibly traceable in the salvation references (1:7; 3:5) and in other redactional additions, which took the original prophetic accusations and threats and applied them to a new situation (4:15a; 5:5b; 6:11a; cf. Wolff, xxxii). However, a more inclusive (i.e., Hoseanic) approach to the salvation sayings and to favorable references to the Davidic dynasty is adopted by Emmerson, 9-116.

3. It has been suggested that 14:1-8[2-9] owes its present form to an adaptation of Hoseanic material by a later (postexilic?) worshiping community whose intention it was to adopt the prophetic words to the needs of the cult (Kruger, *OTE* 1, 1988, 27-48; cf. H. McKeating, *Hosea*, CBC, 1971, 151).

4. 14:9[10] uses "wisdom language" to reflect upon the message of the book and to provide a perspective for an enlightened reading of it. At the same time most of the terms used in the verse occur elsewhere in Hosea (cf. Sheppard, *Wisdom*, 129-36).

BIBLIOGRAPHY
F. I. Andersen and D. N. Freedman, *Hosea*, AB, 1980; J. Blenkinsopp, *A History of Prophecy in Israel*, 1983, 96-106; W. Brueggemann, *Tradition for Crisis: A Study of Hosea*, 1968; M. J. Buss, *The Prophetic Word of Hosea*, BZAW 111, 1969; D. J. A. Clines, "Hosea 2: Structure and Interpretation," in E. A. Livingstone (ed.), *Studia Biblica* 1, 1978, 83-103; H. Donner, *Israel unter den Völkern*, SVT 11, 1964; G. I. Emmerson, *Hosea: An Israelite Prophet in Judean Perspective*, 1984; A. Gelston, "Kingship in Hosea," *OTS* 19, 1974, 71-85; J. Jeremias, *Der Prophet Hosea*, ATD, 1983; D. Kinet, *Baal und Yahwe: Ein Beitrag zur Theologie des Hoseabuches*, 1977; P. A. Kruger, "Yahweh's Generous Love," *Old Testament Essays*, 1988, 1:27-48; J. L. Mays, *Hosea*, OTL, 1969; E. W. Nicholson, *God and His People*, 1986, 179-88; H. H. Rowley, "The Marriage of Hosea," in *Men of God*, 1963, 66-97; G. T. Sheppard, *Wisdom as a Hermeneutical Construct*, BZAW 151, 1980, 129-36; H. Utzschneider, *Hosea: Prophet von dem Ende*, 1980; W. A. VanGemeren, *Interpreting the Prophetic Word*, 1990, 105-20; G. von Rad, *The Message of the Prophets*, ET, 1968, 110-17; H. W. Wolff, *Hosea*, Hermeneia, 1974.

Paul A. Kruger

New International Dictionary of Old Testament Theology & Exegesis

Willem A. VanGemeren, General Editor

If the essays in *A Guide to Old Testament Theology and Exegesis* have given you the hunger to do your own in-depth study of the Old Testament, only the entire five-volume *New International Dictionary of New Testament Theology & Exegesis* will satisfy!

Examine the meaning of words and concepts in the context of the Ancient Near East and the Old Testament, as well as grasp similarities and differences among words within the same semantic field or domain. The *New International Dictionary of Old Testament Theology & Exegesis* is your ideal choice for serious Old Testament study whether you are an academic, pastor, student, or layperson.

In addition to the expert essays, the five-volume set contains:

• The Lexical Dictionary containing over 3,000 separate entries—Discusses each Hebrew word in the context of the Ancient Near East, its use and significance in the Old Testament, its relationship to post-canonical Hebrew and Greek, and New Testament usage.

• The Topical Dictionary

• Comprehensive Indexes

Hardcover Five-volume Set: 0-310-21400-9

Find the New International Dictionary of Old Testament Theology & Exegesis *at your local Christian bookstore.*

ZondervanPublishingHouse

Grand Rapids, Michigan

http://www.zondervan.com

A Division of HarperCollinsPublishers

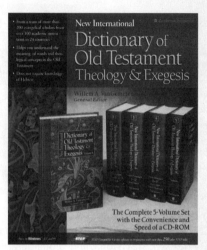

New International Dictionary of New Testament Theology

Colin Brown, General Editor

Understand the theology and message of the New Testament with this translation, extensive revision, and considerable enlargement of the German *Theologisches Begriffslexikon zum Neuen Testament.* On it first publication in German it was recognized as a major reference work, and it has since become widely acclaimed as an important tool for understanding the Bible.

The four-volume *New International Dictionary of New Testament Theology* is a unique and valuable information source that features:

- Concise discussion of the major theological terms of the Bible
- Discussions of each key Greek word in classical Greek, the Old Testament, and the New Testament
- Glossary of technical terms
- Full bibliographies
- Complete indexes
- No need for knowledge of Greek and Hebrew

Hardcover Four-volume Set: 0-310-33238-9

***Find the* New International Dictionary of New Testament Theology**
at your local Christian bookstore.

ZondervanPublishingHouse
Grand Rapids, Michigan
http://www.zondervan.com

A Division of HarperCollins*Publishers*

NOW AVAILABLE ON CD-ROM FOR WINDOWS!

The *NIDNTT* CD-ROM gives you such PC advantages as:

- Lightning-fast word searches by English, transliterated Greek, or Goodrick/Kohlenberger numbering
- Ability to look up any Greek word behind the NIV with the click of a mouse
- Hypertext Bible references
- Convenient drag-and-drop—or cut-and-paste
- Compatibility with more than 250 other STEP titles, including *The NIV Study Bible Basic Library '99, The NIV Study Bible Complete Library '99,* and *The Expositor's Bible Commentary*
- Printable Greek (font provided)
- Ability to import Bible text directly to Microsoft Word or WordPerfect
- Customizable font color and style for text and charts
- NIV text display by paragraph or by verse
- Detailed on-screen help
- User-friendly instruction manual
- Personal, informed, FREE technical support
- Link to the Internet

For Windows 95 or 98
CD-ROM: 0-310-21665-6

We want to hear from you. Please send your comments about this
book to us in care of the address below. Thank you.

ZondervanPublishingHouse
Grand Rapids, Michigan 49530
http://www.zondervan.com